The Impossibilities of the Circular Economy

The fifth Factor X publication from the Federal Environment Agency (Umweltbundesamt, UBA), *The Impossibilities of the Circular Economy* provides an overview of the limits to the circular economy, emphasising the relationship between integrated resource use and more systemic leadership-management approaches.

On a European level, the book ties into the recent European Green Deal and aims to empower actors across sectors and EU member countries to transition from existing linear models of value capture and expression to more systemic-circular solutions of value capture and expression. The volume provides a hands-on contribution towards building the knowledge and skill sets of current and future decision-makers who face these complex-systemic crises in their day-to-day business. The book further provides access to best practices from cutting-edge research and development findings, which will empower decision-makers to develop a more sustainable and equitable economy.

Providing solutions for a more sustainable economy, this book is essential reading for scholars and students of natural resource use, sustainable business, environmental economics and sustainable development, as well as decision-makers and experts from the fields of policy development, industry and civil society.

Harry Lehmann is General Director of the Environmental Planning and Sustainability Strategies Division of the German Federal Environment Agency. He was an early member and is now the President of the Factor 10 Club for resource productivity and sustainable use of natural resources. He is one of the founders of Eurosolar, and since 2011 he has been Executive Chairman of the World Renewable Energy Council.

Christoph Hinske is Associate Professor of System Leadership-Management, SAXION University of Applied Sciences, School of Finance and International Business; Founder of 360° Dialogues. He lectures on societal transformations at the Eberswalde University for Sustainable Development and advises Global Action Networks, financial institutions and Transformation Networks. He is a fellow at the European School of Governance.

Victoire de Margerie is the Founder and Vice-Chairman of the World Materials Forum and Executive Chairman of Rondol. She has spent 35 years in the Materials Industry in Canada, France, Germany, UK and USA, first as an Executive and since 1999 as a Board Director (now Arkema and Eurazeo). She was elected an Academician at the National Academy of Technologies of France in 2020.

Aneta Slaveikova Nikolova is the Climate Policy Lead, Environment and Development Division, Economic and Social Commission for Asia and the Pacific UNESCAP. Ms Nikolova heads a climate action team focusing on climate finance, Paris Agreement implementation and review of national GHG reduction commitments. She has vast experience in sustainable development policy and advocacy, capacity development and technical assistance to developing countries and countries with economies in transition.

Factor X: Studies in Sustainable Natural Resource Management

'Factor X' promotes good and best practices to enable significant savings in natural resource use and ways to improve resource efficiency. In collaboration with the German Environmental Agency (Umweltbundesamt, UBA), and contributions from leading names in policy and academia, this book series proposes innovative strategies for implementing the 'Factor X' concept in order to build a more resource-efficient world.

Sustainable Development and Resource Productivity
The Nexus Approaches
Edited by Harry Lehmann

The Impossibilities of the Circular Economy
Separating Aspirations from Reality
Edited by Harry Lehmann, Christoph Hinske, Victoire de Margerie, and Aneta Slaveikova Nikolova

For more information about this series, please visit: www.routledge.com/Factor-X-Studies-in-Sustainable-Natural-Resource-Management/book-series/FX

The Impossibilities of the Circular Economy

Separating Aspirations from Reality

Edited by
Harry Lehmann, Christoph Hinske, Victoire de Margerie, and Aneta Slaveikova Nikolova

Routledge
Taylor & Francis Group
LONDON AND NEW YORK

earthscan
from Routledge

First published 2023
by Routledge
4 Park Square, Milton Park, Abingdon, Oxon OX14 4RN

and by Routledge
605 Third Avenue, New York, NY 10158

Routledge is an imprint of the Taylor & Francis Group, an informa business

British Library Cataloguing-in-Publication Data
A catalogue record for this book is available from the British Library

ISBN: 978-1-032-15443-5 (hbk)
ISBN: 978-1-032-15446-6 (pbk)
ISBN: 978-1-003-24419-6 (ebk)

DOI: 10.4324/9781003244196

Typeset in Goudy
by Newgen Publishing UK

Contents

Editors bio

Harry Lehmann, PtX Lab Lausitz – practical laboratory for fuels and raw materials from green hydrogen; former General Director Sustainable Strategies Umweltbundesamt (German Environment Agency). He is one of the founders of Eurosolar. He was an early member and is now the President of the Factor 10 Club for resource productivity and sustainable use of natural resources. Since 2011 he has been Executive Chairman of the World Renewable Energy Council.

Christoph Hinske, Associate Professor Ecosynomic Deviance, Activation of Entrepreneurial Ecosystems through High-Performance Agreement Systems, SAXION University of Applied Sciences, School of Finance and International Business; Founder 360° Dialogues on System Leadership. He is a lecturer on system leadership and societal transformations at the Eberswalde University for Sustainable Development. He advised Global Action Networks such as the Forest Stewardship Council or the World Green Building Council, financial institutions such as Santander or Deutsche Bank, Transformation Networks such as the Dutch CleanTech Region, or Build by Nature.

Victoire de Margerie is the Founder and Vice-Chairman of the World Materials Forum and Executive Chairman of Rondol, a DeepTech that develops machinery for drug formulations. She has spent 35 years in the Materials Industry in Canada, France, Germany, UK, and USA, first as an Executive and since 1999 as a Board Director (now Arkema and Eurazeo, previously Italcementi, Morgan Ceramics, Outokumpu, and Norsk Hydro). She was elected an Academician at the National Academy of Technologies of France in 2020.

Aneta Slaveikova Nikolova, D. Eng., Climate Action Theme Lead, Environment and Development Division, Economic and Social Commission for Asia and the Pacific UNESCAP. She is an accomplished sustainable development professional with extensive experience in policy development and advocacy, capacity development, and technical assistance to developing countries and countries with economies in transition. Ms. Nikolova currently leads a climate action team focusing on climate finance, Paris Agreement implementation, and review of national GHG reduction commitments.

Contributors

ANM Safiqul Alam, Lead Researcher, GEOMARK LIMITED, Bangladesh.

Ole van Allen, M.Sc., PhD Student, Inland Norway University of Applied Sciences, Hamar, Norway.

Mariusz Baranowski, Assistant Professor, Adam Mickiewicz University in Poznań, Faculty of Sociology, Department of the Study of Social Dynamics, Poland.

Christopher G. Beehner, Professor, Seminole State College of Florida, USA.

Francesco Boatta, Postdoc, "Vrije Universiteit Amsterdam, Department of Ecological Science, Section Animal Ecology", Netherlands.

Suzana Borshiver, Full Professor at the School of Chemistry, Federal University of Rio de Janeiro (UFRJ), Brazil. Coordinator of NEITEC-Nucleus of Industrial and Technological Studies.

Tom Bosschaert, MSc. MArch., Director and Founder, Except Integrated Sustainability, Netherlands.

Mariana Bozesan, Founder and President AQAL Foundation & AQAL Capital, "Full Member Intl. Club of Rome, Fellow World Academy of Art and Science", Germany.

Alan R. Butcher, Research Professor in Geomaterials & Applied Mineralogy Geological Survey of Finland.

Daniel Dahm, Councilor, World Future Council; Managing Director, United Sustainability Group, Germany.

Lisa Doeland, M.A., PhD candidate and lecturer, Radboud University Nijmegen, University of Amsterdam, Netherlands.

Klaus M. Dosch, Dipl.-Ing., Head of the Factor X Agency, Indeland GmbH, Germany.

Martin Faulstich, Head of Research Group Resource and Energy Systems, TU Dortmund University, Germany.

Henning Friege, Partner N^3 Thinking Ahead Dr. Friege & Partners, Germany and Honorary Professor of Sustainability Sciences, Leuphana University, Lüneburg.

Mario Giampietro, ICREA Research Professor, Universitat Autònoma de Barcelona & Institució Catalana de Recerca i Estudis Avançats (ICREA), Spain.

Monika Gonser, Head of the Intersectoral School of Governance Baden-Württemberg, Intersectoral School of Governance Baden-Württemberg, Cooperative State University Baden-Württemberg (DHBW), Germany.

Floris de Graad, Director, Dutch Vegetarians Association, Netherlands.

Willi Haas, Senior Scientist and Lecturer, Institute of Social Ecology, University of Natural Resources and Life Sciences (BOKU), Vienna, Austria.

Christoph Hinske, Associate Professor Ecosynomic Deviance, Activation of Entrepreneurial Ecosystems, SAXION University of Applied Sciences, School of Finance and International Business.

Sandra Hoomans, Researcher Sustainability & Strategic Decision-making/ Teacher Finance and Control, SAXION University of Applied Sciences, Netherlands.

Jonas Huether, Head of subdivision Circular Economy, Research Group Resource and Energy Systems, TU Dortmund University, Germany.

Charlotte Joachimsthaler, M.Sc., Research Associate, Research Group Resource and Energy Systems, TU Dortmund University, Germany.

Helen Kopnina, Senior Lecturer Sustainable Business, Northumbria University, Newcastle Business School, UK.

Klaus Kümmerer, Professor of Sustainable Chemistry and Resources, Dierctor Institute for Sustainable Chemistry, Leuphana University Lüneburg, Germany and Director Research and Education Insternational Sustainable Chemistry Collaborative Center, Bonn, Germany.

Anran Luo, Dr., Post-Doctoral Researcher, Department of Environmental Politics, Helmholtz Centre for Environmental Research, Germany.

Alexa K. Lutzenberger, Managing Shareholder, ResScore GmbH, Germany.

Reinier de Man, MSc chemistry and PhD social sciences, Sustainable Supply Chain Consultant (retired), Leiden, the Netherlands.

Maureen Metcalf, CEO/Founder, Innovative Leadership Institute, USA.

Simon P. Michaux, Prof., Associate Professor of Geometallurgy, Geological Survey of Finland.

David Ness, Adjunct Professor, University of South Australia.

Aneta Slaveikova Nikolova, D. Eng., Climate Action Theme Lead, Environment and Development Division, Economic and Social Commission for Asia and the Pacific UNESCAP.

Anna Hulda Olafsdottir, Head of the National Knowledge Centre on Climate Change Adaptation at the Icelandic Met Office, Rejkavik, Iceland.

Nathália Fernandes Pimentel, Bachelor in International Relations, Federal University of Goias (UFG), Brazil.

Janez Potočnik, Co-Chair, UNEP International Resource Panel, Partner Systemiq, Slovenia.

James L. Ritchie-Dunham, Prof. Dr., President, Institute for Strategic Clarity (President), Boston College Carroll School of Management (Part-time Faculty), Harvard University (Research Collaborator), Universidad Politécnica de Madrid itdUPM (Advisory Board), USA.

Theodoros Semertzidis, Lecturer (Teaching), Deputy Programme Leader for MSc Sustainable Resources: Economics, Policy and Transitions UCL, UK.

Roger Strand, Professor, University of Bergen, Norway.

Martin Stuchtey, Founder SYSTEMIQ and The Landbanking Group, Professor Innsbruck University, Germany.

Harald U. Sverdrup, Professor of System Dynamics Game Development and Interactive Simulations, Inland Norway University of Applied Sciences, Norway.

Laís Forti Thomaz, Assistant Professor and Head of the International Office, Federal University of Goias (UFG), Brazil.

Tilmann Vahle, Director Sustainable mobility and batteries, SYSTEMIQ GmbH, Germany.

Corinna Vosse, Director Academy for Sufficiency, Center for Cultural Research, Germany.

Martin Welp, Chair of Socioeconomics and Communication, Head of International Master Study Programme Global Change Management "Eberswalde University for Sustainable Development (University of Applied Sciences), Faculty of Forest and Environment", Germany.

Preface

Are we daydreaming or awake?

Since the 1960s, forward-thinking leaders, scientists, and practitioners alike have done nothing less than voice loud wake-up calls to humankind.

Let us recall two of these appeals: The Limits to Growth (Meadows et al., 1972) and the Factor X Manifesto (Schmidt-Bleek, 2000). These two works are just two of the many alarm bells to wake us up from fantasies of endless economic growth through limitless resource exploitation. Did the calls work? Are we awake? Are you awake?

Is the Circular Economy the first act of us being awake? Or are we, using the words of American biologist Edward O. Wilson, "*[…] a waking dreamer, caught between the fantasies of sleep and the chaos of the real world, […]?*" Might it be that we do not dare to recognise that the Circular Economy is the inevitable outcome of what he called: "[...] *a Star Wars civilization, with Stone Age emotions, medieval institutions, and godlike technology*" (Wilson, 2013). Could we be collectively trapped in what Kahneman and Tversky (1973) call the illusion of validity, a cognitive bias that makes us think that what we're doing is valid, even though we know it's not?

The book is for those who cannot let go of the thought that focusing on circularity alone may be an "illusion of validity", leading us down the wrong path for which we will pay dearly in the future. It is for those who want to overcome bureaucratic hurdles and go fast on breakthrough innovations that can significantly impact decoupling continuous economic growth from using our natural resources (Margerie, 2009). It invites us to explore how the actual concept might lure us into believing that only minor changes in production technologies enable us to continue rushing on a path of continuous economic growth.

The 26 articles in this volume help current and future leader-managers to make well-founded decisions by providing facts and arguments from different disciplines and sectors.

However, before ramping up investments that help us move materials around in circles, we should contemplate the notion that economics and the technosphere are not ends in themselves. They serve the wealth of humanity – the fulfilment of humanity's needs. To put it in the words of Erich Fromm (2016), a German social psychologist and psychoanalyst:

> Our consumer and market economy is based on the idea that you can buy contentment and happiness like you can buy anything. However, happiness is completely different; it only comes from inner effort, doesn't cost any money, and is, therefore, the "cheapest" thing in the world. That is something that has not yet dawned on people in a society that makes them pay for everything.

This statement invites us to ask, "How much is enough?" but also: "What kind of wealth should our economy generate?" Is it about "Well-having or well-being?" Thus, this book is for decision-makers who know that more technology does not create more sustainability and happiness but that our mindsets, quality of agreement systems, and behaviours that make the difference (Ritchie-Dunham, 2014).

With that, this book builds and expands on the declaration of Friedrich Bio Schmidt-Bleek:

> System-Policies must become the norm because policies seeking to solve individual environmental, societal, economic, and institutional problems one at a time, without taking inter-dependencies among them into account, cannot protect the environment nor can it lead to a sustained human economy.
>
> (Schmidt-Bleek, 2014)

Let us recall that humanity crossed an estimated four out of nine planetary boundaries, which will drive the Earth system into a much less hospitable state. The tragedy is that improvement in the global trends is not in sight. Every year, it gets more dramatic. Urgent action is needed to preserve the life-giving functions of our natural environment (Lehmann, 2020).

By taking its impossibilities seriously and making it a robust tool, we believe the Circular Economy to be an important stepping stone to the dematerialisation of our economies, a concept broadly discussed in the four previous Factor X publications. We are hopeful that the Circular Economy can become part of our Civilization Project, allowing us to live within the planetary boundaries and give Earth time to regenerate, allowing humankind to survive!

With this book in hand, you have a strong starting point to form your opinion to advance the Circular Economy at a fundamental and systemic level. The chapters enable you to see through the marketing and policy charade, selling the Circular Economy as a silver bullet and realising specific barriers insurmountability.

It is your turn to assess if we are daydreaming or awake.

We profoundly thank all authors for spending many hours writing interesting articles contained in this 5th Factor X edition. We would also like to thank the reviewers and Mrs Martina Eick, Mr Eben Anuwa-Amarh, Mr Timber Haaker, and Mr Joey Willemse for their thoughtful and insightful comments that led to an improvement of the book.

Note: The chapters in this book do not necessarily reflect the opinion or policy of the Federal Environment Agency or the editors.

References

Fromm, E. (2016). *Locarneser Interviews* (R. Funk, Ed.; German Edition ed.). Edition Erich Fromm.

Kahneman, D., & Tversky, A. (1973). On the psychology of prediction. *Psychological Review*, 80(4), 237–251. https://psycnet.apa.org/doi/10.1037/h0034747

Lehmann, H. (Ed.). (2020). *Sustainable Development and Resource Productivity: The Nexus Approaches*. Routledge.

Margerie, V de (2009). *Strategy & Technology Towards Technology Based Sustainable Competitive Advantage*. L'Harmattan.

Meadows, D. H., Meadows, D. L., Randers, J., & Behrens III, W. W. (1972). *The Limits to Growth: A Report for the Club of Rome's Project on the Predicament of Mankind*. Universe Books.

Ritchie-Dunham, J. L., & Pruitt, B. (2014). *Ecosynomics: The Science of Abundance* (B. Pruitt, Ed.). Vibrancy Ins, LLC.

Schmidt-Bleek, F. (2014). *Grüne Lügen: nichts für die Umwelt, alles fürs Geschäft – wie Politik und Wirtschaft die Welt zugrunde richten*. Ludwig. www.penguinrandomhouse.de/leseprobe/Gruene-Luegen/leseprobe_9783453280571.pdf

Schmidt-Bleek, F. B. (2000). *Factor 10 Manifesto*. Factor 10 Institute. Retrieved December 28, 2021, from www.factor10-institute.org/files/F10_Manifesto_e.pdf

Wilson, E. O. (2013). *The Social Conquest of Earth*. Liveright Publishing Corporation.

Part I

What we dream of!

1 Circularity dreams

Denying physical realities

Reinier de Man

Introduction

The central question of this chapter is: how realistic is the idea of a 'circular economy' from a physical perspective? It will be shown that the often exaggerated claims based on this concept contradict the limits set by down-to-earth physical realities. The ideas of 'Cradle-to-Cradle' (C2C) product designs, important building blocks of 'circular economy' thinking, will be more closely discussed here.

'Circular economy' was developed largely after 2000. However, the conflict between the 'circular economy' concept and physical realities is much older. For example, proponents of endless recycling were heavily criticised on the basis of thermodynamics as early as the 1960s. This more than 60 years old debate is highly relevant for understanding the limits of the 'circular economy'. Therefore, a summary of that debate will precede the discussion of 'circular economy' in this chapter.

Thermodynamics and the economy

Limits to growth

Later in this chapter, the exaggerated claims of the so-called circular economy will be discussed. It will be shown that these claims conflict with physical reality, particularly with the Second Law of Thermodynamics.

Already in the late 1960s, the intensive discussions about the physical limits to economic growth took place. The main themes then were the availability of natural resources and energy and the negative effects of pollution. The book *The Costs of Economic Growth*, published by Ezra Misham in 1967, was a best seller. The discussion became even more intense in the 1970s. In 1972, the Club of Rome published its *Limits to Growth Report*, and the first United Nations *Conference on the Human Environment* took place.

The declaration of the UN Conference set an agenda with ambitious goals for safeguarding natural resources and limiting pollution and at the same time

DOI: 10.4324/9781003244196-2

stimulating worldwide economic growth, an agenda with many questions. To what extent would it be possible to move towards these goals and at the same time to provide the growing world economy with the natural resources it requires? Would it be possible at all or is there a need to question economic growth itself? Whereas mainstream economists framed the question and, consequently, their optimistic answers in classical terms of market and price mechanisms, others, mainly scientists with a natural science background, pointed at the fundamental and inescapable limitations posed by the physical world to the economic system. As a consequence, they were far less optimistic.

The arguments put forward by natural scientists in the early 1970s are not less important today as they show hard physical limits that any design of economic systems should take into account. The central element of these arguments is given by the Second Law of Thermodynamics.

Entropy and economics

Georgescu-Roegen's book *The Entropy Law and the Economic Process*, published in 1971 and based on ideas developed in the second half of the 1960s (Georgescu-Roegen 1971, 1986), marks the beginning of an intense debate on the physical conditions under which the economic process can work. From a natural science point of view, the arguments presented in this book and related publications were nothing new, but they were new to economics. Georgescu-Roegen convincingly showed that, for a proper understanding of the physical basis of the economic world and the limitations created by this physical basis, insight into the implications of the laws of thermodynamics is indispensable.

Based on the First and Second Law of Thermodynamics, the basic argument is straightforward: In an isolated system, the amount of energy remains constant (the First Law), while the available energy continuously and irrevocably degrades into unavailable states (the Second Law). Similarly, highly available materials (low entropy) irreversibly degrade into less available materials (high entropy). The concept of availability is important here. Highly concentrated ores, for example, represent a form of high availability or, formulated in thermodynamic terms, low entropy. Waste streams represent high entropy: the materials contained in them are much less available than in the original ore, for example. The same for energy sources: natural gas deposits represent low entropy/high availability.

Recycling waste into more valuable materials always implies purification, creating a more available from less available material, from high to low entropy. This will always require adding energy. Recycling always means energy use, either by depleting fossil energy resources or using solar energy. Georgescu-Roegen warns, in this context, against exaggerated expectations of recycling. Not only does he point at the enormous amounts of energy needed to extract valuable materials from waste. He also points to the time needed: 'Perhaps, we could recycle everything if and only if we could dispose not only of a limitless amount of energy but also of an infinite time' (Georgescu-Roegen 1986).

The economists' resistance

Anyone with some basic knowledge of natural science understands that the limits posed by the Second Law of Thermodynamics are real and non-negotiable. The increase in entropy – i.e. the degradation of any material or form of energy from available to unavailable states – cannot be avoided. Only by adding energy can this process be reversed. Technologies that claim otherwise are impossible. It is interesting that even prominent economists often fail to recognise the absolute character of these physical limitations. Georgescu-Roegen gives a beautiful anecdote:

> Especially after the miraculous technological advances of the recent decades, our faith in technology ... to go beyond or even to refute any known law became a general obsession. For a glaring example: I portrayed the working of the entropy law in an isolated system by an hourglass in which the stuff in the upper half stands for low entropy and by pouring down it degrades into high entropy (waste). To express the irrevocability of the process, I specified that, in contrast to the usual ones, the 'thermodynamic hourglass' cannot be turned over. Paul A. Samuelson, as he finally came to speak of entropy in the last edition authored by him alone of his celebrated textbook, Economics ... asserted that 'Science can temporarily turn the [hour] glass over'. ... Sir Arthur Eddington ... advised that 'if your theory is found to be against the second law of thermodynamics ... there is nothing for it but to collapse in deepest humiliation'. Albert Einstein also opined that thermodynamics 'is the only physical theory of universal content [that] will never be overthrown'. That is, heat will never pass by itself from the colder condenser to the hotter boiler.
>
> (Georgescu-Roegen, 1986: 14)

The situation has not much changed between the early 1970s and today. The thermodynamic arguments brought forward by various authors cannot be dismissed to be merely opinions, as is also underlined in the above quote. They are irrefutable facts grounded in universally valid theories. Nonetheless, these facts are still being denied by economists and practitioners who base their actions on standard economic theory. They are also denied by consultants who sell attractive stories about endless recycling that are too good to be true, such as 'circular economy'.

Circular economy

Immodest claims

Introduction

The idea of a so-called 'circular economy' is being embraced by national governments, the EU, private sector companies and many others. It has become a cornerstone of the European Commission's thinking, not only in dealing with resources and waste but also in the context of promoting continued, 'sustainable' economic growth.

A 'circular economy' is being presented as the systemic alternative to the traditional model of a 'linear economy'. The idea was summarised, for example, in the communication from the Commission of July 2014: *Towards a Circular Economy: A Zero Waste Programme for Europe*:

> Pumping resources back into productive use, again and again, cutting waste and reducing dependence on uncertain supplies is a direct route to improving resilience and competitiveness. By helping to decouple economic growth from resource use and its impacts, it offers the prospect of sustainable growth that will last.
>
> (p. 3)

Even more radical is the narrative given by the Ellen MacArthur Foundation:

> Such an economy is based on a few simple principles. … First, at its core, a circular economy aims to design out waste. Waste does not exist: products are designed and optimised for a cycle of disassembly and reuse. These tight component and product cycles define the circular economy and set it apart from disposal and even recycling, where large amounts of embedded energy and labour are lost. Second, circularity introduces a strict differentiation between consumable and durable components of a product. Unlike today, consumables in the circular economy are largely made of biological ingredients or 'nutrients' that are at least non-toxic and possibly even beneficial, and can safely be returned to the biosphere, either directly or in a cascade of consecutive uses.
>
> (Ellen MacArthur Foundation, 2013a, p.14)

In such publications by policy makers and their consultants, 'circular economy' is presented as a radical solution for radically reducing resource use and at the same time stimulating ('green') economic growth. These claims are based on a set of so-called 'principles'. Whether sticking to these principles really leads to the claimed results is not proven. It is not even made plausible. It appears that 'circular economy' is more popular because of the big promises it makes than of the results it can reasonably produce, which will be shown in the following paragraphs.

The so-called 'principles' of Cradle-to-Cradle

The basis for the present 'circular economy' ideas was laid by the work of Braungart and McDonough on 'Cradle-to-Cradle' (or 'C2C') and the subsequent work by the Ellen MacArthur Foundation. Two of the key principles on which the C2C framework was based are still the accepted basis for circular economy thinking (Bjørn & Hauschild, 2012: 322):

1. *Waste Equals Food* 'The first key principle calls for the elimination of the very concept of waste and encourages inspiration by nature's seemingly perfect nutrient cycles. The focus is to design systems with emissions that other processes can take up as nutrients instead of trying to reduce the amount of waste as advocated by ecoefficiency. This applies to emissions during the production and use stage of a product and also to the product itself when it reaches its disposal stage. To ensure that such emissions can undergo recycling in continuous loops without loss of quality, materials should either be defined as technical or biological nutrients. Technical nutrients should be designed for industrial recycling, whereas biological nutrients should be designed to return to the soil and feed environmental processes. … If biological and technical nutrients are mixed beyond easy separability, a product is created that neither fits the biological nor the technical nutrient cycle. Such a product can never truly be recycled and the result is a "downcycled" product of lower quality and value' (Bjørn & Hauschild, 2012: 322).
2. *Use current solar income* 'The second key principle dictates that the energy required to fuel a continuous-loop C2C society must all originate from "current solar income", defined as photovoltaic, geothermal, wind, hydro, and biomass. These are commonly defined as renewable energy sources. There are no quantitative constraints on the amount of energy used throughout the life cycle of a C2C product. The quantity of energy used is irrelevant as long as the energy quality (i.e., energy source in this context) meets the requirements of current solar income' (ibidem: 323).

Weaknesses

Design rules, not reality

The 'circular economy' is based on the idea that products and production systems should be designed in a way that 'waste equals food' (principle 1) and that we do not need more energy than solar power provides (principle 2). The principles are design rules for the economy: 'Products, production systems and supply chains should be designed in a way that no waste is generated other than materials that can be fed again productively into biological or technical cycles without negative impacts'.

Unfortunately, policy makers and their advisers mistake the design rules for a description of reality. They erroneously claim (or at least convey the impression) that waste does not exist and always represents a useful raw material. As a consequence, they systematically underestimate the seriousness of present waste problems.

Theoretical weaknesses

Suppose we manage to apply the 'circular economy' design principles as postulated by the C2C school of thought. Will we succeed in creating material cycles that contribute to value creation, enabling economic growth without creating any waste (apart from nutrients that can be fed into biological and technical cycles) and without creating any adverse impacts on the environment and climate? Close examination of the assumptions on which the C2C model is built shows no certainty that the answer is positive.

The model shows at least the following fundamental weaknesses:

1. *Neglect of energy requirements* of maintaining materials pure. Just assuming that 'Waste equals Food' is misleading. Only in rare cases, in which materials are used without mixing so that they can easily be recollected after use, will waste equal 'food', nutrients that can be fed into new cycles. In all other cases, if one does not accept downcycling, purification steps will be required. In simple thermodynamic terms, entropy has to be lowered, which necessarily costs energy. Thus, removing the last tiny fraction of pollution will cost a disproportionally high amount of energy. In the C2C logic, the use of energy is supposed not to pose any problem if it comes from 'current solar income', but the amount of energy needed to prevent downcycling in all material cycles may not be available, see next point.
2. *Neglect of limited availability of energy from regenerative sources*. The C2C school of thought simply postulates that energy will not be a problem since it will be from regenerative sources, the so-called 'current solar income'. However, there is no guarantee that the energy needed will be available or can be made available in time. As a result, designs based on C2C may have the unintended consequence that more fossil fuels will be needed.
3. *The incorrect assumption that the ecological footprint of regenerative energy sources can be neglected*. Building wind turbines and solar cells does have negative ecological impacts. They may largely be outweighed by their positive contribution to sustainability, but they cannot be neglected.
4. *Lack of attention to the negative impacts created by the logistics needed for closing all material cycles*. Llorach-Massana et al. (2015: 245) remark: '… the 100% closed cycle is difficult (or even impossible) to implement. The full waste recovery would require an extraordinary increase of transport and management of goods that are associated with higher energy consumption. The energy requirements may result in a scenario where materials' management for closing nutrient cycles could represent a higher environmental impact than other waste management solutions'.
5. The incorrect assumption that 'natural' nutrients can be fed into natural systems without adverse effects on biodiversity and other ecological factors, Reijnders (2008) points at Braungart et al.'s misconception with regard to biological nutrients: 'Contrary to what Braungart et al. suggest … increased emissions or wastes consisting of "biological nutrients" are not ecologically irrelevant. That "biological nutrients" participate in cyclical flows (biogeochemical cycles) does not mean that there are no negative effects of increased inputs in those cycles. Both the occurrence of negative effects due to increased emissions of "biological nutrients" and the occurrence of

hazardous substances in biological materials suggest that there is often a case for management of natural materials in a way that tries to minimise negative impacts'.

6. *The incorrect assumption that growth of material use can be completely decoupled from economic growth.* Even if the C2C approach resulted in endlessly circulating material cycles (technical and/or biological), economic growth would result in the need for additional resources to create new cycles (see Bjørn & Hauschild, 2012; Llorach-Massana, 2015).

If we correct these weaknesses, we immediately understand that the promise of virtually unlimited economic growth without adverse impacts on ecology and climate is close to outright nonsense. Interestingly, the scientific debate about the strengths and weaknesses of the C2C approach is limited to a handful of articles, which, with no exception, are critical and do recognise the points mentioned above. Apparently, this criticism has not influenced the debate in circles of public policy and private sector strategies at all.

Practical limitations

Apart from the fundamental problems with the 'circular economy' concept, there are huge practical problems that need to be addressed. Even if endless recycling loops were possible, there is the problem that there is no guaranteed demand for certain recycled materials in the future. Materials used today may not be used in 10 or 20 years' time. Other problems relate to product and material information systems needed for optimal recycling. These and other issues will be addressed in other chapters of this book.

Strengths

C2C design principles do have their strengths, not as a basis for policy but as a creative design tool. The highly idealistic principles on which C2C thinking is based should not be considered to represent goals that can be reached in reality but as tools to guide our thinking on systems that deal qualitatively differently with material cycles and waste. On the basis of the C2C methodology, the designer of a product, a production process, or a supply chain will ask: 'What solutions can I imagine that keep biological and technical cycles completely separate and that allow to exclude the generation of any "waste" that cannot be fed into the system as a "nutrient"?'. Creative thinking will most probably produce a number of alternative system designs. The end result may be an improved design that leads to less waste, better recycling and other advantages.

The strength of the 'circular economy' (or C2C) language in a design context is at the same time its weakness in a policy context. It is based on an absolute, utopian vision that certainly guides the design process in the right direction but will create illusions in a policy context.

Conclusion and recommendations

From a scientific and technical viewpoint, we conclude that the concept of a 'circular economy', largely based on the C2C design 'principles', is very weak. Moreover, from a policy point of view, the concept is dangerous as it not only creates illusions of a waste-free world but also fails to address the huge efforts that are really needed to create a sustainable economy, including the need for slowing down the depletion of natural resources, reducing the demand for energy and radically changing the design of products and production processes.

Oversimplified and therefore misleading fairy tales of a rapid transition to a circular economy do not help. On the contrary, they deny the seriousness of the problem and the difficulty of its solutions. It is time to fully recognise the assertion that 'waste is food' is a lie today and will remain a lie in the future.

Policy makers should no longer be misled by empty slogans such as 'circular economy'. They should focus on real problems, real developments and real solutions in the real world instead of ideal solutions in an idealised world. Instead of dreaming about unlimited green growth in a waste-free world, they should focus on the intelligent design of products, production and recycling processes and minimisation of natural resource use.

References

Bjørn, Anders and Michael Z. Hauschild, Absolute versus Relative Environmental Sustainability – What Can the Cradle-to-Cradle and Eco-efficiency Concepts Learn from Each Other? *Journal of Industrial Ecology*, 17.2 (2012), 321.

Commission, *Towards a Circular Economy: A Zero Waste Programme for Europe*, Communication from the Commission to the European Parliament, The Council, The European Economic and Social Committee and the Committee of the Regions, Brussels 2.7.2014, COM(2014) 398 final.

Ellen MacArthur Foundation, *Towards the Circular Economy – Accelerating the Scale-up across global supply chains*, prepared in collaboration with the World Economic Forum and McKinsey & Company, August 2013.

Georgescu-Roegen, Nicholas, The Entropy Law and the Economic Process. Harvard University Press, Cambridge, Massachusetts (1971). ISBN 978-0674257801.

Georgescu-Roegen, Nicholas, The Entropy Law and the Economic Process in Retrospect, *Eastern Economic Journal*, Volume XII, January–March (1986).

Llorach-Massana, Pere, Ramon Farreny, and Jordi Oliver-Solà, Are Cradle to Cradle Certified Products Environmentally Preferable – Analysis from an LCA Approach, *Journal of Cleaner Production*, 93 (2015), 243–250.

Reijnders, L., Are Emissions or Wastes Consisting of Biological Nutrients Good or Healthy? – Letter to the Editor, *Journal of Cleaner Production*, 16 (2008), 1138–1141.

2 Does waste equal food?

Examining the feasibility of circular economy in the food industry

Helen Kopnina, Francesco Boatta, Mariusz Baranowski, and Floris de Graad

Introduction: the (im)possibilities of circular food

Environmental problems, from climate change to biodiversity loss and pollution, are recognized to be caused by an increase in human population, production, and consumption (Victor and Jackson 2015; Sullivan 2020). One of the largest challenges to meet sustainable development is feeding almost eight billion people without compromising the needs of future generations to meet their own needs (Brundtland 1987) and in a more ambitious ecocentric vision, without compromising the other species' survival (Piccolo et al 2018; Washington et al 2018; Taylor et al 2020). This also highlights how our choices as consumers have an indirect consequence on biodiversity.

We are becoming aware that it is impossible to rely on finite resources and that our economy should shift from a linear to a circular approach. The circular economy promises more efficient and effective use of resources and waste, based on the Cradle-to-Cradle (C2C) framework (McDonough and Braungart 2010; Stahel 2016).

However each type of waste has its features and its recycling efficiency might change, making it less "durable" after multiple cycles (Converse 1997; Craig 2001). Provided that energy is added to the process, inorganic materials such as glass, aluminum, or copper can efficiently and indefinitely be recycled and repurposed into new products. Other materials, such as paper or plastic, can be recycled for only a limited time before not being anymore suitable for utilization, resulting in "downcycling" and resource loss (McDonough and Braungart 2010). The food production for a single species causes a deficit in other species' food chains, from top predators to insects down the food chain. Also, packaging "for billions of consumers presents a challenge, especially if the alternative is to be found to petrochemical waste, which is cheap" (*The Economist* 2018). Existing solutions, such as RePack (www.repack.com/news/carbon-footprint-of-reusable-packaging), are not used on a mass scale and do not represent a real alternative to the global industrial economy with mass-scale value chains (Geng et al 2019).

The energy required to recycle makes full circularity a "thermodynamic impossibility" (Man and Friege 2016: 6), and the absolute decoupling of natural resources from economic activity rarely occurs (Victor and Jackson 2015;

DOI: 10.4324/9781003244196-3

Washington and Maloney 2020). Thus, the optimism about absolute decoupling or upcycling is rarely warranted in the case of consumables.

This is particularly true for the food industry and the waste associated with food production and consumption. Industrial agriculture and animal husbandry present challenges ranging from climate change (greenhouse gas emissions) to biodiversity loss due to the use of fertilizers and insecticides (Garnett et al 2013), exacerbating the need for a sustainable approach to waste management in the food industrial sector.

Different from the aforementioned inorganic materials which can be effectively recycled, the waste from the food industry is mainly composed of nutrients whose composition can vary depending on their source (Jurgilevich et al 2016). The sources of food waste can be divided into two big domains: waste of industrial origin (food loss) that derives from all the processes before the consumer (e.g., production, post-harvest, and processing – approximately 30% to 50% of food intended for human consumption is wasted at different stages of the food system) and waste of consumer household origin (food waste) (Stuart 2009, Gustavsson et al 2011; Jurgilevich et al 2016; FAO 2020). The losses are much more extensive and also include energy, greenhouse emissions, other pollutants, and feces (Ibid).

Therefore, the main objective of the chapter is to explore possible solutions such as the closed-loop systems C2C and circular economy in the context of the food production and sustainability perspective. The sections below engage with C2C principles and the 9-R strategy for the circular economy but also discuss the danger of subversion. Consequently, we turn to Lindeman's (1942) rule and Moerman's ladder. Lindeman's rule states that there is only a 10% transmission of energy from one trophic level to the next. Moerman's ladder indicates how much value can still be extracted from food that is lost. Following that, we discuss alternatives, such as vegan diets, meat substitutes, lab-grown meat, and, in particular, insects. The chapter centers on the question: is circularity in food production possible?

Food waste has a composition that does not allow the same conversion efficiency obtained with inorganic materials. The increased global population further drives the demand for natural resources (Lidicker 2020; Washington and Maloney 2020), and the increased demand for food produces waste. Additionally, industrial agriculture and animal husbandry present environmental challenges due to excessive use of fertilizers and insecticides (Garnett et al 2013). This scenario exacerbates the need to be more effective to implement the circular economy approach in the food sector.

C2C principles and 9-R strategy for the circular economy: literature review

Circular economy evaluations using the 9-R scale (Figure 2.1) and C2C accreditation and certification are intended to inform producers' choices. These evaluations also address the inputs associated with all the production outputs, use, and disposal, including the product itself, byproducts, and delivery (Ünal and

Shao 2019). C2C identifies three key principles of alternative production systems, starting with *the Waste equals food* principle (e.g., a cherry tree's berries and leaves are nutrients for other species or soil when decomposed). *The use renewables principle* supports only infinite source renewables such as wind and sun. *Celebrate diversity* refers to complex relations within ecosystems. In the biological cycle, the principle of "waste equals food" becomes especially salient (McDonough and Braungart 2010). Yet food, organic material, can hardly be shared between species unless the waste of one species is used as food by others (dung beetles) that contribute to soil formation.

Similar to C2C, a circular economy is based on design principles aimed to eliminate waste and pollution, keep products and materials in use, and regenerate natural systems (EMF 2015). There are various levels of the 9-R hierarchy of circular production. Refuse (R-1) means "doing without," thus stimulating a steady-state economy (Daly 1991) and degrowth (O'Neill 2012; Smith et al 2021).

Notably, in the original hierarchy (RLI 2015; Kirchherr et al 2017; Potting et al 2017), Reduce (R-2) still comes before Re-use (R-3), which is corrected in Figure 2.1 below, as shown by arrows.

Infinite Re-use can be said the best promise of absolute decoupling, satisfying the ultimate goal of the closed-loop systems (Ghisellini et al 2016). Other Rs can counter the take-make-waste system of production and the built-in obsolescence (Bulow 1986). While recovery of metals in electronics has significant sustainability gains (Geng et al 2019), it is difficult if not impossible in the food industry and packaging (Aarnio and Hämäläinen 2008). Refuse (R-1) in food consumption means starvation.

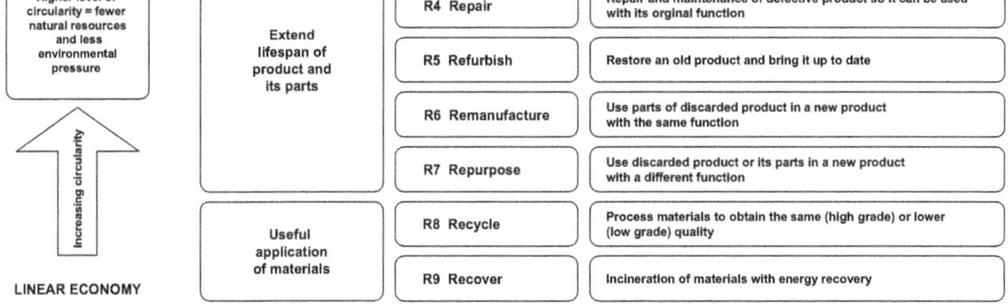

Figure 2.1 The 9-R hierarchy of circular economy.

Source: Adopted and changed from RLI (2015: 15) and Potting et al (2017) with modifications made by the chapter authors.

The "circular packaging" is challenging since most plastic used today is made of petrochemical waste, which is cheap (*The Economist* 2018). Much of food packaging is a "monstrous hybrid" combining organic and nonorganic materials (McDonough and Braungart 2010). Alternative "organic" or bioplastic packaging is often single-use and requires monoculture plantations (Kopnina 2017). Also, advanced recycling technologies for biodegradable bioplastics are still underdeveloped (Borrello et al 2016).

The danger of subversion

Yet, not all is green or circular what is so labeled; for example, the ISO CE standards, which are (in some countries) lacking the involvement of all sectors (www.iso.org/committee/7203984.html). The concept of CE (Circular Economy) and its practice has almost exclusively been developed and led by practitioners, that is, policy-makers, businesses, business consultants, business associations, and business foundations (Korhonen et al 2018: 37). Many of the "good practice" companies on the list of the largest promoter of circular economy, Ellen MacArthur Foundation (EMF), focus on continuing production, *not* infinite reuse (Kopnina 2019; 2021). The circular economy is touted as the "new engine of economic growth" (EMF 2015), inspiring optimism but also opening the door for greenwashing.

McDonough and Braungart's book, *The Upcycle* (2013), illustrates unrealistic optimism. Rather than continuously reusing materials as proposed in the *Cradle to Cradle* book, *The Upcycle* suggests that humans can have a net positive effect on ecosystems. This optimism seems unwarranted in the case of biodiversity (Buchmann-Duck and Beazley 2020). While the upcycled food industry may be worth $46.7 billion (Shirvell 2019), upcycling, in this case, refers to companies that, for example, produce beer from old bread, obviously charging more for the former (Kopnina and Blewitt 2018). While the volume of the material decreases in the process of conversion, the monetary value increases – which is not the same as upcycling the original resource (e.g., grain) or contributing to biodiversity conservation.

De Man and Friege (2016) note that in reality waste is rarely "food" due to thermodynamic laws. Producing massive quantities of insects or other food for a single species is unlikely to preserve habitats and food for other species. Thus, claims of circular economy as being ecologically beneficial seem optimistic at best.

Lindeman's rule and Moerman's ladder

Lindeman's rule in ecology refers to energy flow and nutrient cycling two processes of paramount importance for an ecosystem (Lindeman 1942). Contrarily to nutrients that can be cycled, the energy flow is unidirectional and dissipated while transferred through the trophic levels. According to Lindeman's 10% rule, only a small proportion of the energy intake is fixed into the trophic level and available for the next one. The remaining energy is used by the organisms to maintain the basic metabolic requirements (respiration, maintenance of homeostasis, or investment in growth and reproduction). Therefore the close the trophic level is to the primary production (e.g., herbivores), the lower the solar energy waste is (Lindeman 1942).

Moerman's ladder indicates how much value can still be extracted from food that is lost, thus "the higher up the ladder, the better." Considering Moerman's ladder (cf. Rood et al 2017:33) the greatest value in economic and energy terms is the use of the food product for human consumption. Lower in the hierarchy is the use of these products as animal feed (Lucassen 2019). At the bottom of the ladder is food incineration, a common practice in the agri-food sector (Rood et al 2017). The use of residue streams in a food context is more complex than the conceptual framework suggests as "the devil is in the detail of a production process and the environmental impacts associated with it, as well as any lock-in effects from previous investments" (Rood et al 2017:32). In any policy aimed at promoting a circular economy, it would therefore be sensible to provide room for tailored solutions and flexibility. Instruments are therefore needed which can be used to "substantiate why it would be better to deviate from the 'rule of thumb,' in a particular case" (Rood et al 2017:32). A major problem is that these instruments are still being developed.

Alternative protein research and products

Even if reasoning starts from the human needs, and not the needs of multiple nonhuman species, considerable effort is needed. These needs are reflected in the "food pyramid" of which some components need more labor and resources, and others less. Proteins often need the most labor and resources for production. However, this is mainly so because of the choice of animal protein as an important source. A lot can be won when we change our diets. If the whole global population would choose a plant-based diet, an agricultural area as big as Africa would be "saved" (Poore and Nemecek 2018).

Several alternatives, including vegan diets, vegetable meat substitutes, lab-grown meat, and insect food, have been developed. The quantity of protein needed can roughly be specified: the average protein needed per person multiplied by the human population is what is needed, given that the recommended dietary allowance has already a safety margin built in (Harvard Health Publishing 2020).

However, a lacto-vegetarian diet with a strong plant-based component seems to be the optimum from the perspective of land use (Peters et al 2016; De Boer et al 2019). In the last decade, many plant-based meat substitutes started to play an important role in consumer choice, justifying billions that have been invested in research (Chiorando 2019). From the nutritional and environmental perspective, a well-chosen vegetarian diet contains all nutrients necessary (De Waart 2018). Meat substitutes offer consumers a balanced diet composed of various ingredients. The same holds for lab-grown meat, which some research showed has no nutritional advantage compared to a well-chosen lacto-vegetarian diet, and it is unclear if it is better than the meat it seeks to replace (Jiang et al 2020).

Insects

Insects have an excellent nutritional profile (Makkar et al. 2014) and are rich in protein and lipids, and some insect species (*Hermetia illucens*, the black soldier fly, and *Musca domestica*, the housefly) have an essential amino acid profile and protein content that resembles that of fish meal (Makkar et al. 2014). These characteristics coupled with a low environmental impact required for their production (van Huis and Oonincx 2017) make insect-based ingredients excellent sources of valuable nutrients.

One insect species (the mealworm, *Tenebrio Molitor*) has been recently listed among the novel food by the European Union (Regulation 2015/2283) and is thus safe for human consumption. In addition to that, insect meal and insect oil are also seen as excellent raw materials for the formulation of animal feed (aquaculture, poultry industry). The use of seven insect species as ingredients for the formulation of livestock feed formulation has been recently approved by the European Union (Regulation 2017/893).

Many studies suggest that insect-based conversion of organic waste might also improve the management of the increasing problem of food waste (Cheng et al. 2017; van Huis and Oonincx 2017; van Huis et al. 2013). Therefore insects-fed organic waste might represent an excellent solution to transform low-quality organic waste into high-quality feed ingredients.

However, insects are considered farmed animals by the European Union (Regulation 1069/2009) and can be fed neither manure nor catering food waste, ruminant proteins, or meat-and-bone meal. This is to prevent the potential vertical transmission of harmful organisms present in the organic residues which could represent a health risk for humans and livestock. Therefore the current legislative framework impedes the use of insects-fed organic waste for food and feed applications (Pinotti et al. 2019).

Insect-based products can be used also for the production of secondary industrial compounds (e.g., biofuel, lubricants, pharmaceuticals, and dyes) (Fowles and Nansen 2020) whose regulations might be more relaxed toward the presence of specific pathogens. Therefore, despite the insects used to upcycle organic waste might not yet find a safe application in the food and feed sector they could still upcycle valuable organic products useful for different industrial applications.

Discussion: is circularity in food production possible?

Applying circular economy principles to food production requires, first and foremost, a holistic transformation (Waddal et al 2015) of the food chain. Some Rs from Figure 2.1 are not applicable here but some can be, such as information about what type of energy is used for food production (e.g., growing insects in The Netherlands). There is a big difference between, for example, solar energy and biofuels derived from incinerating wooden pallets or garbage (the lowest R on the 9R scale, Recovery).

One of the larger issues is that the *waste equals food* principle does not apply *after* consumption. In the case of consumables, circularity is impossible without considering what happens to end products. When animals digest food, their waste fertilizes the ground, spreading the seeds. Human toilet waste is hardly used to satisfy the needs of other species, it is either chemically treated and destroyed or burned to produce biofuel, which is the lowest R on the R-hierarchy scale. Refusing food is not an option, but more sustainable (e.g., emissions or water and soil use) or ethical (e.g., animal welfare or labor conditions) food can be seen as a step forward. However, it might be presumptuous (if not to say misleading) to call food circular, especially as feces and urine are not serving as food for endless nutrient cycles.

More indirectly but very importantly, solutions to food shortages include a reduction in the number of people to feed. While the global population has increased due to the advancements in medical and food production technology, we still rely on finite resources (Meadows et al 1972). This reflects on the much-earlier concerns of Thomas Malthus (1826) about the growing population resulting in starvation, war, and disease. Despite the compounding effects of population on global sustainability of resources and food supplies (even if non-human species' interests are discounted), recently much discussion has veered toward consumption in the rich countries (Ganivet 2020). Campbell (2012: 46) points out that the issue of population growth becoming taboo, with the term "Malthusian" becoming derogatory.

Yet, as medical and food production technologies increase life expectancies, it has adverse repercussions on the world's climate and ecosystem's quality, exceeding many of the planetary boundaries (Bogardi et al 2013; Hughes et al 2013). While conscious food movements, including veganism, expanded in some countries, some historically vegan or vegetarian communities (e.g., Hindus) are consuming more meat (Belasco 2014; Devi et al 2014; Pothering 2020), while bushmeat hunting causes the "empty forest syndrome" (Crist et al 2017). Supporting almost 8 billion large omnivores without increasing land conversion for intensive farming and livestock make the interaction between population, food, and biodiversity more pressing (Crist et al 2017; Favre 2019; Shyam 2019), including in mangroves habitats (Boone Kauffman et al 2017). Thus, the population still needs to be considered along with consumption (Kopnina et al 2020; O'Sullivan 2020). Attending to human reproductive rights, avoiding child marriages and unwanted pregnancies through education and information campaigns on family planning offer win-win solutions (Crist et al 2017).

Conclusions

Making food "circular" presents a specific challenge as what needs to be considered is not just how and where food is produced but what happens to the end product (kitchen or toilet waste). The steady-state economy (Daly 1991) and degrowth (O'Neill 2012) have been particularly challenging in the case of food as the first

R of the circular hierarchy, Refuse, is not possible. Existing solutions for closed-loop or circular food products do not and cannot meet all expectations but can provide a more sustainable way of food production. These solutions are nowhere near absolute decoupling or upcycling, given the complex production chain that also involves the use of energy and land.

The insect industry could offer a promising solution for the sustainable management of food waste. Both the insects (as adults or larvae) or the residual substrate after the larval growth can be valuable resources for animal feeds and fertilizers for crops. However, insects-fed food waste and manure do not yet find a concrete application in industry since they are still limited by the legislation aimed at protecting the livestock and consumer's health. While eating insects is much better in terms of greenhouse gas emissions than livestock farming, it still requires tailored feeds for the insects which take up land and uses energy, making the direct consumption of vegetables still more efficient. All considered, a diet without animal protein, vegan substitutes with high protein value, and ecologically restorative agriculture appear more sustainable practices than insects as food. Further investigation in ecological and health effects (use of pesticides, biodiversity loss induced by monocultures, water use and soil erosion, packaging of alternative products, etc.) and social and political acceptance is needed. Decisive and innovative solutions in food production and food waste management are necessary given the growing population and the shift in eating habits occurring in the aspiring middle classes.

References

Aarnio, T. and Hämäläinen, A. (2008). Challenges in packaging waste management in the fast-food industry. *Resources, Conservation and Recycling*, 52(4):612–621.

Belasco, W.J. (2014). *Appetite for Change*. Cornell University Press.

Bogardi, J.J., Fekete, B.M. and Vörösmarty, C.J. (2013). Planetary boundaries revisited: a view through the "water lens." *Current Opinion in Environmental Sustainability*, 5(6):581–589.

Boone Kauffman, J., Arifanti, V.B., Hernández Trejo, H., del Carmen Jesús García, M., Norfolk, J., Cifuentes, M., Hadriyanto, D. and Murdiyarso, D. (2017). The jumbo carbon footprint of a shrimp: carbon losses from mangrove deforestation. *Frontiers in Ecology and the Environment*, 15(4):183–188.

Borrello, M., Lombardi, A., Pascucci, S. and Cembalo, L. (2016). The seven challenges for transitioning into a bio-based circular economy in the agri-food sector. *Recent Patents on Food, Nutrition and Agriculture*, 8(1):39–47.

Brundtland, G.H. (1987). Our common future – Call for action. *Environmental Conservation*, 14(4):291–294.

Buchmann-Duck, J. and Beazley, K.F. (2020). An urgent call for circular economy advocates acknowledging its limitations in conserving biodiversity. *Science of the Total Environment*, 727:138602.

Bulow, J. (1986). An economic theory of planned obsolescence. *The Quarterly Journal of Economics*, 101(4):729–749.

Campbell, M. (2012). Why the silence on population. *Life on the Brink: Environmentalists Confront Overpopulation*. Edited by P. Cafaro and E. Crist. University of Georgia Press, pp.41–56.

Cheng, J. Y., Chiu, S. L., and Lo, I. M. (2017). Effects of moisture content of food waste on residue separation, larval growth, and larval survival in black soldier fly bioconversion. *Waste Management*, *67*:315–323.

Chiorando, M. (2019). *$13 Billion Invested In US Vegan Meat, Egg, And Dairy In 2 Years*, Plant-Based News, https://plantbasednews.org/news/13-billion-invested-us-vegan-meat-egg-dairy-2-years/?fbclid=IwAR1y8mS4L1ae3rE8_DExjn03yovGq_Ohif_s2zqt xUvmvHeh763IZVvtUsM

Converse, A. O. (1997). On complete recycling, 2. *Ecological Economics*, *2*(1):1–2.

Craig, P. P. (2001). Energy limits on recycling. *Ecological Economics*, *36*(3):373–384.

Crist, E., Mora, C. and Engelman, R. (2017). The interaction of the human population, food production, and biodiversity protection. *Science*, *356*(6335):260–264.

Daly, H. (1991). *Steady-State Economics*. Island Press.

de Boer, I.J.M., Van Ittersum, M.K., and Van Zanten, H.H.E. (2019). The role of farm animals in a circular food system, *Global Food Security*, *21*:18–22.

de Man, R. and Friege, H. (2016). Circular economy: European policy on shaky ground. *Waste Management and Research*, *34*(2):1–9.

Devi, S.M., Balachandar, V., Lee, S.I., and Kim, I. H. (2014). An outline of meat consumption in the Indian population-A pilot review. *Korean Journal for Food Science of Animal Resources*, *34*(4):507.

The Economist. (2018). An enzyme that digests plastic… www.economist.com/science-and-technology/2018/04/16/an-enzyme-that-digests-plastic-could-boost-recycling

Ellen MacArthur Foundation (EMF) (2015). Towards a Circular Economy: Economic and Business Rationale for an Accelerated Transition. Ellen MacArthur Foundation. https://emf.thirdlight.com/link/ip2fh05h21it-6nvypm/@/preview/1?o

FAO (2020). The state of food and agriculture. www.fao.org/documents/card/en/c/cb1447en/

Favre, D. (2019). The growing reality of legal rights for companion animals. *Society Register*, *3*(3):143–150.

Fowles, T. M. and Nansen, C. (2020). Insect-based bioconversion: value from food waste. In *Food waste management* (pp. 321–346). Palgrave Macmillan.

Gahukar, R.T. (2011). Entomophagy and human food security. *International Journal of Tropical Insect Science*, *31*(3):129–144.

Ganivet, E. (2020). Growth in the human population and consumption both need to be addressed to reach an ecologically sustainable future. *Environment, Development, and Sustainability*, *22*(6):4979–4998.

Garnett, T., Appleby, M.C., Balmford, A., Bateman, I.J., Benton, T.G., Bloomer, P., … and Herrero, M. (2013). Sustainable intensification in agriculture: Premises and policies. *Science*, *341*(6141):33–34.

Geng, Y., Sarkis, J., and Bleischwitz, R. (2019). Globalize the circular economy. *Nature*, 565:153–155.

Ghisellini, P., Cialani, C., and Ulgiati, S. (2016). A review on circular economy: the expected transition to a balanced interplay of environmental and economic systems. *Journal Cleaner Production*, *114*:11–32.

Gustavsson, J., Cederberg, C., Sonesson, U., van Otterdijk, R., and Meybeck, A. 2011. *Global Food Losses and Food Waste – Extent, Causes, and Prevention*. FAO, Rome. Harvard Health Publishing, 2020 www.health.harvard.edu/nutrition/when-it-comes-to-protein-how-much-is-too-much

Hughes, T.P., Carpenter, S., Rockström, J., Scheffer, M. and Walker, B. (2013). Multiscale regime shifts and planetary boundaries. *Trends in Ecology and Evolution*, *28*(7):389–395.

Jiang, G., Ameer, K., Kim, H., Lee, E.J., Ramachandraiah, K., and Hong, G.P., 2020. Strategies for sustainable substitution of livestock meat. *Foods*, 9(9):1227.

Jurgilevich, A., Birge, T., Kentala-Lehtonen, J., Korhonen-Kurki, K., Pietikainen, J., Saikku, L., and Schosler, H. (2016). Transition towards Circular Economy in the Food System. *Sustainability*, 8(69):1–14.

Kirchherr, J., Reike, D. and Hekkert, M. (2017). Conceptualizing the circular economy: An analysis of 114 definitions. *Resources, Conservation, and Recycling, 127*:221–232.

Kopnina, H. (2017). European Renewable Energy. Applying Circular Economy Thinking to Policy-Making. *Visions for Sustainability* (8) www.ojs.unito.it/index.php/visions/article/view/2331

Kopnina, H. (2019). Green-washing or best case practice? Using circular economy and Cradle to Cradle case studies in educational practice. *Journal of Cleaner Production, 219*:613–623.

Kopnina, H. (2021). Towards ecological management: Identifying barriers and opportunities in transition from linear to a circular economy. *Philosophy of Management, 20*(1):5–19.

Kopnina, H., Washington, H., Lowe, I., and Irvine, S. (2020). Scientists' warning to humanity: strategic thinking on economic development, population, poverty, and ecological sustainability in the Mediterranean and beyond. *Euro-Mediterranean Journal for Environmental Integration*, 5(1):1–15.

Korhonen, J., Honkasalo, A., and Seppälä, J. (2018). Circular Economy: The Concept and its Limitations. *Ecological Economics*, *143*:37–46.

Lidicker, W.Z. (2020). A scientist's warning to humanity on human population growth. *Global Ecology and Conservation*, *24*:p.e01232.

Lindeman, R.L. (1942). The trophic-dynamic aspect of ecology. *Ecology*, *23*(4):399–417.

Lucassen, S. (2019). Animal-based measures: A step towards rights for farm animals? *Society Register*, 3(3):159–166.

Makkar, H.P., Tran, G., Heuzé, V., and Ankers, P. (2014). State-of-the-art on use of insects as animal feed. *Animal Feed Science and Technology*, *197*:1–33.

Malthus, T. (1826). *An Essay on the Principle of Population*, 6th edition. London: John Murray.

McDonough, W. and Braungart, M. (2010). *Cradle to Cradle: Remaking the way we make things*. North Point Press.

McDonough, W. and Braungart, M. (2013). *The Upcycle: Beyond Sustainability – Designing for Abundance*. Macmillan.

Meadows, D.H., Meadows, D.L., Randers, J., and Behrens III. W.W. (1972). *The Limits to Growth*. Universe Books.

O'Neill, D. (2012). Measuring Progress in the Degrowth Transition to a Steady State Economy. *Ecological Economics*, 84:221–231.

O'Sullivan, J.N. (2020). The social and environmental influences of population growth rate and demographic pressure deserve greater attention in ecological economics. *Ecological Economics*, *172*:106648.

Piccolo, J., Washington, H., Kopnina, H., and Taylor, B. (2018). Back to the future: Why conservation biologists should re-embrace their ecocentric roots. *Conservation Biology*, 32(4):959–961.

Pinotti, L., Giromini, C., Ottoboni, M., Tretola, M., and Marchis, D. (2019). Insects and former foodstuffs for upgrading food waste biomasses/streams to feed ingredients for farm animals. *Animal*, *13*(7):1365–1375.

Pothering, J. (2020). "No alternative": India embraces a meat-based future and other 2030 food trends. https://agfundernews.com/no-alternative-india-embraces-a-meat-based-future-and-other-2030-food-trends.html

Potting, J., Hekkert, M.P., Worrell, E., and Hanemaaijer, A. (2017). Circular Economy: Measuring innovation in the product chain. Planbureau voor de Leefomgeving (PVL, Netherlands Environmental Assessment Agency), 2544. www.pbl.nl/en/publications/circular-economy-measuring-innovation-in-product-chains

Peters, C.J., Picardy, J., Darrouzet-Nardi, A.F., Wilkins, J.L., Griffin, T.S., and Fick, G.F. (2016). Carrying capacity of U.S. agricultural land: Ten diet scenarios, *Elementa: Science of the Anthropocene* https://online.ucpress.edu/elementa/article/doi/10.12952/journal.elementa.000116/112904/Carrying-capacity-of-U-S-agricultural-land-Ten

Poore, J. and Nemecek, T. (2018). Reducing food's environmental impacts through producers and consumers, *Science*, 360:987–992.

Regulation 1069/2009. Laying down health rules as regards animal by-products and derived products not intended for human consumption and repealing Regulation (EC) No 1774/2002 (Animal by-products Regulation). European Parliament, Council of the European Union. http://data.europa.eu/eli/reg/2009/1069/oj

Regulation 2015/2283. Novel foods, amending Regulation (EU) No 1169/2011 of the European Parliament and of the Council and repealing Regulation (EC) No 258/97 of the European Parliament and of the Council and Commission Regulation (EC) No 1852/2001. European Parliament, Council of the European Union. http://data.europa.eu/eli/reg/2015/2283/oj

Regulation 2017/893. Amending Annexes I and IV to Regulation (EC) No 999/2001 of the European Parliament and of the Council and Annexes X, XIV and XV to Commission Regulation (EU) No 142/2011 as regards the provisions on processed animal protein. European Parliament, Council of the European Union. http://data.europa.eu/eli/reg/2017/893/oj

RLI (Raad voor de Leefomgeving en Infrastructuur) (2015). Circular Economy: From Wish to Practice. The Council for the Environment and Infrastructure www.rli.nl/sites/default/files/advice_rli_circular_economy_interactive_def.pdf

Rood, T., Muilwijk, H., and Westhoek, H. (2017). *Food for the Circular Economy*. PBL Publication.

Shirvell, B. (2019). The Upcycled Food Industry Is Worth $46.7 Billion. *Forbes*, Dec 19. www.forbes.com/sites/bridgetshirvell/2019/12/19/the-upcycled-food-industry-is-worth-467b-here-are-11-products-you-can-try-at-home/?sh=353191a9340d

Shyam, G. (2019). How community attitudes can strengthen arguments for changing the legal status of animals. *Society Register*, 3(3):67–82.

Smith, T.S.J, Baranowski, M., and Schmid, B. (2021). Intentional degrowth and its unintended consequences: Uneven journeys towards post-growth transformations. *Ecological Economics*, *190*:107251.

Stahel, W.R. (2016). Circular economy. *Nature*, *531*:435–438.

Stuart, T. (2009). *Waste: Uncovering the Global Food Scandal*. Penguin Books.

Taylor, B., Chapron, G., Kopnina, H., Orlikowska, E., Gray, J., and Piccolo, J. (2020). The need for ecocentrism in biodiversity conservation. *Conservation Biology*, 34(5):1089–1096.

Ünal, E. and Shao, J. (2019). A taxonomy of circular economy implementation strategies for manufacturing firms: Analysis of 391 cradle-to-cradle products. *Journal of Cleaner Production*, *212*:754–765.

van Huis, A. and Oonincx, D.G. (2017). The environmental sustainability of insects as food and feed. A review. *Agronomy for Sustainable Development*, *37*(5):1–14.

van Huis, A., van Itterbeeck, J., Klunder, H., Mertens, E., Halloran, A., Muir, G., and Vanthomme, P. (2013). *Edible Insects: Future Prospects for Food and Feed Security*. Rome: Food and Agricultural Organisation of the United Nations. www.fao.org/docrep/018/i3253e/i3253e.pdf

Victor, P. and Jackson, T. (2015). The problem with growth. In: Starke, L. (Ed.), *2015 State of the World Report, Confronting Hidden Threats to Sustainability*. Worldwatch Institute, Washington.

Washington, H. and Maloney, M. (2020). The need for ecological ethics in new ecological economics. *Ecological Economics*, *169*:106478.

Washington, H., Piccolo, J., Chapron, G., Gray, J., Kopnina, H., and Curry, P. (2018). Foregrounding ecojustice in conservation. *Biological Conservation*, *228*:367–374.

3 'The impossible dream'

Can the circular economy alone solve waste management complexities of the Global South?

Aneta Slaveikova Nikolova and David Ness

Introduction

Fast-growing, low-income (LI) cities across the Asia-Pacific region are struggling to implement waste management policies and practices, confronted by burgeoning amounts of waste, while waste prevention is often unknown, and the circular economy (CE) seems an impossibility. This dire situation, compounded by the export of waste by high-income (HI) societies of the Global North, impacts sanitation, health, and the environment while preventing communities from escaping the poverty trap.

Ironically, the concept of a CE grew out of waste management within the Global North, where it was intended to deal with circumstances of low population growth, low demand, and saturated supply. While far removed from the waste crises of the Global South, a transition from a linear to a CE was seen to rely heavily on effective waste management and how waste is treated as a potential future resource (Ranjbari et al., 2021). As Stahel (2020) explained, "waste management and recycling are the *final* phase of the linear industrial economy (LIE) ..., whereas waste prevention and recovering molecules is part of the Circular Industrial Economy (CIE)".

Against current scientific knowledge, the chapter identifies the 'impossibilities' that need to be recognised for the CE to effectively address the challenges of waste management in developing countries of the Asia-Pacific region. It seeks to highlight aspects that the CE cannot achieve by itself and suggests ways in which the CE may be strengthened by integration with complementary theories and programs.

First, in Section 'Circular economy, resource efficiency, and waste management', current scientific understandings of the theory and principles of the CE, resource efficiency, and Factor X are outlined. Section 'The waste management crisis in the Global South' highlights waste management challenges in LI countries of the Asia-Pacific region, while Section 'Case studies' provides a critical examination of case studies and UNESCAP pilot projects that apply the resource efficiency concept to 'pro-poor and sustainable development' programs. Next, in Section 'The impossibilities of a circular economy alone within low-income

DOI: 10.4324/9781003244196-4

countries', the inability of current CE theory and principles to overcome barriers and pitfalls are assessed, with consideration to other aspects that may need to be integrated with the CE to increase the chances of success. Finally, pointing the way forward, some strategies are suggested in Section 'A way forward', whereby LI communities may be supported to lift themselves out of poverty and utilise their resources and attributes in a socially inclusive manner.

Circular economy, resource efficiency, and waste management

The CE is commonly understood as 'closing the loop', whereby technical and biological resources are kept in circulation and avoid going to waste through recovery and recycling. This has been illustrated by the Ellen MacArthur Foundation (EMF, 2021) in Figure 3.1.

Unfortunately, many jurisdictions and organisations see the CE solely in terms of recycling while overlooking other strategies and their potential benefits in terms of job creation, carbon reduction, and increased economic value. Proponents of the CE, such as Prof. Walter R Stahel, view recycling as a last resort, with reuse, remanufacturing, and repair – known as 'slowing' the CE – being preferred; they claim that more value can be gained from resources by extending their life. 'Narrowing' resource flow is also gaining attention (Bocken et al., 2016), as a way of reducing consumption of new resources and delivering more services or output per unit of material input, reducing carbon, and more jobs. This is most closely

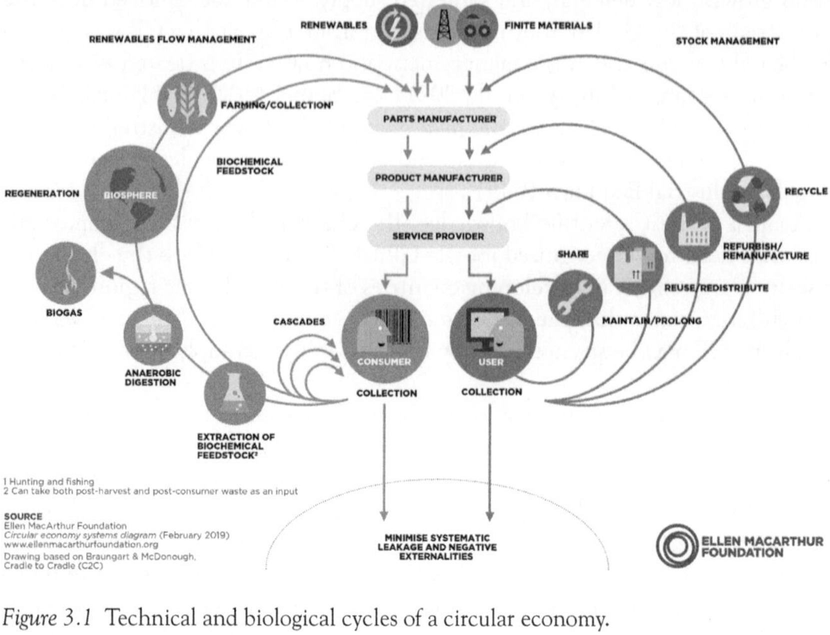

Figure 3.1 Technical and biological cycles of a circular economy.
Source: EMF, 2021.

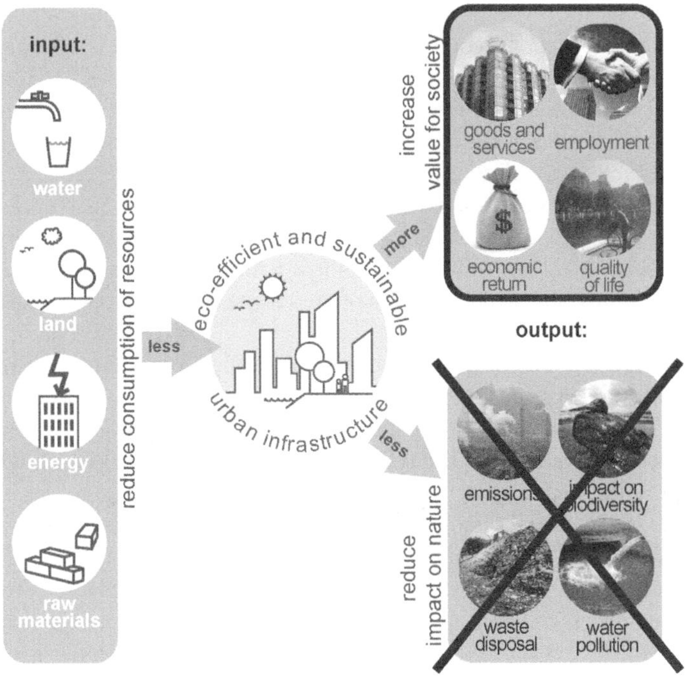

Figure 3.2 Representation of urban metabolism model.
Source: UN, 2011.

allied to the concept of Factor X, using fewer resources per unit of output, which originated in the work of Prof. Dr Ernst Ulrich von Weizsäcker and others in the 1990s (von Weizsäcker et al., 1994).

The UN (2011) has used the notion of resource or eco-efficiency to underpin its approaches to sustainable and inclusive urban infrastructure and greening of the economic growth or Green Growth (UNESCAP, 2012). This seeks to obtain increased value for society by reduced consumption of resource inputs, with less impact on nature in terms of emissions, biodiversity, waste, and water pollution (Figure 3.2).

This approach has much in common with 'narrowing' resource flows in a CE, as the EEB (2020) explained:

> The objective of a true circular economy means reducing the absolute quantity of natural resources that enter our economy, and reducing the quantity of waste coming out. Only with a smaller [narrower] and slower circle of material throughput will we manage to stay within ecological limits and a safe operating space.

In this regard, the most well-known CE diagram (EMF, 2021) is deficient in that it fails to mention the need to reduce absolute consumption. While this may prove impossible for LI countries, where economic growth is sustained by increasing consumption based on their needs, it assumes significance for HI countries that continue to consume resources beyond their needs (despite claiming to be 'circular'). In addition, HI countries increase exports of their solid waste, often labelled as 'recycled', to LI countries – exacerbating their waste crisis, contravening the Basel Convention, and creating 'ecologically unequal exchange' (Dorninger et al., 2021; Liu et al. 2018; Albaladejo et al. 2021). In addition, the over-consumption by HI societies of the North is the root cause of most of the world's carbon emissions, which again is often assigned to the producers located in the Global South.

CE theory has been criticised as a means of justifying continued economic growth in HI countries (Spash, 2020), lacking social, cultural, and ecological dimensions. With regards to a 'transformative social and solidarity economy', Friant et al. (2020) found that the social dimension is often lacking in CE literature, especially with regard to issues of governance, access to resources, justice, power, and cultural change. Similarly, Garcia (pers. comm. 2021) noted that CE literature has largely ignored contextual social and economic specifics of the Global South, such as the high levels of informality. He is currently finalising research on the role of the informal economy in catalysing a CE in cities. Meanwhile, Eitel (2021) is one of the few researchers who have 'got their hands dirty' on this topic, having studied the 'infracycles' of waste management in Phnom Penh.

In some quarters, though, the CE is seen as more relevant to the Global North. Walter Stahel, recognised as the founder of the CE, distinguished between the CE and the Circular Industrial Economy (CIE), mostly applicable to durable products. However, he admitted that the CIE "mainly applies to industrialised economies with markets near saturation" (Stahel, 2020).

Against this background, the following discussion examines whether the implementation of CE principles can improve current solid waste management activities in LI countries of the Asia-Pacific and, if not, how they may need to be extended and supplemented.

The waste management crisis in the Global South

Ferronato and Torretta (2019) highlighted that solid waste management is a significant global issue in terms of environmental contamination, social inclusion, and economic sustainability. They urge more attention to be paid to 'developing' and transition countries, where mismanagement is common and advocate integrated assessments and holistic approaches for its solution.

A substantial percentage of the growing world population is concentrated in urban areas. In 2015, the total population of the 10 largest metropolitan areas in the world (most of which are in developing countries) was approximately 228 million. Exacerbated by rising incomes, this has generated increasing quantities of municipal solid waste, including organics, food waste, packaging, single-use plastics, and electronic waste (e-waste). Based on an approximate waste generation of 0.5 kg per capita per day, Diaz (2015) estimated the global amount of municipal solid waste as around 1.3 billion tonnes per year. An overwhelming portion of that is actually plastic waste, the majority of which leaks into our oceans every year (UNESCAP, 2020).

Although many industrialised countries have established policies to reduce the amount of waste generated and maximise diversion, many LI nations are still unable to manage their solid wastes properly and rely on open dumps for waste disposal. As Schröder (2020) pointed out, at least 2 billion people lack access to solid waste collection. As a result, fast-growing cities in the Asia-Pacific region contribute to over 60 per cent of the plastic waste leakage into the environment.

Preston et al. (2019) emphasised the importance of 'developing' countries, which are "the current dominant centres of production and the future centres of consumption in the global economy". Large informal sectors, which involve about 70 per cent of the population, already practice 'circular' activities – in areas such as electronic waste (e-waste), phone and vehicle repairs – and could engage in higher-value CE supply chains.

Eitel (2021) is one of the few who have attempted to gain a deep understanding of the complexities of the challenge, especially by highlighting the importance of the informal sector. Via a close-up empirical and ethnographic investigation of the City of Phnom Penh, following the daily practices and waste-pickers and the movements of recyclable waste, she discovered "a unique recyclable waste collection system" that she described as "*infracycles*: socio-material constellations through which the quotidian flows of persons, goods, tools, narratives and ideas are organised in a recurrent and circular manner, thereby functioning as an actually lived infrastructure" (Eitel, 2021, 135). This bottom-up system, including waste-pickers, depot owners, and others, keeps the city 'somewhat clean'. However, it is not a closed system: in the same process, "oozy materials leaking from *infracycles* also create new versions of the city in the form of urban nature cultures". What oozes is often tiny fragments of broken-down, deteriorated synthetic materials, often toxic, which percolate through the air, along the streets, or in canals, forming part of urban landscapes. As Eitel (2021, 151) noted, "this may give the misleading impression that no political action is necessary at all", when that is most definitely not the case.

There have been many attempts to redress such challenges by financially and technically supporting the informal sector, such as in Thailand and Vietnam (Eitel, 2021). In addition, pilot schemes involving 'integrated waste management systems' (IWMSs) have been subsidised and supported. These have concentrated on organic waste, which represents up to 70 per cent of all waste, and have sought to sort, treat, and convert this waste to organic compost for use as agricultural fertilisers or biogas. While such schemes have seemed promising in theory and from initial pilots, few have been sustained after external subsidies and support were withdrawn. Meanwhile, the mountains of waste in developing countries continue to grow (Waste Atlas Partnership, 2014).

Case studies

The following case studies – focused on solid waste management – seek to highlight the challenges when introducing a CE to LI countries of the Asia-Pacific region beyond basic recycling. In many jurisdictions of LI countries, even basic waste collection systems are lacking, often resulting in waste being improperly disposed, or even burned. This poses serious challenges for those societies while adversely impacting health, sanitation, and the environment.

Some of the studies received support from the UNESCAP 'Pro-poor and eco-efficient solid waste management' program, which employed resource efficiency principles, as previously described. The pilots implemented in several countries within the Asia-Pacific region have helped to process the increasing organic waste, comprising 60–70 per cent of solid waste, and to turn that into a new higher-value product – renewable energy source-biogas by capturing methane creating access to cheap, clean cooking fuel. This approach was also coupled with composting, which improved the soil quality and the food security of the local community. The programme also helped the informal workers to improve their waste handling safety by providing protective clothing. Some of these approaches are illustrated in several case studies.

Bangladesh

The waste concern

This program sets the benchmark for responsible waste management in an LI country context. The NGO developed an approach to reduce government costs, while providing a business opportunity for a local entrepreneur, improving services to households, and managing waste in a more eco-efficient manner. Organic waste collected from surrounding farms and the township is treated and converted into biogas. This has multiple benefits for all involved, including less territory required for landfills, improved health and sanitation, and jobs for previous waste-pickers. Perhaps its most innovative feature is the gaining of carbon credits via emission reductions under the UN Clean Development Mechanism.

Sri Lanka

Lack of effective waste management strategy

According to the Environment Foundation (2017), attempts for over 20 years to develop an effective waste management strategy for the country – including sanitary landfills and waste-to-energy projects – have been unsuccessful. In 2008, the Central Environment Authority initiated a 10-year Waste Management Program named 'Pilisaru', with the goal of a 'Waste Free Sri Lanka by 2018'. Unfortunately, "the lack of a unified, coherent strategy has led to inconsistent and ineffective practices". This is exacerbated by the myriad of institutions concerned with waste management at different stages.

Meethotamulla and Kotikawatte

Sri Lanka generates 7,000 metric tonnes of solid waste per day, with the Western Province accounting for almost 60 per cent of this – an average of 10.4 kg of waste per day. Only half of the waste is collected. This led to a calamity at Meethotamulla, where a 'mountain of garbage' collapsed on 14 April 2017. The Environment Foundation has identified 'unsanitary eye sores' in at least four provinces, and the degradation of wetlands, coastline, rivers, and streams, which become dumping sites for plastic and polythene waste, and other mixed waste. The open garbage dump at Kotikawatte, located in a wetland and near a highly residential area and school, severely affects the health and hygiene of over 500 people and damages the environment and ecosystem.

Matale

Matale is an urban centre in central Sri Lanka. It generates 21 tons of municipal waste per day, of which 17 tonnes are disposed at an open dumpsite. Seventy per cent of the waste is organic and can be used for composting and biogas generation, while 10 per cent is recyclable, and only 10 per cent needs to go to landfill. Since 2006, the solid waste management in one ward of the city, involving 600 households and small businesses, has improved through a pilot project co-financed and supported by the municipality, the Sevanatha Urban Resource Centre and UNESCAP, based upon the Integrated Resource Recovery Centre approach developed by the Waste Concern. However, establishing a market for the compost has proved a challenge for Matale. Although there is increasing interest in organic farming and the added value of compost or organic fertilisers, chemical fertilisers are still subsidised, distorting the market (UN, 2011). Consistent with the urban metabolism model shown in Figure 3.1, the UN (2011, 157–164) saw solid waste management in Matale as increasing value for society, while reducing resource input and reducing the impact upon nature.

Indonesia

Makassar City

In a study of the sustainable solid waste management (SSWM) project in Makassar City, Indonesia, Permana et al. (2015) showed that community practices on waste reduction and separation were strongly correlated to a sense of cleanliness and a positive environmental image within an enthusiastic community. However, households were engaged in SSWM solely through their own initiatives and efforts and were highly critical of the performance of the waste management authority, which blamed insufficient budget, infrastructure, and personnel. The authors concluded that, within such constraints, the authority should develop a strategy to prioritise currently in-place waste separation, waste recycling, and waste banking practices and increase them to their maximum utility. They should increase the proportion of SSWM households from only 0.65 per cent of the total households in Makassar up to 30 per cent (the present quantity of recyclable wastes). In the meantime, the local government should also develop recycling centres and material recovery facilities. Based on this study and lessons from the success of other cities such as Surabaya and Palembang, Permana et al. (2015) found that the local government should exercise its power to promote community-based recycling businesses as a fundamental step towards more comprehensive SSWM.

Plastic waste management

South-East Asian nations are responsible for as much as 60 per cent of plastic waste leakage into the environment and the ocean. UNESCAP (2020) supports four fast-growing South-East Asian cities to tackle the challenge of reducing plastic waste using innovation and smart technology to monitor, assess, and manage the waste. The 'closing the loop' project, in partnership with the Government of Japan, involves Da Nang (Vietnam), Kuala Lumpur (Malaysia), Nakhon Si Thammarat (Thailand), and Surabaya (Indonesia). For example, biodegradable bags are being used at markets in Da Nang, while in Kuala Lumpur, plastic bags are not provided for free. The private sector plays a role, too, with PlasticBank Asia seeking to make plastic 'too valuable to become ocean pollution'.

The scourge of plastic waste constitutes up to 12 per cent of Thailand's total waste every year, with toxins released when plastic waste is burned or dumped into waterways – causing severe air and marine pollution. It is recognised that tackling these interconnected issues will require systemic change and new ways of engaging and collaborating among stakeholders across the entire value chain. The Bangkok Hub of Global Shapers, a youth-led network of hubs initiated by the World Economic Forum, seeks to tailor CE solutions to local needs through *grassroots* efforts, mainstreaming existing actions, and better persuading policy makers (Kumar et al., 2021).

The UNDP (2021) Plastic Waste Programme in India is claimed to have reprocessed around 85,000 metric tonnes of plastic waste in the City of Indore by keeping the value of plastics in a perpetual 'closed loop' cycle claimed to be "rooted in the principle of circular economy". The programme organises fairs and other mass awareness campaigns, partnering with retail chains and supermarkets, accompanied by mobile vehicles and folk songs to spread the message. India is said to recycle about 60 per cent of post-consumer plastic waste, but this is done mostly by the informal sector. "Recognising and incorporating informal workers into circular economies is critically important to generate jobs…", but a key objective "to help move the sector from informal to formal" may be questionable.

The impossibilities of a circular economy alone within low-income countries

As we have seen from the above examples, waste management remains an insurmountable challenge for many countries in the Asia-Pacific region and elsewhere.

Apart from the Waste Concern and other sporadic programs and projects led by social entrepreneurs, the isolated examples of success have been swamped by a sea of waste, with limited replication and failure to be sustained after the withdrawal of initial support and subsidies.

From a technical perspective, Cobo et al. (2018) found that two major lines of action could be taken to overcome the depletion of natural resources and growing waste: the application of waste prevention policies and the shift from the classical linear IWMSs, which focus solely on the treatment of municipal solid waste, to circular IWMSs (CIWMSs) that combine waste, resource recovery, and materials management, incentivising the circularity of resources. This relies on the expansion of the typical IWMS boundaries to include the upstream subsystems, which reflect the transformation of resources and its interconnections with the waste management subsystems. As Barczak (EEB, 2021) said, it is also important to bear in mind that "waste should be reduced at source and reused and recycled as close as possible, to benefit the local community and make local waste generators responsible". This is known as 'the proximity principle'.

According to Ferronato et al. (2019), the definition of a CE requires additional components: re-circulation of resources and energy, thereby recovering value from waste; implementation of a multi-level approach; and assessing the innovation introduced within society – principles that are followed in HI and emerging economies, but absent in LI countries. Moreover, as Mayers et al. (2021, 2) explained,

> it is important to understand that materials can never progress through life purely in 'lines' or 'circles'. Instead, they move through highly complex supply networks, and the popularly conceived repeating circular motion of reuse and recycling is in fact a downward spiral.

While recognising that "the task facing middle- and low-income societies is enormous", the Global Waste Management Outlook (UNEP, 2015, 294) presented a staged approach ranging from 'bringing wastes under control' towards a 'move from a linear to a circular economy' (Figure 3.3). Importantly, UNEP (2015) also acknowledges that "building on existing, informal recycling systems by integrating them more into the mainstream waste management sector often forms a relatively low-cost, win-win component of an integrated solution".

However, given the complexities of the waste management challenge, such extended approaches towards a CE are unlikely to be sufficient. For such waste management schemes to succeed, it is evident that they will require embedding in a wider support system and policy framework, linked with other goals such as healthcare, childcare, education, and economic development, and involving a much wider group of stakeholders – not least of which is the local communities themselves. Furthermore, Schröder (2020) highlighted that the CE does not automatically address many of the UN Sustainable Development Goals (SDGs), including SDG 2 (Zero Hunger), SDG 5 (Gender Equality), SDG 10 (Reduced Inequalities), coupled with targets under SDG 8 on creating decent work and SDG 4 for quality education.

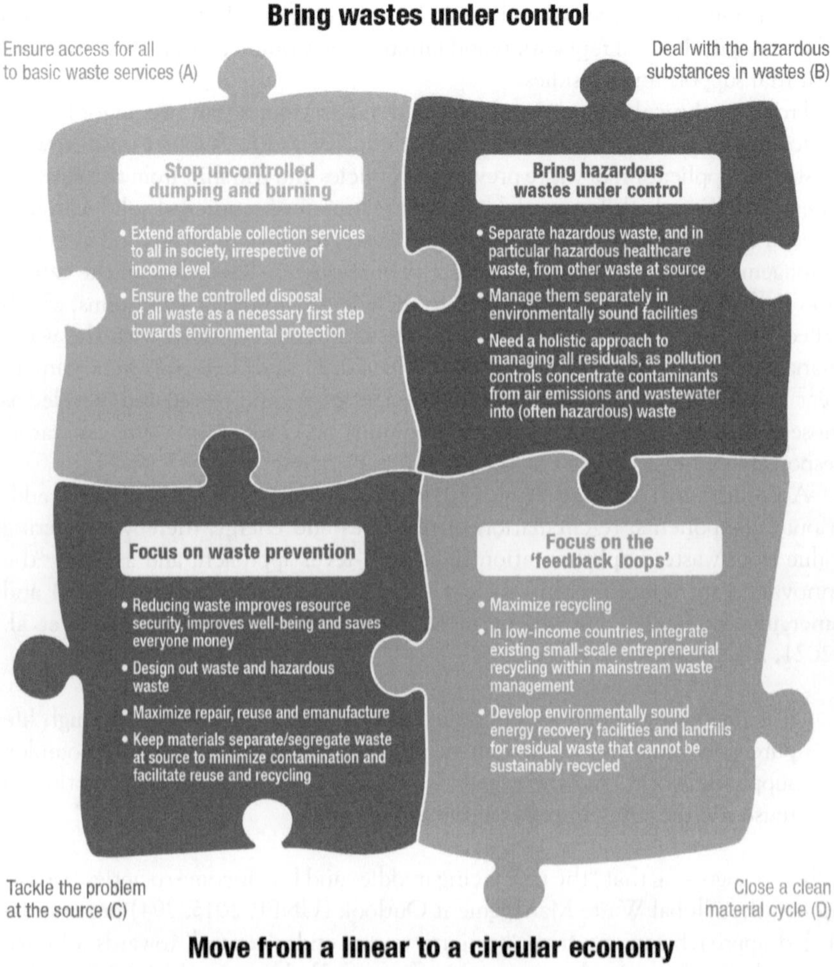

Figure 3.3 Bringing wastes under control: move from a linear to a circular economy. Source: UNEP, 2015, 294.

Diaz (2015) also emphasised the necessity for a wider, multi-dimensional approach:

> Based on my experience, some of the most critical needs include lack of political will to deal with the problem, lack of a national policy related to solid waste management, absence of rules and regulations, insufficient funds dedicated to solving the problem, a severe absence of educational programs at all levels, and last, but not least, no policies related to preserving or creating a 'circular economy'.

Similarly, Preston et al. (2019) emphasised that for the CE to gain political traction and attract investment in 'developing' countries, it is crucial that strategies be aligned with the existing priorities of governments and businesses: There has yet to emerge a compelling narrative on the CE as a strategy for delivering on developing-country policy priorities such as economic diversification, job creation, agricultural development, or energy security.

Although the CE continues to be understood primarily in terms of waste management and recycling, it could – with the right enabling conditions and integration with other programs as discussed above – provide new opportunities for economic diversification, value creation, and skills development, especially as a component of a green post-COVID-19 recovery. This possibility is explored in the next section.

A way forward

Despite its current impossibilities, there is 'a unique opportunity' to use the CE concept as a tool or catalyst for transformative change, especially when it considers 'systemic socio-ecological implications'. When the CE discourse fosters plurality and openness to other visions, including less prominent voices, it can promote more holistic and systemic thinking, including different circular futures. Current practices and actions can be contrasted with "a plurality of alternatives" (Friant et al., 2020).

This can open the way to local, community-based waste management cooperatives and social enterprises, supported by overall policies, regulations, frameworks, education, and finance and investment. Policy makers should be mindful, however, that a CE may not necessarily foster social justice and solidarity; as Leipold et al. (2021, 6) have reminded us from their study of the French food sector, "CE narratives promote profit-oriented rather than charitable actors" and may exacerbate both social and environmental problems.

The enlightening study by Eitel (2021) of the many 'infracycles' within the informal sector within Phnom Penh provides some clues on the way forward. It highlights not only the extreme complexity but also the important and engrained role of 'waste-pickers' and their acceptance by the more formal solid waste collection sector. However, as Eitel emphasised, reliance on the informal sector alone is not enough: political action is 'most definitely' required. Preston et al. (2019) also remind us that waste-picking is rarely the most effective means of processing waste, especially when dealing with e-waste – often made up of complex composites. Additional skills and technology are required to optimise recycling and repair processes (Preston et al., 2019), as well as behaviour change of consumers.

Thus, as UNEP (2015) also explained, we can see that the activities of the informal sector may provide a base upon which to build more effective policies and approaches to waste management in LI-income cities. Garcia (2021) hopes to show from his research within the city of Kigali, Rwanda, that the informal economy may 'catalyse' a CE in such contexts. As Eitel (2021, 136) affirmed, "waste must always be seen within its context, its environment into which it is embedded and from which it emerges".

Finally, it is necessary to question the term 'circular economy' in the context of the Global South. As Leipold et al. (2021, 6) recommended, "narratives calling for a 'circular society' instead of a CE could help to place social problems centre stage and acknowledge the social changes required for CE transformations".

Closing remarks

This chapter has revealed the impossibilities of the CE alone as a solution to the mountains of waste growing in many LI cities of the Asia-Pacific region and elsewhere. However, if accompanied by political will, integration with other key social, environmental, and economic policies, and building upon the dominant informal sector, a CE – or preferably circular society – may serve as a catalyst for societal transformation.

Clearly, as other authors of this book have shown, a more system-wide approach is necessary, with the CE and waste management seen as interconnected with sanitation, health, hygiene, childcare, education, environmental and biodiversity protection, reducing carbon emissions, affordable housing, and lifting communities out of the poverty trap. Such an approach may also assist in meeting many of the SDGs in an integrated manner.

References

Albaladejo, M., Mulder, N., Mirazo, P., and I. M. Jauregi. 2021. The Circular Economy: from waste to resources through international trade, UNIDO, July. The Circular Economy: From waste to resource through international trade | Industrial Analytics Platform (unido.org).

Bocken, N., de Pauw, I., Bakker, C., and B. van der Grinten. 2016. Product design and business model strategies for a circular economy, *Journal of Industrial and Production Engineering*, 33(5), pp. 308–320. www.tandfonline.com/doi/full/10.1080/21681015.2016.1172124

Cobo, S., Dominguez-Ramos, A., and A. Irabien. 2018. From linear to circular integrated waste management systems: A review of methodological approaches, *Resources, Conservation and Recycling*, 135, pp. 279–295. www.sciencedirect.com/science/article/pii/S0921344917302422?via%3Dihub

Diaz, L. 2017. Waste management in developing countries and the circular economy, *Waste Management and Research*, 35(1), pp. 1–2. Waste management in developing countries and the circular economy – Luis F Diaz, 2017 (sagepub.com)

Dorninger, C., Hornborg, A., Abson, D., von Wehrden, H., Schaffartzik, A., Giljum, S., Engler, J.O., Feller, R., Hubacek, K., and H. Wieland. 2021. Global patterns of ecologically unequal exchange: implications for sustainability in the 21st century, *Ecological Economics*, 179 (C), September, DOI: https://10.1016/j.ecolecon.2020.106824

EEB. 2020. A circular economy within ecological limits – Why we need to set targets to reduce EU resource consumption and waste generation in the new Circular Economy Action Plan. European Environmental Bureau. https://mk0eeborgicuypctuf7e.kinstacdn.com/wp-content/uploads/2020/02/A-circular-economy-within-ecological-limits.pdf [Accessed 26 March 2021].

Eitel, K. 2021. Oozing matters: Infracycles of 'waste management' and emergent naturecultures in Phnom Penh, *East Asian Science, Technology and Society: An International Journal*, 15(2), 1350152.

EMF. 2021. *The butterfly diagram*, Ellen MacArthur Foundation.

Environment Foundation. 2017. Status of waste management in Sri Lanka, Environment Foundation (Guarantee) Ltd, Columbo, Sri Lanka, 14 June. https://efl.lk/status-waste-management-sri-lanka/

Ferronato, N., and V. Torretta. 2019. Waste Mismanagement in Developing Countries: A Review of Global Issues, *International Journal of Environmental Research and Public Health*, 16, 1060. https://doi.org/10.3390/ijerph16061060

Ferronato, N., et al. 2019. Introduction of the circular economy within developing regions: A comparative analysis of advantages and opportunities for waste valorization, *Journal of Environmental Management*, 230, pp. 366–378. www.sciencedirect.com/science/article/pii/S0301479718311058?via%3Dihub

Friant, M. C., Vermeulen, W., and R. Salomone. 2020. A typology of circular economy discourses: navigating the diverse visions of a contested paradigm, *Resources, Conservation, and Recycling*, 161, October. https://doi.org/10.1016/j.resconrec.2020.104917

Garcia, F. C. 2021. Pers. comm. on role of informal economy in catalyzing a CE in cities, August.

Kumar, A., Sutiono, I., and L. Olsauskaite. 2021. *How changemakers in Bangkok are popularising the circular economy*, World Economic Forum, 19 July.

Leipold, S., Weldner, K., and M. Hohl. 2021. Do we need a 'circular society'? Competing narratives of the circular economy in the French food sector, *Ecological Economics* 187 www.sciencedirect.com/science/article/pii/S0921800921001440

Liu, Z., Adams, M., and T Walker. 2018. Are exports of recyclables from developed to developing countries waste pollution transfer or part of the global circular economy? *Resources, Conservation and Recycling*, 136, pp. 22–23. www.sciencedirect.com/science/article/pii/S0921344918301368?via%3Dihub

Mayers, K., Davis, T., and L. van Wassenhove. 2021. The limits of the 'sustainable' economy, *Harvard Business Review*, 16 June.

Permana, A., et al. 2015. Sustainable solid waste management practices and perceived cleanliness in a low-income city, *Habitat International*, 49, pp. 197–205. www.sciencedirect.com/science/article/pii/S0197397515001095?via%3Dihub

Preston, F., Lehne, J., and L. Wellesley. 2019. An Inclusive Circular Economy: Priorities for Developing Countries, *Chatham House Research Paper*, Energy, Environment and Resources Department, May. www.chathamhouse.org/sites/default/files/publications/research/2019-05-22-Circular%20Economy.pdf

Ranjbari, M., et al. 2021. Two decades of research on waste management in the circular economy: insights from bibliometric, text mining, and content analyses, *Journal of Cleaner Production*, 314 https://doi.org/10.1016/j.jclepro.2021.128009

Romero-Hernández, 0., and S. Romero. 2018. Maximizing the value of waste: From waste management to the circular economy, *Thunderbird in Business Review*. 60, pp. 757–764. DOI: https://10.1002/tie.21968

Schröder, P. 2020. *Promoting a just transition to an inclusive circular economy*, Energy, Environment and Resources programme, Chatham House, April. www.chathamhouse.org/2020/04/promoting-just-transition-inclusive-circular-economy

Spash, C. L. 2020. Apologists for growth: passive revolutionaries in a passive revolution, *Globalisations*. www.tandfonline.com/doi/full/10.1080/14747731.2020.1824864

Stahel, W. 2019. *The circular economy: a user's guide*, Routledge, 24 June. www.routledge.com/The-Circular-Economy-A-Users-Guide/Stahel/p/book/9780367200176

Stahel, W. 2020. The future direction of study about the circular economy. What should the Society do? IS4CE, 29 June. www.is4ce.org/en/news/is4ce-news-and-articles

The Waste Concern. 2021. Carbon footprint https://wasteconcern.org/carbon-foot-print/

UN. 2011. Are we building competitive and liveable cities? Guidelines for developing eco-efficient and socially inclusive infrastructure, United Nations, Thailand.

UNDP. 2021. In India, a circular economy creates value from plastic waste, UN Development Programme, August.

UNEP. 2015. *Global waste management outlook*. UN Environment Programme and International Solid Waste Association (ISWA).

UNESCAP. 2012. Low Carbon Green Growth Roadmap for Asia and the Pacific.

UNESCAP. 2020. Closing the loop. Cities and marine plastic pollution, in *Building a Circular Economy Handbook*.

Von Weizsäcker, E., Lovins, A., and H. Lovins. 1994. Factor 4: Doubling wealth, halving consumption. A Report to the Club of Rome. Routledge.

Waste Atlas Partnership. 2014. *Waste atlas: the world's 50 biggest dumpsites*, 2014 Report.

4 The entropic nature of the economic process

A scientific explanation of the blunder of circular economy

Mario Giampietro

Introduction

In the sixth century, the book *Christian Topography* described the Earth as a flat structural element on which very high walls were supporting heaven. This belief was held at the time by essentially all of European society in spite of the fact that a full millennium earlier Greek scientists had showed convincingly that the Earth was spherical (APS, 2006). In this chapter, I claim that the current social endorsement of the plausibility of a circular economy presents a sort of a *déjà vu* situation. In both cases, flat Earth and circular economy, we are dealing with a phenomenon referable to as: "[s]ocially constructed ignorance in science and environmental policy discourse" (Rayner, 2012). As explained in his paper, Rayner (ibid, emphasis added) writes:

> *To make sense of the complexity of the world so that they can act, individuals and institutions need to develop simplified, self-consistent versions of that world. The process of doing so means that much of what is known about the world needs to be excluded from those versions, and in particular that knowledge which is in tension or outright contradiction with those versions must be expunged.* ***This is uncomfortable knowledge***.

This mechanism explains why the availability of robust information about the implausibility of a narrative used to justify a knowledge claim or a given policy, if sufficiently uncomfortable, may rather become an "unknown known" in the policy arena than be given due consideration. Such uncomfortable knowledge, even if easily available to those willing to find it, is simply expelled from the discourse.

In relation to this mechanism, a European project, Moving Towards Adaptive Governance in Complexity (MAGIC, https://magic-nexus.eu/), has been tracking the systemic exclusion of uncomfortable knowledge in the different processes used to select European Union (EU) policies across several policy domains relevant to sustainability. The policy domain of "circular economy" was one of the case studies of MAGIC. Findings from that case study are used to inform the text of this chapter. Those interested in the presentation of the results

DOI: 10.4324/9781003244196-5

of MAGIC in video format (as well as in scientific paper format) are invited to check the Uncomfortable Knowledge Hub (https://uncomfortableknowledge.com/) website.

The text of this chapter is structured as follows. Section "Essential knowledge from the field of non-equilibrium thermodynamics" presents what is scientifically known about the process of self-organization of complex adaptive systems, a class of open systems to which social-ecological systems belong. Section "What happens if we use this knowledge to study the circularity of the economy?" illustrates a proper characterization scheme, which should at a minimum be followed when accounting for the metabolic pattern associated with the economic process. This characterization scheme is required to check the level of circularity of the economic flows in a social-economic system. When properly assessed, we can see that there is indeed no significant circularity in the metabolic process associated with the economic process. Section "The prophecy of Habermas" addresses the ideological reasons pushing our modern welfare democracies to deem the findings of non-equilibrium thermodynamics as "unknown knowns". This social construction of ignorance serves to steer the political discussion away from the implications of this uncomfortable knowledge. The final section concludes.

Essential knowledge from the field of non-equilibrium thermodynamics

We all know that complex adaptive systems (e.g., living systems and social systems) require a continuous process of energy and material conversions to preserve their identity and express their functions. However, the relation between identity preservation within this class of systems and the continuous process of dissipation has proven difficult to study within the field of classical physics (Giampietro et al., 2013). In fact, when considering the term "energy" in physics—standardly "the ability to do work"—we are faced with a tautological definition. That is, the apparent definition of energy requires a separate, pre-analytical definition of a special type of work. Work in physics is moreover about the effect of a "force", but its quantification does not make any reference to the time dimension. In relation to this impasse in the ability to deal with energetic transformations, the field of classical thermodynamics entered as a first attempt to generate a systemic classification of patterns of energy transformations, that is, thermodynamic cycles. However, the development of classical thermodynamics was based on the adoption of a series of "heroic assumptions" about the functioning of these cycles—no frictions, infinite time durations, and conditions of equilibrium to allow the measurement of the value of the relevant variables. Despite its heavy reliance on theoretical assumptions, equilibrium thermodynamics "represented a first departure from mechanistic epistemology by introducing new concepts such as irreversibility, symmetry breaking and indeterminacy: when describing real world processes nothing can be the same (e.g., the same state) when it happens for the second time" (Giampietro et al., 2013). The concept of entropy was key in this revolution. In classic thermodynamic analysis, the concept of entropy was associated with the idea of unavoidable decay of thermodynamic systems operating out of equilibrium. That is, sooner or later the gradients that allow the system to be perceived as an entity distinct from its environment are bound to disappear, meaning, according to equilibrium thermodynamics, complex patterns of energy and material transformations are transient patterns destined to disappear. A flame goes out when it runs out of fuel, a tornado dissolves when it loses the energy that formed it, living systems die without food, and so forth.

Unfortunately, the general conclusion that complex patterns dissipating energy are bound to disappear and the resulting prophet-of-doom association with the concept of entropy was inconsistent with experience. In our daily experience, we find that complex adaptive systems thrive all around us in the biosphere. Classical thermodynamics was providing an unsatisfactory analysis of the phenomenon of life and, more in general, of the existence of complex adaptive systems. Hence, not surprisingly, the field of thermodynamics experienced a second, more profound revolution in the scientific analysis of energy transformations, that of non-equilibrium thermodynamics. The curse of decay associated with entropic processes applies only to closed systems in which functional organization will be eliminated by a continuous and inexorable growth of entropy. For this reason, the focus of analysis in non-equilibrium thermodynamics moved to *open* dissipative systems in which a given dissipative structure can maintain its own identity due to the interaction with its context. Schrödinger (1967, in an added note to Chapter VI of *What is Life*, first published in 1945) provided the solution to the problem: open systems can compensate for the harmful pace of generation of positive entropy if they have available a negative flux of entropy coming from their environment. That is, open systems can export internally generated entropic surplus to the environment wherever and whenever their environment can absorb it. This idea was developed further by the work of the Prigogine school (Prigogine, 1961; Glansdorf & Prigogine, 1971; Nicolis & Prigogine, 1977; Prigogine & Stengers, 1984) with the introduction of a new class of physical systems—*dissipative systems*. Dissipative systems are *open systems* that can preserve a given identity expressed by specific dissipative structures—structures that can be observed as distinct from their environment and can be predicted in terms of expected attributes. This conceptual framing standardly indicates the relation between a dissipative structure and its environment using the following iconic equation, pointedly describing the condition of stability of the dissipative system:

$$+dSi - dSe \leq 0.$$

It should be noted that this discussion of positive internal entropy generation (+dSi) and external negative entropy fluxes (−dSe) is based on concepts in which the distinction between ontology and epistemology is blurred (Mayumi & Giampietro, 2004). Indeed, the term entropy has been an attractor of scientific discussions giving different meanings and different definitions to it, such as in classical thermodynamics, information theory, non-equilibrium thermodynamics, and so forth. Hence, we should not expect an uncontested agreement over how to define quantities of positive or negative entropy, but we must use these semantic relations to develop heuristic methods of analysis (more on this below). In any case, a given dissipative structure: (i) requires a continuous flow of energy and material (metabolic inputs) taken from its context, such as humid air for a tornado, food for an organism, a mix of commodities for a city; and (ii) generates a continuous flow of degraded energy and materials (metabolic outputs) dumped into its context. The establishment of this metabolic pattern—the stabilization of a metabolic flow—entails the ability to establish an expected set of relations over the set of transformations of different energy and material elements associated with the interactions the dissipative structure has with its admissible environment.

How does this discussion relate to the circular economy? When considering the factors determining the stability of a dissipative structure, we must first observe that the narrative of "circular economy" represents a major step forward compared with the old framing of neo-classical economics. This new economic narrative finally admits that the economic process requires a continuous flow of material and energy (those that must be recirculated). However, this narrative is unfortunately based on the exclusion of a very "well-known fact": dissipative systems *must be open*. That is, the concept of circularity is based on the erroneous assumption that it is possible to maintain the identity of a dissipative system by recirculating inside it the primary flows (those flows coming from and going to its environment) needed to preserve its identity. In fact, every time we add a new activity to an economic system (e.g., to increase the level of recycling of internal material and energy flows), we introduce a new source of +dSi. Obviously, the increase of +dSi caused by recycling activities can reduce the pace of generation of +dSi from other activities. Regardless, to explore the plausibility of the "circularity solution", it is important to properly frame the analysis over the factors determining the sustainability of a dissipative structure.

What happens if we use this knowledge to study the circularity of the economy?

Before getting into an illustration of the application of the rationale of non-equilibrium thermodynamics to the analysis of sustainability, it should be noted that, primed by the pioneering work of Kenneth Boulding (1966) and Georgescu-Roegen (1971), there is a line of research on the application of thermodynamic reasoning to the study the sustainability of the economy, among others Dyke (1988), Mayumi (2001), Giampietro et al. (2012), Friend (2012). For an overview of applications of the concept of entropy in the field of ecological economics, see Mayumi and Giampietro (2004).

To study the factors determining the sustainability of the economic process, we must start from the conceptual definition of a *dissipative structure*—the observable aspect of a dissipative system. A dissipative structure is generated by the establishment of a dynamical regime that can be considered as a reproducible steady state determined by the interaction with the context. Examples include a tornado, an organism, and a city. When dissipative structures are able to store information to guide their own reproduction (e.g., using genetic information or a language), they can learn how to adapt (expanding the set of meaningful behaviors they can express). In this case, we are dealing with complex adaptive dissipative systems (Giampietro, 2018). The possibility of storing information about how to preserve and adapt the identity of a dissipative structure is key as it allows the definition of the expected set of energy and material forms that are degraded inside the system. That is, the identity of a dissipative structure defines the mechanisms associated with the production of +dSi requiring a given mix of inputs. For example, inside terrestrial ecosystems: (i) plants need a mix of inputs including solar radiation, water, CO_2, and other nutrients; (ii) herbivores need a mix of water and plants; (iii) carnivores need a mix of water and herbivores; and (iv) detritus feeders have yet another definition of the mix of inputs they need internally to reproduce themselves and express their expected functions. In human societies, we can identify the required mix of inputs needed for sustaining both the physiological processes taking place inside the human body and the technological processes under human control. We cannot define in general terms a quantitative definition of +dSi and −dSe that is applicable to any dissipative systems. However, the conceptualization provided by non-equilibrium thermodynamics allows to "tailor" this quantification on any given type of dissipative structure. The identity of the dissipative structure, that is, a rural community or a post-industrial economy, can be associated with a given requirement and consumption of a mix of inputs needed for its positive entropy production (+dSi)—what is called in the jargon of energetics "exergy degradation". Then by tracking the primary flows needed to generate these inputs, we can identify the environment's capacity required to stabilize these primary flows both on the supply side (flows coming from the environment) and the sink side (flows going into the environment). In this way, we can generate a quantitative characterization of the flux of "negative entropy" (−dSi).

In conclusion, the expression of a dissipative structure entails establishing a relationship between two different categories of material and energy flows, which are observable either from inside or outside the given metabolic pattern, as illustrated in Figure 4.1:

1) Flows in the internal STATE. Inside the system, we can observe what is happening, that is, the pattern of dissipation of known exergy forms (+dSi). Here secondary and tertiary flows produced and used under human control are represented. These secondary and tertiary flows are needed for reproducing structural elements and expressing the set of required functions.
2) Flows determining an external PRESSURE. Outside the system we can observe the flows exchanged by the system with its context (−dSe). The interaction between the technosphere and the biosphere can be characterized by tracking primary flows. The stabilization of these flows requires a given quantity of supply and sink capacity (a flux of negative entropy coming from nature) capable of compensating for the production of positive entropy in the technosphere.

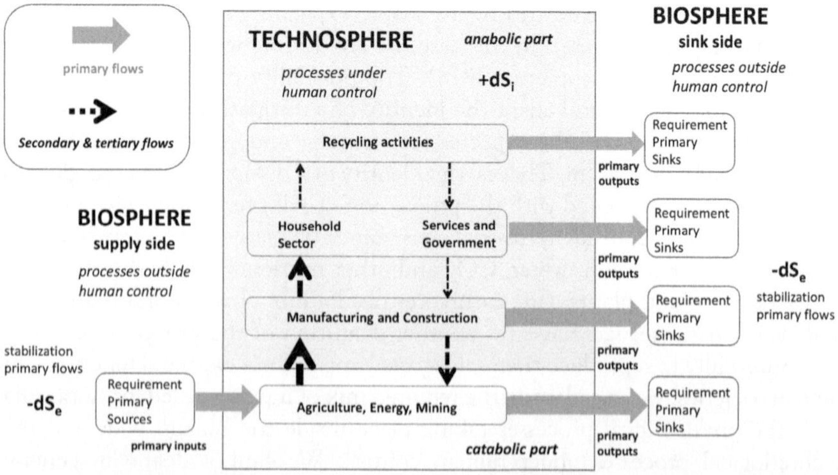

Figure 4.1 Different typologies of flows in the metabolic pattern of the economy: primary flows between the biosphere and the technosphere as well as secondary/tertiary flows between the economic sectors.

Source: own figure.

As illustrated in Figure 4.1, the sustainability of the economic process depends unavoidably on the existence of natural processes capable of maintaining stable boundary conditions. The pressure associated with a given metabolic state must remain admissible in relation to the integrity of environmental processes. Excessive pressure can damage the stability of favorable boundary conditions by damaging the life support system of the dissipative structure—generating an excessive impact on the environment, such as major soil erosion, depletion of a water table, accumulation of greenhouse gases in the atmosphere, or so forth. This distinction between the different categories of flows is essential to clear the confusion about the accounting of water, energy, mineral, and food flows in the "circular economy". Note that the terms "water", "energy", "mineral", and "food" are mere semantic labels in the narrative of metabolic flows and cannot be used as such to carry out a quantitative study on circularity (Giampietro, 2019).

In the analysis of the metabolism of social-ecological systems—a new class of systems proposed to help with the analysis of the interaction of the economic process with the biosphere (Berkes et al., 1998, 2003)—we must make a distinction between the activities of the catabolic part and the anabolic part in the metabolic process. Within the socio-economic process, these two parts handle different types of "water", "energy", and "food". The activities of the catabolic part take place in the primary production sectors of the economy (agriculture, energy, and mining). They destroy gradients freely provided by nature (primary resources and services) to make available secondary flows to the rest of society. The activities of the anabolic part take place in the remaining sectors of the economy (residential, manufacturing and construction, service and government, recycling). This part generates products and materials needed to build and maintain the structural elements of the society, guarantee the reproduction and the quality of life of humans, and produce adaptable institutions.

Note that the secondary and tertiary flows within the metabolic pattern are at the same time inputs and outputs: "In the anabolic compartment secondary inputs are both produced and consumed in the economic process". The secondary outputs of a given primary sector (e.g., the supply of electricity, food, materials, or products) become secondary inputs to other sectors in the catabolic part but also in the anabolic part itself (e.g., the consumption of electricity, food, mineral, or products in the economy). The production of secondary outputs is conditional on their being useful as input by some other metabolic elements; otherwise, they would not be produced in the first place (Giampietro, 2019). This fact may explain the idea of "circularity" in the economic process. Indeed, when adopting a conventional economic narrative of the economic process, we only allow ourselves to observe secondary and tertiary flows inside the technosphere (the ones regulated by market transactions). However, looking at Figure 4.1, it is obvious that there is no recycling of primary flows in the technosphere.

A last, important piece of information given by the relations shown in Figure 4.1 is that recycling is not a panacea. That is,

> According to the first principle of thermodynamics energy cannot be produced. We cannot increase the size of primary energy sources, but only learn how to use them better. According to the second principle of thermodynamics irreversible processes alter the qualitative characteristics of material flows. Recycling can be done, but only to a certain extent and at a certain cost, and only if the corresponding primary resources are available. Hence, the amount of primary waste outflows of an economy can be reduced by recycling (provided the inputs required by the recycling process itself do not exceed the waste outflow recycled), but a continuous production of wastes is unavoidable.
>
> (Giampietro, 2019)

The prophecy of Habermas

It is at last time to go back to the phenomenon of socially constructed ignorance discussed in the introduction, which works to explain the desperate need of the current establishment to expunge uncomfortable knowledge from policy discussions over sustainability. In relation to this point, it is relevant to recall the prophetic concern of Habermas (1979) about the existence of a systemic legitimation problem in social welfare state mass democracies. Habermas argued that, after abandoning the "dangerous" nationalistic mechanism of formation of a common identity adopted in the past, modern states base their legitimacy on the claim that they can solve all the sustainability challenges perceived by their constituent members, thereby keeping their stress low. This point is extremely clear when reading the justifications used by the EU to defend its policies. Looking at the ecological transition promised with the European Green Deal "the European Green Deal will transform the EU into a modern, resource-efficient and competitive economy, ensuring: no net emissions of greenhouse gases by 2050; economic growth decoupled from resource use; no person and no place left behind" (European Commission, 2021). The only possible solution when faced with this implausibly tall order is endorsement of and reliance on socio-technical imaginaries, which can be defined as "collectively held, institutionally stabilized, and publicly performed visions of desirable futures, animated by shared understandings of forms of social life and social order attainable through, and supportive of, advances in science and technology" (Jasanoff and Kim, 2015). Socio-technical imaginaries are effective not only in reducing feelings of stress in society ("yes, we can") but also in allowing a transformation of extremely delicate political issues into mere technical ones (Strassheim & Kettunen, 2014; Funtowicz & Ravetz, 1990; Wynne, 1992; Schumaker, 1973; Winner, 1989) which can be solved without major confrontation. To paraphrase the idea, to fix all our problems we need a continuous flow of "new business models" and "technical innovations".

The Cartesian dream of prediction and control (Guimarães Pereira & Funtowicz, 2015) has led modern societies into a serious predicament: they must now endorse a dubious belief in the unlimited power of scientific knowledge, an act that has profound consequences for the functioning of the science-policy domain. The choice of policies prioritizes control over adaptability, so that an overdose of rosy scenarios is used to prevent an informed discussion over concerns.

Conclusion

First, I would like to make clear that a critical appraisal of the blunder of "circular economy" does not entail that we should reduce our efforts in recycling, reusing, and reducing. On the contrary, through adoption of a sobering narrative about our total dependence on nature—after acknowledging that the economic process is entropic—we can better understand that recycling, reusing, and reducing waste are the only strategies we have to deal with the unsustainability of the current pattern of economic growth. It is the hubris associated with the concept of circular economy—the assumption that we can substitute nature by generating our own life support system—that represents a danger to our own sustainability. In relation to this point, Giampietro and Funtowicz (2020) explain that an aggressive mobilization of expectations having the goal of colonizing the future translates into an endorsement of ideological justification narratives and a systemic suppression of criticism, thus locking in chosen normative narratives.

> Once they have attained normative status, assumptions are taken for granted, they neither must be justified nor reflected upon (*Bakker & Budde, 2012*; *Konrad, 2006*). The danger here is that the myths underpinning the

reference points become naturalized, the result being that space for critical and hesitative reflection diminishes and it is socially discouraged (*Buclet & Lazarevic, 2014*). The all-encompassing expectations the concept brings together carry persuasive and performative power (*Brown & Michael, 2003; Lazarevic & Valve, 2017*). For these reasons those proposals perceived as implausible should be deemed irresponsible (*Strand, 2012*).

In conclusion, it seems safe to say that the flat Earth blunder in the sixth century was analogous to but perhaps more innocent and more harmless than the circular economy blunder of the twenty-first century. This stands true especially when considering that the quality of scientific inquiry available at the time of the flat Earth blunder was much lower. The dangerous intoxication of modern scientific inquiry in the field of sustainability can be explained by the hegemonic use of obsolete narratives endorsed by orthodox economic assumptions about the unlimited power of science and the market.

References

APS (2006). June ca. 240 B.C. Erathosthenes measures the Earth. *APS News*, 15 (6), 2. www.aps.org/publications/apsnews/200606/upload/June2006.pdf

Bakker, S., & Budde, B. (2012). Technological hype and disappointment: lessons from the hydrogen and fuel cell case. *Technology Analysis and Strategic Management*, 24 (6), 549–563. https://doi.org/10.1080/09537325.2012.693662

Berkes, F., Colding, J., & Folke, C. (1998). *Linking social and ecological systems. Management practices and social mechanisms for building resilience*. Cambridge University Press.

Berkes, F., Colding, J., & Folke, C. (2003). *Navigating social-ecological systems: Building resilience for complexity and change*. Cambridge University Press.

Boulding, K. (1966). The Economics of the Coming Spaceship Earth. In H. Jarrett (Ed.), *Environmental Quality in a Growing Economy* (pp. 3–14). John Hopkins University Press.

Brown, N., & Michael, M. (2003). A sociology of expectations: retrospecting prospects and prospecting retrospects. *Technology Analysis and Strategic Management*, 15 (1), 3–18. https://doi.org/10.1080/0953732032000046024

Buclet, N., & Lazarevic, D. (2014). Principles for sustainability: the need to shift to a sustainable conventional regime. *Environment, Development and Sustainability*, 17 (1), 83–100. https://doi.org/10.1007/s10668-014-9539-4

Dyke, C. (1988). Cities as dissipative structures. In J.D. Smith, D.J. Depew & B.H. Weber (Eds.), *Entropy, information, and evolution: New perspectives on physical and biological evolution* (pp. 355–367). MIT Press.

European Commission (2021). A *European Green Deal*. https://ec.europa.eu/info/strategy/priorities-2019-2024/european-green-deal_en

Friend, A. (2012). System of accounts for global entropy-production (sage-p): The accounting in the topological domain space (tds) of the econosphere, sociosphere, and the ecosphere. In S. Shmelev & I. Shmeleva (Eds.), *Sustainability analysis: An interdisciplinary approach* (pp. 25–51). Palgrave Macmillan. https://doi.org/10.1057/9780230362437_3

Funtowicz, S., & Ravetz, J. (1990). *Uncertainty and quality in science for policy*. Kluwer Academic Publishers.

Georgescu-Roegen, N. (1971). *The entropy law and the economic process* (1st ed.). Hardvard University Press.

Giampietro, M. (2018). Anticipation in agriculture. In R. Poli (ed.), *Handbook of Anticipation*. Springer. https://doi.org/10.1007/978-3-319-31737-3_23-1

Giampietro, M. (2019). On the circular bioeconomy and decoupling: Implications for sustainable growth. *Ecological Economics*, 162, 143–156. https://doi.org/10.1016/j.ecolecon.2019.05.001

Giampietro, M., & Funtowicz, S.O. (2020). From elite folk science to the policy legend of the circular economy. *Environmental Science and Policy*, 109, 64–72. https://doi.org/10.1016/j.envsci.2020.04.012

Giampietro, M., Mayumi, K., & Sorman, A.H. (2012). *The metabolic pattern of societies: Where economists fall short*. Routledge.

Giampietro, M., Mayumi, K., & Sorman, A.H. (2013). *Energy analysis for a sustainable future: Multi-scale integrated analysis of societal and ecosystem metabolism*. Routledge.

Glansdorff, P., & Prigogine, I. (1971). *Thermodynamic theory of structure, stability and fluctuations*. Wiley-Interscience.

Guimarães Pereira, A., & Funtowicz, S. (2015). *Science, philosophy and sustainability: The end of the Cartesian dream*. Routledge.

Habermas, J. (1979). *Communication and the evolution of society*. Beacon Press.

Jasanoff, S., & Kim, S.-H. (2015). *Dreamscapes of modernity—Sociotechnical imaginaries and the fabrication of power*. University of Chicago Press.

Konrad, K. (2006). The social dynamics of expectations: the interaction of collective and actor-specific expectations on electronic commerce and interactive television. *Technology Analysis and Strategic Management*, 18 (3–4), 429–444. https://doi.org/10.1080/09537320600777192.

Lazarevic, D., & Valve, H. (2017). Narrating expectations for the circular economy: towards a common and contested European transition. *Energy Research and Social Science*, 31, 60–69. https://doi.org/10.1016/j.erss.2017.05.006

Mayumi, K. (2001). *The origins of ecological economics: The bioeconomics of Georgescu-Roegen*. Routledge.

Mayumi, K., & Giampietro, M. (2004). Entropy in Ecological Economics. In J. Proops & P. Safonov (Eds.), *Modeling in ecological economics* (pp. 80–101). Edward Elgar.

Nicolis, G., & Prigogine, I. (1977). *Self-organization in nonequilibrium systems: From dissipative structures to order through fluctuations*. Wiley.

Prigogine, I. (1980). *From being to becoming*. W.H. Freeman.

Prigogine, I., & Stengers, I. (1981). *Order out of chaos: Man's new dialogue with nature*. Bantam Books.

Rayner, S. (2012). Uncomfortable knowledge: the social construction of ignorance in science and environmental policy discourses. *Economy and Society*, 41 (1), 107–125. https://doi.org/10.1080/03085147.2011.637335

Schrödinger, E. (1967). *What is life & mind and matter*. Cambridge University Press.

Schumacher, E.F. (1973). *Small is beautiful: Economics as if people mattered*. Harper & Row Publishers.

Strand, R. (2012). Doubt Has Been Eliminated. In S.A. Oyen, T. Lund-Olsen, & N. Sorensen Vaage (Eds.), *Sacred science? On science and its interrelations with religious worldviews* (pp. 55–64). Wageningen Academic Publishers.

Strassheim, H., & Kettunen, P. (2014). When does evidence-based policy turn into policy-based evidence? Configurations, contexts and mechanisms. *Evidence and Policy: A*

Journal of Research, Debate and Practice, 10 (2), 259–277. https://doi.org/10.1332/174426514X13990433991320

Winner, L. (1989). *The whale and the reactor: A search for limits in an age of high technology*. University of Chicago Press.

Wynne, B. (1992). Uncertainty and environmental learning: Reconceiving science and policy in the preventive paradigm. *Global Environmental Change*, 2 (2), 111–127. https://doi.org/10.1016/0959-3780(92)90017-2

5 The impossibility of circular recycling

Jonas Huether, Charlotte Joachimsthaler, and Martin Faulstich

Introduction

The vision of a holistic circular economy demands an industrial and societal system in which all phases of the value chain and product life cycle are restorative or regenerative. Among possible opportunities are reuse, recycling, refurbishment, sharing and, embracing all three, measures to extend the service life of products (Ellen MacArthur Foundation, 2013). Yet, none of these opportunities and measures promises a holistic circular economy as some technical-physical impossibilities remain. The ubiquitous challenge is that any kind of production, processing and recycling requires energy and usually emits greenhouse gases. Even if the question of energy availability is disregarded, challenges arise in terms of material science and life cycle assessment. In this chapter, these will be examined in detail by using three instructively examples.

Strictly speaking, when we talk about recycling, we are frequently referring to downcycling. Thermodynamically and physically, it is not possible to keep a product or material in a true infinite cycle and circle. In addition, the better a material is re-processed, the more energy is required.

Therefore, the terms recycling and downcycling are briefly defined in the following section. Then, the impossibilities of a circular economy are illustrated by means of three examples. Dissipation is introduced: materials, for example, valuable metals, become part of blends and alloys and are thus lost as usable raw materials. For composites, it is shown why it is impossible to recycle fibres and polymers in a consistent quality. The difficulties and the impossibility of all-encompassing life cycle assessments are discussed.

Downcycling

In the German Circular Economy Act ("Kreislaufwirtschaftsgesetz"), recycling is defined as any recovery procedure aiming at the transformation of waste into products, materials or substances that are subsequently used for either the original purpose or another, indicating that the recycled material needs to fulfil a purpose. Following this thought, downcycling is a phenomenon that may occur along with recycling but does not necessarily have to. Commonly, the label downcycling is

DOI: 10.4324/9781003244196-6

used when the quality of products, materials or substances processed from waste is reduced compared to the original quality or when the technical or economical value is decreased (Geyer et al., 2016). Yet, quality is no objective material property and can be understood from many perspectives, including stiffness, strength, wear resistance or conductivity. Scientific literature and laws are vague and ambiguous about the differences between both, recycling and downcycling, and about material quality. In addition, no differentiation between the original and other purposes is shown.

As downcycling is important for the three exemplary impossibilities highlighted in this chapter, the following operational definitions are used in the work at hand in order to approach the phenomenon of downcycling: downcycling emerges when the range of possible applications of a material or product is reduced. Downcycling also occurs when the specific use value (usually commercial price) of a product or material processed from waste is lower than the value of the same product or material produced with primary raw materials. Downcycling is also apparent when the reprocessing and reuse of a material consume more energy than production based on using virgin sources would. In terms of sustainability, downcycling appears when the ecological footprint of a material based on re-used material exceeds that of the virgin counterpart. Yet, for a more comprehensive and quantifiable definition of the downcycling phenomenon, the reader may refer to respective literature.

In conclusion, downcycling means that after a certain amount of recycling cycles, recycled raw materials cannot be fed into the original material cycle anymore. In addition, environmental impacts that hinder the achievement of the social development goals and climate neutrality, decelerating the transition to a holistic circular economy, occur due to downcycling.

The impossibility of closed loops due to dissipation

Dissipative losses are defined as materials, which cannot be regained due to economical or technical impossibilities. They are permanently lost and do not re-enter the original material and processing flow. Reasons for dissipation are manifold. They range from merging of materials that makes recovering individual materials impossible to entire losses during the use phase (Seelig et al., 2015; Zimmermann & Gößling-Reisemann, 2013).

The following paragraph will show that dissipation is a severe antagonist of a holistic circular economy. Circular economy is based on the principle that every material circulates forever and that all systems regenerate themselves. While nature provides biological cycles where infinite circulation is the norm, humankind's technical cycles are prone to losses. Nonetheless, not only the loss is of importance but also every dissipative loss is compensated by new material in the next cycle. This implicates an additional use of materials and, as a consequence, the additional extraction of resources, the emergence of emissions and environmental risks and consequences.

Dissipation can be considered the worst case of downcycling and thus both are commonly based on the same causes.

An example of these phenomena is industrial design. When it contradicts the aforementioned principles of recycling-fair construction, dissipation is more likely to occur. Nevertheless, the technical development partly proceeds contrary to the recommendations of recycling-fair construction as material diversity and product complexity are still rising. Nowadays, all but the radioactive elements are used in engineering, which means that approximately 75% of all elements known to humankind are directly used in our products (Faulstich, 2020). Advances in technology and miniaturisation cause the use of rare earth elements and particular metals in ever-lower concentrations and increasing complexity (Behrendt, 2015; Felipe et al., 2012). Such small amounts are commonly not recovered from components and are often neglected in life cycle assessments. The more tramp materials remain, the less homogeneous the primal material becomes. Material diversity creates a challenge for the recycling companies as collection, analysis, sorting and separation become more difficult and expensive. Due to the long bonding times and technological reasons, metals are difficult to separate. This applies in particular to steel and aluminium alloys. Reuter et al. designed the so-called metal wheel, which shows the recycling compatibility resulting from losses and potential recoveries of various metal combinations. For instance, neither tin, silver, platinum nor copper can be recovered by recycling steel or aluminium, and some might additionally have a negative impact on the material properties (Reuter et al., 2018). The results are high rates of downcycling and dissipation. To compensate for the effect of undesired alloying elements, the base alloy has to be diluted and base elements, for instance, iron or aluminium, have to be added and therefore need to be mined and processed. To reduce both dissipation and downcycling, sorting must be as accurate as possible (Fendel & Kempkes, 2014). Nonetheless, there are several aspects that interfere with optimised recycling: our consumption and disposal behaviour, technical limits in terms of machine precision and the fact that the development of high-precision sorting technology usually lag behind the development of products and materials that are to be recycled. A rising material diversity and increasingly complex products demand for a high sorting depth to fully recycle all materials. Today, analysing and sorting are commonly based on binary single sorting methods that do not provide enough sorting depth. Analysing technologies specialise on certain material classes or elements. All others might remain undetected, causing dissipation and downcycling. Criteria for high-performance detection are high throughput, in-depth information and accuracy. However, comprehensive combinations of sensors and inline analysis tools are yet to be developed. The better the analysis of scrap flow, the higher the probability that pure materials are regained. Nowadays, reprocessing of scrap and used products is widely designed for huge mass flows and is not appropriate for consumer goods that contain complex electronic components. For instance, if these components are not demounted prior to shredding, parts of the electronic components and thus a variety of critical and valuable metals are spread in the output flows and lost by dissipation. With metal prices being highly volatile, investments in the sorting and recycling technology are risky (Behrendt, 2015).

Another example of truly closed loops is given by the thermodynamics of metals. For instance, tinplate cans are molten during recycling and several alloy elements are regained by evaporation. Yet, as the flash point of tin is rather high, it remains within the steel alloy. Thus, tin is not only lost and must be replaced for producing new tin cans but also the steel's properties might be affected (Gleich & Brahmer-Lohss, 2004; Seelig et al., 2015). Another example highlighting the impossibility of closing all material loops is dissipative losses due to abrasion and corrosion (Seelig et al., 2015). Materials interact with the environment and with humans: rust caused by rain and saltwater devours the steel of ships, cars and buildings. Each steel wheel running and braking on a track will cause the release of tiny amounts of metal particles. By driving a car, we constantly lose rubber particles and when we break, infinitesimal fractions of the brake discs and pads are lost. It is evident that by no means of today's technology, we could regain those dissipated particles and feed them to our production cycles. So the best we can do is to ensure that these particles do not harm the ecological systems. In a real world, where friction, abrasion and weather are ubiquitous, circular economy's dream of perfectly closing all loops remains an impossibility.

While it is impossible to prevent dissipation completely, it is our duty to increase our effort to reduce it: we need quantitative analyses to measure dissipative losses and to understand their occurrence. Based on that, methods for reducing dissipation can be developed to allow high-quality recycling of materials.

With regard to circular economy and the well-known butterfly diagram, we need inspiration from nature: the biological cycle is a fully closed loop, and we would do well to design our technical cycles in the same way.

The impossibility of complete recycling of composite materials

Downcycling is found across all material classes and its complete prevention seems to be impossible when approaching the phenomenon holistically and considering all relevant factors (material, energy, emissions, etc.). Yet, for some materials such as glass and gold, procedures to minimise downcycling are established. For others, particularly fibre-reinforced plastics, high-quality recycling and restoring the materials to serve the primal purpose is an impossibility.

Composites combine two or more individual materials, which are permanently joined during the initial fabrication. The reinforcing material, frequently fibres, is embedded in the matrix, and it contributes high strength and stiffness and is therefore the load-bearing component. The matrix offers processability, freedom of geometries and protection against environmental impacts. Particularly, it passes external loads into the reinforcing fibres. Composites and among them especially fibre-reinforced plastics were developed to fulfil a requirement profile that no monolithic material can promise. For applications in vehicles and airplanes, wind turbine blades, sports equipment and so on, high-performance composites based on glass or carbon fibres and polymeric matrices, preferably thermosets, have become the material of choice (Woidasky, 2013). Those polymer-matrix composites are at the centre of attention in this chapter. In many years of development, the focus was on engineering performance rather than sustainability and recyclability. The art of engineering and tailored lightweight products outshone ecological concerns. During processing, fibres and (thermoset) matrix join permanently. While a high durability of the interface between the materials is a promising goal for the engineers, it is the reason for the impossibility of complete composite recycling.

In the following, the focus lies upon the fibres most commonly used in polymer-based composites, glass and carbon fibres. To regain those fibres from a composite, the polymeric matrix is decomposed by heat (pyrolysis), chemically (solvolysis and hydrolysis) or can be melted when being thermoplastic. Therefore, the matrix is taken from closed-loop recycling and has to be replaced by virgin material. The fibres are more valuable than the matrix and can be recovered (Pimenta & Pinho, 2014).

Yet to this day, a multitude of challenges remains unsolved, leading to severe downcycling effects: the fibre properties, particularly the tensile strength, are significantly reduced which limit the subsequent usability. The fibres lose their protective coating and become more brittle, making further processing more complicated. The fibre surface is altered, causing unpredictable variation in the fibre–matrix interface (Pimenta & Pinho, 2014). These effects are more severe for glass than for carbon fibres. While glass fibre strength is reduced by up to 70% (Feih et al., 2011), carbon fibres are typically reduced by about 10% to 20% (Huether, 2020). Yet for both, the loss in strength depends significantly on the applied recycling parameters (Pimenta & Pinho, 2012). Today's manufacturing routes for high-performance composites rely on continuous fibres. Continuous fibre rovings are either used directly for processes such as filament winding or are processed to non-woven and woven fabrics to be used in processes such as resin transfer moulding. As fibre reclamation causes a severe loss in fibre length and geometry, recycled fibres cannot directly feed any of these routes. There are ideas to apply hybridisation technology to re-enter recycled fibre yarns to these routes, but industrial upscaling is not proven yet. Replacing virgin fibres directly by recycled fibres is only feasible in routes such as injection moulding, where the fibre length is only a few millimetres anyway and thus low mechanical properties are intended and accepted from the outset. Here, recycled fibres can substitute short virgin fibres. However, as they are not returned to the primal cycle of high-performance continuous fibre composites, downcycling occurs (Huether, 2020; Pimenta & Pinho, 2014).

Finally yet importantly, the recycling of composites minimises the economic value of the fibres compared to their virgin counterparts. Recycled carbon fibres are still more expensive than the matrix and regaining them can turn out as an economic benefit. However, with costs of about 1€ per kilogram, virgin glass fibres are already as cheap as typical polymer-matrix systems and therefore their recycling becomes economically unattractive (Huether, 2020). Pulverisation of glass fibre composites without fibre reclamation and reusing them as filler becomes a viable option, despite the fact that it is severe downcycling.

To regain fibres, only pyrolysis has reached industrial dimensions, yet, leading to the aforementioned challenges. Improvements in pyrolysis as well as upscaling developments of solvolysis, hydrolysis and new fibre reclamation technologies will most likely increase the potential of reusing fibres. Nonetheless, closed-loop recycling of composites without downcycling effects remains out of reach.

In the context of a sustainable material use in a circular economy, engineers and designers have to examine systematically whether monolithic materials which are easier to recycle can provide the same function as the composite. From a strict recycling perspective, composites should be avoided wherever possible. Nonetheless, one must bear in mind that composites offer sustainability benefits: to name a few, lightweight vehicles and planes reduce fuel consumption and today's large wind turbine rotor blades could not be engineered without using glass and carbon fibre composites (Woidasky, 2013). If composites are the material of choice, new concepts of durability and design-for-recycling must be considered from the beginning to minimise the ecological harm and to acknowledge the thinking of a circular economy. Politics and society should demand a greatly reduced use of fibre-reinforced plastics wherever they are not necessary, and engineers should develop appropriate guidelines.

The impossibility of a holistic life cycle assessment

Life cycle assessment is a method to analyse potential environmental impacts of products and services and is defined in standards ISO EN 14040 and 14044. The method is divided into the following four phases: the definition of scope and goal, the inventory analysis, the impact assessment and the interpretation of the results (DIN EN ISO 14040:2006, 2009). In terms of impossibilities, the first phase is key, as will be elucidated in this paragraph.

In the first phase, the user defines the scope and goal of the life cycle assessment (LCA). Here, technical, temporal and geographical system boundaries are set. Cut-off rules to delimit the chosen system from the setting are defined. In addition, the functional unit of the system is defined and the reference flow required for this is quantified. Furthermore, the type of impact assessment is described (DIN EN ISO 14040:2006, 2009). Cut-off rules and boundaries are used to decrease complexity and to set the focus correctly. As a side effect, this might reduce computing effort and improve data availability (Klöpffer & Grahl, 2009).

In the second phase, the inventory analysis, inputs and outputs, such as material and energy flows, are monitored. Collected data is related to individual processes and to a reference. The third phase includes a quantitative analysis of the impacts resulting from the inventory analysis. For instance, the system might be reduced or enlarged and references are studied. The fourth phase is used to summarise the life cycle inventory and impact assessment, interpretation and discussion, as well as to derivate recommendations for action (DIN EN ISO 14040:2006, 2009; Klöpffer & Grahl, 2009).

It becomes obvious that the scientific quality and all results greatly depend on the initial set of scope, goal, cut-off rules and boundaries. On the one hand, this explains why results of LCAs for the same system or material might differ depending on the software, data quality and the user itself. On the other hand, one can derive that the quality of the results of an LCA is significantly affected by the initial assumptions. In other words, to obtain a holistic LCA, the initial settings have to be selected with great care.

Cut-off rules defined in phase 1 serve to exclude minor inputs of the product system. This is due to the fact that the product systems are embedded in the technosphere and the environment as large systems (Klöpffer & Grahl, 2009). Different subsystems are linked to each other and interact to varying degrees. If a system is delimited from its environment, some of these links are inevitably separated in order to meet the goal. The guidelines for this are based on cut-off rules that apply to individual process modules, as well as to the entire product system.

Common cut-off criteria are masses, energy and environmental impact. For instance, it is common practice to exclude input variables which account for less than 1% of either material mass, energy flow or environmental impact. To do so, all shares have to be acquired (Klöpffer & Grahl, 2009). This shall be demonstrated in the following, firstly, with a fictional example: consider a technical component that contains both a structural element and an electronic subcomponent. In total, it consists of 13 different materials in varying amounts. Here, the basic structure could contain epoxy resin as matrix (1), glass fibres as reinforcement (2) and calcium carbonate (3) as a filler. Copper (4) is used for electrical conduction and rubber (5) for cable insulation. Mountings are made from two different polymers (6, 7), steel (8) and an aluminium-magnesium alloy (9+10). Furthermore, polymeric glue (11) and tin-lead solder (12+13) are used, yet, both account for less than 1% in weight. In this example, the investigator might set the cut-off rule in a way so that all materials that have less than 1% mass fraction are neglected. Consequently, the tin-lead solder and the glue would not be investigated and would not appear in phases 2, 3 and 4 of the LCA. Thus, the possible environmental impacts, particularly that of lead, are not observed in this LCA. Yet, materials with minor mass fractions are frequently those with critical impacts, like lead, gold and platinum (impacts on the environment and water usage), or rare earths, gallium and indium (social and environmental impacts). In addition, the availability of these elements is commonly low and they are likely to dissipate.

In addition to the fictional example, a second, more specific example concerning wind turbines shall be used to emphasise the impossibility: in wind turbines, neodymium is a critical metal but commonly not considered in LCAs due to its low mass fraction (Moss et al., 2013). Consequently, environmental impacts related to the mining and processing of neodymium are overseen. Therefore, existing LCAs are barely helpful for investigations linked to the potential environmental impacts of rare earths (Davidsson et al., 2012).

A third issue arises from the aforementioned downcycling and dissipation. LCAs need defined input and output flows, which are hardly obtainable for dissipating materials traces such as rubber tyre wear particles, precious trace elements becoming undesired alloy contents during recycling or lubricants in production and use.

These examples not only demonstrate the challenges and the impossibility of a comprehensive LCA, but they also hint for possible improvements: phases 2 and 3 of the LCA build directly on phase 1 and allow few degrees of freedom. Phase 4 can be used to discuss the LCA and to adapt variables. In the example at hand, the LCA can be customised so that in phase 1, smaller quantities are also considered for the lead solder and neodymium, respectively, and the LCA is repeated. For LCA, not only the technical correctness but also the skill and experience of the investigator are of great importance. Yet, both compete with computational power and expenditure of time, and sensible trade-offs may be required.

Another impossibility is to fully encompass our entire globalised world: With product trade and production all around the globe, and with high-tech devices and products containing almost all the stable elements known to humankind, it becomes (almost) impossible to track and evaluate every milligram of it. In addition, an LCA run in Germany might differ vastly from one in France or China. Thinking on a global scale, it must be acknowledged that, for instance, inputs and outputs related to transportation and the energy supply will vary significantly from region to region. Again, LCA must be tailored to a certain scope and goal, but it remains impossible to provide a solution that holds in principle.

In summary, system boundaries, selected cut-off rules and limited data availability result in the fact that not all material flows can be included in LCA. This is a particular concern as circular economy and the associated zero-waste philosophy require managing all material in closed loops. Thus, it would be necessary to include all materials in the LCA to allow for holistic assessments and comprehensive guidance. In this context, it is essential to further develop LCA methods to adapt to ever-increasing complexity of material systems (for instance, fibre composites). Yet, this would demand for infinite data acquisition and unlimited computing power. As both are impossibilities, it is deduced that LCA is an important and powerful tool to discuss the environmental impact of human production and consumption and our interaction with the planetary resources and boundaries. Yet, it remains impossible to detect even the smallest impacts and flows and to discover all the weak points in our technological systems.

In the context of LCAs for a circular economy, engineers and scientists are to optimise all assessment tools. Yet, they should question all results with rhyme and reason and, where possible, decide on the technological option that is best for the planet. It always remains to be scrutinised whether, under certain circumstances, small mass flows were excluded in the first phase, which could lead to undesirable effects on the environment.

Conclusion

To conclude, it shall be briefly and graphically summarised why the three chosen examples lead to impossibilities within the circular economy (see also Figure 5.1).

Consider a product consisting of the four materials a, b, c and d. *In a perfect circular economy, all materials would circulate infinitely*. As elucidated, this is not feasible for real products and materials.

For downcycling and dissipation, tramp elements and contaminations are both cause and effect, at the same time. The more contamination a material contains, the lower its quality is expected to be and the lower the will for high-level recycling. Yet, the lower the endeavour in better recycling, the more contaminations remain within the base material. Instead of a material cycle, a vicious circle is established. *Fractions of a material, in the figure α and γ, vanish in the environment*.

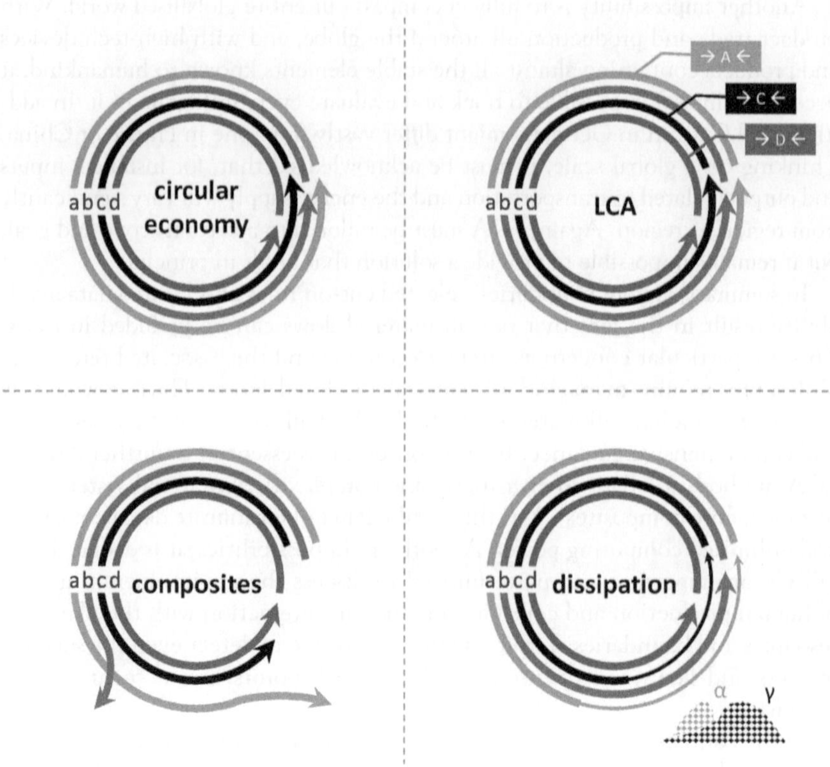

Figure 5.1 Graphical representation of a perfect circular economy compared to impossibilities arising in our real world.

Source: Illustration by J. Huether.

For composites, the impossibility of circularity lies within the engineering idea itself. When engineers strive to permanently and irretrievably bond material without having its end-of-life in mind, it becomes an engineering impossibility to separate the components without loss. By design, some materials, here a and b, cannot circulate and are lost at the end of life.

In life cycle assessment, the impossibility lies within the fact that criteria and cut-off rules are needed to make LCA viable. Furthermore, the results of LCA differ between regions and studies, and it is impossible to define a universal LCA. *In the figure, criteria A, B and D are set and materials a, b and d are investigated. Yet, material c is not considered due to cut-off rules or unavailable data.*

References

Behrendt, S. (2015). Recycling von Technologiemetallen: Transformationsfeldanalyse im Rahmen des Projekts Evolution2Green – Transformationspfade zu einer Green Economy. Adelphi, www.researchgate.net/profile/Siegfried-Behrendt/publication/340341311_ARBEITSPAPIER_Recycling_von_Technologiemetallen_Transformationsfeldanalyse/links/5e846a894585150839b2e0a5/ARBEITSPAPIER-Recycling-von-Technologiemetallen-Transformationsfeldanalyse.pdf

Davidsson, S., Höök, M., & Wall, G. (2012). A review of life cycle assessments on wind energy systems. *The International Journal of Life Cycle Assessment, 17*(6), 729–742. https://doi.org/10.1007/s11367-012-0397-8

DIN EN ISO 14040:2006 (2009). Umweltmanagement – Ökobilanz – Grundsätze und Rahmenbedingungen (ISO 14040:2006): Deutsches Institut für Normung: DIN.

Ellen MacArthur Foundation (2013). Towards the Circular Economy: Economic and business rationale for an accelerated transition.

Faulstich, M. (2020). Circular economy. *Nachhaltige Industrie* (1) n.p.

Feih, S., Boiocchi, E., Mathys, G., Mathys, Z., Gibson, A. G., & Mouritz, A. P. (2011). Mechanical properties of thermally-treated and recycled glass fibres. *Composites Part B: Engineering*, 42(3), 350–358. https://doi.org/10.1016/j.compositesb.2010.12.020

Felipe, J., Kumar, U., Abdon, A., & Bacate, M. (2012). Product complexity and economic development. *Structural Change and Economic Dynamics*, 23(1), 36–68. https://doi.org/10.1016/j.strueco.2011.08.003

Fendel, A., & Kempkes, P. (2014). Die veränderte Welt des Metallrecyclings – Steigende Vielfalt der Funktionswerkstoffe – Entropie und Dissipation in Schrotten. *Uwf UmweltWirtschaftsForum*, 22(2–3), 207–212. https://doi.org/10.1007/s00550-014-0329-0

Geyer, R., Kuczenski, B., Zink, T., & Henderson, A. (2016). Common misconceptions about recycling. *Journal of Industrial Ecology*, 20(5), 1010–1017. https://doi.org/10.1111/jiec.12355

Gleich, A. von, & Brahmer-Lohss, M. (2004). *Nachhaltige Metallwirtschaft Hamburg: Erkenntnisse – Erfahrungen – praktische Erfolge*. Effizienzgewinne durch Kooperation bei der Optimierung von Stoffströmen in der Region Hamburg.

Huether, J. J. (2020). *The Impact of Recycling on the Fibre and the Composite Properties of Carbon Fibre Reinforced Plastics*. https://doi.org/10.5445/KSP/1000098911

Klöpffer, W., & Grahl, B. (2009). *Ökobilanz (LCA)*. WILEY-VCH Verlag.

Moss, R., Willis, P., Tercero, E. L., Tzimas, E., Arendorf, J., Thompson, P., Chapman, A., Morley, N., Sims, E., Bryson, R., Pearson, J., Marscheider-Weidemann, F., Soulier, M., Lüllmann, A., Sartorius, C., & Ostertag, K. (2013). Critical metals in the path towards the decarbonisation of the EU energy sector: Assessing rare metals as supply-chain bottlenecks in low-carbon energy technologies. *EUR, Scientific and Technical Research Series, 25994*. Publications Office.

Pimenta, S., & Pinho, S. T. (2012). The effect of recycling on the mechanical response of carbon fibres and their composites. *Composite Structures*, 94(12), 3669–3684. https://doi.org/10.1016/j.compstruct.2012.05.024

Pimenta, S., & Pinho, S. T. (2014). Recycling of carbon fibers. *Handbook of Recycling* (pp. 269–283). Elsevier. https://doi.org/10.1016/B978-0-12-396459-5.00019-2

Reuter, M. A., van Schaik, A., & Ballester, M. (2018). *Limits of the circular economy: Fairphone modular design pushing the limits*. World of Metallurgy – ERZMETALL 71 (2018) No. 2: 68–79.

Seelig, J. H., Stein, T., Zeller, T., & Faulstich, M. (2015). Möglichkeiten und Grenzen des Recycling. In K. J. Thomé-Kozmiensky & D. Goldmann (Eds.), *Recycling und Rohstoffe*. TK-Verl: 55–69.

Woidasky, J. (2013). Weiterentwicklung des Recyclings von faserverstärkten Verbunden. In K. J. Thomé-Kozmiensky & D. Goldmann (Eds.), *Recycling und Rohstoffe*. TK-Verl: 241–259.

Zimmermann, T., & Gößling-Reisemann, S. (2013). Critical materials and dissipative losses: A screening study. *The Science of the Total Environment, 461–462*, 774–780. https://doi.org/10.1016/j.scitotenv.2013.05.040

Part II

What are our blind spots?

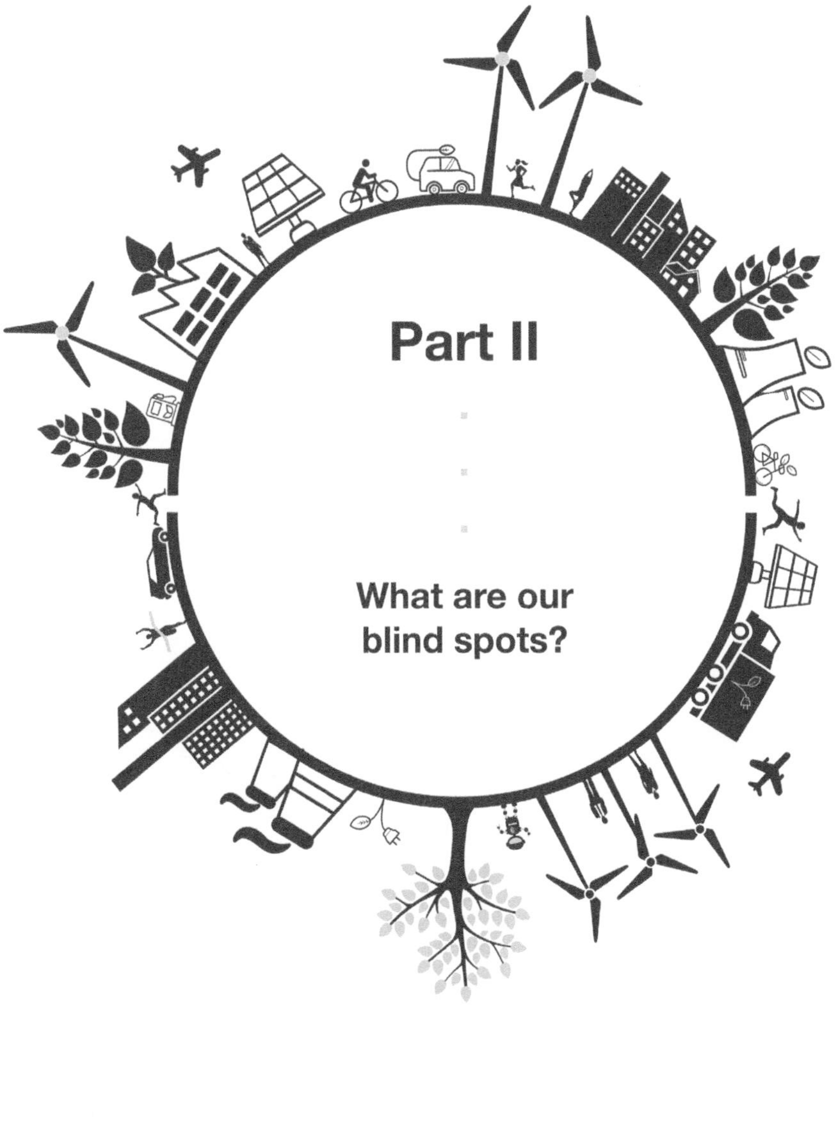

6 Circular economy, sustainability and functional differentiation

An impossibility and its strategic-methodological implications

Monika Gonser and Christoph Hinske

Introduction

In recent years, the circular economy has been lauded as one possible contribution to overcome the ever-increasing impacts of the excessive exploitation of natural resources by humanity expressing itself in climate change, the decrease of biodiversity, the pollution of the natural environment and so on. In order to fully understand and adapt the production, usage and recycling process to a closure of the often-cited product loop, circular economy calls for the inclusion and application of a multi-stakeholder perspective, among other things (Ellen Mac Arthur Foundation 2016; Webster 2017; Stahel 2019). Stahel (2017: 79) equates circular with sustainable (Geissdoerfer et al. 2016) and shows that most such solutions "are intersectoral and interdisciplinary" (2017: 79). This claim follows an intuitively understandable logic since the producers (e.g. policymakers) and consumers play an essential role in the adaptation process of product life cycles to circularity and sustainability. At second – and deeper – thought, however, a contradiction appears that deserves a closer look: Intersectoral – ideally holistic – approaches (i.e. the inclusion of sector perspectives from politics, business, public administration, civil society etc.) come with the inclusion of different, possibly contradicting, possibly mutually exclusive (i.e. particularistic) logics of action, core values, professional ethos, quality management approaches and risk definitions (Gonser et al. 2019; Webster 2017; Ritchie-Dunham 2022; Metcalf & Hinske 2022). Do these varying, sometimes contradicting, logics and characteristics impede the closure of the loop, thus actually masking an impossibility of the circular economy? If so, are there other perspectives on intersectoral coordination of action that can explain how to overcome these impediments? Furthermore, from a practical viewpoint, does this result in any relevant consequences for the multi-stakeholder process of 'doing circular economy'?

For this purpose, the article first briefly explains the understanding of the 'circular economy' it is based on and explains why the inclusion of multi-stakeholder perspectives in the process of 'doing circular economy' can be understood as an intersectoral governance process. It then briefly explores relevant sociological perspectives on multi-stakeholder governance processes and explains which

DOI: 10.4324/9781003244196-8

process implications for 'doing circular economy' follow from these theoretical viewpoints.

The concepts of circular economy and intersectoral/collaborative governance

The concepts of *circular economy* and *intersectoral governance* and their juxtaposition are the focus of this chapter, thus demanding their brief introduction and independent reflection. The Ellen McArthur Foundation introduced one of the most widespread definitions of the circular economy: "an industrial economy that is restorative or regenerative by intention and design" (2013: 14). It puts forward the idea of a circular, systemic approach to the production of goods that strategically focuses on "waste prevention, regional job creation, resource efficiency, dematerialization of the industrial economy" (Geissdoerfer et al. 2016: 759) and utilization instead of ownership (Stahel 1982: Tonelli & Cristoni 2019). Circular economy as a concept represents an ideal type where resources do not go to waste and can be entirely reused for other purposes at the end of the product's life cycle. Although the practical implications and obstacles that accrue to implementing the approach from the focus on this ideal type are relevant (Man 2022), it goes beyond the scope of this chapter.

The notion of circular economy is often used almost synonymously with the notion of sustainability. Although taken by itself, this might not always be adequate (Geissdörfer et al. 2016); for this article, we explicitly understand sustainability as a central dimension of the circular economy since the multi-stakeholder perspective becomes most relevant when this is the case. Most commonly, sustainability – a term initially stemming from forestry (Grober 2010) – is defined as a societal "development that meets the needs of the present without compromising the ability of future generations to meet their own needs" (Brundtland et al. 1987: OECD 2003). This definition shows that if sustainability as a normative concept is inherent to the circular economy, perspectives of other stakeholder groups than market participants need to be included. This approach ensures to appropriately respect future needs not only of economic but also of political, civic and cultural actors, thus referring to the sustainable aspect of the circular economy as a public good. Secondly, it clarifies that an expression of the particular *perspective* of any such actor will not be sufficient. Instead, it is necessary to coordinate and align the *actions* of these actor groups (i.e. sectors – be it business, civil society, public administration or others) to close the product life cycle so that it will not compromise the options for future generations. So, what is needed is the inclusion of multi-stakeholder perspectives and the coordination of the sectors around the product under concern, that is, intersectoral or collaborative governance.

Intersectoral governance is the German translation of 'intersektorale Governance', the most common English term being that of 'collaborative governance'. According to Kooiman (1999, 2000),

> The role of the state shifts from that of 'governing' through direct forms of control (hierarchical governance), to that of 'governance', in which the state must collaborate with a wide range of actors in networks that cut across the public, private and voluntary sectors, and operate across different levels of decision making.

Straßheim (2013: 347) goes further by reporting collaborative governance as a summarization of different coordination modes in the deliverance of (public) goods, the provision of infrastructure, the implementation of funding programmes, the coordination of political expertise and the design of governance tools. These conceptualizations show that governance as a notion often focuses on the government or public administration as the central actor. However, it does not necessarily have to be – intersectoral action coordination can also be thought of as relying heavily on business or civil society.

As the previous paragraphs show, the inclusion of multi-stakeholder perspectives and the coordination of intersectoral action are relevant for 'doing circular economy'. Sustainability as a normative core to the circular economy concept serves as a quality mark for the results of the intersectoral coordination process. However, theory on the hallmark of modern societies – functional differentiation – informs us that communication between the sectors resulting from cooperation and alignment on ethical grounds is an unrealistic expectation, that is to say an impossibility.

Functional differentiation is an impossibility in the circular economy

'Functional differentiation' can be understood as one of the central characteristics of modern, industrialized societies – it means a division of labour between different societal spheres based on function. Essential societal functions like the production of knowledge, collective decision-making, allocation of goods and so on are delivered by separate societal systems. Societies become functionally differentiated in reaction to the increasing complexity of modern societies. A specific theoretic approach, systems theory based on Luhmann (1984), understands the formation and specification of different sectors as distinct and de-limited communication systems (e.g. the political system, the economic system, the academic system and the system of law and jurisdiction). In its strict interpretation, these different societal systems can only exchange and process expressable information following each system's specific core values. Core values and core differentiation (e.g. profit – no profit, true – untrue) form the action logic within the specific systems as expressed by Luhmann (1984). Communication between the systems on a topic not expressable in a system's logic of action is impossible unless a societal system manages to cause a disturbance in the functioning of another system, for example, due to the introduction of a law that prohibits profits based on wasting ecological resources. Only in this case, the system disturbed would adapt to the changing societal conditions. Joint communication and thus any kind of pro-active, ethically inspired and aligned exchange and action on matters of the circular economy not expressable in the logic of all systems involved and not necessitating instant adaptations in all systems involved strictly speaking is an impossibility within the concept of functional differentiation. Ethics, or an overarching moral in particular, is not considered an issue particularly relevant to functional differentiation. Of course, political focuses and rules are set by the political system. Due to the cross-cutting nature of the sustainability concept in the circular economy, Luhmann, the sociological mastermind of this strand of systems theory, would have doubted whether modern societies can adapt to the concept as he doubted their ability to adapt to ecological hazards in general (1990; Reckwitz 2001; Schneidewind 2019).

The relevance of functional differentiation to the circular economy discourse

Admittedly, theory informs but does not predict reality, so the question, where functional differentiation is relevant to the establishment of the circular economy, in reality, is valid. Its relevance expresses itself in its potential to explain disturbances and dysfunctions we can observe in the collaborative governance of the circular economy: When giving the product life cycle the lead and including any stakeholder's perspective on it along the way, the necessity to cope with the complexity of interdependent logics of actions and contradicting, possibly mutually excluding core values and core differentiation increase decisively, enhancing disturbances and dysfunctions between the systems (Gonser et al. 2019). Within the concept of functional differentiation, the two most promising practical approaches to overcoming inter-system contradictions and non-communications are: (1) to translate action logics between societal systems, that is, to express the purpose of one system e.g. empowerment in the civil society to another system's purpose e.g. profit in the economy and (2) to construct disturbances in systems by including sustainability issues into the legislation thus changing the environment of the economic system and resulting in its adaptation. However, not all central issues of one societal system are easily translatable into another system's logic. Think of the differences in quality control between academia, business and community-based organizations. Whereas in academia, quality is ensured through an elite-dominated, peer-review process (Anderson et al. 2015; Hoffman 2021b), in business, it is defined through the quantifiable outcomes expressed in the business case. In community-based organizations, it is defined by spirit, justice and long-term sustainability (Waddell 2011).

These disturbances and dysfunctions are still further intensified because many strategic planning and administration methodologies are adapted to the logic of action of only one societal system, for example, a business plan or an administrative procedure (Scott 2018, Waddell 2011). So, not only do interdependencies and contradictions between actors exist but also existing methodologies blind them to the logic behind another actor's position even if they are willing and ready to contribute to the process (Rumelt 2017, Berger 2019).

Complementary perspectives on intersectoral/collaborative governance and 'doing circular economy'

Does the conclusion that the circular economy, sustainability and functional differentiation strictly speaking form an impossibility indicate an end of discussion? This is not the case since social theory offers other approaches that highlight collaboration and coordination of collective action that complement the picture and result in impossibilities. In particular, we would like to follow a categorization by Reckwitz (2001) and include institutional economics (Buttkereit 2009), the deliberative process (Habermas 1981) and culturalistic approaches (e.g. Rorty 1989).

Intersectoral alliances within the perspective of *institutional economics* are analytically split into two levels: the individual and the collective level. While the collective level refers to all actors involved in a coordination or cooperation process – i.e. the multi-stakeholder perspective – the individual level refers to an individual actor from one specific sector – i.e. a stakeholder like a firm, a non-governmental administration or an agency. The lens of institutional economics then defines how benefits and losses of a given process (e.g. adaptation towards a circular product cycle) are distributed across all stakeholders compared to the benefits the community might gain from the adaptation. Buttkereit (2009), based on Ostrom (1990), assumes that intersectoral alliances always include individual benefits and a collective benefit or public good to be gained. This fits into the standpoint on sustainability as a central dimension of the circular economy. For the successful coordination of intersectoral alliances, Buttkerkeit shows that the existence of a collective benefit and an individual benefit for each stakeholder involved is of central relevance. Suppose a careful analysis of the given situation shows otherwise. In that case, the regulatory agreements guiding the interactions and relationships need to be rearranged, for example, by compensations or the distribution of shares, thus creating a win-win situation. This approach overcomes the impossibility of the circular economy, sustainability and functional differentiation by dividing the arena of action into an individual and a collective sphere and creating a regulation system around it that overcomes asymmetries in benefits and harms for the stakeholders involved. However, this approach is not unconditional and depends on the strength of the interdependency between the stakeholders, the exclusiveness of the problem-solving forum, the sets of rules applied, the quality of their adaptation and the extent of initial asymmetries (Ansell & Gash 2007).

While institutional economics focuses on the collective and individual stakeholder *results* and reflects necessary adaptations of the distribution system, Habermas' deliberative process focuses on the cooperation process between the stakeholders involved (Reckwitz 2001). He establishes the "post-traditional morale of communication" (Reckwitz 2001: 211) and defines rules that need to be adhered to when an ethically justifiable, fair and truthful communication result is to be reached. Practically, Habermas asks for a joint world of debate and argument between the stakeholders, believing that the knowledge brought to the table transparently and respectfully will produce a consensual solution to the stakeholders' problem or innovative attempt. The creation of the third space of deliberation between two actors where the better argument can unfold its effect is an intellectually compelling idea and is taken as the basis in particular of methodology development of American authors (Forrer 2015; Innes & Booher 2018). This idea seems to be relevant for the circular economy, which requires collaboration along and across supply chains (Webster 2017). However, the ability to create a "third space" depends on persons' mindset and behaviours that allow them to build trust among stakeholders, engage in cooperation and develop shared beliefs (Metcalf & Hinske 2022).

So while from the perspective of functional differentiation, the closure of the loop of circular economy with the aim of improved sustainability must be considered an impossibility, formal-rationalistic approaches to the coordination of collective action like institutional economics or Habermasian deliberative processes do offer ways of communicating on value-based adaptations to existing societal spheres and processes (Reckwitz 2001). However, the widespread practical and effective application is still doubted in literature (Reckwitz 2001). Current conditions like social polarization and disruptions and, for example, asynchronous meeting necessities due to geographical distances, for example, along supply chains, could pose a threat.

Accordingly, Reckwitz discusses the third strand of approaches to the coordination of collective action – culturalistic approaches – that, in our opinion, is relevant in the circular economy literature as well. In this concept, engagement in the circular economy is driven by striving for an ethically 'good life'. It captures the "complex of meaningful positive and negative assessments based on which individual actors see their specific conduct as concrete or abstract representation of a morally 'good' way of living" (Reckwitz 2001: 213). Thus, culturalistic approaches create a link between personal and collective identities. Furthermore, they define an individual's idea of 'purpose'. So, pragmatic approaches are relevant and allow for an analysis of how social environments integrate the functioning of other systems like business or the media into their interpretation of a 'good' way of living and purpose. The reflection of good life and purpose is part of the individual identity and comes before the coordination of collective action (Reckwitz 2001). Analysing interpretations of purposes thus can be understood as a key to reaching out to individual actors or particular social environments and to including them in collaboration on the circular economy. In the governance literature, we find this approach in particular in newer literature on organizational forms of self-regulating, possibly intersectoral teams (e.g. Laloux 2014, Edmondson & Harvey 2017), new work and leadership (e.g. Breidenbach & Rollow 2019) and transformation towards a sustainable society (e.g. Schneidewind 2019; Göpel 2020; Parkin 2010, Hoffman 2021a).

Strategic-methodological implications

The article has shown that various theoretical lenses allow reflecting the coordination of multi-stakeholder settings with the aim of a circular economy and sustainability. All bring specific characteristics, developments and frictions to the fore and overlook others. In our opinion, the one 'intersectoral' lens by which to best understand multi-stakeholder settings in the circular economy does not exist. Instead, the different approaches inform us about different aspects, and their reflection and comparison highlight the central dimensions any strategy development or methodology that is applied to the circular economy should incorporate:

Dimension 1: System complexity of society

Management in a circular economy is exposed to much higher levels of complexity (Webster 2017; Stahel 2019), making the ability to handle complexity a vital issue. Consequently, up-to-date management approaches need to enable actors (individuals and groups) to do so. Paradoxically, functional differentiation was initially interpreted to decrease complexity. However, it simultaneously adds to it by causing additional disturbances at sectoral interfaces. Additionally, interdependencies of only evolving processes and feedback loops are difficult to predict, and unknown variables impacting the process need to be dealt with (Snowden 2007).

So to appropriately deal with complex matters and systems, methodologies are needed that acknowledge their typical features and are capable of grasping them. Boulton et al. (2015:36) characterize complex systems with the following features: They tend to be

> *systemic and synergistic, they are multi-scalar, show variety, diversity, variation and fluctuations that may give rise both to resilience and adaptability, are path-dependent, contingent on the local context and on the sequence of what happens, change episodically and can tip into new regimes, and can self-organize, self-regulate and new features can emerge.*

Accordingly, analytical and enabling methodologies for complex projects need to allow the actors to see and alter the interactions between the various parts of the system, from multiple, for example, disciplinary angles, and not only the elements and their characteristics alone (Webster 2017: 62). Methodologies that reflect specific characteristics of complexity are methods that address strategic questions based on dynamic uncertainty and impacts with contingent outcomes (Ritchie-Dunham & Rabbino 2001, Collins 2019, Borgert 2019, Hinske 2021a, Hinske 2021b).

Dimension 2: Individual and collective costs and benefits

As mentioned above, one dimension in which the impossibility of, for example, the circular economy in a functionally differentiated world can be overcome is to analytically split the sphere of action into the individual and the collective sphere. Individual costs and benefits within a particular functional logic can be aligned with collective costs and benefits, thus 'translating' functional logics via institutional rearrangements that create win-win situations.

Analytical and strategic methods need to help its users to determine which stakeholders are relevant to the process. It needs to show the individual or collective costs-benefits stakeholders have from a given process (Fligstein 2012). It then needs to give a detailed analysis of all relevant stakeholders' resulting costs/benefits share and inform the analyst about existing disbalances that need to be altered by the institutional setting to create win-win situations.

The institutional setting is based on a mixture of measures that, on the one hand, set and measure objectives and interaction parameters to have a robust overview over any disbalances. On the other hand, the institutional setting defines and institutionalizes rewards and penalties to the stakeholders in order to overcome disbalance-causing effects as, e.g. a lack of information objectivity, information asymmetries, moral hazard and adverse selection, risk-increasing, in-transparency, free-riding behaviour, stereotypes in mental models inhibiting cooperation and so on. (Buttkereit 2009: 93ff.). Ritchie-Dunham and Puente (2008) described a mental model mapping that helps to identify and correct gaps in mental models, needs and wants. As Sandfort and Moulton's purpose mapping, it can be applied to get a more detailed overview of the balance between individual and collective costs and benefits (Sandfort & Moulton 2015).

Dimension 3: Process quality

A third dimension that seems relevant in overcoming the impossibility of a circular economy in a functionally differentiated world is the dimension of process quality. It allows changing the focus from functional logics to a joint interpretation of the world and a shared understanding of the relevant facts. Creating the above-mentioned third space establishes a deliberative context in which objectives, meaning and impact of a process ideally are negotiated on a level playing field.

To ensure process quality, essential conditions of communication must be met to the best extent possible:

- Communication, central to the process, should be "conducted face-to-face,
- all statements must be comprehensible to all participants,
- they must be true to the speaker's best knowledge,
- statements must be made sincerely, and the speakers must have the legitimacy to make their statements.
- Coercion cannot be part of the process, and all participants must be treated equally and have equal access to information.
- Wherever possible assumptions must be made explicit, and participants must be persuaded by the force of the better argument and not by power, ignorance or peer pressure" (Innes & Booher 2018:25).

Methodologies that focus on this kind of transparency, robust knowledge and better argument are expert-driven process designs. They prevent limiting the space of deliberation and interaction between the participants. This so-called principled engagement usually is established by clear rules of procedures, joint fact-finding processes and so on (Emerson & Nabatchi 2015, Crislip 2002).

Dimension 4: Purpose and meaning

The last dimension to be mentioned here for overcoming the impossibility of the circular economy in a functionally differentiated world is the dimension of purpose and meaning. Culturalistic approaches assume that increasing complexity results in an overall loss of structures, which necessitates a more direct link between the individual and the collective level. Reflecting individual identity in the context of a collective identity allows for creating an inner value structure that – based on continuous self-reflection and contact with the emotional self – allows to reach collective objectives, thereby replacing the need for outer structures. A methodology that supports strategic analysis and action in this dimension promotes self-reflection and self-contact, empathy, co-creation and constructive conflict resolution. It allows combining the individual with a multiperspective meta-interpretation of a given problem or situation. Methods that focus on all of these dimensions are, e.g. the AQAL-Model (Wilber 2000) or the collaborative governance regime model (CGR) by Emerson and Nabatchi (2015) based on the collaborative governance dynamics of principled engagement, shared motivation and capacity for joint action.

Conclusion

This article discussed the theoretical impossibility of a circular economy in a functionally differentiated world. It showed that the circular economy causes an increase in complexity and thus calls for the application of methodologies capable of appropriately modelling complexity. It gave examples of corresponding methods for strategic analysis and design of circular economy processes. Besides, it discussed what other social theory approaches could shed light on collaborative planning and decision-making questions in systemic conditions and exemplarily discussed relevant dimensions according to methodology.

References

Anderson, L.; Gold, J.; Stewart, J.; & Thorpe, R. (2015). Chapter 3. Concepts and Theory Building. In: A Guide to Professional Doctorates in Business and Management (pp. 35–56). London: SAGE.

Ansell, C.; Gash, A. (2007): Collaborative Governance in Theory and Practice. Journal of Public Administration Research and Theory 18 (4), S. 543–571. DOI: 10.1093/jopart/mum032.

Berger, J. G. (2019). Unlocking Leadership Mindtraps. Stanford, CA: Stanford Briefs.

Borgert, S. (2019). Unkompliziert! (4th ed.). Offenbach: GABAL.

Boulton, J.; Allen, P.; Bowman, C. (2015): Embracing Complexity. Strategic Perspectives for an Age of Turbulence. Oxford: Oxford University Press.

Breidenbach, J.; Rollow, B. (2019): New Work needs Inner Work. München: Verlag Franz Vahlen.

Brundtland, G. et al. (1987): Our Common Future. World Commission on Environment and Development, New York: United Nations.

Buttkereit, S. (2009): Intersectoral Alliances. An institutional economics perspective. Berlin: WVB.

Collins, J. (2019). Turning the Flywheel. Random House.

Crislip, D. (2002): The Collaborative Leadership Fieldbook. A Guide for Citizens and Civic Leaders. San Francisco: Jossey-Bass.

Edmondson, A.; Harvey, J. (2017): Extreme Teaming. Lessons in Complex, Cross-Sector Leadership. Bingley: Emerald Publishing Limited.

Ellen MacArthur Foundation (Ed.). (2016). A New Dynamic 2 – Effective Systems in a Circular Economy. Ellen MacArthur Foundation.

Emerson, K.; Nabatchi, T. (2015): Collaborative Governance Regimes. Washington D.C.: Georgetown University Press.

Fligstein, N.; McAdam, D. (2012): A Theory of Fields. Oxford: Oxford University Press.

Forrer, J.; Kee, J.; Boyer, E. (2014): Governing Cross-Sector Collaboration. San Francisco: Jossey-Bass.

Geissdoerfer, M.; Savaget, P.; Bocken, Nancy M.P.; Hultink, E. (2017): The Circular Economy – A new sustainability paradigm? Journal of Cleaner Production 143, S. 757–768. DOI: 10.1016/j.jclepro.2016.12.048

Göpel, M. (2020): Unsere Welt neu denken. Eine Einladung. 5. Aufl. Berlin: Ullstein.

Gonser, M.; Eckart, J.; Eller, C.; Köglberger, K.; Häußler, E.; Piontek, F. (2019): Unterschiedliche Handlungslogiken in transdisziplinären und transformativen Forschungsprojekten – Welche Risikokulturen entwickeln sich daraus und wie lassen sie sich konstruktiv einbinden? In: Rico Defila und Antonietta Di Giulio (Hg.): Transdisziplinär und transformativ forschen, Band 2. Wiesbaden: Springer Fachmedien Wiesbaden.

Grober, U. (2010). Die Entdeckung der Nachhaltigkeit – Kulturgeschichte eines Begriffs. München: Kunstmann.

Habermas, J.(1981): Theorie des kommunikativen Handelns. Frankfurt/ Main: Suhrkamp Verlag.

Hinske, C. (2021a, July 27). The Ecosystem Decision-Making Radar. Innovative Leadership Institute. Retrieved October 11, 2021, from www.innovativeleadershipinstitute.com/the-ecosystem-decision-making-radar/

Hinske, C. (2021b) 360°Strategieprozess FSC Deutschland [Unpublished report], FSC Deutschland – Verein für Verantwortungsvolle Waldwirtschaft e.V.

Hoffman, A. J. (2021a). Management as a Calling. Stanford, CA: Stanford Business Books.

Hoffman, A. J. (2021b). The Engaged Scholar. Stanford, CA: Stanford University Press.

Innes, Judith E.; Booher, David E. (2018): Planning with Complexity. An Introduction to Collaborative Rationality for Public Policy. New York: Routledge.

Kooiman, J. (1999), 'Social-political governance: overview, reflections and design', Public Management, 1: 1, March, 67–92.

Kooiman, J. (2000), 'Societal governance: levels, models and orders of social-political interaction', in J. Pierre (ed.), Debating Governance: Authority, Steering and Democracy, London: Sage.

Laloux, Frédéric (2014): Reinventing organizations. A Guide to Creating Organizations: Nelson Parker.

Luhmann, N. (1984). Die Wirtschaft der Gesellschaft als autopoietisches System. Zeitschrift für Soziologie, 13 (4) (S. 308–327).

Luhmann, N. (1990): Ökologische Kommunikation. Kann die moderne Gesellschaft sich auf ökologische Gefährdungen einstellen? 3. Aufl. Opladen: Westdeutscher Verlag, zuletzt geprüft am 07.09.2021.

Man, R. d. (2022). Circularity dreams denying physical realities. In The Impossibilities of the Circular Economy (Vol. 5). London: Routledge.

McGuire, J. B.; & Rhodes, G. (2009). Transforming Your Leadership Culture. San Francisco: John Wiley & Sons.

Metcalf, M.; & Hinske, C. (2022). Circular Economy Leadership – Leadership Mindsets and Behaviours – the Unseen Impossibility. In The Impossibilities of the Circular Economy (Vol. 5). London: Routledge.

OECD (2003, March 14). OECD Glossary of Statistical Terms – Sustainability Definition. OECD Statistics. Retrieved December 1, 2021, from https://stats.oecd.org/glossary/detail.asp?ID=2625

Ostrom, E. (1990): Governing the Commons. The evolution of institutions for collective action. Cambridge: Cambridge University Press.

Parkin, S. (2010). The Positive Deviant. Abingdon, Oxon: Routledge.

Reckwitz, A. (2001): Die Ethik des Guten und die Soziologie. In: Jutta Allmendinger (Hg.): Gute Gesellschaft? Zur Konstruktion sozialer Ordnungen. Verhandlungen des 21. Kongresses der deutschen Gesellschaft für Soziologie in Köln: Opladen (A), S. 204–224.

Ritchie-Dunham, J. (2022). Truly Circular Economies Require Deep Collaboration. In H. Lehmann (Ed.), The Impossibilities of the Circular Economy (Vol. 5). London: Routledge.

Ritchie-Dunham, J. L.; & Puente, L. M. (2008). Strategic Clarity: Actions for Identifying and Correcting Gaps in Mental Models. Long Range Planning, 41(5), 509-525.

Ritchie-Dunham, J. L.; & Rabbino, H. T. (2001). Managing from Clarity. Chichester: Wiley.

Rorty, R. (1989). Kontingenz, Ironie und Solidarität. Frankfurt/Main: Suhrkamp.

Rumelt, R. (2017). Good Strategy Bad Strategy. London: Profile Books.

Sandfort, J.; Moulton, S. (2015). Effective Implementation in Practice. Integrating Public Policy and Management. San Francisco: Jossey-Bass.

Schneidewind, U. (2019): Die Große Transformation. Eine Einführung in die Kunst des gesellschaftlichen Wandels. 4. Aufl. Frankfurt: FISCHER Taschenbuch.

Scott, R. (2018). Group Model Building. Springer.

Snowden, D.; Boone, M. (2007): A Leader's Framework for Decision Making. In: Harvard Business Review (November 2007). https://hbr.org/2007/11/a-leaders-framework-for-decision-making

Stahel, W. R. (2019). The Circular Economy – A User's Guide. London: Routledge.

Straßheim, H. (2013): Collaborative Government. Mehrebenendynamik und Mechanismen des Wandels. In: dms – Der moderne Staat – Zeitschrift für Public Policy, Recht und Management 6 (2), S. 345–360, zuletzt geprüft am 02.05.2021.

Tonelli, M., & Cristoni, N. (2019). Strategic Management and the Circular Economy. London: Routledge.

Waddell, S. (2011). Global Action Networks. New York: Palgrave Macmillan.

Webster, K. (2017). The Circular Economy – A wealth of flows (2nd ed.). Ellen MacArthur Foundation.

Wilber, K. (2000). A theory of everything: An integral vision for business, politics, science, and spirituality. Boston: Shambhala.

7 Circularity is not sustainability

How well-intentioned concepts distract us from our true goals, and how SiD can help navigate that challenge

Tom Bosschaert

I begin with a confession; when I give lectures around the world, often to rooms full of sustainability experts, I like to ask the question, 'Who here is tired of the word "sustainability"?'. Without fail, a substantial number of people raise their hands. This is a manifestation of actual 'sustainability fatigue' even in circles of the intimately knowledgeable, the most hardened sustainability pioneers. It does not come as a surprise.

The very word itself sits atop a range of concepts and ideas that still can cause debate about their meaning within such circles.

It does not come as a surprise either that other words pop up vying to take its place. Language is a reflection of human behaviour, it is alive in itself, and here it clearly shows. Talking about sustainability has become stale. Today, it is more interesting to step into a room and talk about Cradle to Cradle, Circularity, Societal Resilience, Natural Capital, or Climate Neutrality. Notwithstanding that these words mean something different, there is genuine competition between these ideas for attention and popularity and the concepts they represent in all major fields and industries. While this is unavoidable to some degree, and innovation and evolution of language are valuable in their own right, how does this affect our mission to survive on this planet?

Please note—this is not some idle speculation—words matter.

One of the most beautiful words I know is 'sublime'. I love it because of its original meaning, arising out of the 18th century together with the 'invention' of Romanticism. I am not an etymologist, rather someone who spent most of his life working on sustainable transitions and innovation, and I apologise for any inaccuracies in advance. Despite this, I request your permission to use the history of this word to make a point. Sublime once meant, freely interpreted, 'beauty and awe in the face of God and certain death', the feeling you get when standing on the edge of the Grand Canyon and looking down. Some consider it as part of the emotional spectrum of 'terror', even. In our current times, it has eroded to become just another synonym for 'excellent'. As its original meaning faded, some of its power disappeared with it. Words erode, and by doing so, show us the character of humanity, society, and our past. Humans habitually exaggerate and (over) use superlatives. We oversimplify and can be opportunistic. By doing so and by

DOI: 10.4324/9781003244196-9

Figure 7.1 Painting, 'Wanderer above the Sea of Fog', Caspar David Friedrich, Ca. 1818. This romanticist painting is often associated with the original meaning of the word 'sublime'.

Source: Public domain, retrieved from https://en.wikipedia.org/wiki/File:Caspar_David_Friedrich_-_Wanderer_above_the_sea_of_fog.jpg

mis-attributing words in the process, we erode their meaning. Consequently, we need new words to replace the eroded terms to regain the meaning they once had. Awesome. Captivating. Terrific. Thrilling.

Words shape our reality. Language, beyond anything else, enabled us to evolve to become the top predator on this planet. Language has shaped our destiny, for better or worse. Our ability to use abstract concepts in language has especially enabled us, *Homo sapiens*, to rise above the other 'humans' (e.g. the Neanderthals), develop math, art, medicine, and land on the moon. For this reason, abstract concepts matter. Their definitions matter. They are the foundations of all we do, build, and hope to achieve.

'Circularity' is such an abstract concept. Nonetheless, so is 'sustainability'. Yet theoretical and conceptual as they may be, properly understanding and agreeing on the meaning of these terms is critical. It lies at the core of overcoming our challenges now and in the coming centuries. After all, if we cannot agree on what they are, how can we hope to achieve them?

Sustainability as a word has been around in small circles for a few centuries. Its current global journey started in the 1980s, referring to the continued survival of humans on this planet. This is most notably captured in what has become the official United Nations definition of sustainability, written by the Brundtland committee, to be; 'sustainable development is development that meets the needs of the present without compromising the ability of future generations to meet their own needs' (Our Common Future, Brundtland, 1987). Gently stepping over the fact that this defines 'sustainable development' rather than 'sustainability', this definition was only granted its UN definition status a decade after it was written. Gro Brundtland, the head of the commission, shared that when it was written, this sentence was never intended to be, or become, the definition of the term 'sustainable development'. What is more, it shows.

While inspiring as a goal, as a definition, it is particularly useless. It is similar to defining basketball by stating that whoever has more points wins the game. This is a statement of the successful outcome of the goal of basketball, not its definition. This lack of a definition of sustainability has not served humanity well. Arguably, sustainability is the most crucial abstract concept of our time, but its meaning has been eroding quickly. Nobody polices the meaning of the term; few authorities point out that the recycled plastic bags from the local supermarket are far from being 'sustainable', despite that word being printed right on top of it.

And now we come to Circularity. As a term, the 'Circular Economy' first appeared in 1988, but it has gained serious societal traction only in the last decade or so, doubling as a search term each year on Google from about 2013 (Google 2021). From its inception, the Circular Economy defines human activity aimed at the closed-loop re-use of resources within our material industrial systems, called the 'technosphere'.

In and of itself, the Circular Economy is a term aimed to help us think about this particular part of the challenge while 'externalising' a range of aspects of reality, allowing us to focus. While useful as a concept to discuss specific aspects of the challenge ahead, we have reached a point where the term has also replaced 'Sustainability' in many areas and many practitioners' understanding. For example, in a recently published book release on 'Lessons on Circularity', the introduction states, 'It used to be called sustainability, and now it's called Circularity'.

This is a problem—a serious one.

The Circular Economy requires us to rethink and rebuild our society's supply and value chains, which is a massive challenge. It requires a shift in perspective from a world organised at the object level to one operating on a network level, which is already a big step for some. In that, Circularity is a worthwhile goal and concept to strive for. That being said, Circularity is only a particular subset of sustainability, and it is a limited perspective on the entirety of the systemic challenge we face. The Circular Economy does not by itself integrate aspects such as social justice, societal resilience, biodiversity regeneration, or nature-inclusive development. To put it clearly, following the majority of 'Circular Economy' tools, texts, and projects, if we achieve this, we will not necessarily end up with a just and resilient society. We may not even improve the network-level aspects of our society all that much either, since network parameters, such as redundancy, flexibility, regeneration, and stability, are not considered.

When we realise that these are essential components of a sustainable society, we fall short of our goal.

While one can argue that we need to tackle one problem at a time to move forward, it is a fallacy to think that aiming for just a subset of our larger challenge will help. Suppose we have learned anything from the industrial revolution. In that case, we cause our downfall by considering reality from a reductionist perspective and externalising impacts just for the sake of simplicity. One cannot simplify the sustainability challenge in a reductionist way.

The whole point of the 'Sustainability' movement is its holistic properties and its roots in systems thinking. This is why 'Sustainability' originated hand-in-hand with the systems thinking movement in the 1960s and 1970s. As the term has eroded in some circles, we can discern our use of the word 'Sustainability' from the eroded meaning by indicating that we are talking about 'integrated' and 'systemic' sustainability. Adding the adjective 'integrated' to the word signals that the approach includes all aspects of the challenge (not just energy and materials, but also social and ecological, among others). The word 'systemic' is added to indicate that it uses systems thinking and systems dynamics as its theoretical basis to arrive at a holistic perspective. For us to succeed, Circularity must always be clearly positioned as a part of, and in relation to, this larger integrated systemic sustainability challenge. This challenge has interrelations and systemic connections to other areas of our reality that, in some cases, matter a great deal more than 'simple' Circularity.

I do not pass judgement upon those who replace the two words, or who do not wish to deal with the interdisciplinary requirements of Sustainability; I understand fully why some are summoned by the siren call of Circularity. Sustainable development is hard work. Indeed, sustainability can be complex, confusing, frustrating, tiring, and exhausting. It is far easier, comfortable, and popular to talk about Circularity instead, as it is a more simple, concrete term. Yet as innocent as this seems, this 'replacement' of terms poses a clear and present danger to us and as such must be prevented.

In a time where every decade counts, to be distracted by a dozen years or so focusing on Circularity alone is a humanitarian disaster waiting to happen. This is no exaggeration.

In our reality, as sustainability consultants, the number of 'Circularity roadmaps' developed by major industrial companies and cities and governments outnumbered 'Sustainability roadmaps' two to one. Circularity roadmaps are planning documents that often have milestones to 2050 and beyond, which primarily focus on energy and material resource cycles. A few Circularity roadmaps include some aspects of climate adaptation, but aspects such as societal resilience and social inclusion, to name a few, are virtually absent. This is a significant missed opportunity. While we're fiddling with the dials of our systems, we should be planning to look at them in an integrated fashion. It is good news that an increasing number of practitioners join the growing movement towards a better, long-term future and start learning how to participate. While this happens, we need to ensure that the foundations of this movement are secured and not eroded by distractions created by the need to sound 'new', thereby missing the goal, or slowing down our pathways to get there.

While the United Nations has helped to empower the conversation with the Sustainable Development Goals (SDGs), the unfortunate reality that the SDGs on release lacked a coherent systemic framework for understanding what they are, how to use or evaluate them has not helped to get us very far yet. This has resulted in cherry-picking of the SDGs, where organisations choose to focus on one or just a few of the SDGs, while the whole point was to indicate that everything we do reflects on all of these goals. As it goes, losing the 'integrated' part of the idea, and through the lack of a practical framework, means losing the 'systemic' part altogether.

All of this is understandable. The Circular Economy has received a significant boost in popularity for its adaptation into concrete, helpful tools by organisations such as the Ellen MacArthur Foundation, which has been indispensable work. These tools are practical and valuable, for sure, but we cannot use them in a vacuum. Since these Circular Economy tools and programs tend to focus on the object material plane, system dynamics seem to fall out of their scope. Nevertheless, real and present threats to projects exist in this systemic sustainability domain, such as system dynamics, which includes the rebound effect, the tragedy of the commons, and the law of diminishing marginal returns. For projects that impact our material world, industries, policies, and economy, if these system dynamics are not taught, studied, and analysed alongside, we are not simply moving the hole, but rather we are digging our own grave.

As confusing as 'Sustainability' may be, it is the only word and, therefore, a mental tool we have as humans to truly face our challenges. Being a more complex challenge, sustainability requires more effort. It is a surmountable challenge, however, but spending this effort is simply a necessity. The expression to 'embrace complexity' is often found among systemic sustainability practitioners as a helpful mental framing to enable handling its systemic depth. In our experience, building a Circularity roadmap versus a proper integrated systemic sustainability roadmap takes about the same amount of time once you have the experience in doing so. The learning how to work on systemic sustainability, without a doubt, takes years instead of the weeks that Circularity requires to learn. Once known, however, the steps to identify the goals and vision investigate stakeholder networks, form partnerships, and look for innovative solutions for implementation are all similar. The depth and complexity involved are an order of magnitude larger in systemic sustainability than with Circularity. Just as there are tools for Circularity, concrete frameworks to support systemic sustainability have been made and are increasingly sophisticated.

Since 1999, a range of sustainability experts, researchers, and developers have made a concerted effort to develop practical frameworks for integrated systemic, sustainable development. One of these frameworks that we have worked on in our practice is Symbiosis in Development (SiD) which is freely and publicly available under an open-source license. One may not be surprised that one of the first and core aspects of the framework has been to define 'sustainability' properly. Over the past decades, the definition received several revisions, and the framework with evaluation tools, application methods, and co-creation processes was built around it.

> Sustainability is a state of a complex, dynamic system. In this state, a system can continue to flourish resiliently, in harmony, without requiring inputs from outside its system boundaries.
>
> Applied to our civilization, this state is consistent with societies powered by renewable energy and closed loop material systems, living in thriving ecosystems, on a biodiverse planet, with healthy and happy individuals living in just, tolerant, and diverse cultures, supported by open and transparent economies.
>
> SiD Sustainability Definition v4.0 (Bosschaert, 2019)

With sustainability as the core goal for long-term human survival, the definition and framework also define subsets of sustainability, including Circularity, Resilience, and Harmony (including social justice). Figure 7.2 shows the relationship these terms have, arranged on the systemic, network, and object layers. Let us look at this structure a bit further to gain insight into how Circularity and Sustainability are related to one another.

The SiD System-Network-Object (SNO) hierarchy shows a systemic interrelation of terms on different levels of scale and impact. The system is the highest, most impactful, complex, and abstract level of interrelationships, going down via the network level, to the concrete object level. As the structure shows, 'Sustainability' is defined on the system level as a 'sweet spot' between Autonomy, Resilience, and Harmony. Circularity is defined as one of the parameters that contributes to the Autonomy system indicator, along with parameters such as Self-governance and Efficiency. Being on the network level, Circularity interacts with the other network parameters to jointly form the system's dynamics and performance. Within those dynamics, balances need to be struck for systems to move towards their own sweet spot in Autonomy, Resilience, and Harmony. While each complex system behaves differently, there are still commonalities in most real-world situations.

For example, the network parameters Redundancy and Efficiency affect each other. A certain amount of Redundancy helps systems to become more Resilient, especially for critical functions, such as water supply, or telecommunications. Having these systems be Redundant (having multiple of each that perform the same function), increases the chance these services remain available, even if some of them are impacted. However, an increased Redundancy automatically reduces Efficiency. As it goes, in many western economies, Redundancies are therefore actively sought out and reduced, which as a consequence can reduce Resilience. A good case study here is the difference in Intensive Care (IC) beds that are available per capita in Germany (600+ per 100.000), versus those in

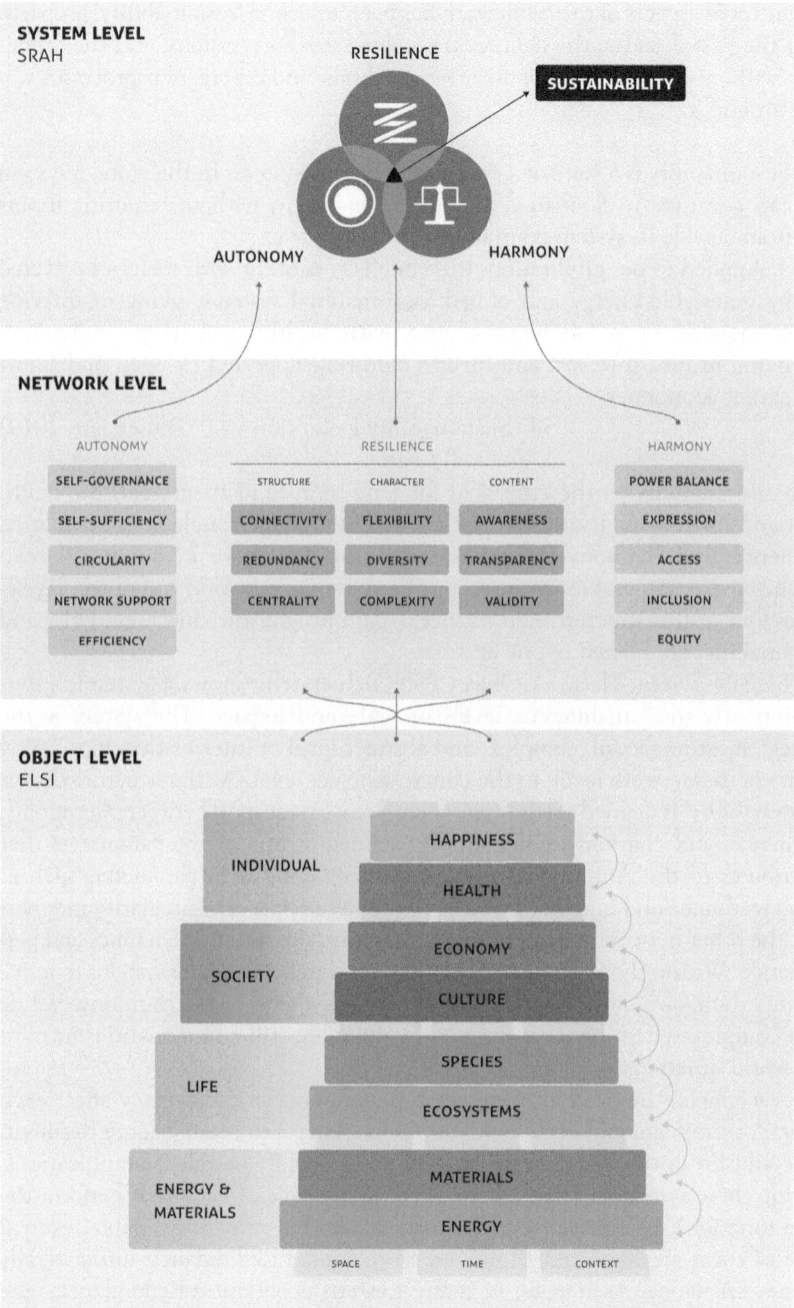

Figure 7.2 The Symbiosis in Development (SiD) SNO hierarchy showing the relationships between the system, network, and object-level subject categories.

Source: Own depiction.

the Netherlands (330+). The Netherlands' drive for Efficiency helped it to save money (increasing its Autonomy), but when Covid came around, its resilience was too low, forcing it to use German IC beds at great financial and time cost, which risked human life as well.

When Efficiency is increased, Autonomy is typically increased with it. Consequently, when Efficiency is increased at the cost of Redundancy, Autonomy may increase at the cost of Resilience. Striving for maximised Autonomy will negatively affect Resilience in most real-world circumstances. This in turn may decrease systemic sustainability overall. As follows, pushing Circularity towards a maximum without evaluating the effects on these other network and system parameters may inadvertently hurt the overall sustainability of the system.

SiD's structure allows existing tools for Circular Economy development to be used within its context. It also enables practitioners from different fields to work side-by-side and speak a shared language. In that sense, SiD works as a Rosetta Stone for mutual understanding across disciplines, sectors, entities, languages, and cultures. In this framework as well, language forms the basis of our understanding of the world and how we can begin to talk with each other about how to deal with our challenges. For this purpose, SiD's toolset includes definitions of all terms, co-creation methods, complex systems analysis, agile-based process management, and serious gaming aspects that enable holistic understanding. Within this and other frameworks, it is the holistic systemic overview that truly matters. Without this, the tools of the Circular Economy are naked, vulnerable, and without true purpose.

In the last decades, we have been able to witness the effects of SiD in practice on several hundred projects worldwide, in different cultures and contexts, for industry, policy, cities, products, and strategy. These often involved dozens of external stakeholders and experts. From this experience, we have seen an increasing number of external practitioners choosing to learn about sustainability by focusing on Circularity alone. Due to its more narrow focus, Circularity allows practitioners to get up to speed quickly, with a few workshops and tools. This fast learning process is a great advantage of Circularity, allowing those that focus on this subset to become effective in a short amount of time. However, as the above suggests, we repeatedly see a limited domain understanding with these practitioners of Circularity. Moreover, we see that many, with notable exceptions of course, remain in what we call an 'object-oriented' perception of the challenge. In this perception, we can achieve our global sustainability challenges by replacing the material objects that pervade our society with circular ones. If only everything was circular, we would have a perfect sustainable world, the thought goes. With systemic sustainability practitioners, however, this is observed as a clear fallacy.

Sustainability requires a holistic, systemic overview, including all relevant factors. It is often not the material objects in our society that make the difference but the dynamics of the systems in which we have placed them. This cannot be focused merely on material resources or business models alone but rather requires the inclusion of social, cultural, and environmental considerations as a given. The payoffs of a systemic sustainability approach, however, are enormous. We see those focused on Circularity fall into 'system traps' frequently, gaining only short-term, object-level impacts and becoming stuck in heavily compromised reductionist scenarios (e.g. 'Let us only focus on our carbon footprint for now'.). Meanwhile, systemic transition opportunities, business models built on holistic understanding, and vastly improved long-term performance pass by unnoticed. With pressure building and time not being on our side, we cannot afford to miss these opportunities.

Other articles in this publication will explore various shortcomings of Circularity as a principle or practice. There is no need to repeat these in this article. Suffice it to say, according to our argument, Circularity as a concept is a valuable tool. However, if not used within a more holistic framework, it falls short of being useful for our global challenges. Since it is not on its own referring us in a holistic, integrated direction, Circularity may even pose a danger to our progress, functioning as a 'red herring' that distracts us from the real challenge more than the valuable tool it sets out to be.

Instead of an increasing focus on Circularity, we argue for placing Circularity squarely inside a more holistic framework of systemic sustainability, thereby promoting a renewed understanding of both terms. Sustainability captures the challenge for us as human beings to continue to thrive on this planet in a meaningful way. Circularity can only ever be a means to an end and one to carefully weigh on where it is appropriate or relevant.

From a holistic understanding, and by learning to fathom the beautiful intricacies of system dynamics, the meaning of the word 'Sustainability' moves once more. Discovering the vast opportunities, beauty, might, and magic of a systemic sustainable world may even start to lend flavour to the original sense of the word 'sublime'. It certainly has and remains in doing so for me.

Discovering the path to expedite the transition of our society to one that is built on resilient and just systems and is in harmony with nature is nothing short of 'sublime'. That is because such a society provides us with the opportunities to tackle age-long issues that perpetually have crippled humans, such as famine, poverty, greed, and corruption. Let us not deprive ourselves of the opportunity to move the foundations of our society in the right direction, in favour of a circular rearranging of the deck chairs on the Titanic.

References

Bosschaert, Tom 2019, Symbiosis in Development, http://thinksid.org/?p=125

Google 2021, Google Trends, Circular Economy, https://trends.google.com/trends/explore?date=all&q=%22Circular%20Economy%22

8 Circular Economy

From panacea for sustainability to conceptual and resource realities

Theodoros Semertzidis

The appeal of Circular Economy

Humans exert an immense pressure on the natural environment by extracting materials and generating waste. Thanks to our better comprehension of this, compared to a few decades ago, there have been attempts to improve the situation. One of these attempts is the emergence of the Circular Economy (CE) concept, as a solution to better utilise resources and improve environmental pressure. CE is a technology-focused concept, which can also generate economic gains. Due to this, it has gained a perception of great appeal from academia, public, and private sectors (Velenturf and Purnell, 2021). The development of CE has been strongly practitioner-led (e.g., Ellen MacArthur Foundation), and it is positioned squarely within the Green Growth discourse, meaning that primary resource consumption and emissions can be decoupled from Gross Domestic Product (GDP) to legitimise continued economic growth (Parrique et al., 2019).

It is understandable where the appeal of CE is steaming from, since Lacy and Rutqvist (2016) forecasted $4.5 trillion in global economic benefits by 2030, and $25 trillion by 2050, when the global economy was $80 trillion in 2017 (World Bank, 2019). However, the appeal is not just financial, since circular business models create more value from each unit of natural resource compared to traditional linear models (Di Maio et al., 2017; Robaina et al., 2020). Additionally, recycling is a big part of CE, and it is not just about keeping waste out of landfills, but it is also about energy conservation. All products contain embodied energy, which is the total amount of energy required to produce a product (mining, transportation, manufacturing, and distribution). The recycling process also consumes energy, added to the transportation of waste; however, even taking this into account, there is a difference of three orders of magnitude between the amount of energy needed to produce products from raw materials and the amount of energy needed to recycle them from the old ones (Johnson, 2015).

Due to these, and other, very positive aspects, the Circular Economy Action Plan (EC, 2015), and later the second Circular Economy Package (EC, 2019), introduced measures to stimulate Europe's transition into a CE, "closing the loop" of product lifecycles through greater recycling and reuse, benefitting both the environment and the economy (Robaina et al., 2020).

DOI: 10.4324/9781003244196-10

Definition and indicator issues

At first glance, CE is appealing, and it is worth striving for, but based on current understanding and practice, there are a lot of things to consider, before we get invested in it too deeply. It is logical to try and minimise resource exploitation, while decreasing waste, but CE has received as many definitions as there are CE researchers and practitioners (Kirchherr et al., 2017). A common motto is to strive to make better use of resources, but what constitutes "better" remains debatable. CE has undoubted sustainability potential documented in literature, but its limited conceptual grounding and weak connection to sustainable development can prove to be detrimental (Velenturf and Purnell, 2021).

Furthermore, indicators can be useful in assessing CE, and although the European Commission has been developing a wide variety of quantitative indicators (Huysveld et al., 2019), there is still a scarcity of adequate metrics for performance measurements. The trouble is that what should be measured to assess compliance with CE principles is debatable, since CE definition is rather qualitative and ambiguous, and different indicators can lead to different conclusions. Some authors have reviewed tools and methodologies already in use and argued that most of them are not capable of measuring all CE characteristics (Moraga et al., 2019).

Additionally, as mentioned earlier, CE is positioned within the Green Growth discourse and the decoupling from GDP discussion. However, decoupling itself is also vague as a term. Frequently, there is no distinction between "relative" and "absolute", but even if "absolute decoupling" is achieved, this doesn't mean we have solved our problems. A rise in GDP with a drop (no matter the percentage) in emissions is considered "absolute decoupling", but sustainability-wise this is somewhat parodical, because it does not solve the issue, nor does it make growth sustainable (Parrique, 2021).

Conventionally, an economy's resource use is measured through Domestic Material Consumption (DMC), which is the total weight of raw materials extracted from the domestic territory, plus physical imports, minus physical exports. Many governments have adopted the division of GDP by DMC to assess the "resource efficiency" of their economy. If the GDP grows faster than DMC, then we have "relative decoupling" and a more resource-efficient economy. GDP/DMC is also used by the European Union and the OECD to monitor progress towards Green Growth. However, and without opening a discussion about the suitability of GDP as an indicator, DMC is problematic itself, since it does not include material impact involved in the production and transport of imported goods (Wiedman et al., 2015). If we alternatively look at the total resource impact of consumption by any given nation (referred to as "material footprint" by Wiedmann et al.), the perception changes. Wiedmann et al. (2015) show that although the EU-27, USA, UK, Japan, and the OECD have achieved "relative decoupling", their material footprint has been rising at a rate equal or greater than GDP. This shows that perhaps decoupling is not actually occurring, depending on the chosen definition (Hickel and Kallis, 2020).

The Jevons Paradox also has a place in this discussion, since according to it, in the long-term, an increase in efficiency in resource use will generate an increase in resource consumption rather than a decrease. It is important to understand the nature of the Jevons Paradox when it comes to our attempt to achieve a CE (Hickel and Kallis, 2020). Additionally, societal success evaluated through indicators of growth assumes that affluence correlates with well-being (Cobb et al., 1995; Robra and Heikkurinen, 2019). The problem though is that economic growth is very closely correlated with environmental damage (IPCC, 2014). Despite efforts to develop technology and increase efficiency of production, economic growth has not achieved decoupling from global resource and energy use, nor from the rise of emissions and waste (Robra and Heikkurinen, 2019).

Different resource aspects and shifting of problems

Aside from the actual definition of CE, which is vital to exist and be accepted widely, and the ongoing issue with indicators, there are also more practical issues to consider. It needs to be noted here that CE is not a new concept, it has been implemented for economic purposes for hundreds of years, and there are examples of "industrial symbiosis" where the by-products of one industry are used as inputs for another (Desrochers and Leppala, 2010). Although industrial symbioses can be sustainable, they can also lock in unsustainable material systems like the petrochemical industry infrastructure, perpetuating a dependency on fossil fuel extraction (Velenturf and Purnell, 2021).

There is an ongoing concern about evidence of the feasibility and environmental benefits of circularity in general, and specifically recycling. Waste recycling does not and cannot create a perfect circle due to the growing demand for materials, which exceeds the waste available from past consumption, while materials are lost and degraded during processing (entropy), and the energy required for processing rises with higher collection rates (van Ewijk, et al., 2021). Resource efficiency cannot improve forever, as eventually it approaches physical limits (Ward et al., 2016). In general, indefinite growth of any material category is not compatible with ecological principles.

An interesting example is recycled concrete (RC-concrete). Mostert et al. (2021) assessed RC-concrete regarding its potential in CE. They found that it can decrease the material footprint by up to 50%, but the reduction potential for the climate footprint is limited, while the water footprint can be up to ten times higher with the wet processing of concrete waste. Although RC-concrete can save natural aggregates, the deconstruction and treatment process of concrete waste is energy-intensive and could require a great quantity of water, depending on the treatment technology used. In the case where additional amounts of cement are needed, the overall Green House Gas (GHG) emissions can surpass that of Business As Usual concrete (Mostert et al., 2021). CE has decarbonisation potential, but it is important to avoid shifting emissions from one part of the system to another. If for example biological materials are used in place of mineral resources, it is possible to require water resources well beyond sustainable levels of supply (Giampietro and Funtowicz, 2020).

In another example, van Ewijk et al. (2021), in their analysis of recycling pulp and paper, found that landfill practices mattered more than material flows, and energy use mattered the most, showing that greater circularity through recycling and recovery is not a straightforward recipe for reducing GHG emissions and that circular use of materials cannot remove the requirement for clean energy (van Ewijk, et al., 2021). These two different examples show that there are other resources that need to be considered in the whole CE discussion and that the outcomes of engaging in CE are anything but clear-cut.

Another very important issue to consider is the shifting of problems from one place to another. For example, the reuse and recycling rate of plastics in Europe is still very low, especially in relation to paper, glass, and metals. In particular, Europe produces 25.8 million tonnes (Mt) of plastic waste annually, with <30% of this being collected for recycling (EC, 2018). A significant part of this quantity, however, is exported to third countries, which sometimes apply different and less friendly environmental standards (Robaina et al., 2020). In another more specific example, 46% of separated Polyethylene (one of the most common types of plastic) waste is exported outside of the source country, and although the fate of this export is not well-known, a study by Bishop et al. (2020) estimated that 83,187 tonnes, or 3% of exported European Polyethylene, in 2017, ended up in the ocean. Also, the European Environment Agency reports that 250,000 tonnes to 1.3 Mt of cast-off electrical products are exported annually from Europe, and the most frequent destinations are West Africa and Asia (Sahajwalla and Gaikwad, 2018).

All these examples, among many others, significantly affect CE studies. In general, 92% of all decoupling studies only use production-based measures, instead of consumption-based indicators (Wiedenhofer et al., 2020), which create an illusion of absolute decoupling when the environmental pressures are just shifted elsewhere (Parrique, 2021). Since this shift is also usually happening from the Global North to the Global South, it creates a sort of discrimination and an unjust burden on the Global South.

Since a relationship between the Global North and South is already established, it is important to notice that waste, for example, differs from country to country, geographical region, population, social conditions, economic situation, local habits, climate, and so on. High-income countries generate less organic waste (32% of total) than low- and middle-income countries (56% and 53% of the total, respectively), while high-income countries generate a high percentage of plastic, paper, metal, glass, and so on as waste (51% of the total) (Kaza et al., 2018). This makes it clear that depending on the case study, different waste and potentially materials are more critical and should receive priority. Not all case studies are the same, and they need to be treated as such.

Moreover, despite the fact that CE is frequently associated with sustainability, it is still unclear if it actually contributes towards the achievement of the Sustainable Development Goals (SDGs), particularly regarding their social aspects. This is an aspect that is true in general, but even more so for the future of the Global South. Although scholars have started to explore the assessment of social sustainability within CE practices, Walker et al. (2021) in their assessment of CE's social sustainability practices in industry in Italy and the Netherlands concluded that the majority of firms do not conduct any type of social assessment. Even the companies that did implement some sort of assessment did so in a qualitative manner or used industry-based sustainability indicator frameworks. Frequently, the only indicator mentioned in CE literature, regarding the social aspect, is "job creation" (Kravchenko et al., 2019), discounting other important aspects, from health to corruption (Walker et al., 2021).

Ways forward?

Some of EC's issues have been identified above, but is there a way they can be alleviated? The first step is to start with the concept itself. Which alternatives exist, and are there any possible inputs from elsewhere? From the multitude of conceptual approaches to sustainable development, three stand out since they discuss the relationship between environment, society, and development (Belmonte-Ureña, et al., 2021) and these are CE, Degrowth, and Green Growth. However, it is not that clear which of these embraces the breadth of topics found in the SDGs. CE advocates for an economic system dissociating environmental pressure from economic growth by replacing linear production for a circular one, with waste as a resource (Sanguino et al., 2020). Green Growth focuses on economic growth through investments in activities that protect or restore the natural environment (Vazquez-Brust et al., 2014), while Degrowth assumes resource limitations and advocates for smaller growth rates (even negative as the name suggests) to balance the natural and economic systems (Sandberg et al., 2019).

The CE and Green Growth concepts are increasingly taken into account in policies, while Degrowth is seen as too controversial by decision makers (Sandberg et al., 2019). Additionally, CE theory of addressing the challenge is weak, as was discussed earlier, since it doesn't accept boundaries, and it is ambiguous about how to deal with industries that cannot be made circular (Belmonte-Ureña et al., 2021). Giampietro and Funtowicz (2020) go a step further and argue that "the belief in the ability of technology and markets to achieve a decoupling from economic growth through a CE is essentially a 'folk tale'". This has in part to do with Degrowth scholars and activists being sceptical of growth itself (Kallis, 2019). This is not to say that a Degrowth perspective is necessarily a legitimate alternative, since, according to critics, it has not engaged with real-world dynamics of class politics, and it has simply chosen to highlight the problem of growth and proposed to abandon it altogether (Arsel, 2020).

Nevertheless, there are lessons learned from Degrowth, since the concept claims that growth is not possible on a finite planet, while at the same time economic growth is not a prerequisite for human well-being (Demaria et al., 2013; Robra and Heikkurinen, 2019). The main aim of Degrowth is to reduce economic activity to a point where it can be considered ecologically sustainable (Demaria et al., 2013). Practically, what this ecological sustainability would mean for a society is to "keep [its] wastes within assimilative capacities; harvest within re-generative capacities of renewable resources; deplete non-renewables at the rate at which renewable substitutes are developed" (Goodland and Daly, 1996, p. 1002). It is more important to meet human needs than to meet ever-increasing human wants (Bonnedahl and Heikkurinen, 2019).

Additionally, and perhaps on a more practical note, it is important for CE to take the Resource Nexus into account. For example, Nerini et al. (2017) identified 113 SDG targets requiring actions to change energy systems, finding evidence of relationships between 143 targets (synergies and trade-offs); this being for SDG7 (Affordable and Clean Energy) alone. Trying to take more Goals into account, the synergies and trade-offs would rise significantly. This is not something trivial, and it signifies that there is still a lot of work to be done, but also shows that there are a lot of opportunities for research and action. These relationships strongly indicate that substantial changes are in order, to be able to deliver the SDGs. CE would have a lot to gain from embracing a Resource Nexus perspective in its modelling.

Conclusions

The CE concept has been proposed as a solution to better utilise resources and improve environmental pressure, but its definition is weak and not consistent. Consequently, its metrics are lacking when it comes to performance measurements because it is debatable what actually needs to be measured. CE is in line with Green Growth discourse and the decoupling from GDP, but decoupling is also vague, and even "absolute decoupling" does by no means suggest that we have achieved sustainability. In addition to conceptual and definition aspects, it is important to account for physical/natural limitations to recycling and reusing of materials. Waste recycling cannot create a perfect circle, since firstly the materials degrade with time (due to processing), and secondly, the demand for materials is constantly increasing.

Furthermore, sustainability is not just GHG emissions; water, food, land, materials, pollution, waste, biodiversity loss, they all need to be considered. "Which other resources do we need to use in order to recycle/reuse a specific material?" is a question that needs to constantly be asked. It has been shown that it is possible, for example, to use significant energy and water in order to reutilise certain materials. This connection between resources (the Resource Nexus) is vital when it comes to CE. The impact of greater circularity needs to be assessed for individual materials and products, and each product, different aspect, and so on deserves its own research.

Another important aspect is that of shifting some of the burden (waste, processing, etc.) elsewhere, and this usually happens from the Global North to the Global South. This is something that needs to be considered in all forms of modelling of the CE. Imports and particularly exports need to be taken into account, therefore consumption-based indicators might be more useful. Additionally, the social aspect of the CE literature is weak, and so are its social metrics, since apart from "job creation", nothing else stands out.

Additionally, Degrowth, which is considered to be a lot more controversial than CE, does take into account the simple fact that growth is not possible on a finite planet and that economic growth is not necessarily a prerequisite for human well-being. Therefore, Degrowth should not be dismissed, since sufficiency-oriented strategies can be valuable for developed countries, but also developing ones to some extent. At the end of the day, the three Rs of CE are Reduce/Reuse/Recycle, and the first part goes very well with Degrowth thinking.

Despite the issues mentioned above, CE and Green Growth are both increasingly used in policies, and this is the reason why we have a responsibility of pointing out their defects and suggesting how they can be improved. There are a lot of aspects that need to be considered simultaneously to aim towards true sustainability. CE has potential, but if one thinks that it can help towards true sustainability, it is wishful thinking at best. Concepts like the Resource Nexus and Degrowth can greatly assist in improving CE in many ways, by firstly achieving a worthwhile definition of the concept, and secondly by improving on its metrics. Lastly, it is important to understand that a "perfect solution" is not possible, CE does have limitations, some of which cannot be improved by much, and we need to accept this.

References

Arsel M. (2020) The myth of global sustainability: Environmental limits and (de)growth in the time of SDGs. ISS Working Papers – General Series 129596, International Institute of Social Studies of Erasmus University Rotterdam (ISS), The Hague.

Belmonte-Ureña L.J., Plaza-Úbeda J.A., Vazquez-Brust D., Yakovleva N. (2021) Circular economy, degrowth and green growth as pathways for research on sustainable development goals: A global analysis and future agenda. Ecological Economics, 185, 107050.

Bishop G., Styles D., Lens P.N.L. (2020) Recycling of European plastic is a pathway for plastic debris in the ocean. Environment International, 142, 105893.

Bonnedahl K.J. and Heikkurinen (eds) (2019) Strongly sustainable societies: Organising human activities on a hot and full earth, 1st edn, Routledge, London.

Cobb C., Halstead T., Rowe J. (1995) If the GDP is up, why is America down? Atlantic-Boston, 276, 59–79.

Decrochers P., Leppala S. (2010) Industrial symbiosis: Old wine in recycled bottles? Some perspective from the history of economic and geographical thought. Int. Reg. Sci. Rev., 33, 338–361.

Demaria F., Schneider F., Sekulova F., Martinez-Alier J. (2013) What is degrowth? From activist slogan to social movement. Environ. Values, 22, 2, 191–215.

Di Maio F., Rem P.C., Baldé K., Polder M. (2017) Measuring efficiency and circular economy: a market value approach. Resour. Conserv. Recycl., 122, 163–171.

EC (2015) Closing the loop – An EU action plan for the circular economy.

EC (2018) A European strategy for plastics in a circular economy. COM/2018/028 Final. Communication from the commission to the European Parliament, the Council, the European Economic and Social Committee and the Committee of the Regions. European Commission, Brussels.

EC (2019) Press release – Circular economy package report: Questions & Answers.

Giampietro M., Funtowicz S.O. (2020) From elite folk science to the policy legend of the circular economy. Environ. Sci. Policy, 109, 64–72.

Goodland R., Daly H. (1996) Environmental sustainability: universal and non-negotiable. Ecol. Appl., 6, 4, 1002–1017.

Hickel J. & Kallis G. (2020) Is Green Growth Possible? New Political Economy, 25, 4, 469–486.

Huysveld S., Hubo S., Ragaert K., Dewulf J. (2019) Advancing circular economy benefit indicators and application on open-loop recycling of mixed and contaminated plastic waste fractions. J. Clean. Prod., 211, 1–13.

IPCC (2014) Climate change 2014: synthesis report. Contribution of Working Groups I, II and III to the Fifth Assessment Report of the Intergovernmental Panel on Climate. IPCC.

Johnson A. (2015) Recycling energy: An exploration of recycling and embodied energy, Penn Sustainability Review, 1, 6, 5.

Kallis G. (2019) Socialism Without Growth. Capitalism Nature Socialism, 30, 2, 189–206.

Kaza S., Yao L., Bhada-Tata P., van Woerden F. (2018) What a Waste 2.0 – A global snapshot of solid waste management to 2050. World Bank Publications, the World Bank Group.

Kirchherr J., Reike D., Hekkert M. (2017) Conceptualizing the circular economy: An analysis of 114 definitions. Resour. Conserv. Recycl., 127, 221–232.

Kravchenko M., Pigosso D.C.A., McAloone T.C. (2019) Towards the ex-ante sustainability screening of circular economy initiatives in manufacturing companies: consolidation of leading sustainability-related performance indicators. J. Clean. Prod., 241, 118318.

Lacy P., Rutqvist J. (2016) Waste to wealth: the circular economy advantage. Palgrave Macmillan UK.

Moraga G., Huysveld S., Mathieux F., Blengini G.A., Alaerts L., Karel V., van Meester S., Dewulf J. (2019) Circular economy indicators: what do they measure? Resour. Conserv. Recycl., 146, 452–461.

Mostert C., Sameer H., Glanz D., Bringezu S. (2021) Climate and resource footprint assessment and visualization of recycled concrete for circular economy. Resource, Conservation & Recycling, 174, 105767.

Nerini F.F., Tomei J., To L.S., Bisaga I., Parikh P., Black M., Borrion A., Spataru C., Broto V.C., Anandarajah G., Milligan B., Mulugetta Y. (2018) Mapping synergies and trade-offs between energy and the Sustainable Development Goals. Nature Energy, 3, 10–15.

Parrique T. (2021) From green growth to degrowth. Global Policy, April 2021.

Parrique T., Briens F., Kerschner C., Kraus-Polk A., Kuokkanen A., Spangenberg J.H. (2019) Decoupling debunked: evidence and arguments against green growth as a sole strategy for sustainability. Eur. Environ. Bureau., https://eeb.org/wp-content/uploads/2019/07/Decoupling-Debunked.pdf

Robaina M., Murillo K., Rocha E., Villar J. (2020) Circular economy in plastic waste – Efficiency analysis of European countries. Science of the Total Environment, 730, 139038.

Robra B., Heikkurinen P. (2019) Degrowth and the Sustainable Development Goals. In: Leal Filho W., Azul A., Brandli L., Özuyar P., Wall T. (eds) Decent Work and Economic Growth. Encyclopedia of the UN Sustainable Development Goals. Springer, Cham.

Sahajwalla V., Gaikwad V. (2018) The present and future of e-waste plastics recycling. Curr. Opin. Green Sustain. Chem., 13, 102–107.

Sandberg M., Klockars K., Wilén K. (2019) Green growth or degrowth? Assessing the normative justifications for environmental sustainability and economic growth through critical social theory. Journal of Cleaner Production, 206, 133–141.

Sanguino R., Barroso A., Fernández-Rodríguez S., Sánchez-Hernández M.I. (2020) Current trends in economy, sustainable development, and energy: A circular economy view. Environ. Sci. Pollut. Res., 27, 1–7.

van Ewijk S., Stegemann J.A., Ekins P. (2021) Limited climate benefits of global recycling of pulp and paper. Nature Sustainability, 4, 180–187.

Vazquez-Brust D., Smith A.M., Sarkis J. (2014) Managing the transition to critical green growth: the 'green growth state'. Futures, 64, 38–50.

Velenturf P.M., Purnell P. (2021) Principles for a sustainable circular economy. Sustainable Production and Consumption, 27, 1437–1457.

Walker A.M., Opferkuch K., Lindgreen E.R., Simboli A., VErmeulen W.J.V., Raggi A. (2021) Assessing the social sustainability of circular economy practices: Industry perspectives from Italy and the Netherlands. Sustainable Production and Consumption, 27, 831–844.

Ward J.D., et al. (2016) Is decoupling GDP growth from environmental impact possible? Plos one, 11, 10, e0164733.

Wiedenhofer et al. (2020) A systematic review of the evidence on decoupling of GDP, resource use and GHG emissions, part I: bibliometric and conceptual mapping. Environ. Res. Lett., 15, 063002.

Wiedmann T.O., et al. (2015) The material footprint of nations. Proceedings of the national academy of sciences, 112, 20, 6271–6276.

World Bank (2019) World Bank National Accounts Data, and OECD National Accounts Data Files.

9 Some observations on the current Circular Economy model

In particular, the mineral-metal-material stream blind spots

Simon P. Michaux and Alan R. Butcher

Material flows in the industrial ecosystem

The Circular Economy has been proposed as a way of transforming European society in how it manages raw material flows internally into a more sustainable architecture (European Commission, 2011). The Circular Economy is a systems framework that provides a set of systems-based principles to transition from the current dominant linear economy (extract metal from mining, manufacture, ending in waste stored in landfill) to a high-value industrial economy. Further, the Circular Economy designs waste at the outset and keeps products and materials in use at the highest value for the longest time by applying waste management strategies, typically the so-called 3Rs: reduce, re-use and recycling. In doing so, this would greatly reduce the pollution waste plume from industrialisation. As a result, a more sustainable relationship with the environment is to be actively developed. A successful Circular Economy, in theory, should reduce demand for virgin (raw) materials and dramatically increase resource productivity at all stages of the value chain.

The current system, Linear Economy (LE), based on economic growth, with monetary value as the metric, is stressed in multiple sectors. There is a very real need to develop a replacement system for a practical level of operation while the current system is still productive. It is also apparent that the Circular Economy is structurally flawed. The visible flaws have serious implications and mean our best, and brightest scientists and engineers are possibly working on the wrong projects. This chapter attempts to discuss these flaws. A replacement for the existing system is also needed. The current system, which the Circular Economy was designed to replace, is seriously unbalanced and unsustainable. If the flaws of the Circular Economy are understood, a new system can be proposed that would attempt to address those flaws.

Creating a truly sustainable system requires the creation of optimal industrial ecological systems with optimally linked best available techniques and methodologies. This must maximise the recovery of minerals from ores and materials from industrial waste residues, all within the boundaries of consumer behaviour, product design/functionality, thermodynamics, legislation, technology and economics.

DOI: 10.4324/9781003244196-11

Recycling is not effective enough to be the only source of materials

Recycling has been proposed as the main source of raw materials to supply feedstock to manufacturing needs in the Circular Economy ecosystem. This will not be possible in the context of the sophistication of recycling technology at the time of writing.

Not everything is recycled

Figure 9.1 shows three different waste stream products. They each contain many different useful metals and materials. Which metal or material should be prioritised? For example, gold or copper? To what metric should this be decided?

Figure 9.1 Three different waste product streams after the first stage of waste collection. Source: Own figure.

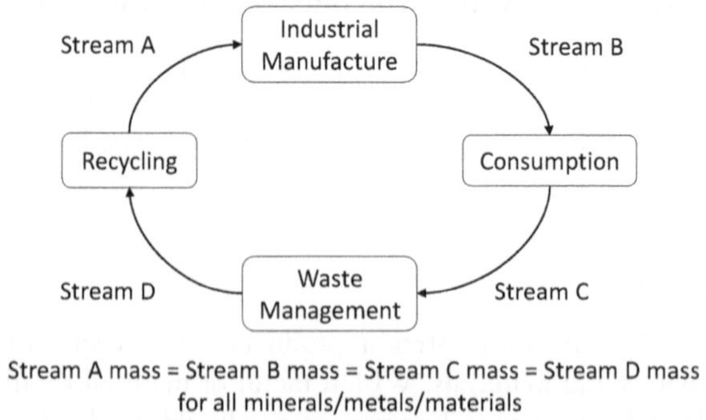

Figure 9.2 The idealised Circular Economy material streams.
Source: Own figure.

Economic value or industrially usefulness? Each processing path has efficiency windows, where process units are optimised to extract a target metal. Each metal has a slightly different process optimisation engineering requirement. This means that when extracting more than one metal in the same process plant, efficiency trade-off decisions are made, usually to favour the most economical metal. Historically, a polymetallic process path to extract several different metals is often very inefficient, especially for the secondary and tertiary target metals.

An ideal Circular Economy would collect 100% of the industrial ecosystem waste and then recycle 100% of all the different metals/minerals/materials in each stream, where there is no final waste at all. Thus, the mass and metal/material content of all internal macro streams shown in Figure 9.2 would be equal. The mass of metals and materials sourced from recycled waste would equal the mass of metals and materials required for manufacture to match consumption demand.

This is not possible under the current standard practices for several reasons:

1) Any given recycling process plant will be optimised to recover one primary metal. Sometimes, a polymetallic plant is constructed that also targets two or three secondary metals, accepting a reduction in recovery efficiency. The rest of the material (which could be 95% of the stream mass) is considered waste that is not economic to process and is often put in a landfill. The implications here are that most of the material masses of the internal material flows that could be subject to recycling would still end up in landfill, losing most of the metals and materials.
2) There are enormously practical logistical challenges in collecting all the waste streams that can be recycled. This is partly due to the nature of each waste stream and due to not enough of the community participating in recycling at the collection point.

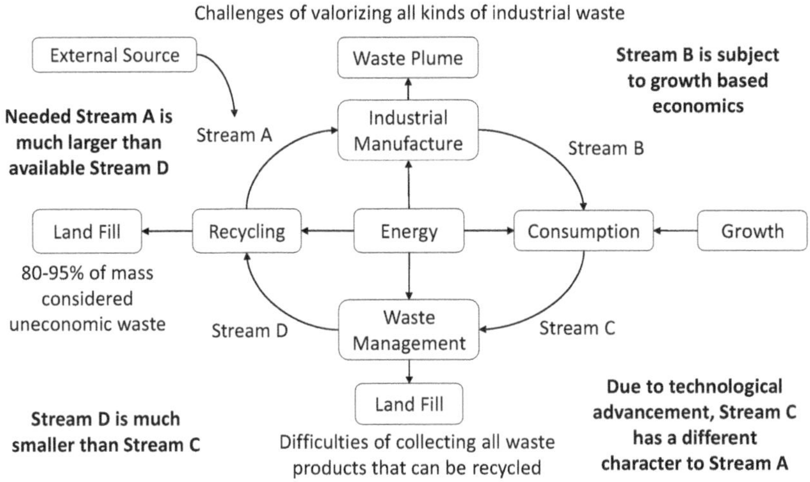

Figure 9.3 Material streams in a fully functioning Circular Economy.
Source: Own figure.

3) For a recycling process plant to deliver effective recovery, its feedstock must be mostly made up of the same EOL waste product, of which the process plant has been designed to recover a target metal from that waste product. Ideally, the EOL waste products should be sorted in appropriate streams, and the 'right' waste streams are sent to the 'right' process plant. Unfortunately, achieving this has been logistically very difficult, with only very basic sorting being achieved for some of the waste streams. In addition, each process plant usually has highly variable feedstock in the context of what the process plant has been optimised to process. As a result, recoveries are generally lower than they could be if the feedstock was more optimised.

Perhaps a more realistic macro-scale flowchart of the material streams of a Circular Economy is shown in Figure 9.3. Each of the streams is very different in mass, raw materials are required from an external source (from mining, for example), and large masses of materials are lost to landfill.

No recycling process is 100% efficient. There are always losses

Current recycling technology not only has been developed to recycle a limited number of materials but their thermodynamical limitations for each process are less than 100% efficient in recovery (Kaya, 2019). Today, any given recycling process cannot extract all target metal because a proportion of the feedstock has a texture that is not amenable to extraction by that method (Reuter et al., 2006). Future developments could work to create processes that target several products but that increases the complexity of the processes. For this to be viable, the metric of control for what is worthwhile and what is not will have to be something other than economic viability.

Figure 9.4 shows a thought experiment around a recycling process flow chart for the recovery of gold (Au) from printed circuit boards (PCB), with a recovery of 90%. This process was used to recycle a PCB, and the gold recovered was used to manufacture an identical PCB, where 10% of the needed gold would have to be sourced from some external source. The same process was used to recycle the PCB product several times. Each time, some gold is lost, and some would have to be sourced externally. At each stage, all of the material in the PCB that is not gold was put in the landfill.

This highlights how there will always be losses, materials sourced externally to the Circular Economy are always needed, and there are thermodynamic limits to the Circular Economy concept (Cooper et al. 2017).

Demand will always increase

In the current industrial ecosystem, the underlying metric for operational success is growth. Current economic ecosystems are geared to a growth of 2% per annum. Growth in all its forms is a metric of the current system (The Linear Economy). Considering that physical products represent a large part of such economic growth, the consumption of natural resources has steadily increased.

The Circular Economy is an attempt to be sustainable while maintaining economic growth and technological complexity. When it was first proposed, the Circular Economy at its foundation was based on market growth. It used money made as the metric for success while attempting to reduce material feedstock requirements and be more efficient in energy consumption. In the current industrial ecosystem, the money language and economic growth are the decision-making system. To make the most sustainable choice often means accepting a less economically cost-effective outcome. A future form of a Circular Economy could operate to a different metric, but it would require a completely different business model to the current industrial ecosystem, where the fundamental unit of comparison could be exergy, for example (Szargut, 2005).

Products are not designed to be recycled

Metals are theoretically infinitely recyclable. In practice, the functionality and design of consumer products complicate recycling due to their ever more complex structures producing unliberated low-grade and textural complex recyclates (Reuter, 2011). Metallurgical smelting technology has been developing in sophistication with the more effective use of thermodynamics and transfer processes to achieve better final recovery. However, the Second Law of Thermodynamics provides a limit of what can practically be recycled which is determined by the complexity of the recyclates. It could be possible to design products for more effective recycling, yet current practices are designed for product performance and low cost of production. So recycling waste is a function of recycling

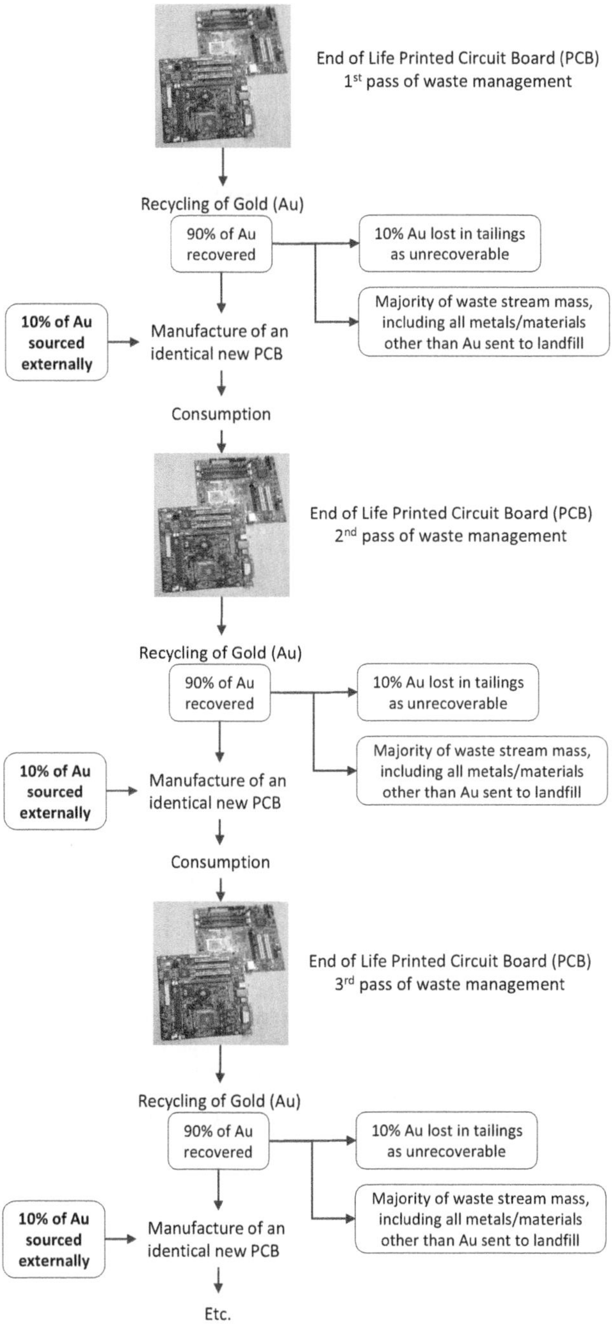

Figure 9.4 Implications of less than 100% recycling – regular sourcing of material from external sources.

Source: Own figure.

thermodynamic limitations and product designs that are difficult to recycle. So recycling (in its current form) will never be able to supply the needed volume of metals and materials demanded by manufacturers. As such, it will be very difficult to develop a truly closed-loop industrial ecosystem that does not extract any resources from the environment nor discards any waste into landfills.

Examples of non-circularity behaviour and losses in the Circular Economy

There are many examples where the Circular Economy model is not working, will never work or where technology needs to catch up to make it work more efficiently in the future. Listed below are a few examples.

Loss-by-design

This is an interesting concept developed by Ciacci et al. (2015), where certain metals and materials are lost by intent. Several examples are cited by them, including brake pads, in which the metal plates are worn out by design and are

Table 9.1 Ten examples of non-circularity leading to loss of minerals, metal and materials

Area of non-circularity	*Example*	*Cause*	*Lost minerals/metals/ materials*
Loss-by-design	Brake pads	Consumable surfaces, by design	Steel, copper
Loss-by-funeral	Human teeth, bones	Incineration, burial	Precious metals, titanium
Loss-by-heating	Bricks & ceramics	Irreversible firing clay in a kiln	Clay Group minerals
Loss-by-landfill	Electronic waste	Non-recycled household waste	Gold, PGM's, copper
Loss-by-extraction	Waste rock, tailings	Inefficient mining & processing	Base, precious & industrial minerals
Loss-by-melting	Metal in slags	Inefficient metal extraction	Iron, base & precious metals
Loss-by-consumption	Paint, some paper products	Products are unrecyclable	Mineral pigments, mineral fillers
Loss-by-waste water	Sewerage	Dumping of e-waste	Precious metals
Loss-by-weaponry	Bullets, explosives, pellets	Conflict, wars, country sports	Lead, high-tech metals, copper
Loss-by-catalysis	Automobile catalytic converters	Emission of exhaust fumes	PGM's

therefore considered to be consumable surfaces. Compositions of brake pads vary depending on the manufacturer, but most are combinations of copper, steel, graphite and brass, all of which are to some degree lost to the environment during wear, never to be recovered. This might not sound very important, but a study carried out in Stockholm (Westerlund & Johansson, 2002) calculated that in this one city alone, 3,300 kg of brake linings are used by buses per year!

Another automobile-related consumable is the studded tyre, pioneered by the Scandinavians and allowing for safe driving in the most extreme winter conditions. Again, by design, the studs wear down as the vehicle travels across road surfaces, releasing tungsten and aluminium (both EU critical metals) into the environment. An unfortunate extra side effect of studded tyres is the generated fine dust that can pose health risks to humans (Kupiainen et al. 2016), particularly in Springtime during the thaw.

Loss-by-funeral

Disposal of human bodies after death is treated in many different ways around the world, depending on cultural factors and religious practices. Most common are incineration (cremation) or burial. This is a sensitive area for obvious reasons. However, metals are inevitably lost in the process of laying a loved one to rest, including gold, silver and palladium from teeth and jewellery, and titanium and aluminium from various metal hip implants, as well as other metals, originating from ornaments on coffins. The same goes for burial sites in graveyards, cemeteries and mausoleums. Some crematoria practise recycling, and families are made aware that this process is taking place, and general consent needs to be given, but cremation rates in various countries vary considerably. For example, in the Nordics, cremation rates are as follows: Norway 36%, Finland 51%, Sweden 70% and Denmark 76%, so there is likely to be considerable loss of metals in these areas, at least.

Loss-by-heating

One of the most common examples in everyday life of how minerals are lost due to non-circularity activities might be the one-way conversion of clays into useable everyday items that we take for granted, such as ceramic and pottery ware and the common brick and roof tiles for building construction. After the clay has been fired in a kiln, there is no process known to get it back to clay again. This irreversible reaction of heating a mineral is analogous to thermal metamorphism in nature. Worse still, bricks are not easily recycled, as they are often damaged during building demolition and have little value as a crushed product. Furthermore, the clay deposits on earth are becoming depleted, and the processes required for their formation take millions of years (hydrothermal alteration of previously formed minerals), and so the mining of them cannot be considered (along with many other minerals) to be either a sustainable or a renewable activity. Clay deposits are precious and need to be carefully managed now and into the future for these reasons.

Loss-by-landfill

We are all aware these days that we must try and recycle everything as far as possible. However, historically there has been much loss of valuable metals and minerals in the form of discarded household and industrial waste, which could not be recycled and ended up in landfill sites. To put a positive spin on this, one could argue that these sites are the metal deposits of the future. Disturbingly, the practice of dumping materials in landfills continues today, even for items such as used rubber tyres (in which the zinc coatings on steel cord reinforcements are lost) in countries such as Australia (Commonwealth of Australia, 2014). However, there is some research on how to valorise waste tyres as a fuel (Singh et al., 2009) and a secondary source of metal (Riedewalda et al., 2016).

Wind turbine blades – one of the good news stories for renewable energy supporters, one would have thought – have been featuring heavily in the press recently, unceremoniously being lowered to their final resting places – again, landfill sites. This is happening because at the end of their life (around 15–20 years), the material that makes up the blades – thermosetting composites, mostly with glass and carbon fibre – cannot be easily recycled at an industrial scale, at least according to current technology, and so they are being stored for future use or re-use. In addition, they are non-combustible, by design, and, thus, cannot be used as a fuel, and they cannot either be remoulded to form new composites (Bloomberg, 2020). So, to date, all of the materials used in wind farm blades are not part of the Circular Economy.

Other examples of metals and materials lost to the world's landfill sites include: aluminium medicine blister sheets (plastic + foil), yoghurt lids (foil), ring pulls (aluminium) and beer bottle crown tops (steel or aluminium), as they are too small or difficult to separate them from a present commercial perspective, although promising research is always on-going (Wang et al., 2015).

Loss-by-extraction

The extraction of minerals, no matter how efficient and eco-friendly it may be, involves the inevitable loss of materials. Firstly, ore is often left behind in the ground as extraction is typically grade-controlled and driven by profitability. Some minerals are therefore always left *in situ*.

Secondly, so-called waste rock is generated – that is, rock which has no obvious commercial value at the time of extraction and is therefore discarded (even stockpiled) on waste rock dumps. For example, it may have come from the overburden or the footwall and hangingwall rock sequences to the mined ore bodies. Historically, there has been no incentive to find a use for this material, but today mining companies are looking at alternative uses. Thirdly, it is now known that there are considerable useful materials stored in tailings dams – that part of the mineral processing stage which was deliberately rejected in the process of concentration of the minerals of most commercial interest. Here the challenges for recycling are significant, especially if the tailings material in the dam has been stored in a wet state for years and further damaged by reagents during initial processing. Thus many tailings facilities remain to this day unexploited, though they have huge potential for valorisation (Van der Ent et al., 2020).

Loss-by-melting

After mining, comminution and concentration (by combinations of flotation, gravity, magnetic and leaching techniques), ores then go off to the metal refining stage. The rejected material at this point is a waste referred to as slag, and it is well-known that slags often contain metals that have not been efficiently separated during the pouring processes and continue to be stored in so-called slag heaps. Valorisation of slags is becoming a discipline in its own right, and there are some excellent studies in the literature where they are being valorised at an industrial scale (Van Schalkwyk et al., 2018).

Loss-by-consumption

This section might seem a little obscure to some readers, but paint of course typically is made from mineral fillers (for consistency of application and drying, or as pigments for colour effects). Paint is not easily taken off surfaces once applied, and it is therefore not a circular material in the context of the present discussion. The same is true for many wood products (such as papers and cardboard), which also rely on minerals (clays) for achieving their specific performance requirements (ability to take on inks, thickness, whiteness), and which are not, or cannot, be easily recycled because of their additives. Finally, cement is an outstanding example of a non-circular material. It is typically made from crushed and calcined limestone, and it is well-known that most buildings today continue to be made largely from virgin cement (as opposed to recycled cement). This is largely because of the exacting safety specification required for new buildings. Performance and price also come into the equation, which are difficult to reconcile with current recycling technologies. Cement that has been added to concrete (cement + aggregate) cannot easily be reconstituted back into its original dry powdered state for re-use.

Loss-by-waste water

Extraordinarily, you may not be aware that significant metal loss can take place through sewer systems in major cities. For example, it has been estimated that a city of roughly one million inhabitants flushes $13 million worth of precious metals down toilets and sewer drains on an annual basis (Westerhoff et al., 2015). Dried sewage sludge typically contains gold, platinum, silver and copper. The metals are believed to have come from electronics and jewellery manufacturers, mining, soil, electroplating and industrial catalysts. Researchers estimate that, globally, 360 tons of gold accumulates in sewage sludge every year. A sewage treatment facility in Japan already harvests gold from incinerated sludge – roughly 1,890 g/t (see Yoshikawa, 2009).

Loss-by-weaponry

It might be expected zones of conflict might produce anomalies in metal contents in soils following the detonation of missiles, bullets, bombs and so forth. All of these are typically made from metals, some of them High-Tec. Perhaps what is more unlikely is that country sports are also a source of non-circularity. For example, more than 6,000 tonnes of lead ammunition in the United Kingdom alone are discharged by guns every year, and up to 100,000 swans, ducks, geese and other wildfowl in Britain are estimated to be killed after accidentally ingesting poisonous spent shot pellets. Some estimates suggest that 19,000 tonnes of lead shot are discharged onto European soil every year (see the European Chemical Agency, ECHA, 2017).

Loss-by-catalysis

Finally, we mention here that the use of catalytic converters is a little-known source of metal leakage into the environment. In 1998, a researcher in the UK, Hazel Pritchard (University of Cardiff) was one of the first to collect and systematically analyse roadside dust, such as at roundabouts, in the city of Cardiff, Wales, UK. She showed that there was metal loss in the form of Platinum Group Metals (PGMs) that had come off catalytic converters and were being deposited by exhaust fumes along roadsides. The values reported in the dust were: Pt 126 ppb, Pd 99 ppb, Rh 22 ppb and Au trace (Pritchard and Fisher, 2012). This was extraordinary given that the natural background level for Pt in Britain is <1 ppb! Such observations have now been confirmed elsewhere, especially in the USA, where 6.7 g/t were found in 2016 on USA freeway I80 (Reeder, 2016).

How do we know that these metals have come from catalytic converters and not some other sources? Well, dust collected by the side of the road has been further refined, and it was found that the levels of PGM match almost exactly the ratios of the metals used in the manufacture of catalytic converters, so the provenance is highly indicative.

Summary

The current Circular Economy model is an ideal one, and in reality, it is neither circular nor an economy. The reasons for this are complex but are mainly due to current technology not being sufficiently advanced to capture all minerals that we are extracting from the Earth, and all the metals and materials that we are using to make our everyday products. This chapter attempts to highlight where there are losses and where future research and development needs to be focussed to change this. It does not offer all the possible solutions as that would be beyond the scope of this contribution, but we hope that this will drive further debate, discussion and much-needed action to rectify the current misunderstood paradigm.

References

Ciacci L, Reck, BK, Nassar, NT, and Graedel TE (2015). Lost by Design. Environmental Science & Technology 2015, 49, 16, 9443–9451. https://doi.org/10.1021/es505515z

Commonwealth of Australia (2014). Factsheet – Product stewardship for end-of-life tyres.

Cooper, S. J. G., Giesekam, J., Hammond, G.P., Norman, J. B., Owen, A., Rogers, J. G., Scott, K. (2017).Thermodynamic insights and assessment of the 'circular economy', Journal of Cleaner Production 162 (2017) 1356e1367.

European Chemical Agency (ECHA) (2017). https://echa.europa.eu/documents/10162/13641/restrictions_lead_shot_axv_report_en.pdf/6ef877d5-94b7-a8f8-1c49-8c07c894fff7.

European Commission (2011). Tacking the challenges in commodity markets and on raw materials, Communication from the commission to the European Parliament, The Council, The European Economic and Social Committee and the Committee of the Regions, Brussels, 2.2.2011 COM(2011) 25 final, https://eur-lex.europa.eu/legal-content/EN/TXT/PDF/?uri=CELEX:52011DC0025&from=EN

European Commission (2017). Study on the review of the list of Critical Raw Materials: Criticality Assessments. Deloitte, BGS, BRGM, TNO. Luxembourg. Accessed as http://hytechcycling.eu/wp-content/uploads/Study-on-the-review-of-the-list-of-Critical-Raw-Materials.pdf

Kaya, M. (2019). Electronic Waste and Printed Circuit Board Recycling Technologies (The Minerals, Metals & Materials Series) 1st ed. 2019 Edition, Springer publishing ISBN-13: 978-3030265922

Kupiainen K., Denby B.R., Gustafsson M., Johansson C., Ketzel M., Kukkonen J., Norman M., Pirjola L., Sundvor I., Bennet C., Blomqvist G., Janhäll S., Karppinen A., Kauhaniemi M., Malinen A., Stojiljkovic A. (2016). Road dust and PM10 in the Nordic countries Measures to reduce road dust emissions from traffic. ISBN 978-92-893-4800-3 (PRINT) ISBN 978-92-893-4801-0 (PDF) http://dx.doi.org/10.6027/ANP2016-790 ANP

Martin C (2020). Accessed as www.bloomberg.com/news/features/2020-02-05/wind-turbine-blades-can-t-be-recycled-so-they-re-piling-up-in-landfills

Pritchard, H.M. & Fisher PC (2012). Identification of Platinum and Palladium Particles Emitted from Vehicles and Dispersed into the Surface Environment. Environ. Sci. Technol.46, 6, 3149–3154 https://doi.org/10.1021/es203666h

Reeder, C. (2016). https://hackaday.com/2016/06/06/mining-platinum-from-the-road.

Reuter, M. (2011). REVIEW PAPER: *Limits of Design for Recycling and "Sustainability"*: A Review. Waste and Biomass Valorisation. 2. 183.

Reuter, M., van Schaik, A., Ignatenko, O., and de Haan, G.J. (2006). Fundamental limits for the recycling of end-of-life vehicles, Minerals Engineering 19 (2006) 433–449.

Riedewalda, F., Goodea K., Sexton A, Sousa-Gallagher MJ (2016). Scrap tyre recycling process with molten zinc as direct heat transfer and solids separation fluid: A new reactor concept. MethodsX. http://dx.doi.org/10.1016/j.mex.2016.05.003

Singh, S., Nimmo W, Gibbs, BM, Williams PT (2009). Waste tyre rubber as a secondary fuel for power plants. Fuel 88 (2009) 2473–2480.

Szargut, J. (2005). *Exergy Method.* Technical and Ecological Applications, 192p. WitPress, Southampton, Boston

Van der Ent, A, Parbhakar-Fox, A and Erskine, PD. (2020). Treasure from trash: Mining critical metals from waste and unconventional sources. Science of The Total Environment, 758 143673, 143673. doi: 10.1016/j.scitotenv.2020.143673

Van Schalkwyk, RF, Reuter MA, Gutzmer J, Stelter M. (2018). Challenges of digitalising the circular economy: Assessment of the state-of-the-art of metallurgical carrier metal platform for lead and its associated technology elements. Journal of Cleaner Production. 186, 585 – 601. https://doi.org/10.1016/j.jclepro.2018.03.111

Wang, C-Q, Wang H, and Liu Y-N. (2017). Separation of aluminum and plastic by metallurgy method for recycling waste pharmaceutical blisters. Journal of Cleaner Production 102, 378–383. http://dx.doi.org/10.1016/j.jclepro.2015.04.067

Westerhoff P, Lee S, Yang Y, Gordon GW, Hristovski K, Halden RU, Herckes P (2015). Characterisation, Recovery Opportunities, and Valuation of Metals in Municipal Sludges from U.S. Wastewater Treatment Plants Nationwide. *Environmental Science & Technology*, 49, 16, 9479 – 9488. https://doi.org/10.1021/es505329q

Westerlund & Johansson (2002). Emission Of Metals And Particulate Matter Due To Wear Of Brake Linings In Stockholm. www.witpress.com/elibrary/wit-transactions-on-ecology-and-the-environment. doi: 10.2495/AIR020791

Yoshikawa, M (2009). Sewage yields more gold than top mines. Accessed from Reuters. www.reuters.com/article/us-gold-sewage-odd-idINTRE50T56120090130

10 Circular economy leadership

Leadership mindsets and behaviours – the unseen impossibility

Maureen Metcalf and Christoph Hinske

Introduction

There is no doubt that new technologies, governance structures, values, and interaction dynamics are fundamental to implementing the Circular Economy. However, it is leaders who build and run the house on this foundation. The chapter discusses how applying well-tested leadership frameworks provide a crucial piece of the puzzle required to turn the Circular Economy from an impossibility to a probability.

Using the Innovative Leadership Mindset and Competency model (Cannon et al., 2015), this chapter tries to understand the leadership needed for the Circular Economy. The authors argue that the leadership required to succeed in a Circular Economy is fundamentally different from traditional leadership. To succeed in the Circular Economy, leaders must evolve how they think, their presence as leaders, and what they do to progress circular economies successfully. In addition, they must understand the complexity of the underlying cause and effect behind interactions between actors, events, and structures and whether these influence their actions and strategies (Busulwa et al., 2019, 8).

Furthermore, the chapter claims that the Circular Economy will not deliver against its promises if leadership mindsets and behaviours remain unchanged. We have seen little progress globally to give evidence of this needed change. That is why the authors believe that under current circumstances, the implementation of the Circular Economy is an impossibility. While the Circular Economy advocates are overpromising its impact, working on leadership mindsets and associated behaviours is essential to move this critical agenda forward and improve its environmental, economic, and social effects.

The concepts of Circular Economy and Innovative Leadership

This chapter focuses on the concepts of the *Circular Economy* and *Leadership* and how the framework of Mindset and Competency Development can help identify impossibilities. Thus, this chapter introduces and reflects the two concepts.

DOI: 10.4324/9781003244196-12

The Circular Economy

The Ellen MacArthur Foundation established the Circular Economy early on as an alternative industrial model (as cited in Tonelli & Cristoni, 2019), whereby taking a dynamic (Ellen MacArthur Foundation, 2016) and a systemic approach (Webster, 2017). It "*manages stocks and manufactured assets […] to maintain their value and utility as high as possible for as long as possible; and stocks of resources at their highest purity and value*" (Stahel, 2019). The *Circular Economy and Sustainability Journal* merges the Circular Economy concepts with sustainability as a new approach to achieve sustainable development. It states that the practical and scientific disciplines underlying the Circular Economy "*are not independent to each other, but […] relations, interactions, and synergies exist and should be further developed and studied*" (Springer, n.d.). According to Springer, integrating these approaches allows for achieving the Sustainable Development Goals, solving various environmental problems, expanding technological limits, overcoming potential economic disturbances, and making linear business models circular.

Putting the Circular Economy on such an ambitious foundation requires it to be transdisciplinary (Otten & Sint Nicolaas, 2021; Lieder & Rashid, 2016) and Nexus approach (Lehmann, 2020). Ken Webster, Director of the International Society for the Circular Economy, goes one step further by establishing that system thinking, system dynamics, and complexity science are foundational principles for achieving the transition from linear to circular. Additionally, he argues that being empathetic, understanding feedback and interdependence, and seeing our economy as a complex adaptive system are vital (Webster, 2017).

This framing puts forward the relevance to making system dynamics and systems thinking (Stahel, 2019) and, in particular, complexity principles such as "non-linearity, feedbacks, thresholds, hierarchies, emergence and self-organisation" (Wells, 2013) the primary modus operandi of current and future decision makers. In other words, leaders have to execute strategies and transform operations despite disruption and complexity (Busulwa et al., 2019). They have to accomplish deep levels of collaboration in multi-stakeholder ecosystems (Rincón-Moreno et al., 2020, Takacs et al., 2020, Ritchie-Dunham, 2022) and System Leadership (Beehner, 2022; 2020, 23).

The Innovative Leadership Mindset and Behaviour Framework

Building a genuinely Circular Economy going beyond "serving old wine in new bottles" requires leaders with a mindset of navigating complexity, empathy, and collaboration. The Innovative Leadership Mindset and Behaviour Framework (the Framework) consists of a cohesive set of models facilitating leadership development and organisational transformation in complex environments.

The Framework is grounded in constructive-developmental psychology (Brown, 2011). It asserts that individuals evolve to increased capacity to navigate higher complexity, longer time horizons, greater emotional intelligence, and more ethical behaviour referred to as Strategist. As Webster (2017) and Stahel

(2019) described, the economy we need to build is more complex, dynamic, and ambiguous. Thus, individuals and leaders need to develop the capacity to create new ways of how to process information, lead teams, organisations, and navigate entrepreneurial ecosystems (Moore, 1997; Anuwa-Amarh et al., 2020; Takacs et al., 2020). The Circular Economy demands leaders reassess their mental models as it has a dramatic impact on their direct and indirect decision context (Webster, 2017). Its implementation, however, is an impossibility unless we evolve the leadership required to create the frameworks and develop leaders who successfully implement them at a global scale rife with competing commitments and self-interest.

Scholar-practitioners in leadership development define leadership maturity stages of combined cognitive-affective-behavioural growth using accurately measurable, statistically verified instruments (Cannon et al., 2015). There are seven mindsets and behavioural traits associated with the Strategist's level of maturity: humility, commitment to right action, strategic perspective, versatility, authenticity, ability to inspire followership, and innate collaboration.

Prevailing leadership models are an impossibility to the Circular Economy

A Strategist is a person who can grasp, navigate, and act within highly entangled and conflicting relationships that change over time. They are "*passionate and unbiased, detailed and strategic, hard-driving and sustainable, fact-focused and intuitive, self-confident and selfless*" (Cannon et al., 2015). The strategists competencies enable leaders to execute highly effective actions (Kegan & Laskow Lahey, 2009) to solve challenges and perform tasks in transforming our economy towards sustainability (Beehner, 2022, Hinske, 2013, 2016). The architects of the Circular Economy seem to take the ability to grasp and navigate entangled relationships for granted. We state that this is plain dangerous. Taken for granted, it is not on the minds of the Circular Economy architects. As a result, it fades out of the academic, policy, and investment discourses causing the Circular Economy to be built on the old mindsets, making it impossible to deliver against its new promises. However, Webster and Stahel frame the Circular Economy as being "*a complex adaptive system*" (Webster, 2017, 12) and "*the new normal*" (Webster, 2017, 43; Stahel, 2019). They see "*simple, linear*" systems as the exception to the norm (Webster, 2017) consequently positioning the Circular Economy in the domain of complexity, the realm to which most contemporary business has shifted (Moore, 1997; Snowden & Boone, 2007; Cooper Ramo, 2016; Ramírez & Mannervik, 2016; Heimans & Timms, 2018; Meyer & Williamson, 2020).

Regardless of how much policymakers and academics push the Circular Economy concept, it will not deliver against its goals as long as leaders are not developed to navigate this new realm. To make it work, it needs leaders with

> *The understanding of dynamic systems, systems with feedback but uncertainty [and] the skills of seeing the big picture, of being empathetic, seeing from another's*

> *point of view since one of the lessons of feedback and interdependence is that of unforeseen or unexpected outcomes in both near but also distant parts of the system.*
> (Webster, 2017, 62)

Webster affirms that most systems are in a state of "*ordered complexity*" with "*intricate dynamic patterns, intertwined casualties and feedback loops*" (Webster, 2017, 63). Consequently, the rules and interaction patterns defining our economy have to be based on the insights of non-linear systems. However true, that is, Ritchie-Dunham (2022) argues that the three basic requirements of "*explicit feedback loops, (2) coordination across a set of these feedback loops, and (3) the capacity to learn and adjust across this set over time*" do not exist within the "*linear-causal worldview of mainstream economic thinking; they have literally been integrated out of mainstream thinking*". Against this background, it becomes apparent that most leaders cannot make high-quality decisions in complex situations. They lack the understanding of how factors interrelate, form dynamics, and how their fundamental emotions and belief systems influence their choices and stakeholder systems (Hinske, 2021). Moreover, few low threshold and practitioner-oriented tools combine strategic decision making in complex situations with emotional intelligence, business ecosystem thinking, and system dynamics (Hinske, 2021).

Shading out the foundational impact of vertical leadership development to achieve the Circular Economy is a self-induced impossibility, though not less potent than the laws of thermodynamics. One can conclude that society requires these skills now, at scale, and not tomorrow for only a few.

The relevance of leadership development to implement the Circular Economy

Leaders are crucial in global efforts to move the Circular Economy efforts forward. This section uses a leadership mindset and behaviour model to discuss the relevance of leadership development to implement a Circular Economy.

As mentioned above,

> The qualities of effective leadership can be paradoxical – requiring effective leaders to be passionate and unbiased, detailed and strategic, hard-driving and sustainable, fact-focused and intuitive, self-confident and selfless – often at the same time. Such complexity is rarely found in leaders, even under optimal conditions.
> (Cannon et al., 2015)

As we implement a Circular Economy, we will face new challenges beyond the abilities of most leaders. The Circular Economy presents such new contexts and conditions, demanding leaders to develop horizontally and vertically. Unlike horizontal development, which is about expanding the toolkit and training skills by adding new ones, vertical growth is concerned with expanding persons' mindset, thus, transforming a leader to be more adaptive, self-aware, collaborative, and span boundaries and networks (Hinske, 2009, Henley, 2020).

The leader in the Circular Economy needs to move from our traditional focus on driving results, often at any cost, to taking on the thinking and behaviour of a scientist. They must continually make accurate observations, ask informed questions, form comprehensive hypotheses or testable explanations, make predictions based on the hypothesis, test the predictions, and use the results to make new hypotheses or predictions. For leaders to shift from traditional behaviour to taking on the mindset of a scientist, they must shift how they see themselves and the world and how they make meaning in the world. This shift requires a significant change and can only be achieved through efforts of vertical development (Cannon et al., 2015).

A recent report by PricewaterhouseCoopers profiled over 6,000 leaders across industries and sectors in the UK, identifying those who have applied the appropriate capabilities in the right situations to prepare them to lead business change in complex environments successfully. According to PricewaterhouseCoopers (2015), the number of Strategist leaders has only increased by 1% over the past ten years. It becomes evident that those able to understand the complexity of the underlying cause and effect behind interactions between actors, events, and structures, able to integrate it into strategy execution are in short supply. The data varies by country. However, not more than 8% of leaders in the UK are at this developmental level. Other countries have far fewer people (PricewaterhouseCoopers, 2015). Earlier research confirmed that such leaders are rare (Brown, 2011), as the action logics exist in only 5–7% of the general population. To implement the Circular Economy, we need Strategist leaders with highly complex meaning-making abilities (Brown, 2011; Webster, 2017; Beehner, 2022). Therefore, considerable work needs to be done to build leadership development programs that appropriately prepare such leaders.

With the limited number of leaders at the Strategist level and the slow rate of development, the challenge is the focus, scale, and time requirements. Vertical growth is usually incremental and gradual, and growing from one vertical level to the next is believed to take from three to five years (Brown, 2013; Murray, 2017; Rooke & Torbert, 2005). Even though recent development programs aimed at accelerating vertical growth have reported statistical success in shortening this time horizon to as little as one year (Braks, 2020; Brown, 2011; Vincent et al., 2015), individuals and organisations must be willing to make a long-term investment of time and money. This investment has to happen globally to develop the kind and amount of leaders capable of successfully implementing the Circular Economy.

Strategic-methodological recommendations

Our contribution to this discussion is to translate the developmental maturity models referenced above and again referenced in the research by PricewaterhouseCoopers, Barret Brown, and others to a set of seven mindsets and corresponding behaviours. It is important to note that it is not enough to mimic a list of behaviours. Leaders must evolve how they grasp and process information to perform at this new level.

Our recommendations focus primarily on the mindset of leaders as it is the mindset that governs the meaning-making algorithm, how leaders make sense of the world, informing the actions they take or do not take.

1. **Professionally humble**, caring more about system success than personal success or image. A professionally humble leader is committed to their organisation's purpose and, at the same time, their values and sense of legacy. This leader delivers results while also living their values. As it relates to leading in a Circular Economy, this leader will balance delivering on the company mission, including sustainability and stewardship for the planet. The humility part comes in when the leader puts their commitment above their image. The path to building a Circular Economy is a complicated one. Leaders will need to update their ways forward continually. Leaders will make commitments that they find are unattainable in the time frames they want or at the cost they think is reasonable. They learn through this experimentation.
2. **Unwavering commitment to right action** – unstoppable and unflappable when on a mission. Right action is an interesting phrase. Right according to who? If we look back at professionally humble, we see that the leaders are committed to their mission and personal values. Additionally, we need to engage with one another and have honest conversations, and some are not easy. We are also talking about right today vs. right to create the future we want to see. Finally, we are asking about the longer-term implications of our current actions. If, as leaders, we list our stakeholders, including the future inhabitants of the planet and the environment, we expand our thinking about what is right. How would decisions change if we considered the planet's health in scorecards along with profit and employee satisfaction? Will this shift guide thinking about the right action?
3. **360-degree thinker** – taking a systems view and seeing the interconnectedness of people and systems. Being a 360-degree thinker offers obvious value in creating a Circular Economy. Leaders need to be systems thinkers as they must take a systemic view of inputs, processes, and outputs of a wide range of ecosystems to identify the optimal shift towards circularity. Once leaders and organisations make these shifts and conduct experiments, they will continue collecting data and gaining insights to optimise and move towards a more robust circular impact. This process will unfold at varying rates in different industries, and some are already making progress while others are less engaged.
4. **Intellectually versatile** – develops interests, curiosity, and expertise beyond their organisation. Because the Circular Economy is a new pursuit, leaders need to build the skills required to succeed. The most effective ones will draw from a wide range of interests and synthesise their divergent ideas into a cohesive perspective. This perspective will inform the subsequent experiments and actions. A relentless commitment to learning fuels these

leaders, allowing them to continually update their internal meaning-making algorithm to be increasingly more effective and insightful.

5. **Authentic and reflective** – focused on personal growth and emotional courage. Reflection is one of the essential skills to allow people to grow and develop. This time in our history certainly requires courage and skill to accept and support our colleagues who see the world differently. As leaders, we must continually evaluate how we lead our organisations and balance the many competing commitments, including building a circular ecosystem. This means leaders will need to transform organisations and, in many cases, will also need to change how they think about their role as leaders. As they embark on the Circular Economy journey, they will learn a great deal of information about creating a circular ecosystem, updating their business processes, and navigating resistance to the changes. Leaders will need to model commitment and flexibility simultaneously, pushing to hit targets and allowing people to learn and grow at an accelerated pace to address global pressures without burning people out.
6. **Inspire followership** – connects with a broad range of people around a shared vision. Leaders need to set an inspirational image of what a booming Circular Economy looks like, feels like, and benefits the organisation. Telling people what to do may generate short-term compliance, but it also runs the risk of causing disengagement. Purpose, autonomy, and mastery inspire people. They want to do work that matters in a way that allows them to feel empowered. They also need to trust their leaders to act with integrity, be transparent, and act in good faith. Leaders must lay out the story of why the Circular Economy benefits employees as well as the world. They want to feel part of the journey and see a direct line between their efforts and the positive impact; in short, they want to connect their actions to the larger purpose. They also want to receive truthful information about what is working and what needs to change.
7. **Innately collaborative** – seek input from diverse points of view to create novel solutions. As leaders and organisations implement a Circular Economy, they will be creating solutions that did not previously exist. They will need to collaborate with a broad range of experts and stakeholders to evaluate the ecosystem, identify opportunities, and develop experiments to test the hypothesis. This collaborative process circles back to humility. Leaders will rely on their expertise as part of a broader solution. Each will need to balance a strong foundation of knowledge with an open mind and curiosity about what others bring to the solution. Leaders who master this skill can synthesise a broad range of information and divergent perspectives into a cohesive approach.

Closing remarks

The authors firmly believe that the Circular Economy is a needed frame of reference for our industrial evolution if framed by the United Nations Sustainable Development Goals (United Nations, n.d.). However, to make it happen requires leaders to develop their mindsets and behaviours, unlocking the power of shared beliefs for societies (Strand, 2022). This ability is essential! History has shown again and again what *Homo sapiens* is capable of when sharing an idea and what happens if not (Harari, 2015; Clifford, 2015; Cooperation, 2019). Leadership that can inspire shared belief is essential for transforming educational, business, financial, political, or social systems (to name a few) as they help society to collaborate across sectors and supply chains (Hinske, 2009, 2016; Ellen MacArthur Foundation, 2016; Webster, 2017; Stahel, 2019; Systemic & The Club of Rome, 2020; Takacs et al., 2020).

The bad news is that the Circular Economy, as described by its current architects, is impossible to build quickly and at scale. The good news is that the solutions are out there, and if we find them, we will achieve transformational changes at scale (Ritchie-Dunham & Pruitt, 2014; Ritchie-Dunham, 2022).

In line with the reasoning by Nonaka and Takeuchi (2021), this chapter concludes that the Circular Economy requires leaders who can handle complex dynamic systems, polarities, ambiguities, feedback, uncertainty, and integrate these into a cohesive strategy. To do so, they need to see the big picture and be empathetic, humble, innately collaborative, and unstoppable. Balancing and aligning these elements without favouring some are essential for the Circular Economy efforts to succeed. Furthermore, as leaders navigate the complexities of building Circular Economy ecosystems (Takacs et al., 2020), they will draw on many skills not required in our previous economic conditions (McGuire & Rhodes, 2009). For example, to ensure leaders make high-quality decisions in complex transformations, such as moving from the linear to the Circular Economy, they must understand how interrelated strategic resources produce flywheels (Collins, 2019) and complex dynamics (Ritchie-Dunham & Rabbino, 2001). In addition, decision makers need to know how fundamental values, emotions, and belief systems of themselves and their group influence their success over time (Hinske, 2021; Nonaka & Takeuchi, 2021).

Using the Innovative Leadership Mindset and Behaviour Framework, we intended to inspire you, the reader, to evaluate how to effectively and efficiently develop Circular Economy efforts and what mindsets and behaviours are required. Suppose you agree that we need leaders with these mindsets and behaviours. In that case, we suggest identifying an approach to attract and retain them as we believe it is essential to balance recruiting, promoting, and developing leaders to create a solid team to move a Circular Economy from an impossibility into a probability. Following the tradition of mode three knowledge production and transdisciplinary research (Anderson et al., 2015), we, the authors, developed an easy-to-use and open-access process that helps you, the leaders, execute strategies in complex circular ecosystems (Metcalf, 2013; Hinske, 2021).

References

Anderson, L., Gold, J., & Stewart, J. (2015). *A Guide to Professional Doctorates in Business and Management* (J. Stewart, L. Anderson, R. Thorpe, & J. Gold, Eds.). SAGE Publications.

Anuwa-Amarh, E. et al. (2020). The Kwawu resilient entrepreneurial ecosystems: A complex adaptive systems approach to achieving the Sustainable Development Goals. In *Sustainable Development and Resource Productivity The Nexus Approaches* (Vol. 4, pp. 317–328). Routledge.

Beehner, C. G. (2020). System Leadership for Sustainability. Routledge.

Beehner, C. G. (2022). System Leadership for Overcoming the Impossibilities of a Circular Economy. In H. Lehmann (Ed.), *The Impossibilities of the Circular Economy* (Vol. 5). Routledge.

Braks, A. J. (2020). Leadership Coaching Leads to Later Stage Development. *Integral Review*, *16*(1), 332–356.

Brown, B. C. (2011). Conscious Leadership for Sustainability – How Leaders with late-stage action logic design and engage in sustainability initiatives. Fielding Graduate University | Dissertation.

Brown, B. C. (2013). *The Future of Leadership for Conscious Capitalism* [White Paper]. MetaIntegral Associates.

Busulwa, R., Tice, M., & Gurd, B. (2019). Strategy Execution and Complexity – Thriving in the Era of Disruption. Routledge.

Cannon, S., Morrow-Fox, M., & Metcalf, M. (2015). The Strategist Competency Model: The Future of Leadership Development. In *Leadership 2050, Critical Challenges, Key Contexts and Emerging Trends* (Chapter 12). Emerald Publishing.

Clifford, M. (2015). The Greening of Asia: The Business Case for Solving Asia's Environmental Emergency. Columbia University Press.

Collins, J. (2004). Good to Great: Why Some Companies Make the Leap... and Others Don't (37th ed.). Random House UK Ltd.

Collins, J. (2019). Turning the Flywheel: A Monograph to Accompany Good to Great. Penguin Random House.

Cooperation. (2019). In S. Parrish (Ed.), *The Great Mental Models – Physics, Chemistry and Biology* (Vol. 2, pp. 326–339). Latticework Publishing Incorporated.

Cooper Ramo, J. (2016). The Seventh Sense: Power, Fortune, and Survival in the Age of Networks. Hachette Book Group.

Ellen MacArthur Foundation (Ed.). (2016). *A New Dynamic 2 – Effective Systems in a Circular Economy*. Ellen MacArthur Foundation.

Freeman, R. E., Harrison, J. S., & Zyglidopoulos, S. (2018). *Stakeholder Theory*. Cambridge University Press.

Garvey Berger, J. (2019). *Unlocking Leadership Mindtraps – How to Thrive in Complexity*. Stanford University Press.

Harari, Y. N. (2015). *Sapiens: A Brief History of Humankind*. Vintage Books.

Heimans, J., & Timms, H. (2018). *New Power – How Anyone Can Persuade, Mobilize, and Succeed in Our Chaotic, Connected Age*. Anchor Books.

Henley, D. (2020). *Research Says Vertical Development Can Make You A Better Leader*. Forbes. Retrieved 09, 2021, from www.forbes.com/sites/dedehenley/2020/01/31/vertical-development-can-make-you-a-better-leader-in-todays-world/?sh=75f14cfb76ca

Hinske, C. (2009). Triple-Loop Learning in the context of global environmental change – 21st-century competencies of global-change agents to facilitate third-order change, Master Thesis for the M.Sc. Program Global Change Management. University of Applied Sciences Eberswalde, Faculty of Forest and Environment.

Hinske, C. (2013). Core Resources of Paradigm-Change Facilitation. *The Systems Thinker – | Pegasus Communications*, *24*(2), 6–9.

Hinske, C. (2016). Agreements of Transformation – Experience-based research exploring the patterns and specifics of societal-scale transformations in different cultures. The Institute for Strategic Clarity, United States of America.

Hinske, C. (2021). *The Ecosystem Decision-Making Radar*. Innovative Leadership Institute. Retrieved October 11, 2021, from www.innovativeleadershipinstitute.com/the-ecosystem-decision-making-radar/

Kegan, R. (1994). *In Over Our Heads – The Mental Demands of Modern Life*. Harvard University Press.

Kegan, R., & Laskow Lahey, L. (2009). *Immunity to Change – How to overcome it and unlock the potential in yourself and your organisation*. Harvard Business Press.

Lehmann, H. (Ed.). (2020). *Sustainable Development and Resource Productivity The Nexus Approaches* (Vol. 4). Routledge.

Lieder, M., & Rashid, A. (2016, March 1). Towards Circular Economy implementation: a comprehensive review in the context of the manufacturing industry. *Journal of Cleaner Production*, *115*, 36–51. 10.1016/j.jclepro.2015.12.042

McGuire, J. B., & Rhodes, G. B. (2009). *Transforming your Leadership Culture*. Jossey-Bass and The Center for Creative Leadership.

Metcalf, M. (2013). *Innovative Leaders Guide to Transforming Organizations*. Integral Publishers.

Meyer, A. D., & Williamson, P. J. (2020). *Ecosystem Edge – Sustaining Competitiveness in the Face of DISRUPTION*. Stanford Business Books.

Moore, J. F. (1997). *The Death of Competition – Leadership & Strategy in the Age of Business Ecosystems*. Harper Business.

Murray, T. (2017). Sentence completion assessments for ego development, meaning-making, and wisdom maturity, including STAGES. *Integral Leadership Review*. https://bit.ly/3xisOFD

Nonaka, I., & Takeuchi, H. (2021, Fall). Strategy as a Way of Life – businesses must root strategy and moral purpose to thrive in a complex, rapidly changing world. *MIT Sloan Management Review*, 63(1), 56–63.

Otten, A., & Sint Nicolaas, R.C. (2021). The energy transition in Deventer – A Hanseatic approach. In *Sustainable Development and Resource Productivity, The Nexus Approaches*. Routledge.

PricewaterhouseCoopers. (2015). *The hidden talent: Ten ways to identify and retain transformational leaders*. PricewaterhouseCoopers LLP. https://osca.co/pubs/pwc-hidden-talent

Ramírez, R., & Mannervik, U. (2016). *Strategy for a Networked World*. Imperial College Press.

Rincón-Moreno, J., Ormazabal, M., Álvarez, M. J., & Jaca, C. (2020). Shortcomings of Transforming a Local Circular Economy System through Industrial Symbiosis: A Case Study in Spanish SMEs. *Sustainability*, *12*(Special Issue Circular Economy in Small and Medium Enterprises), 1–18. https://doi.org/10.3390/su12208423

Ritchie-Dunham, J. (2022). Truly Circular Economies Require Deep Collaboration. In H. Lehmann (Ed.), *The Impossibilities of the Circular Economy – Lessons from the Hunt to Square the Circle* (Vol. 5). Routledge.

Ritchie-Dunham, J. L., & Pruitt, B. (2014). *Ecosynomics: The Science of Abundance* (B. Pruitt, Ed.). Vibrancy Ins, LLC.

Ritchie-Dunham, J. L., & Rabbino, H. T. (2001). *Managing from Clarity: Identifying, Aligning and Leveraging Strategic Resources*. Wiley.

Rooke, D., & Torbert, W. R. (2005). *Seven Transformations of Leadership*. Harvard Business Review. Retrieved 08 10, 2021, from https://hbr.org/2005/04/seven-transformations-of-leadership

Scott, R. (2018). *Group Model Building – Using System Dynamics to Achieve Enduring Agreement*. Springer.

Snowden, D. J., & Boone, M. E. (2007). *A Leader's Framework for Decision Making*. Harvard Business Review – Decision Making and Problem Solving. Retrieved 09, 2021, from https://hbr.org/2007/11/a-leaders-framework-for-decision-making

Spigel, B. (2020). *Entrepreneurial Ecosystems – Theory, Practice and Futures*. Edward Elgar Publishing.

Springer (n.d.). *Circular Economy and Sustainability*. Circular Economy and Sustainability. Retrieved October 06, 2021, from www-springer-com.saxion.idm.oclc.org/journal/43615

Stahel, W. R. (2019). *The Circular Economy – A User's Guide*. Routledge.

Strand, R. (2022). Can there be a responsible narrative about the Circular Economy? In *FactorX, The Impossibilities of the Circular Economy – Separating aspirations from reality* (Vol. 5). Routledge.

Systemiq & The Club of Rome (2020). *A System Change Compass: Implementing the European Green Deal in a time of recovery*. Club of Rome. Retrieved August 03, 2021, from www.clubofrome.org/publication/a-system-change-compass-implementing-the-european-green-deal-in-a-time-of-recovery/

Takacs, F., Stechow, R., & Frankenberger, K. (2020). *Circular Ecosystems: Business Model Innovation for the Circular Economy* [White Paper of the Institute of Management & Strategy, University of St. Gallen.].

Tonelli, M., & Cristoni, N. (2019). *Strategic Management and the Circular Economy*. Routledge.

Torbert, B. (2004). *Action Inquiry – The Secret of Timely and Transforming Leadership*. Barrett-Koehler Publishers, Inc.

United Nations (n.d.). *THE 17 GOALS | Sustainable Development*. Sustainable Development Goals. Retrieved August 2021, from https://sdgs.un.org/goals

Vincent, N., Ward, L., & Denson, L. (2015). Promoting post-conventional consciousness in leaders: Australian community leadership programs. *The Leadership Quarterly*, *26*(2), 238–253. https://doi.org/10.1016/j.leaqua.2014.11.007

Waddell, S. (2016). *Change for the audacious: a doer's guide – Large Systems Change for a flourishing future*. NetworkingAction Publishing.

Webster, K. (2017). *The Circular Economy – A wealth of flows* (2nd ed.). Ellen MacArthur Foundation.

Wells, J. (2013). *Complexity and Sustainability*. Routledge.

11 Can there be a responsible narrative about the circular economy?

Roger Strand

Is the circular economy a contradiction in terms?

According to a dictionary of good reputation, a contradiction in terms is "a phrase that contains words which have very different or opposite meanings" (Merriam-Webster, n.d.). The dictionary provides an example: "working vacation". Students of logic are often given another example, namely that of the "married bachelor".

The married bachelor is a particular type of contradiction in terms, namely an oxymoron. There is an adjective (married) that explicitly contradicts the definition of the noun (bachelor = unmarried man). In a course on logic, one would learn that the term "married bachelor" is logically impossible; all meaning breaks down if we say such things, that is, unless we are doing poetry. The working vacation is different, though, at least in practice. A very strict logician might think of it as a logical impossibility. Yet, many if not most employees in neoliberal, post-industrial societies know what it means. It means that you can be on vacation, but still you are expected to check your e-mail and keep an eye on at least some work tasks. "Work" and "vacation" once meant something quite opposite. In contemporary societies, however, the boundary between work and leisure is dissolving, and so "working vacation" is becoming an increasingly meaningful term and no longer an impossibility. We have got used to it. Yet, there is an unpleasant element of contradiction, or at least tension, in the expression.

The expression "circular economy" bears some similarity with the "working vacation". It is not an oxymoron per se; "economy" is not defined as a type of non-circular system or activity. Indeed, in some textbooks of economics, the economic system is depicted as two concentric circles that represent the flow of money (from consumer expenditure to revenue, producer expenditure, wages and back to consumer expenditure) and the opposite flow of labour, goods and services, respectively. The circles in such diagrams are not meant to be taken in their literal, geometrical sense; rather, they are meant to depict repetitive patterns in monetary flows and the creation of economic value. To express the desire for a circular economy, however, is something else. It expresses an ideal of a system of production and consumption where materials and other natural resources are

DOI: 10.4324/9781003244196-13

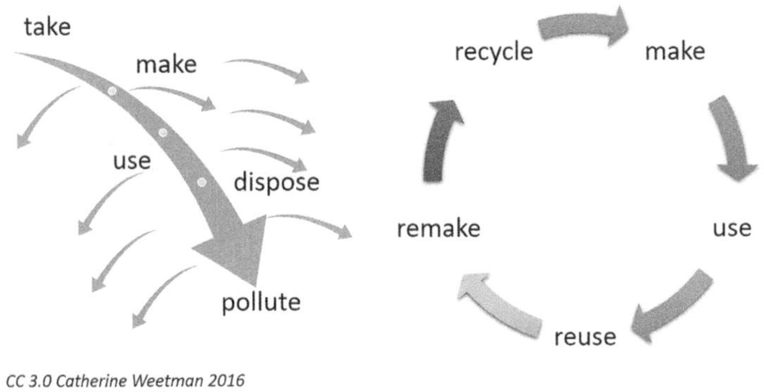

Figure 11.1 Linear versus circular economy.
Source: By Catherine Weetman – Own work, CC BY-SA 4.0, https://commons.wikimedia.org/w/index.php?curid=67945876

recycled so as to continue to be used over and over again, see Figure 11.1, so that no waste is produced and no virgin resources are needed (perfect circularity), or alternatively, that as little waste as possible is produced and little virgin resources are needed (Figure 11.2).

At first sight, there seems to be no contradiction in terms here. Ecological economists and researchers within the field of material flow analysis, however, have argued otherwise (Giampietro, 2019; Kovacic et al., 2019). What they claim is that economic activity by definition cannot be (perfectly) circular because its purpose is to produce order – refined goods and services – and accordingly have to degrade order elsewhere. Economic activity has to utilize naturally occurring gradients of high-order materials or energy to be possible. For these scholars, this is a logical implication of the Second Law of Thermodynamics: Production is neg-entropic, and accordingly it has to be coupled to entropic processes of decay in order to take place (Daly, 2005). This is true in principle, they would claim, but also in matters of degree and for practical purposes. For example, one could in principle collect and recycle used silver nanoparticles, but to do so will require huge amounts of work in the form of labour and high-order energy. Another example is recycling of food. In the very literal sense, we cannot eat the food twice. We can of course collect our excretions from the sewer system and use it as fertilizer, and in that sense there is a recycling. However, this process of recycling is slow because it has to go through the nutrient cycles of the biosphere; it is not an "economic activity" that we humans can undertake as such (Giampietro, 2019). We may change our economic activities so that they become "more" circular (where "more" has to be defined in terms of indicators or other variables), but this change is incompatible with expectations of continuous economic growth as it is normally defined. Fast-growing economies are linear and with high throughput of resources; this property is the reason why we are having a high throughput and

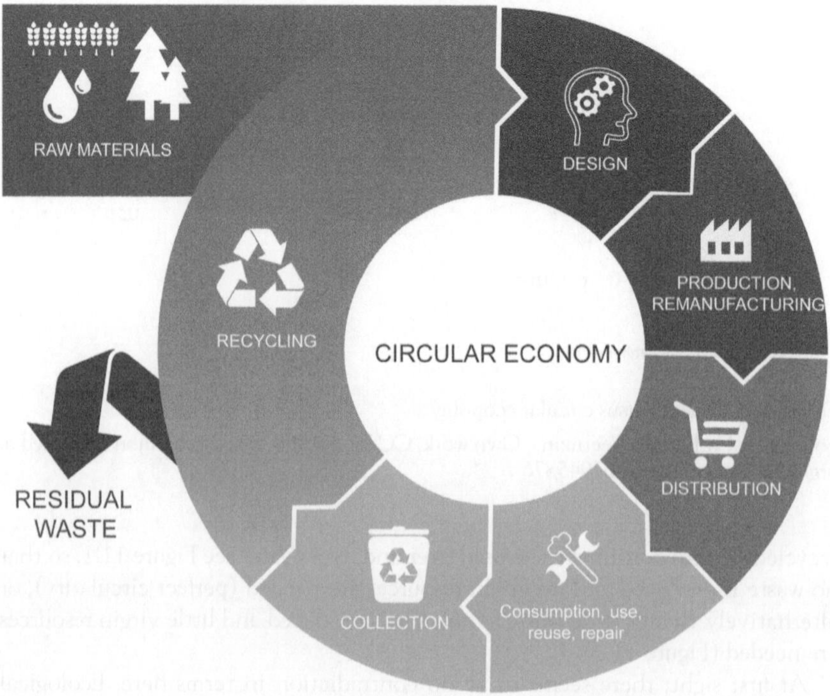

Figure 11.2 The circular economy as depicted by the European Union.

Source: Located at www.europarl.europa.eu/news/en/headlines/economy/20151201STO05603/circular-economy-definition-importance-and-benefits

why contemporary civilization became so unsustainable in the first place. A fossil fuel-based, linear, wasting economy makes for faster growth.

Still, we have got used to the expression "the circular economy" just as we got used to talking about a "working vacation", though, for some of us, with a similarly unpleasant sense of contradiction or tension. The tension is of a different flavour, though. When vacation gets the new predicate "working", the resulting idea changes employees' behaviour by undermining the concept of what a vacation is and should be. The predicate "circular" does not change or undermine the idea of the economy. Rather, it is the opposite. The expression is more likely to undermine the idea of circularity. This can happen by degree, so that the economy "is" circular if we *try* to reduce waste (but our circularity rate still remains at, say, 14%) and we *try* to reduce the need for virgin resources. Or it can happen by emptying the signifier "circular" from its original meaning, so that "circular economy" can mean anything that for instance the European Union wants it to mean. We are reminded of Humpty Dumpty in Alice in Wonderland. For instance, one of the Eurostat indicators for the circular economy is "Private investments, jobs and gross value added related to circular economy sectors" (https://ec.europa.eu/eurostat/web/circular-economy/indicators/monitoring-framework). By the grace of irony, this indicator indeed has a circular definition.

Emptying and filling the concept with content

When ecological economists get upset by current circular economy policies – and in my personal experience, they do – we can understand their upset in terms of the discussion in the previous section. The question about linearity and circularity of economic activities is an important one in the literature on ecological economics, material flow analysis and bioeconomics, and there have been serious scientific debates going back to the 1970s and 1960s with the Club of Rome, Hermann Daly, Kenneth Boulding, Nicholas Georgescu-Roegen and many others, with predecessors in the 19th and even 18th centuries. When governing bodies such as the EU now claim that their circular economy policies will decouple resource use from economic growth, ecological economists and their like may feel that their body of knowledge is not taken seriously and that the word "circular" is being emptied with meaning. In my opinion, it is not unreasonable to think so.

As soon as a concept has lost its original meaning, it may be filled up again with a new and different meaning. Kirchherr (2017) compiled and analysed 114 different definitions of the circular economy. Zora Kovacic, Thomas Völker and myself (Kovacic et al. 2019) studied how the concept is currently being filled with meaning in policy work within the European Union. In particular, we studied the role of *imaginaries* and *indicators*. By imaginaries, we do not mean fantasies or denials of reality. Imaginaries may be more or less realistic, but their main feature is that they are oriented towards the future: they are future visions of a social and technical order, in the words of Jasanoff and Kim (2015). Especially with regard to innovation and other activities that are intended to create a future that is qualitatively different from the present, the creation of imaginaries is in part *how politics is done* and has to be done. One cannot do a cost-benefit analysis or impact assessment of future technologies and practices before they are even imagined. The emerging imaginaries of the circular economy may have little or nothing to do with what ecological economists have to say about it. They are imaginaries of eco-design, of alternative food and feed sources, of the right to repair, of sophisticated waste management systems and so on. Together with the development of imaginaries, there is a development of indicators to be used to measure and monitor the effects of the policies, such as the above-mentioned monitoring framework of Eurostat. The creation of imaginaries and indicators is not one and the same or necessarily strictly coordinated. The actors are not the same: while innovators, entrepreneurs and perhaps activists may participate in the process of imagining the future. The construction of indicators is more often a task for statisticians and civil servants with other types of technical expertise. Still, the two processes are not independent. Lines of action for which there can be no reliable data will have a disadvantage in the formulation of the policy. One example that has been mentioned in the case of the circular economy is that

Europe has much better data on domestic waste than industrial waste. This can in part explain the focus on domestic waste in the policy.

Irresponsible narratives

Even if the economy cannot be circular – strictly speaking – policies about the right to repair, better waste management or eco-design can be meaningful, legitimate and important. Furthermore, it seems reasonable to subsume them under the same label. If the European Union, China or other countries wish to use the label of the circular economy, why not? It could have been called the elliptic or quadratic economy, or perhaps the downward spiralling economy, but such terms might not have gained much acclaim. Pathos is part of rhetorics, and rhetorics is a legitimate dimension of political life.

The issue becomes more critical when unrealistic claims about the prospects of the circular economy are used to justify political choices. In the Communication on the European Green Deal, it was introduced as:

> a new growth strategy that aims to transform the EU into a fair and prosperous society, with a modern, resource-efficient and competitive economy where there are no net emissions of greenhouse gases in 2050 and where economic growth is decoupled from resource use.
>
> (EC, 2019, p. 2)

The Communication proceeds to identify its circular economy policies as a major component of this new growth strategy and refers to the circular economy 20 times in the document.

At this point, ecological economists, material flow analysts and their like would protest. It is contrary to existing knowledge to claim that economic growth can be decoupled from resource use. It is not legitimate to argue in favour of a policy by stating a goal that is impossible. The narrative, so proposed, is *irresponsible*. We may compare it to Toyota's corporate philosophy of stating impossible goals (Osono et al 2008), for instance to produce a car that would make the air cleaner by driving it. The difference, however, is that decision-makers in Toyota knew and accepted that the goal was impossible. Their reason for stating it was to become inspired. In this sense, it was a kind of poetry.

In the public political sphere, there is also room for inspiration and creativity, but it is irresponsible demagoguery when politicians are not clear on what is poetry and what is intended to be prose. In the Horizon 2020 project MAGIC – Moving towards Adaptive Governance In Complexity (https://magic-nexus.eu/) – Mario Giampietro and coworkers worked to specify the conditions for responsible policy narratives. In order for a policy narrative to qualify as responsible, it should be biophysically feasible and socio-economically viable. These conditions do not hold for the narrative proposed by the Green Deal: Perfect decoupling (and perfect circularity) is known to be biophysically unfeasible. Moreover, a very high degree of (imperfect) circularity is known to be unviable within a larger frame of policies for growth, because it would imply degrowth. As mentioned above, modern societies have grown fast exactly because they were not circular. Turning to the indicators, one can also question how responsible they are in terms of the real challenges of sustainability. In order to answer that question, one needs to study the causal relationships between what the indicators measure and the footprint of these activities on the actual state of the natural environment, ecosystems, climate and so on. As far as I am aware, there is no compelling evidence to conclude that improvements in recycling rates, green public procurement and private investments in the circular economy sector will solve the grand challenges that the Green Deal promises to solve.

Towards a responsible narrative of the circular economy

This book is about impossibilities. It is important to mobilize the courage to dwell for at least some moments in the sustainability challenges faced by our civilization and not immediately jump into solutionist promises. Still, at the end of this chapter, I would like to point towards possibilities. It may be possible to develop different, hitherto underdeveloped, indicators. *What if* Eurostat and other agencies decided to abandon the indicators that are there for historical reasons (because data is available) or for political reasons (because they are very closely linked to the proposed actions)? *What if* for instance ecological economists were put in charge of developing radically different indicators that were not defined in terms of human activity but in terms of ecosystem health and the integrity of what Georgescu-Roegen called biophysical *funds*, that is the naturally regenerating sources of ecosystem services? Perhaps we would like to keep the term "circular economy", but then "circular" would change meaning again, no longer mainly denoting the recycling-like activities in the economy and instead denoting activities to support the integrity of circular processes in nature.

Together with such alternative indicators, one could develop responsible policy narratives, that is, narratives that are both biophysically feasible and socio-economically viable. I would also like to add a third criterion, in line with Mario Giampietro's thinking, namely that a responsible narrative should in some sense be desirable. This is a complicated criterion because what is desirable for some may be very undesirable for others. Here I simply mean it in a weak sense: It is irresponsible to offer nothing but despair for the future. A responsible narrative has to offer some hope.

This recipe may sound trivial. It is not. Hope should not be false hope. In an ongoing collaboration (2020–2021) between the European Environment Agency (EEA) and the European Centre for Governance in Complexity (ECGC), we have developed the concept of *Narratives for Change*, www.eea.europa.eu/themes/sustainability-transitions/drivers-of-change/about-the-series. The underlying idea is an old one, namely that if status quo, the old normal, is unsustainable, our societies have to abandon practices and values that are part of that unsustainable state of affairs in order to sustain practices and values that we deem more important. The first of these narratives was called "Growth without Economic

Growth", and it was published by the EEA in January 2021 (www.eea.europa.eu/publications/growth-without-economic-growth/growth-without-economic-gro wth). Our explicit goal was to develop a responsible narrative in Giampietro's sense that does not deny the stark realities of environmental degradation nor the impossibility of full decoupling of economic growth from resource use, but still maintain that the future may be bright. It may require that society redefines what bright means, however, and adopts a broader concept of progress and growth than just economic growth. The narrative received considerable attention, also in policy circles, even if it expresses sentiments quite different from EU economic policy (Kovacic et al. 2021). The next narrative, published Autumn 2021, took a similar critical perspective on innovation policies and finds hope in the thought that humans are citizens and not just consumers and the prospect that "citizens and governments meet grand challenges also through what they do and not only through what they buy" (Rommetveit et al., 2013, p. 77).

So far, the EEA-ECGC collaboration has not developed a responsible narrative for the circular economy. I believe this to be an important task but also a task that everybody can engage in. From the initial contradiction in terms, the expression was almost emptied of content before it was filled again. The challenge now is to give it a renewed content, content that inspires agency and creativity and at the same time actually can make a difference in the transition to sustainability.

References

Daly, H. E. (2005). Economics in a full world. *Scientific American*, 293(3), 78–85.

European Commission (2019). The European Green Deal. COM(2019) 640 final.

Giampietro, M. (2019). On the circular bioeconomy and decoupling: implications for sustainable growth, *Ecological Economics*, 162, 143–156, https://doi.org/10.1016/j.ecolecon.2019.05.001

Jasanoff, S., & Kim, S.-H. (2015). *Dreamscapes of Modernity: Sociotechnical Imaginaries and the Fabrication of Power*. University of Chicago Press.

Kirchherr, J., Reike, D., & Hekkert, M. (2017) Conceptualizing the circular economy: An analysis of 114 definitions, *Resources, Conservation and Recycling*, 127, 221–232, https://doi.org/10.1016/j.resconrec.2017.09.005.

Kovacic, Z., Strand, R., & Völker, T. (2019). *The Circular Economy in Europe: Critical Perspectives on Policies and Imaginaries* (1st ed.). Routledge. https://doi.org/10.4324/9780429061028

Kovacic, Z., Benini, L.; Jesus, A.; Strand, R., & Funtowicz, S. (2021) When the unspeakable is no longer taboo: growth without economic growth. *Issues in Science and Technology* 37(4), 16–18.

Merriam-Webster. (n.d.). Contradiction in terms. In Merriam-Webster.com dictionary. Retrieved November 9, 2021, from www.merriam-webster.com/dictionary/contradiction%20in%20terms

Osono, E., Shimizu, N., & Takeuchi, H. (2008). *Extreme Toyota: Radical Contradictions That Drive Success at the World's Best Manufacturer*. Wiley & Sons.

Rommetveit, Kjetil, Strand, R., Fjelland, R., Funtowicz, S., & Saltelli, A. (2013). *What can history teach us about the prospects of a European Research Area?* https://doi.org/10.2788/1057

12 Who has discursive agency to change global environmental narratives?

Insights from the China–EU cooperation discourse on circular economy

Anran Luo

Introduction

A circular economy (CE) is impossible given the inability of key stakeholders to co-create narratives that enable communication or negotiation of political differences in current governance systems at national, supranational and international scales (Leipold, 2021; Luo et al., 2021; Simoens & Leipold, 2021). CE scholars have argued that international cooperation is particularly important for upscaling the CE from fragmented networks to the macro systems required to achieve its resource efficiency and waste management goals (Geng et al., 2019; Haas et al., 2015). For example, cooperation is needed to set up platforms to share data and experiences as well as to coordinate industrial policies and trade (Geng et al., 2019). While other chapters in this book tackle the impossibilities of a CE based on thermodynamics and entropy (Corvellec et al., 2021; Cullen, 2017), this chapter takes the CE's biophysical constraints as a given and adds to the repertoire of CE critiques from a socio-political perspective (Man & Friege, 2016; Rincón-Moreno et al., 2020). It assesses the political impossibilities of CE based on policy goals of curbing excessive resource extraction and waste generation as stated by the European Union (EU) and China—two CE frontrunners who have been developing CE policy programs within their own jurisdictions (Flynn et al., 2019; McDowall et al., 2017).

Many CE practitioners consider the Memorandum of Understanding (MoU) on CE between China and the EU as a milestone towards global efforts to address pressing environmental problems of extraction, resource use and waste management (Ellen MacArthur Foundation, 2018). However, Luo et al. (2021) show that the cooperation could not move beyond rhetorical agreement to institutionalization and practice. Specifically, the optimist market discourse coalition relied on eco-modernist win-win narratives that depoliticized market exchange and made addressing underlying political tensions an impossible task for the sceptical market discourse coalition. Luo et al. (2021) recommend identifying narrative strategies, or strategic practices, to repoliticize environmental cooperations. Repoliticization is defined as a process involving strategic practices that would support contestation and negotiation on development disparities and open

DOI: 10.4324/9781003244196-14

channels for joint conceptualization of implementation scales for environmental strategies.

This chapter builds on Luo et al. (2021)'s discourse analysis of the first international CE cooperation, which uses the MoU and the preceding EU CE Mission to China as entry points (European Commission and Chinese Development and Reform Commission, 2018). While the former study analyses institutions, narratives and discourse coalitions in the China–EU CE cooperation case, this chapter focuses on stakeholder perspectives of agents, agency and their strategic practices through the Discursive Agency Approach (DAA) (Leipold & Winkel, 2017) and addresses the following research questions:

1. Who do stakeholders perceive to have agency in China–EU CE cooperation?
2. How do these agents' strategic practices support or hinder repoliticizing the cooperation?

As narratives shape countries' sustainability policies, they are therefore also significant for international coordination on such policies (Leipold et al., 2019). Considering stakeholder positions within these narratives is therefore of great importance for understanding communication gridlocks in international cooperation as it creates a political impossibility for a CE. While identifying agents with transformative power and their strategic practices cannot make the impossible possible, it may provide insights for future environmental cooperation, circular or otherwise.

The chapter is structured according to the following: The following section explains the materials and methods. Section 'Background' gives an overview of the China–EU CE cooperation based on Luo et al. (2021). Section 'Results' builds on Section 'Background', offering an in-depth analysis of agents, agency and strategic practices. Based on the findings, Section 'Discussion' discusses thought spaces for possible pathways for repoliticizing the China–EU CE cooperation and implications for wider environmental politics. The final section concludes.

Materials and methods

This study collected data from key policy, industry, research and NGO stakeholders from international, Chinese and European institutions whose work is related to CE efforts between China and the EU between October 2017 and August 2019. The data set comprises:

- 20 explorative interviews
- 72 semi-structured interviews conducted primarily in Brussels and Beijing, with a select few in Geneva, Helsinki, the Netherlands and Shanghai
    - between 30 and 120 minutes in length
    - 61 were recorded and transcribed
    - 11 could not be recorded because interviewees did not give consent; these have been documented using on-site notes as well as follow-up memory protocol

- 40 documents related to China–EU CE (e.g., environmental dialogues, joint declarations and event programs, press releases, speeches, media articles and publications)
- Participant observation at the International Circular Economy Conference and Exhibition in Beijing (November 2017), Circular Economy Stakeholder Conference in Brussels (March 2019), and the World Circular Economy Forum in Helsinki (June 2019)

The data was analysed by coding the data based on the categories provided by the DAA (Leipold & Winkel, 2017) using MAXQDA. The DAA is based on established discourse analytical theories and analysis techniques while setting a particular focus on agents and strategic practices in discursive policy-making. This makes it a useful heuristic for guiding our analysis of understanding discursive gridlock from stakeholder perspectives and exploring alternative pathways for repoliticizing environmental cooperation.

DAA understands political debates as struggles over interpretations. To present a specific 'political truth' (e.g., what it means for China and the EU to cooperate on CE successfully), stakeholders need to define who they are in relation to the overall discourse (e.g., the discourse about the cooperation) and justify why they should have a voice. To define their discursive position, stakeholders create narratives in which they present their interpretation of the issue and ascribe certain characteristics to themselves and others. Since there are often many stakeholders involved, discourses are characterized by multiple narratives communicating competing truths. Thus, the discursive agency is essentially established if agents become perceived as relevant speakers offering a pertinent political truth. Political stakeholders who seek discursive agency use language and act in certain ways to create a relevant position for themselves and support their position and the connected political truths. I refer to this latter step as strategic practices, including coalition building, discursive strategies, rationalization, scientification and exclusion strategies (cf. Leipold & Winkel, 2017).

To assure the protection of interviewees' personal data, aggregated stakeholder categories (e.g., A = academic institutions) have been developed for the purpose of referencing direct quotes in this article (see Table 12.2). The interviews in each category were numbered according to the interview date (e.g., A1 = first interviewee from this category, P7 = seventh interviewee from this category). The codes do not represent the order of interviewees' affiliations presented in Table 12.2.

Background

The institutional context leading up to China–EU CE cooperation

China–EU CE cooperation is predated by the two political actors' respective CE trajectories that shifted responsibility towards economic institutions and business and trade frameworks. This is evidenced by the key actors involved and the institutional process that led up to the MoU.

In China, CE achieved national recognition in 2002 through projects under the State Environmental Protection Agency (subsequently reorganized into the Ministry of Ecology and Environment since 2018). China's 11th Five-Year Plan (2006–2010) made CE its explicit goal, which led to the CE Promotion Law of 2008 and an expansion of CE pilots (State Council of the People's Republic of China, 2013). As the National Development and Reform Commission (NDRC) became the main government body responsible for CE (Chinese National Development and Reform Commission, 2015), its CE work is supported significantly by the China Association of CE (CACE) and its advisors, many of whom are scientists from top Chinese academic institutions (China Association of Circular Economy, 2014).

In Europe, CE promotion began with the EU CE Action Plan of 2015 (European Commission, 2015). Alongside the European Commission's Directorate-General for Environment (DG ENV) and for Internal Market, Industry, Entrepreneurship and SMEs (DG GROW), NGOs such as the Ellen MacArthur Foundation, and specific strands of the business community, represented by Business Europe have also been key CE stakeholders in the EU (Leipold, 2021).

In 2016, the EU began its CE Missions, a series of 'high-level political and business meetings to communicate and promote sustainable and resource-efficient policies' (European Commission, no date), with China as one of the CE Missions' first target countries. This Mission was coordinated together with the CACE in Beijing and attended by many EU industry associations, business representatives, NGOs and academics and select China–EU business groups. The Dutch representation in the EU delegation was perceived to be CE frontrunners and particularly influential in China–EU CE discussions. Scholars from several Chinese academic institutions were also perceived as particularly influential in facilitating China–EU CE discussions (Luo et al., 2021).

The CE Mission in China paved the way for the signing of the CE MoU in 2018 at the 20th China–EU Summit. While the MoU is not legally binding, it is significant because it is the first official joint declaration of intent from China and the EU to begin high-level cooperation on CE. Various international organizations, including the World Economic Forum (WEF), the United Nations Conference on Trade and Development (UNCTAD) and the Organisation for Economic Cooperation and Development (OECD), applauded the signing of the CE MoU from the sidelines (cf. Luo et al., 2021).

Table 12.1 shows the main CE-related actors in China and the EU as well as those related to the China–EU CE MoU according to interviews, documents and participant observation data.

China–EU CE discourse coalitions, narratives and actors

Luo et al. (2021) demonstrate two discourse coalitions as shown in Figure 12.1: 'CE Market Optimists' ('Optimists') and 'CE Market Sceptics' ('Sceptics'). The 'Optimists' comprise actors who use optimistic CE narratives to structure their arguments for how a market-driven China–EU CE cooperation would be beneficial for all parties: the EU, China, the economy and the economy in the

Table 12.1 Main CE-related actors in the EU, China and for the China–EU CE Memorandum of Understanding according to interviews, documents and participant observation data

EU	*China*	*International*
European Commission (DG ENV and GROW)	National Development and Reform Commission (NDRC)	WEF
Ellen MacArthur Foundation	China Association of Circular Economy (CACE)—under NDRC	UNCTAD
Business Europe	Chinese academic institutions—e.g., Tsinghua, Tongji University	OECD
GIZ in China	Chinese Ministry of Industry and Information Technology	
EU Delegation in China	Ministry of Ecology & Environment	
Dutch Embassy in China		

context of trade promotional practices and the environment. European and international actors drew more on these narratives, especially favouring 'CE as Trade Cooperation' and 'Market Exchange'. In particular, European actors affiliated with industry trade associations, policy actors in the Commission, the Dutch government, an EU member state embassy representative in China, regional governments, NGOs such as the Ellen MacArthur Foundation, but also international organizations including UNCTAD, WTO, OECD, the International Resource Panel and the Bureau of International Recycling drew on optimist narratives. Chinese actors also subscribed to optimist narratives, especially that of 'CE Tech Exchange' and 'CE as Trade Cooperation'. This optimist discourse coalition converges actors' diverse understandings of CE behind an optimistic perception that China–EU business and regulatory cooperation will boost the trade of circular goods and services on a global market, thereby resulting in positive diplomatic, economic and environmental outcomes.

'Sceptics' is a discourse coalition ascribing to sceptical CE narratives that are critical of the trade cooperation meta-narrative the 'Optimists' favour. They question whether a market-driven CE between the EU and China can achieve cooperation goals given bilateral tensions. Institutional actors from policy, research and NGOs draw on sceptical narratives of 'Development Disparity' and 'Distrust' more than industry actors, while industry actors subscribe more to narratives of 'Negative Competition'. Specifically, the discourse coalition comprises Chinese actors conducting research for government and in environmental NGO; European policy actors working in China: at embassies, on China–EU environmental cooperation projects, and in NGOs; actors from international NGOs such as Greenpeace and ICLEI; as well as some industry actors from non-plastic trade associations, e.g., metals. 'Sceptics' did not propose clear solutions other than suggesting more educational and cultural exchange is needed between China and the EU to foster greater mutual understanding.

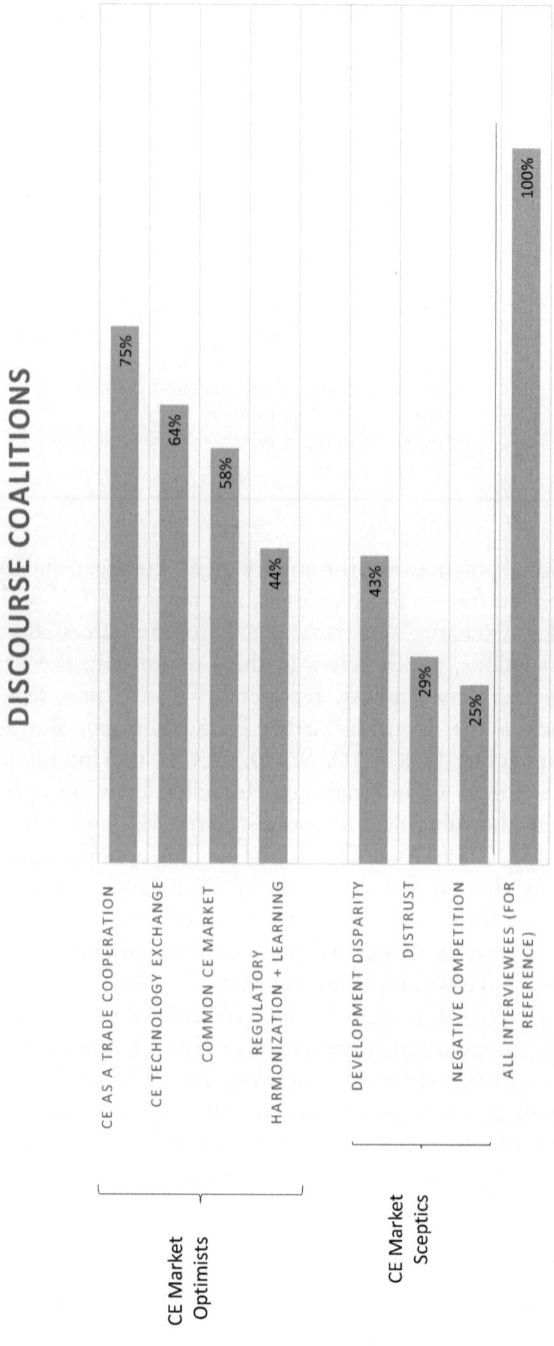

Figure 12.1 Optimist and sceptic discourse coalitions and corresponding narratives.
Source: Adapted from Luo et al. (2021).

Results

In Section 'The institutional context leading up to China–EU CE cooperation', I presented information on the key institutions and actors that paved the way for the CE MoU. Section 'China–EU CE discourse coalitions, narratives and actors' briefly summarized the optimist and sceptic cooperation discourse coalitions and their narratives between China and the EU after the 2018 CE MoU. In the following section, I explain the optimist and sceptic discourse coalitions through discursive agents and their strategic practices. All results are based on the interviews, documents and participant observation.

Official and industry agents: 'coalition building' and 'exclusion' strategies for win-win trade narratives

In the official China–EU CE cooperation, primarily the EU CE Mission and the CE MoU, stakeholders identify 'China' and 'the EU' as discursive agents, but sometimes also name the NDRC and DG ENV as their ministerial representation. In particular, the EU Commission is perceived to assist in providing a bridging platform for EU businesses, both multinationals and SMEs, to China. As a Commission representative expressed,

> (CE) It is one—one positive topic—positive cooperation topic for—for, I mean, for EU and China. If we can move together, we can do something positive for the planet, that's how people will—will be happy of and positive for (EU) companies ... and we hope that there will be business-to-business cooperation (EU_P2).

EU member states and their own delegations are considered to have similar functions though at a more regional and local level. EU industry associations, especially 'green' businesses within Europe, are portrayed as winners of the CE market cooperation as well as strategic partners. For example, when referring to the CE Mission, Umicore and Dutch firms are often touted as CE best practices and as CE leaders (e.g., EU_I3, EU_NGO1, EU_P17). International organizations such as WEF and UNCTAD are also identified as bridging private-public cooperation (e.g., IO_4, IO_1) as well as connecting with international NGOs such as the Ellen MacArthur Foundation. The WTO is seen as a traditional platform for closed-door discussions between official agents on matters of CE trade (e.g., IO_8, IO_4).

'Coalition building' is an important strategy, especially for official agents in the China–EU CE cooperation as the diplomatic success of the CE Mission and the subsequent MoU relied on this practice. Chinese and EU government actors are both keen to be politically correct and thereby stick to the win-win trade narratives (EU_I32, EU_P1, EU_P2, EU_P3)—especially in the context of official CE Missions. 'Rationalization and scientification' strategies are employed to promote the optimist CE narratives as the business sense of CE through technological efficiency; increasing trade and fostering policy exchange are linked to its scientific foundations (CH_I5, EU_I1, CH_I4, EU_P13, EU_I15, EU_NGO5). The cooperation is further legitimated as scientific, backed by data from the International Resource Panel, and is therefore an obvious cooperation point for China and the EU (European Commission and Chinese Development and Reform Commission, 2018). Agents also often 'employ normative power' as CE cooperation will benefit the world: China and the EU can fight for the Sustainable Development Goals together, for example, by combating marine litter and climate change (Luo et al., 2021).

Market-optimist stakeholders actively use 'exclusion' strategies to justify why actors such as the Chinese Ministry of Ecology and Environment and other ministries related to key CE functions are not part of the China–EU CE cooperation. This is done by either articulating that it is the most sensible action for the NDRC to be the only Chinese counterpart on this cooperation and explaining that the trade cooperation will enable China and the EU to access 'low-hanging fruits' such as technology exchange (e.g., IO_4), and bypass any potential intra-ministry political conflicts (e.g., EU_P4). Yet, market-sceptic stakeholders express that excluded actors, such as the Chinese Ministry of Ecology and Environment, could be key to changing the narratives by connecting CE to other environmental concepts and narratives such as low carbon and climate narratives. Excluded industry and social agents, primarily small Chinese waste management firms and 'waste-pickers' engaged in the informal waste sector, are perceived to be the 'losers' as they have no role to play in the CE market exchange between China and the EU.

Unofficial agents have the potential to bridge differences between official agents

Another group of discursive agents, though in a non-official capacity, are perceived to have the potential to bridge diverging understandings between official agents. They include international NGOs working to promote CE, where EMF especially stands out from this group to have strong agency; Chinese academics, here especially CE scholars from top universities such as Tsinghua, are seen to be influential; international organizations such as the OECD, WEF, UNCTAD and ICLEI are also seen to play a bridging role between official agents from the EU and China. While these agents often express barriers to the win-win trade cooperation by emphasizing development disparities, distrust or negative competition, they often fall back on solutions from the optimist discourse coalition and do not propose alternatives. However, they are seen to have the knowledge, cultural background and networks to be able to bridge diverging discourse coalitions and to include currently excluded or external actors (EU_NGO3, EU_NGO4, EU_NGO5, EU_P16, EU_P17, CH_I2, CH_P4, CH_I4, CH_R5, IO_10). These agents have the potential to use such 'coalition bridging' and 'inclusion' strategies to open up new channels of communication.

Discussion

The results from the China–EU CE cooperation narratives suggest that future research should explore the strategic practices of 'coalition bridging' and 'inclusion', discovered through this analysis. Such strategies should be linked to the better-known strategy of 'coalition building' for repoliticizing environmental cooperation in the international context. The core difference between the two is that 'coalition bridging' does not focus on achieving shared narratives or consensus building but rather focuses on providing a discursive space for communication, contestation, negotiation and empathy development. The goal of such a practice is not necessarily cooperation but rather a greater mutual understanding of differences, identifying suitable areas for cooperation and establishing contingency plans for areas of conflict.

This takeaway is based on three main findings, which are as follows:

1) Agents with bridging capacities, the ability to build platforms for communication between different discourse coalitions or stakeholder groups, are perceived to have agency.
2) However, agents who exclusively bridge government and business stakeholder groups enact strategic practices of 'coalition building', 'rationalization and scientification', 'employing normative power', and 'exclusion strategies' focus on achieving win-win trade goals through the optimist narratives and thus depoliticize the cooperation by avoiding underlying political tensions.
3) Agents who seek to bridge government and business to other stakeholder groups, including excluded agents through 'coalition bridging' and 'inclusion strategies' are perceived to have more chances of bringing new elements into the China–EU CE cooperation.

Based on this analysis, discursive agents with the following characteristics may have transformative agency, be well-suited to bridge coalitions and should be prioritized when engaging in bilateral communications for CE or other environmental cooperation.

1) Agents with access to knowledge (e.g., academics);
2) Agents with experience from multiple cultures (agents working in international organizations, agencies who regularly engage with individuals in multiple cultures);
3) Agents with access to large multi-stakeholder networks;
4) International agents with networks to both official and unofficial agents.

Conclusion

Identifying transformative agents and their strategic practices is not enough to make the impossible possible, but it is a first step in the direction to enable new narratives in CE or other environmental cooperation. These findings enhance our understanding of opportunities and challenges for developing narratives that can bridge development disparities between global political actors such as the EU and China, as well as build trust and new mutual environmental identities that drive coordination instead of negative competition. They suggest that official agents' 'coalition building' strategies to connect on 'win-win' market narratives and 'exclusion' strategies to avoid conflicts make it impossible to open channels of negotiation and contestation to discuss political differences necessary for CE cooperation. While unofficial agents hold transformative agency and potential to bridge diverging narratives and include excluded actors, their desire to bridge coalitions often results in 'coalition building': they end up taking up or falling back on dominant win-win narratives.

The results of this study highlight the importance of official agents to make space for unofficial agents to voice new ideas on the one hand, and for transformative agents to find ways to enact 'coalition bridging' without 'coalition building'. This analysis further introduces two strategic practices in addition to those provided for in the DAA typologies: 'coalition bridging' and 'inclusion strategies'. These strategies serve as both analytical tools for further research and practical guides for decision-makers on the ground. To repoliticize CE as environmental cooperation between China and the EU and to pave the way for bringing in new narratives, it is crucial for agents to open up discursive spaces for communicating areas of difference and to bridge active stakeholder groups with excluded stakeholder groups.

Table 12.2 List of interviewees (anonymized and abbreviated)

Affiliation	*Number*	*Abbreviations*
International		
- International Organizations (governmental and non-governmental)	10	IO_1
China		
- Chinese Policy Institutions (Chinese embassies and governmental research institutes)	7	CH_P1
- Chinese Research Institutions	9	CH_R1
- Chinese Industry Associations and Businesses	5	CH_I1
- Chinese Environmental Non-Governmental Organizations	1	CH_NGO1
Europe		
- European Policy Institutions (European Commission, European embassies, Dutch government, regional governments, development agencies and projects)	18	EU_P1
- European Industry Associations and Businesses	15	EU_I1
- European Non-Governmental Organizations	6	EU_NGO1
- European Research Institutions	1	EU_R1
Total	72	

References

China Association of Circular Economy. (2014). *中国循环经济大事记*. China Association of Circular Economy.

Corvellec, H., Stowell, A. F., & Johansson, N. (2021). Critiques of the circular economy. *Journal of Industrial Ecology*. Advance online publication. https://doi.org/10.1111/jiec.13187

Cullen, J. M. (2017). Circular Economy: Theoretical Benchmark or Perpetual Motion Machine? *Journal of Industrial Ecology*, *21*(3), 483–486. https://doi.org/10.1111/jiec.12599

Ellen MacArthur Foundation. (2018). China-EU agreement paves way for global adoption of circular economy.

European Commission. (no date). *Circular Economy Missions to Third Countries*. European Commission. https://ec.europa.eu/environment/international_issues/missions_en.htm#:~:text=The%20Circular%20Economy%20Missions%20are%20conceived%20with%20three,public%20procurement%20and%20innovative%2C%20sustainable%20and%20inclusive%20growth.

European Commission and Chinese Development and Reform Commission. (July 2018). *Memorandum of Understanding on Circular Economy*. https://ec.europa.eu/environment/circular-economy/pdf/circular_economy_MoU_EN.pdf

Flynn, A., Hacking, N., & Xie, L. (2019). Governance of the circular economy: A comparative examination of the use of standards by China and the United Kingdom. *Environmental Innovation and Societal Transitions*, 33, 282–300. https://doi.org/10.1016/j.eist.2019.08.002

Geng, Y., Sarkis, J., & Bleischwitz, R. (2019). How to globalize the circular economy. *Nature*, 565(7738), 153–155. https://doi.org/10.1038/d41586-019-00017-z

Haas, W., Krausmann, F., Wiedenhofer, D., & Heinz, M. (2015). How Circular is the Global Economy? An Assessment of Material Flows, Waste Production, and Recycling in the European Union and the World in 2005. *Journal of Industrial Ecology*, *19*(5), 765–777. https://doi.org/10.1111/jiec.12244

Leipold, S. (2021). Transforming ecological modernization 'from within' or perpetuating it? The circular economy as EU environmental policy narrative. *Environmental Politics*, *30*(6), 1045–1067. https://doi.org/10.1080/09644016.2020.1868863

Leipold, S., & Winkel, G. (2017). Discursive Agency: (Re-)Conceptualizing Actors and Practices in the Analysis of Discursive Policymaking. *Policy Studies Journal*, 45(3), 510–534. https://doi.org/10.1111/psj.12172

Leipold, S., Feindt, P. H., Winkel, G., & Keller, R. (2019). Discourse analysis of environmental policy revisited: traditions, trends, perspectives. *Journal of Environmental Policy & Planning*, *21*(5), 445–463. https://doi.org/10.1080/1523908X.2019.1660462

Luo, A., Zuberi, M., Liu, J., Perrone, M., Schnepf, S., & Leipold, S. (2021). Why common interests and collective action are not enough for environmental cooperation—Lessons from the China-EU cooperation discourse on circular economy. *Global Environmental Change*, *71*, 102389. https://doi.org/10.1016/j.gloenvcha.2021.102389

Man, R. de, & Friege, H. (2016). Circular economy: European policy on shaky ground. *Waste Management & Research: The Journal of the International Solid Wastes and Public Cleansing Association, ISWA*, 34(2), 93–95. https://doi.org/10.1177/0734242X15626015

McDowall, W., Geng, Y., Huang, B., Barteková, E., Bleischwitz, R., Türkeli, S., Kemp, R., & Doménech, T. (2017). Circular Economy Policies in China and Europe. *Journal of Industrial Ecology*, *21*(3), 651–661. https://doi.org/10.1111/jiec.12597

Rincón-Moreno, J., Ormazabal, M., Álvarez, M. J., & Jaca, C. (2020). Shortcomings of Transforming a Local Circular Economy System through Industrial Symbiosis: A Case Study in Spanish SMEs. *Sustainability*, *12*(20), 8423. https://doi.org/10.3390/su12208423

Simoens, M. C., & Leipold, S. (2021). Trading radical for incremental change: the politics of a circular economy transition in the German packaging sector. *Journal of Environmental Policy & Planning*, *23*(6), 822–836. https://doi.org/10.1080/1523908X.2021.1931063

State Council of the People's Republic of China. (2013). *国务院关于印发循环经济发展战略及近期行动计划的通知*. www.gov.cn/zwgk/2013-02/ 05/content2327562.htm

13 Brazil's structural issues in advancing the circular economy

The case of biogas

Laís Forti Thomaz, Nathália Fernandes Pimentel, and Suzana Borshiver

Introduction

In the last few years, a new trend that entails a transition from a linear economy to a circular one has surfaced (McDonough & Braungart, 2002; Roös, 2021; Oliveira et al., 2020). On this matter, the idea of "waste-to-energy" can be defended as a strategy to circularity, including biogas initiatives (Barros et al., 2020; Bernal et al., 2017; Ximenes et al., 2021).

Circular economy (CE) has been identified as an important approach towards urban development solutions. Therefore, implementing CE within a resource-orientated sanitation and waste systems context could provide outcomes in relation to CO_2 emissions, sustainable urban waste management and environmental benefits (Ddiba et al. 2020b). They could incentivize the production of resources such as clean water and energy and the reduction of residue and sewage (Ddiba et al., 2020b).

Although there are many different views on CE, one of the most accepted definitions was created by Ellen MacArthur Foundation (EMF) and it states:

> A circular economy is an industrial system that is restorative or regenerative by intention and design. It replaces the "end-of-life" concept with restoration, shifts towards the use of renewable energy, eliminates the use of toxic chemicals, which impair reuse, and aims for the elimination of waste through the superior design of materials, products, systems, and, within this, business models.
>
> (EMF, 2013, p. 7)

This concept implies the need for a cooperative ecosystem, in which stakeholders from different industries can communicate with each other to create a continuous flow of materials, as it is described in the "power of cascaded use" section of EMF's 2013 report. On this matter, authors have criticized the inability to have a more holistic perspective within the concept to reach just that: different sectors coordinating at one cohesive system (Homrich et al. 2018).

DOI: 10.4324/9781003244196-15

Furthermore, other difficulties emerge from disregarding the three dimensions of sustainable development: social, economic, and sustainable (Kirchherr et al., 2017); or from failing to understand the complexity of public governance at local level (Ddiba et al., 2020a). In this regard, ecosystems are a relevant topic because the concept refers to the idea of dissipation of energy amongst different actors, considering the interdependence between multiple industry sectors and producing an outcome greater than the actions of individual initiatives.

CE initiatives may be developed in many shapes. An example can be found in biogas, a renewable energy produced from urban waste management and provides solutions to several urban issues in its process. Waste Management and Greenhouse Gas (GHG) emissions reduction can be achieved by implementing biogas. Its technology may also be combined with others, such as green hydrogen, to promote a more sustainable energy grid.

Obtained through an anaerobic digestion process from several possible feedstocks, biogas can be treated and develop other subproducts for numerous other demands. Through upgrading, biogas can be transformed into biomethane, which will be a substitute for natural gas in all its roles (Santos et al., 2018). After upgrading, the remaining byproduct could be used as fertilizer, reducing fossil fuel demands for its production (IEA, 2020).

Studies that analysed the Brazilian entrepreneur ecosystem identified a low level of interaction between institutions and individual initiatives (Inácio Júnior et al., 2016). This challenge, combined with several structural national/regional issues, makes it difficult to visualize a CE implementation within the Brazilian context, especially in the public sector. Such problematics will be further discussed in the following sections of the chapter but are related to geographical, political, technological, and entrepreneur matters.

The potential vs the reality of Biogas in Brazil

Biogas has reached its full production potential neither in Brazil nor worldwide. The global capacity to produce biogas and biomethane is extensive. If effectively used, biogas could guarantee 20% of the global demand for gas. Considering Brazil's potential, in 2017, only 0,83% of the national biomass was met, with 15 biogas power plants producing 114.7 MW of power totally (Santos et al., 2018). In comparison with other European countries' approaches, Brazil's initiatives are insufficient. Nevertheless, biogas and biomethane production is increasing its applicability and, by 2040, its feedstock should grow up to 40% (IEA, 2020).

However, public policies, technology development, and fossil fuels discouragement are necessary for a transition towards sustainability. Within this framework, low-interest rates for the initial investment, lack of support from the government and agribusiness cooperatives, wrong destination of waste, and unfamiliarity with the waste to generate financial and environmental gains are some of the gaps to implement biogas successfully (Barros et al. 2020). Even demonstrating the relevance of public policies and feedstocks for its implementation, the political, technological, and historical aspects of the absence of biogas in Brazil's energy grid (Assunção et al., 2021).

Analysing thoroughly, Brazil's biogas framework is mainly composed of initiatives in agriculture and cattle industries. Brazil is considered an agricultural and livestock power worldwide (Ritchie & Roser, 2020). Several projects have been implemented regarding such stock sources. Furthermore, biogas has a decentralized potential for energy production (FNR, 2013). Ionescu et al. (2013) demonstrated the potential of adopting anaerobic digestion of food waste and sewage sludge to generate energy for the domestic setting. Bernal et al. (2017) and Barros et al. (2020) have presented that biogas production is neither dependent on geographical location nor requires complex or monopolistic technologies.

Biogas can also be implemented as a strategy in rural areas for waste management and tackling poverty within family farms. However, their income is often below the minimum wage, and they struggle with issues related to disposal, including inappropriate measures, such as incineration and grounding. Implementing truly CE strategies within this context could help mitigate their environmental impacts (Velden et al., 2021).

Within the private sector, the number of biogas plants has increased substantially over the years and also their production. From 2008 to 2019, there was an almost 2000% increase in the number of biogas plants in Brazil, while biogas production escalated by more than 900% (EPE, 2020). Although Brazilian biogas production only reached 1,5% of the estimated national potential in 2018 (Abiogás, 2018). In 2019, biogas plants operated mainly with agriculture and livestock sources, representing 79% of the plants' total (Table 13.1). Also, 44 biogas plants were related to urban waste management, representing 8% of Brazil's total which corresponded to 76% of total biogas production, demonstrating its potential if truly used throughout the country (Cibiogás, 2019).

Brazil's set of impossibilities regarding circular economy

Most of Brazil's harnessed potential is related to the private sector. Biogas plants mainly utilize agriculture and livestock resources and waste regardless of lower efficiency in comparison with urban waste solutions. The reasons behind this scenario are vast and will be covered in this section of the chapter. They are related to the lack of (i) cultural and economic incentives for biogas implementation in Brazil; (ii) cooperation between stakeholders in both private and public sectors; (iii) access to knowledge and technology; and (iv) geographical and cultural coherence amongst different regions in the country. All issues are related to historical and structural problems that have been in place during the entirety of Brazil's history and are unlikely or very difficult to change.

First, as aforementioned, there is a lack of biogas incentives, especially in comparison to other biofuels, especially ethanol and biodiesel. Within Brazil's context, biogas' first steps date back to the 1970s. The Energy Mobilization Program is highlighted amongst such projects and entailed the production of biogas within small farms. Although the technology was initially embraced throughout the rural area, most farmers abandoned the idea after a few years because of the lack of a specialized workforce. Furthermore, without a biogas market, farmers could not profit from such production and with lower prices of fossil fuels, it was quickly dismissed (Zanatta, 2020). Therefore, since the beginning of biogas' implementation process, the public sector was not in focus.

Furthermore, it is important to analyse Brazil's energy grid to understand the role biogas could have on this matter. In 2001 and 2013, Brazil faced two massive energy crises due to low hydropower supply – and it is facing again in 2021. In response, Brazil's policy broadened the hydroelectric power production as well as thermal power facilities, as opposed to other alternative energy sources such as biogas. It is estimated that climate change should reduce up to 36% of hydropower productivity. In the 2010s, some of Brazilians' federal units promoted the biogas sector, but incentives within the federal government were insufficient (Prado et al., 2016; Sebrae, 2021).

Therefore, Brazil's energy tradition evolves around hydro and thermal power, and there are no incentives for a more diverse energy matrix, financially or culturally speaking. Furthermore, internationally, Brazil is recognized for its renewable energy grid, although hydropower energy has its consequences on biodiversity and forest preservation. Within this context, there is no reason for international pressure to occur, lowering the incentives for such systematic change.

Second, a culture of cooperation within multiple sectors in Brazil is practically non-existent. Most biogas production relies on big agricultural and cattle companies without any cooperation with other sectors. Although developing an ecosystem of cooperation would be necessary for the achievement of CE within Brazil (Aarikka-Stenroos et al., 2021), most initiatives work in closed-loop solutions. Even considering the importance of closed-loop projects within the agriculture sector, such as cassava processing (Lin et al, 2021), sectors should be incentivized to cooperate towards circularity.

However, as little coordination within Brazilian governance is observed, such a collaboration framework will not be developed. Also, as CE is seen as a path to reduce the expenditure of private sector companies, such a required ecosystem cannot develop spontaneously. This occurrence is not only related to the biogas sector but can be seen in a broader analysis of the cooperation ecosystem within Brazil's sectors and provides yet another structural issue within the country's context (Inácio Júnior et al., 2016).

Third, technological matters should be considered. Several types of reactors are used in Brazil, depending on the sector they are located in. For example, Continuous Flow Stirred Tank Reactors are the main technology for anaerobic digestion, used mainly by agricultural, industrial, and sanitation sectors. Lagoons are also used by these sectors. Upflow Anaerobic Sludge Blanket Reactors are efficiently used in Brazil within the industrial and sanitary sector, feasible due to the Brazilian tropical climate. However, related to urban waste management, the technologies employed either require a more systematic waste collection or a more expensive investment in technology. Both cases are dependent on the municipality's infrastructure, which is scarce and limited (Brasil, 2015). Thus, the public sector experiences challenges towards the implementation of biogas.

Apart from that, urban waste management is disorganized, and regulations are still in progress. Although the National Policy on Solid Waste (PNRS) was adopted in 2010, its implementation was recently redacted in 2020, postponing its implementation up to 2024, dependent on the municipality (Brasil, 2010; 2007; 2020). PNRS is an important regulatory landmark once it presents waste as an economic resource to be actively reused and with the ability to promote social changes. However, it also burdens the municipalities with the process of correct disposal of residues, implementing landfills instead of dumps (Zanatta 2020; Oliveira & Negro, 2019). Hence, the cost of proper residue management is also observed as a challenge in the implementation of biogas.

In 2017, another legislation also supported biomethane provided by landfills and sewage treatment centres to be used in vehicle use and the energy grid (ANP, 2017; 2015). Sanctioned in 2018, the National Biofuels Policy (RenovaBio) also provides a valuable resource for promoting biogas use for transportation. The 2021 Future Fuel Program also had the potential to create conditions for the expansion of the biogas (Brasil, 2021). However, there is still no relevant legislation that specifically deals with biogas in the federal sphere. On November 3, 2021, Deputy Arnaldo Jardim introduced a bill (# 3865/2021) related to biogas incentives.

The potential of urban waste in Brazil is tremendous: in 2018, it produced 79 million tons of municipal solid waste. However, from this amount, little is harnessed. Recycling was responsible for only 2,2% of these materials, while 24,4% was improperly designated and 59,5% went to landfills. Even if landfills sum up almost 60% of the urban waste destinations, biogas production is almost insignificant. The main reason is that few landfills have any kind of material recovery approach. In 2018, of the 621 operating landfills, 22 operated with biogas plants associated with electricity generation. This represents 3,5% of the landfills and 0,08% of the Brazilian energy grid. Furthermore, 13,9% of the municipal solid waste in 2018 is unaccounted for (Mancini et al., 2021).

This brings the topic to another challenge in the Brazilian context: inequality between regions. Although the number of plants has been increasing over the years, most of them are in the South and Southeast regions. Considering the number of biogas plants and the production per year, some states are highlighted (Table 13.1).

As important agriculture and livestock states, Minas Gerais, Paraná, and Goiás are ranked within the five states in the number of biogas plants. Many of the north and northeast regions states did not operate biogas plants in 2019. By 2020, the scenario did not suffer major changes, apart from developing a biogas plant at Pará- northern state. São Paulo is highlighted even if it only hosts 8,4% of Brazilian biogas plants. Goiás and Santa Catarina are excluded from the five most prominent states, and Rio de Janeiro and Pernambuco take their place. The reasons behind this are related to the source of biogas production. Hosting 37,4% of all biogas plants in Brazil, Minas Gerais was responsible for producing only

Table 13.1 Biogas overview by Brazilian Federal Units (2019)

States	*Biogas production*			*Power plants*		*Number of power plants by source*		
	Total (Nm^3/year)	*Percentage (%)*	*Potential*	*Number*	*Percentage (%)*	*Agriculture and livestock*	*Industry*	*Urban waste*
Region: Midwest								
DF	2.114.558	0,16		3	0,57	3		
GO	20.945.021	1,54		38	7,25	35	2	1
MS	20.441.375	1,51		19	3,63	15	4	
MT	27.000.055	1,99		26	4,96	26		
Region: Northeast								
BA	6.394.990	0,47		3	0,57		1	2
CE	31.583.674	2,33		2	0,38	1		1
MA	4.204.800	0,31		1	0,19			1
PB	26.280.000	1,94		1	0,19			1
PE	102.699.253	7,57		5	0,95			5
Region: North								
AM	26.280.000	1,94		1	0,19			1
TO	243.582	0,02		2	0,38	2		
Region: Southeast								
ES	831.307	0,06		2	0,38	2		
MG	163.690.944	12,07		196	37,40	186	2	8
RJ	196.704.277	14,51		8	1,53		1	7
SP	474.444.828	34,99		44	8,40	23	11	10
Region: South								
PR	166.539.645	12,28		110	20,99	66	39	5
RS	63.658.971	4,69		26	4,96	21	4	1
SC	21.941.249	1,62		37	7,06	36		1
Total	1,356	100		524	100	416	64	44

Source: Own elaboration from data of Cibiogás (2019).

12,07% of the national total. Such a pattern can also be observed in Goiás: it hosts 7,3% of biogas plants but produces only 1,54% of Brazil's sum (Cibiogás, 2019).

It becomes apparent that regions that specialized themselves in urban waste sources or have a more diverse portfolio are the most relevant to the national context. Rio de Janeiro was the second state that produced the most biogas in Brazil in 2019, representing 14,51% of the national total, even if it only possesses eight biogas plants. Since seven of its plants utilize urban waste feedstock sources, it can provide a relevant biogas production. Goiás and Minas Gerais mostly focus their biogas production on agriculture and livestock, hence their low contribution to the national total (Cibiogás, 2019).

While the public sector in the Southeast region regarding biogas production is more developed, it is practically non-existent in northern and north-eastern states. Therefore, when the possibility for further development is observed (Table 13.2), the northern and north-eastern states are highlighted for their unharnessed potential.

The Southeast region alone sums up 61,63% of biogas production and 47,71% of biogas plants, surpassing all the other regions. In comparison, the south region produces 18,59% of biogas and possesses 33,02% of the plants. The Midwest region contributes even less: 5,20% of the production with 16,41% of the plants. Lastly, the north region produces only 1,96% of the biogas total with 0,57% of the countries' plants (Cibiogás, 2019). This demonstrates a relevant disparity within the regions of the country.

Final remarks

Brazil possesses many structural issues to overcome before being able to pursue the implementation of circularity in its economy as it is defined in its concept. With several political and legitimacy crises throughout its history, Brazil also has difficulties in ensuring a continuance of policy and having a partnership ecosystem of innovation within the energy sector. Although regulations related to the residue and other biofuels have been developed over the years, specific incentives for biogas and biomethane have been scarce, depending primarily on international cooperation with other countries.

Furthermore, knowledge and funding conditions are highlighted as issues that make it difficult to implement biogas in the agricultural sector. Within the public sector, there is even the question of institutional coordination. Also, knowledge on biogas technologies is insufficient, making it unlikely for the private and public sectors to implement such initiatives. Therefore, awareness creation must be strengthened within Brazil to generate policy instruments to make the spread of biogas possible (Roitman, 2020).

Lastly, the most critical issue refers to how diverse Brazil is, and it reflects on the different realities of its regions. On this matter, some federal units in the country have developed projects and legislation that promotes biogas initiatives, while others have not implemented a biogas reactor. However, no specific federal feed-in tariffs or fiscal incentives have been established yet. Hence, the disparity

Table 13.2 Biogas potential per year by Federal Unit in Brazil

States	*Production (Nm³/2019)*	*Potential*		*Potential by source (% of the total)*		
		Nm³/year	*Harnessed (%)*	*Agriculture and livestock (%)*	*Sugarcane energy industry (%)*	*Urban waste (%)*
Region: Midwest						
DF	2.114.558	34.868.130	6,06	0,014	0,000	99,986
GO	20.945.021	2.641.689.813	0,79	0,007	97,302	2,691
MS	20.441.375	1.651.346.554	1,24	0,005	98,394	1,601
MT	27.000.055	631.351.873	4,28	0,037	94,837	5,126
Region: Northeast						
AL		567.935.323	0,00	0,002	94,797	5,201
BA	6.394.990	293.988.832	2,18	0,021	46,637	53,342
CE	31.583.674	95.207.108	33,17	0,038	0,000	99,962
MA	4.204.800	149.519.909	2,81	0,037	53,769	46,194
PB	26.280.000	263.886.061	9,96	0,004	86,326	13,670
PE	102.699.253	479.655.318	21,41	0,006	81,877	18,116
PI		68.367.644	0,00	0,078	57,489	42,433
RN		119.253.508	0,00	0,009	74,839	25,152
SE		82.807.230	0,00	0,027	77,858	22,115
Region: Northeast						
AC		5.749.277	0,00	0,063	0,000	99,937
AM	26.280.000	52.128.293	50,41	0,015	17,218	82,768
AP		6.104.732	0,00	0,047	0,000	99,953
PA		101.704.974	0,00	0,044	38,094	61,862
RO		12.997.779	0,00	0,338	0,000	99,662
RR		4.854.830	0,00	0,670	0,000	99,330
TO	243.582	89.520.110	0,27	0,033	86,293	13,674

Region: Southeast						
ES	831.307	128.408.777	0,65	0,031	71,420	28,549%
MG	163.690.944	2.460.117.871	6,65	0,011	91,342	8,647%
RJ	196.704.277	245.038.772	80,27	0,008	11,733	88,259%
SP	474.444.828	11.753.448.347	4,04	0,002	94,353	5,646%
Region: South						
PR	166.539.645	1.214.687.657	13,71	0,023	91,342	8,635
RS	63.658.971	87.376.131	72,86	0,246	1,161	98,594
SC	21.941.249	50.632.828	43,33	0,229	0,000	99,771
Total	1.355.998.530	46.585.295.364	2,91	0,009	90,399	9,592

Source: Own elaboration from data of Abiogás (2020).

between regions in the country is overwhelming, especially considering circularity, waste management, and proper disposal of residues. Although recently there have been some efforts to improve the monitoring of residues in the country, there are several challenges in managing urban waste and residue, mainly if not every sector residue is accounted for.

Notwithstanding these issues are manageable at some level, they are also considerably structural ones, dating back from centuries of historical disparities and policy-making differences. Thus, it is unlikely that the loop will ever be closed if these structural issues – such as the historical disparity between the regions, lack of continuity in federal policy, and awareness challenges – are not overcome.

References

Aarikka-Stenroos et al. (2021). Circular Economy Ecosystems: A Typology, Definitions, and Implications. In: *Research Handbook of Sustainability Agency*, 260–76. Edward Elgar Publishing. https://doi.org/10.4337/9781789906035.00024.

Abiogás. (2018). Proposta de Programa Nacional do Biogás e do Biometano (PNBB). https://abiogas.org.br/wp-content/uploads/2021/01/PNBB_Versao_Final.pdf.

———. (2020). Potencial de Biogás No Brasil. Dados Nacionais – Setor de Saneamento. 2020. https://abiogas.org.br/potencial-de-biogas-no-brasil/.

ANP. (2015). Resolução N° 8. January 30, 2015. https://atosoficiais.com.br/anp/resolucao-n-8-2015?origin=instituicao&q=8/2015.

———. (2017). Resolução N° 685. June 29. https://bit.ly/2WgAcqG

Assunção, L et al. (2021). Technology Roadmap of Renewable Natural Gas: Identifying Trends for Research and Development to Improve Biogas Upgrading Technology Management. *Applied Energy* 292 (June): 116849. https://doi.org/10.1016/J.APENERGY.2021.116849.

Barros, M V et. al. (2020). Mapping of Research Lines on Circular Economy Practices in Agriculture: From Waste to Energy. *Renewable and Sustainable Energy Reviews* 131 (October): 109958. https://doi.org/10.1016/J.RSER.2020.109958.

Bernal, A P et al. (2017) Vinasse Biogas for Energy Generation in Brazil: An Assessment of Economic Feasibility, Energy Potential and Avoided CO_2 Emissions. *Journal of Cleaner Production* 151 (May): 260–71. https://doi.org/10.1016/J.JCLEPRO.2017.03.064.

Brasil. (2007). Lei N° 11.445, de 5 de Janeiro de 2007. January 5. www.planalto.gov.br/ccivil_03/_ato2007-2010/2007/Lei/L11445.htm.

———. (2010). Lei N° 12.305, de 2 de Agosto de 2010. August 2. www.planalto.gov.br/ccivil_03/_ato2007-2010/2010/lei/l12305.htm.

———. (2020). Lei N° 14.026, de 15 de Julho de 2020. July 15. www.planalto.gov.br/ccivil_03/_Ato2019-2022/2020/Lei/L14026.htm#art6.

———. (2021). Despacho Do Presidente Da República N°16. Diário Oficial Da União. April 23. www.in.gov.br/en/web/dou/-/despacho-do-presidente-da-republica-320067170.

———, Ministério das Cidades. (2015). Tecnologias de Digestão Anaeróbica Com Relevância Para o Brasil: Substratos, Digestores e Uso de Biogás. www.giz.de/en/downloads/probiogas-tecnologias-biogas.pdf.

Cibiogás. (2019). Biogasmap. https://mapbiogas.cibiogas.org/.

———. (2020). Nota Técnica Cibiogás ER-002/2020: Panorama do Biogás no Brasil em 2019. www.cibiogas.org.

Ddiba, D et al. (2020a). Governing the Circular Economy: Assessing the Capacity to Implement Resource-Oriented Sanitation and Waste Management Systems in Low- and Middle-Income Countries. *Earth System Governance* 4: 100063. https://doi.org/10.1016/j.esg.2020.100063.

———. (2020b). Governing the Circular Economy: Assessing the Capacity to Implement Resource-Oriented Sanitation and Waste Management Systems in Low- and Middle-Income Countries. *Earth System Governance* 4 (June): 100063. https://doi.org/10.1016/J.ESG.2020.100063.

EMF. Ellen MacArthur Foundation. (2013). Towards the circular economy: an economic and business rationale for an accelerated transition (Vol. 1). https://ellenmacarthurfoundation.org/towards-the-circular-economy-vol-1-an-economic-and-business-rationale-for-an

EPE. (2020). Brazilian Energy Balance 2020. https://bit.ly/3i8UPwv

FNR. (2013). Biogas – an Introduction. 2013. https://bit.ly/3o72YW9

Homrich, A S et al. (2018). The Circular Economy Umbrella: Trends and Gaps on Integrating Pathways. *Journal of Cleaner Production* 175 (February): 525–43. https://doi.org/10.1016/J.JCLEPRO.2017.11.064.

IEA. (2020). Outlook for Biogas and Biomethane March. https://doi.org/10.1787/040C8CD2-EN.

Ionescu et al. (2013). Potential of Electricity Generation from Renewable Energy Sources in Standard Domestic Houses. https://doi.org/10.2495/ESUS130211.

Inácio, J. E., Autio, E., Morini, C., Prado, F. A. G. & Avancci, E. D. (2016). Analysis of the Brazilian Entrepreneurial Ecosystem. Desenvolvimento Em Questão, 14(37): 5–36. https://doi.org/10.21527/2237-6453.2016.37.5-36

Kirchherr, J et al. (2017). Conceptualizing the Circular Economy: An Analysis of 114 Definitions. *Resources, Conservation and Recycling* 127 (December): 221–32. https://doi.org/10.1016/J.RESCONREC.2017.09.005.

Lin, H et al. (2021). Life Cycle Assessment of a Biogas System for Cassava Processing in Brazil to Close the Loop in the Water-Waste-Energy-Food Nexus. *Journal of Cleaner Production* 299 (May): 126861. https://doi.org/10.1016/J.JCLEPRO.2021.126861.

Mancini, S D et al. (2021). Circular Economy and Solid Waste Management: Challenges and Opportunities in Brazil. *Circular Economy and Sustainability* 1(1): 261–82. https://doi.org/10.1007/S43615-021-00031-2.

McDonough, W & Braungart, M. (2002). Cradle to Cradle: Remaking the Way We Make Things, 208, Edition. North Point Press.

Oliveira, A C V et. al. (2020). Economia circular: Conceitos e contribuições na gestão de resíduos urbanos. *RDE – Revista de Desenvolvimento Econômico* 3 (44). https://doi.org/10.21452/RDE.V3I44.6386.

Oliveira, L G S & Negro, S O. (2019). Contextual Structures and Interaction Dynamics in the Brazilian Biogas Innovation System. *Renewable and Sustainable Energy Reviews* 107 (June): 462–81. https://doi.org/10.1016/J.RSER.2019.02.030.

Prado, F A et al. (2016). How Much Is Enough? An Integrated Examination of Energy Security, Economic Growth and Climate Change Related to Hydropower Expansion in Brazil. *Renewable and Sustainable Energy Reviews* 53 (January): 1132–36. https://doi.org/10.1016/J.RSER.2015.09.050.

Ritchie, H & Roser, M. (2020). Agricultural Production. *Our World in Data*, March. https://ourworldindata.org/agricultural-production.

Roitman, T. (2020). O Gargalo Sobre o Biogás é o Conhecimento. Abiogás News. March. https://abiogas.org.br/abiogas-news-marco-2020/.

Roös, P B. (2021). Regenerative-Adaptive Design for Sustainable Development. Sustainable Development Goals Series. https://doi.org/10.1007/978-3-030-53234-5.

Santos, I F S et al. (2018). Assessment of Potential Biogas Production from Multiple Organic Wastes in Brazil: Impact on Energy Generation, Use, and Emissions Abatement. *Resources, Conservation and Recycling* 131 (April): 54–63. https://doi.org/10.1016/J.RESCONREC.2017.12.012.

Sebrae. (2021). Biblioteca de Legislação Do Biogás. https://datasebrae.com.br/biblioteca-legislacao-biogas/.

Velden, R et al. (2021). Closed-Loop Organic Waste Management Systems for Family Farmers in Brazil. https://doi.org/10.1080/09593330.2021.1871660.

Ximenes, J et al. (2021). Valorisation of Agri- and Aquaculture Residues via Biogas Production for Enhanced Industrial Application. *Energies* 14 (9): 2519. https://doi.org/10.3390/EN14092519.

Zanatta, H G (2020). The Diffusion of Biogas Technologies in the Brazilian Context: A Comparative Case Study in Two Brazilian States. http://urn.kb.se/resolve?urn=urn:nbn:se:liu:diva-170093.

Part III

What we need to stress more!

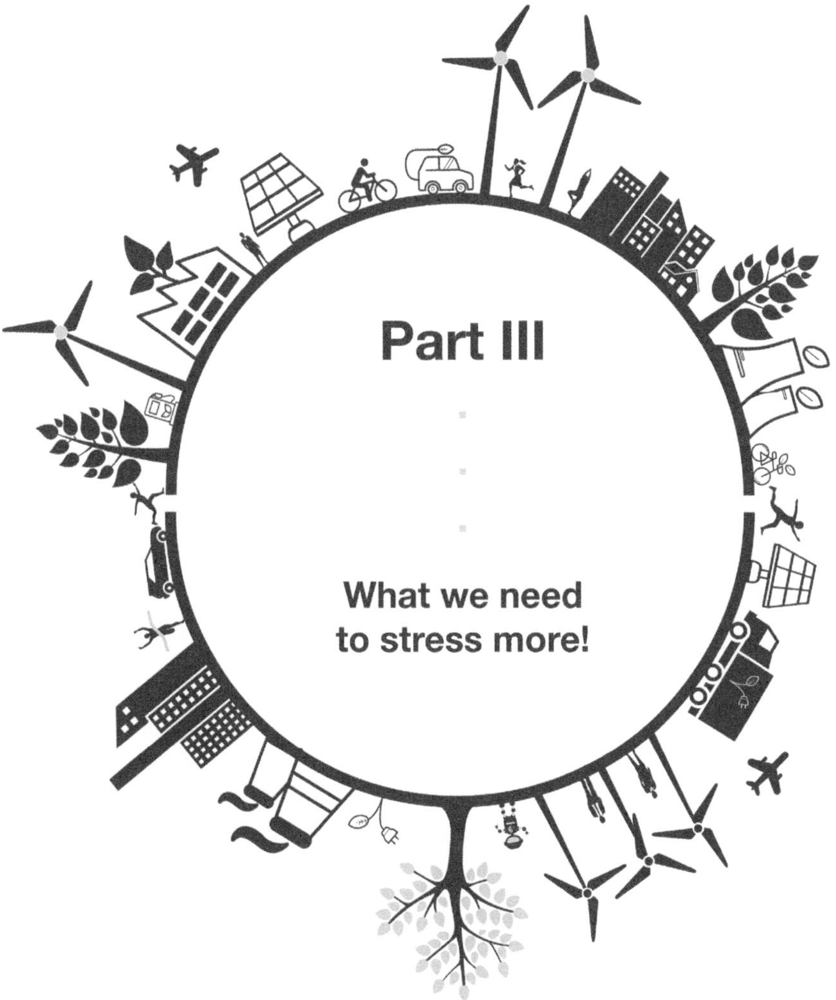

14 The Circular Economy should finally demand the impossible

Lisa Doeland

In the past decade, the Circular Economy (CE) has been heralded as *the* alternative to the unbridled and unsustainable so-called "linear economy" and has become firmly embedded in policy worldwide. At the same time, however, the CE discourse is being contested (Calisto Friant, Vermeulen, & Salomone, 2020; Corvellec, Böhm, Stowell, & Valenzuela, 2020; Korhonen, Seppälä, & Honkasalo, 2018). We should wonder, therefore, if the CE is so very different from the linear economy that it aspires to break with. If the linear economy is characterized by a logic of take-make-waste, that was exposed as unsustainable when it stumbled upon the limits to growth in the 1970s, who can honestly argue that the CE offers an alternative? Since the publication of *The Limits to Growth* (1972), a report issued by the so-called "Club of Rome," we have gone out of our way to *not* take the main conclusion to heart, namely, that infinite (economic) growth is simply impossible and will lead to collapse of the earth systems at some point in the future. As the authors of the report succinctly summarize their main argument against growth:

> The unspoken assumption behind all of the model runs we have presented [...] is that population and capital growth should be allowed to continue until they reach some kind of "natural" limit. This assumption also appears to be the basic part of the human value system currently operational in the real world. Whenever we incorporate this value into the model, the result is that the growing system rises above its ultimate limit and then collapses.
>
> (Meadows, Meadows, Randers, & Behrens, 1972)

Concepts like "sustainable development," "eco-efficiency," "decoupling," "green growth," "green capitalism," "circular (bio)economy," and so on seemingly offer an alternative to the ideology of limitless growth but in reality keep the dream alive.

But what *are* these limits to growth? As I will argue in this chapter, they refer to the "Real of nature" (Stavrakakis, 1997), a Real that reminds us that you cannot have the one – economy – without the other – ecology. It seems that we have

DOI: 10.4324/9781003244196-17

forgotten about the etymological root that economy and ecology share – *oikos* [household]. As Michael Marder aptly puts it:

> If economy is the default organization of our dwellings – whether at the level of the psyche, the household or the planet as a whole – than ecology is the rupture that no longer obeys the economic order and that, within its confines, is experienced, precisely, as disorder, if not chaos, a harbinger of crisis.
>
> (Marder, 2018, p. 142)

You cannot have one without the other. Yes, there will always be this need to control and manage – economy – but there will always also be this uncontrollable, unmanageable real, an "outside" that disturbs our plans – ecology. We should wonder, therefore, whether the linear economy is not a very convenient foe. The problem is not so much the economy being linear, but economy disavowing ecology. As Yannis Stavrakakis observes, "it is easier to fight a single identifiable foe than the inherent division of the social order" (Marder, 2018, p. 127). By turning the linear economy into a scapegoat, the CE has carefully avoided dealing with the real of Nature: the inherent division of our planetary household.

It seems that this avoidance of the ecological side of things is sustained by a misconception of nature and of natural processes. This has the CE seemingly dealing with the Real of nature, without actually doing so. Cases in point are the fantasy of "decoupling" economic growth from ecological impact, which denies the reality of natural limits (Fletcher & Rammelt, 2017), the fantasy of being able to "close the loop" that relies on a misunderstanding of natural cycles (Skene, 2018) and of carbon neutrality that fantasizes about off-setting "excess carbon" so the system can return "back to normal" (Watt, 2021) that relies on a misconception of nature as a balanced and harmonious totality. As long as the CE tries to realize these fantasies, it seems that it indeed demands the impossible. However, it is rather the other way around. With a wink to the battle cry of the 1968 protest movement, my thesis is that the CE should *finally* become realistic and demand the impossible.

What do we talk about when we talk about "the impossible"? Drawing on the work of philosopher Jacques Derrida and psychoanalyst Jacques Lacan, I will argue that the problem of the CE is not that it demands the impossible but, quite the contrary, that it fails to do so. We tend to conceive of the impossible as an unattainable ideal, as something that cannot possibly be realized but that we should nonetheless strive for (like equality, justice and world peace). However, as Derrida argues, the impossible is not so much an unattainable ideal but that which is "most undeniably *real*" (Derrida, 2003), that is, the impossible tells us something about *the way things are*. In a similar vein, one of Lacan's famous recurring formulas has it that "the Real is the impossible." For both Derrida and Lacan "the impossible" is in some way necessary and is concerned with the real.

The question is, however, what we talk about when we talk about the *real*. In both Derrida and Lacan, what we call "real" refers to that which escapes our socio-symbolic orderings and points to what precedes these. It is the cracks in the system, the unmanageable, the incalculable. A case in point is waste that, within CE discourse, is framed as always already managed and manageable (Corvellec, 2014), taken as an economical thing tout court – a resource – and stripped of its ecological dimension. The ultimate fantasy: a "zero waste" CE. I will argue that this "impossible real" refers to ecology as the repressed "other" of *economy* that is returning with a vengeance in our time of ecological crisis. We find that our house is, and has always been (but we've forgotten about that), a *haunted* house. To be is to haunt and be haunted, both from within and without. Nothing is ever fully at one with itself or, sticking with the metaphor of the haunted house, nothing is ever fully at home. As long as the CE disavows this spectrality and tries to close the loop, it both fails to address *and* demand the impossible.

Idealizing nature

Before we turn to "the impossible" in more detail, let us first remain with "the realistic." What is this command to be realistic? As Mark Fisher (2009) argues, we should be wary of claims concerning "realism." He distinguishes what he calls "capitalist realism," which has us belief that, as Margaret Thatcher has famously put it, *there is no alternative* (to capitalism). This twin process of naturalization and depoliticization – capitalism is conceived of as both natural, necessary and a-political – disguises the fact that the command to "be realistic" is itself ideologically charged. As Fisher points out, we should not forget that only a decade earlier the surge of privatization that started in the 1980s and haunts us still today was itself deemed "impossible" (Fisher, 2009). And while we soothe ourselves with the idea that we should indeed be realistic and not demand the impossible, inescapable realities – flooding, heatwaves, droughts, PFAS, to name but a few – start to haunt us and demand our attention ever more fervently, and closer to home

Walking around a garbage dump in the documentary *Examined Life* (2008), philosopher Slavoj Žižek remarks that "this is where we should start feeling at home." He explains that we tend to conceive of nature as a balanced and harmonious whole and think of waste as not being part of that. According to Žižek this idealized conception of nature is ideologically charged – "ecology is the crucial field of ideology today" (Taylor, 2008). Žižek stresses that the problem of ideology is that it addresses real problems but mystifies them. This is exactly what we see happening in CE discourse. It addresses very real problems (such as limits to growth) but mystifies them by suggesting we can decouple economic growth from environmental impact. This mystification, then, works through a flawed concept of nature. As Yannis Stavrakakis points out, this "green ideology"

> is built on the dislocation of the previously dominant view of our right to nature with no hazard and no limits. What is shown by the current environmental crisis is that there are in fact some limits, limits to growth and economic expansion, limits imposed by the Real of nature.
>
> (Stavrakakis, 1997, p. 124)

This ideology, then, offers a symbolization of nature that is of a "totally fantasmatic nature," that is, the phantasmatic representation of nature as a harmonious whole. "If nature is by definition harmonious," remarks Stavrakakis, "all imbalance must be the result of industrialism" (124). In short, nature is good, people are bad. And, we must try and fix people and make them and their (economic) systems "natural" again.

Insofar as the CE and its earlier incarnations rely on a flawed, idealized conception of nature, they do not propose an alternative but in fact strengthen green ideology. If we want to salvage the CE and *actually* have it break with green ideology, we should steer away from conceptualizations that take it (or try to turn it into) a "grand harmonization between industrialization and its natural limits" (Skene, 2018, p. 480), and instead take the (the Real of) nature, that is, ecology into account, not some idealized version of it. In fact, non-ideological green discourse that "accept[s] the inherent imbalance both of the social and the field of human/nature relations" (Stavrakakis, 1997, p. 128) is possible, and Lacan and Derrida can help us sketch its contours.

Disrupting circular exchange

If anything, the aim of Jacques Derrida's "method" of deconstruction was to show the myriad ways in which the house of philosophy is a haunted one. He went about this by, again and again, showing a certain impossibility at work. The concepts we use and the phenomenon we explore never coincide with themselves fully. When we try to define *exactly* how things are and give up the ghost, we rely on binaries and boundaries that in fact render its emergence impossible. Take "nature" that relies on its being opposed to "culture." Our concept of nature is, however, culturally mediated, which means that a strict boundary and opposition cannot be maintained. Moreover, the way in which nature is conceptualized actually changes things "in nature." When you take nature for a resource, oceans (and forests) turn into "carbon sinks," mountains turn into piles of stone, ecosystems provide certain "services." Culture contaminates nature, nature contaminates culture, and changes it. Where to a philosopher like Martin Heidegger, language was "the house of being," and we could make ourselves at home in it, for Derrida language was not so much a place of *being* (ontology), but of *haunting* (hauntology). Derrida, then, conceived of the house of language as a haunted one, and

> [his] style of inhabiting this house was by deconstructing it: by exploring its hidden corners and secret passages, exposing whatever has been swept under the rugs, pulling skeletons out of closets, descending to the basement and showing how the pillars that support it make it, at once, possible and impossible, stable and ready to cave in.
>
> (Marder, 2018, pp. 141–142)

Although Derrida himself hardly wrote about nature and steered clear of the notion of ecology, he can nonetheless be conceived as an environmental thinker. This is also reflected in the upsurge of interest in Derrida's work from an environmental perspective (Fritsch, Lynes, & Wood, 2018; Vitale, 2018). Why, then, did Derrida not write about ecology explicitly? As Michael Marder (2018) argues, the reason for this might well be the fullness of presence promised by both "eco" and "logos" – like we can truly inhabit our house [*oikos*], make it just ours, as if our discourse [*logos*] on it discloses all there is to it. Marder suggests this is why, instead of engaging with ecology, Derrida paid close scrutiny to "economy," showing how the economy disrupts (or in Derridean terms: deconstructs) itself from within, a disruption that points to ecology as the hidden kernel of economy.

One of the ways in which Derrida deconstructs economy is by showing how it relies on something *aneconomic* – the gift. Although the gift is related to economy and to economic exchange, it interrupts it. As Derrida explains:

> For there to be a gift, there must be no reciprocity, return, exchange, countergift, or debt. If the other *gives* me *back* or *owes* me or has to give me back what I give him or her, there will not have been a gift.
>
> (Derrida, 1994, p. 12)

Therefore, we cannot recognize the gift *as gift*. The gift suspends economic calculation and exchange and opens the circle, defying reciprocity and symmetry. Derrida:

> If the figure of the circle is essential to economics, the gift must remain *aneconomic*. Not that it remains foreign to the circle, but must *keep* a relation of foreignness to the circle [...] It is perhaps in this sense that the gift is impossible. Not impossible but *the* impossible.
>
> (Derrida, 1994, p. 7)

Following Derrida, we find there is a strange affinity between the gift and waste. Waste too suspends calculation and exchange. For something to be recognized as waste – useless, unwanted, unvaluable – it must defy economic exchange. We should be wary, therefore, of taking waste for a resource, for something that, without remainder, can be reincorporated in the cycle of economic exchange. Both the gift and waste are "the impossible," that is, the aneconomic that lies at the heart of economics. As Derrida adds later on, "wherever *time as circle* [...] is predominant, the gift is impossible" (Derrida, 1994, p. 9). Just like the gift, waste stands in a certain relation to circularity but should remain exterior to it. The trick is, then, to not try and close the loop but to have waste serve as a reminder of aneconomic ecology being a vital part of economy. As Michael Marder aptly puts it: "the house of economy is haunted. And the specter that disturbs it is that of ecology" (Marder, 2018, p. 157).

A spectre is haunting (circular) economy

In *Specters of Marx* (1993), Derrida explores the figure of the ghost or spectre – it goes by many names – and the ways in which it returns, haunts, is repressed, is conjured up and exorcized. Writing in the aftermath of the fall of the Berlin Wall in 1989, which was heralded as the end of communism, most notably by Francis Fukuyama in his *The End of History and the Last* Man, Derrida asks: what do we do when we say something has ended (in that instance: communism)? We seem to be performing an exorcism. And what happens when we try to banish spectres? We become haunted even more. These conjuring tricks consist of calling upon something – a spectre – making it fully present, saying: this is it! this is all there is to it! – to then try and make it go away. But there is always *more* to these ghosts. Nothing can ever be made fully *present*. We tend to conceive of things being either present or absent, being either this or that. According to Derrida, however, ontology – that which concerns the *being* of things – is itself a "conjuration." He writes:

> To haunt does not mean to be present, and it is necessary to introduce haunting into the very construction of the concept, beginning with the concepts of being and time. That is what we would be calling here a hauntology. Ontology opposes it only in a movement of exorcism. Ontology is a conjuration.
>
> (Derrida, 2006, p. 202)

This play on the homonym of ontology and hauntology – pronounced exactly the same in French – is to make us aware of the fact that when we try and *define exactly what things* are and make them fully present, we are in fact *excluding things that are also there*.

It is precisely these "conjuring tricks" that are vital to (a zero waste) CE. It first calls upon something – waste – putting all kinds of different things into one container – albeit an actual or an administrative one – to then exorcize them by magically turning them into something else: resources. The resourcification of waste comes down, then, to an exorcism. More specifically, to an exorcism of ecology. Just like the aforementioned fantasies about decoupling and carbon offsetting, the fantasy of waste-as-resource relies on the assumption that we can, one way or another, disentangle ourselves from our environment – economy without ecology. Instead, we find that however much we try and find a place or a use for it, waste escapes our managerial grasp and haunts us ever more fervently, demanding our attention. This Derridian spectre of waste (Doeland, 2020) is, then, akin to the Lacanian Real of nature to which we will turn now in a bit more detail.

Lacan and the Real

We have concluded earlier that in Lacanian, psychoanalytic terms, the demanding presence of waste refers to the Real (of nature). We have not, however, explored the relationship between this Real and reality in Lacan. To define reality, Lacan draws on the distinction psychoanalyst Sigmund Freud made between what he called the "pleasure principle" – our seeking pleasure and satisfaction – and the "reality principle" – the external world that thwarts satisfaction. Lacan questions the idea that reality is something "out there," unrelated to our dreams and desires. "Reality," he writes, "isn't just there so that we can bump our heads up against the false paths along which the functioning of the pleasure principle leads us. In truth, we make reality out of pleasure" (Lacan, 1997, p. 225). As Alenka Zupančič explains, Lacan's take on the reality principle draws our attention to the dangers of taking reality as in some way "natural." She writes that "the reality principle is not simply some kind of natural way associated with how things are [...] The reality principle itself is ideologically mediated" (Zupančič , 2003, p. 77). In short, that which we conceive of as given and natural is in fact a construct, a fantasy.

It is important to touch here upon the conceptual separation of three realms in Lacanian theory, one of which is the aforementioned Real, the others being the Symbolic and the Imaginary.

> The Real is Lacan's placeholder name for the fundamentally unknowable (in his terms "impossible") reality that we attempt to make sense of and control in the realm of the Symbolic. Due to the Real's impossibility, however, it inevitably exceeds our Symbolic efforts to bring order to it. Yet, rather than acknowledging this reality, we tend to "suture" this gap in the realm of the Imaginary through recourse to fantasy, which Žižek calls "the frame through which we experience the world as consistent and meaningful."
>
> (Fletcher & Rammelt, 2017, p. 453)

Fantasy is, in short, vital to the smooth functioning of ideology, which in turn constitute what we call "reality."

The Real, then, is what disturbs the smooth functioning of ideology since it cannot be integrated into reality. The Real is that which we cannot conceptualize, symbolize or imagine. As Lacan himself puts it: "The Real is the difference between what works and what doesn't work. What works is the world. The Real is what doesn't work" (Pohl, 2020, p. 70). This is, then, why for Lacan the Real is in a sense "impossible," for it cannot be integrated into the socio-symbolic order. It is the pure paradox of trying to signify (speak, write, think) a complete, functioning reality that can be tamed and managed consistently. Lucas Pohl sums it up nicely when he remarks that, just like the unconscious marks the limits of consciousness, the Real marks the limits of reality (Pohl, 2020, 71).

Just like for Derrida, for Lacan the impossible is both necessary and real. As Zupančič stresses, Lacan's point is precisely that the impossible (Real) *happens*:

> Lacan's identification of the Real with the impossible, however, is not simply that the Real is a Thing that cannot possibly happen. On the contrary: the whole point of the Lacanian concept of the Real is that *the impossible happens* [...] The Real happens precisely as the impossible. It is not something that happens when we want it, or try to make it happen, or expect it, or are ready

> for it. It always happens at the wrong time and in the wrong place; it is always something that does not fit the (established or anticipated) picture. The Real as impossible means that there is no right time or place for it, not that it cannot possibly happen.
>
> (Zupančič 2003, p. 177)

The Real is, then, that which does not fit, that which has no place within the existing order. From a Lacanian perspective, we find that however much the CE tries to manage waste and make it part of "what works in the world" – reality – it finds waste to be a reminder of that which "does not work" – the Real (of nature).

Demanding the impossible?

The CE should, then, try and find a way to make room for spectres, such as the spectre of waste, instead of trying to exorcize them. Demanding the impossible would mean that we do not disavow a vital Real of nature: waste. This brings me to a final, pivotal fantasy of the CE: that of trying to realize recycling without remainders (Doeland, 2019a). This fantasy rests upon the supposition that waste can be reappropriated as a resource without residue. However, such idealized discourse on the being resource of waste bears a fatal flaw, that is, it strips waste of its impossible and spectral dimension, meaning its symbolic capacity to remind us of the real (and catastrophic!) effects of our habits and desires, and even to haunt us if we stay oblivious to our impacts on our environment, while over-indulging these desires. The result is the loss of society's power to curb ever-increasing consumption and growth in a global-capitalist system (Doeland, 2019b).

One can wonder, however, if this means that the CE should indeed "be realistic and demand the impossible." Should we be doing the demanding, or should it rather the other way around? Perhaps it's not so much that we should demand the impossible but that, as Jack Black concludes at the end of his analysis of that other impossible real that haunts us these days – Covid-19 – "the impossible demands a new 'us'" (Black, 2021). If anything, waste reminds us that our times of demand are over. Waste happens. It is most undeniably real. And it is about time we start taking its demands seriously.

References

Black, J. (2021). COVID-19 and the Real Impossible. International Journal of Zizek Studies, 14(2), 1–20.

Calisto Friant, M., Vermeulen, W. J., & Salomone, R. (2020). A typology of circular economy discourses: Navigating the diverse visions of a contested paradigm. Resources, Conservation and Recycling, 161, 1–19.

Corvellec, H. (2014). Recycling food waste into biogas, or how management transforms overflows to flows. In C. Barbara, & R. Orvar, Coping with excess. How organizations, communities and individuals manage overflows (pp. 154–172). Cheltenham: Edward Elgar Publishing.

Corvellec, H., Böhm, S., Stowell, A., & Valenzuela, F. (2020). Introduction to the special issue on the contested realities of the circular economy. Culture and Organization, 26(2), 97–102.

Derrida, J. (1994). Specters of Marx. New York & Oxon: Routledge.

Derrida, J. (2003). Autoimmunity: Real and Symbolic Suicides. In G. Borradori, Philosophy in a Time of Terror (P.-A. Brault, & M. Naas, Trans., pp. 85–136). The University Of Chicago Press.

Derrida, J. (2006). Specters of Marx. New York and London: Routledge.

Doeland, L. (2019a). At Home in an Unhomely World: on living with waste. Detritus, 6, 4–10.

Doeland, L. (2019b). Letting Remainders get Stuck in our Throats. Detritus, 7, 1–3.

Doeland, L. (2020). Turning to the Specter of Waste: a hauntological approach. In R. Ek, & Nils Johansson (Eds.), Perspectives on Waste from the Social Science and the Humanities: Opening the Bin (pp. 21–36). Newcastle upon Tyne: Cambridge Scholars Publishing.

Fisher, M. (2009). Capitalist Realism. London & New York: Zero Books.

Fletcher, R., & Rammelt, C. (2017). Decoupling: A Key Fantasy of the Post-2015 Sustainable Development Agenda. Globalizations, 14(3), 450–467.

Fritsch, M., Lynes, P., & Wood, D. (2018). Eco-Deconstruction. Derrida and Environmental Philosophy. New York: Fordham University Press.

Korhonen, J., Seppälä, J., & Honkasalo, A. (2018). Circular Economy: The Concept and its Limitations. Ecological Economics, 143, 37–46.

Lacan, J. (1997). The Seminar of Jacques Lacan – Book VII. New York and London: W.W. Norton & Company.

Marder, M. (2018). “Ecology as Event.” In M. Fritsch, P. Lynes, & D. Wood, Eco-Deconstruction. Derrida and Environmental Philosophy (pp. 141–164). New York: Fordham University Press.

Meadows, D., Meadows, D., Randers, J., & Behrens, W. (1972). The Limits to Growth. New York: Universe Books.

Pohl, L. (2020). Ruins of Gaia: Towards a Feminine Ontology of the Anthropocene. Theory, Culture & Society, 37(6), 67–86.

Skene, R. K. (2018). Circles, spirals, pyramids and cubes: why the circular economy cannot work. Sustain Sci, 13, 479–492.

Stavrakakis, Y. (1997). Green Fantasy and the Real of Nature: Elements of a Lacanian Critique of Green Ideological Discourse. JPCS: Journal for Psychoanalysis of Culture & Society, 2(1), 123–132.

Taylor, A. (Director). (2008). Examined Life [Motion Picture].

Vitale, F. (2018). Biodeconstruction. Jacques Derrida and the Life Sciences. Albany: SUNY Press.

Watt, R. (2021). The fantasy of carbon offsetting. Environmental Politics, 1–21.

Zupančič, A. (2003). The Shortest Shadow. Nietzsche's Philosophy of the Two. London: The MIT Press.

15 System leadership for overcoming the impossibilities of a circular economy

Christopher G. Beehner

Introduction

According to the European Commission (EC), "climate change and environmental degradation are an existential threat to Europe and the world" (n.d.). The European Union (EU) developed the European Green Deal (EGD) to address the existential threat and transform the EU "into a modern, resource-efficient and competitive economy". The goals of the EGD are: "no net emissions of greenhouse gases by 2050; economic growth decoupled from resource use; and, no person and no place left behind" (European Commission, n.d.). Transitioning to a circular economy is critical for achieving sustainable development and the EGD. While the title of this volume is *The Impossibilities of the Circular Economy*, with the proper tools and leadership, economic circularity is possible. However, humankind must recognise and respond to the impossibilities impeding the transition from a linear to a circular economy.

System leadership describes a model in which influence is exerted beyond the leader's sphere of influence, enabling influence across entire systems (Ghate, 2015; Senge et al., 2015; Timmins, 2015). Advancing progress against society's most impossible problems requires system leadership (Senge et al., 2015), which has been recommended for achieving sustainability (Beehner, 2020). Although scholars have been advocating the circular economy for decades (Reday & Stahel, 1976), this decade may become "the gateway to the transition to a circular economy" (Webster, 2017, p.43). This gateway is not because "humans have come to their senses, it may be that only now do the advantages seem so clear" (Webster, 2017, p. 43). Because sustainability and economic circularity are complementary concepts requiring action across artificial and natural systemic boundaries, system leadership is appropriate for achieving a circular economy. This chapter will explore the application of system leadership to overcome the impossibilities of achieving economic circularity.

Role of the circular economy in sustainability

The dominant economic model throughout modern civilisation has been linear, with resources extracted, processed, consumed, and discarded. Throughout most

DOI: 10.4324/9781003244196-18

of human history, this model posed a limited risk to the sustainability of the planet. However, the exponential human population growth and corresponding overconsumption that began during the Industrial Revolution now threaten the ability of our planet to sustain eight billion consumers.

The business model of the twentieth century was described by Nobel laureate and economist Milton Friedman (1970) as having one responsibility: shareholder profit generation. While many shareholders engaged in socially responsible behaviour, these actions were voluntary and exterior to the business function. Moreover, the environmental focus of organisations was primarily legal and regulatory, with many companies engaging in token environmental activities and sustainability behaviour. However, the ecological and social crises of the latter half of the twentieth century facilitated a change in business focus. Business leaders increasingly recognised responsibility to the environment and society.

The growing recognition that natural resources were finite influenced business and economic models, which supported decoupling economy from resource consumption. The triple bottom line (TBL) was introduced, suggesting a focus on the three Ps: people, planet, and profit (Elkington et al., 2007). According to TBL, business leaders must consider environmental and social costs in addition to economic costs. Circularity, or the circular economy, offers a deliberately restorative and regenerative framework (Ellen MacArthur Foundation, 2021). The 9R framework of the circular economy contains nine strategies on a continuum from circularity to linearity: refuse, reduce, reuse, repair, refurbish, remanufacture, repurpose, recycle, and recover. "Refuse" is the highest level of circularity, describing achievement of product redundancy by elimination of product function or achieving similar functionality with an entirely different product (Potting et al., 2017).

While business activity is often blamed for current global environmental and social crises, businesses possess the human and financial resources necessary to solve them (Beehner, 2020). Businesses influence the social framework of most developed nations through labour and employment (Jones & Upward, 2014) and are integral and essential components of contemporary society. Viewing business as independent of social-ecological systems is inconsistent with the highly interdependent challenges of sustainability (Marcus et al., 2010; Starik & Kanashiro, 2013; Walker et al., 2009; Whiteman et al., 2013). Therefore, businesses should actively engage in mitigating and reversing environmental degradation and threats and achieving sustainable outcomes necessary for human survival.

Circularity reduces waste and adverse environmental impacts, resulting in a more sustainable world. Achieving economic circularity requires leaders capable of influencing beyond their organisations, industries, communities, and nations. Evolving from the existing linear "take–make–waste" system to a circular "borrow–use–return" system requires employees and managers at every level to be intentionally active in business planning and decision-making (Doppelt, 2017). The following section addresses the impossibilities of transitioning from a linear to a circular economic model.

What are the impossibilities of the circular economy?

Circularity offers a solution to the wicked environmental and social problems faced by Europe and the world. However, the impossibilities of circularity are a result of those wicked problems. A wicked problem is a

> Social or cultural problem that is difficult or impossible to solve for as many as four reasons: incomplete or contradictory knowledge, the number of people and opinions involved, the large economic burden, and the interconnected nature of these problems with other problems.
>
> (Kolko, 2012, p. 10)

Knowledge about climate change, sustainability, and the wicked problems of the twenty-first century is prevalent. However, understanding these problems is complicated by the number of people and opinions, the interconnectedness of these problems, and the economic costs of these problems and their solutions. Moreover, there is a misconception that the circular economy will enable continued economic growth while radically reducing waste production (De Man & Friege, 2016). This misconception is the first impossibility of circularity.

The global population was 7.8 billion in 2020 and is estimated to reach 9.9 billion by 2030 (Population Reference Bureau, 2020). While the global poverty rate has declined annually, in 2017, 689 million people lived below the international poverty level income of US$1.90 daily (World Bank, 2020). The global middle class in 2019 was 1.32 billion, and the high-income population totalled 593 million (Kochhar, 2021). Many of the remaining 6.2 billion people living below the middle-class standard of living desire upward economic mobility. However, just for China and India to achieve a middle-class American lifestyle would require four to five additional planet Earths. The desire of billions to exit poverty, combined with the realisation of insufficient resource availability to support present consumption, is the second impossibility of circularity.

A paradigm shift in how goods and services are produced and consumed is required to achieve economic circularity while simultaneously improving the standard of living of the planet's poorest inhabitants. While the circular economy offers a meaningful model to reduce natural resource consumption, the paradigm shift necessary to satisfy the needs of current and future generations is impossible. This impossibility is further compounded by the Jevons paradox: "increasing efficiency doesn't lead to less consumption – it leads to more" (Moss, 2019, p.1). The third impossibility of circularity is believing that nearly eight billion people will agree on any economic model which requires sacrifice or change.

What is system leadership?

Northouse (2018) defined leadership as: "… a process whereby an individual influences a group of individuals to achieve a common goal" (p. 6). The term "leader" is overused and misused in describing any individual occupying a position of power or authority. However, most leadership scholars and practitioners agree that being a leader does not require a formal position of authority, with individuals often unaware they are demonstrating leadership.

System leaders are individuals whose leadership transcends organisational boundaries (Fullan, 2004, 2005). They are unique individuals capable of understanding entire systems and organising collective leadership for collaborative efforts (Senge et al., 2015). System leaders can influence across internal and external systems of entire organisations, industries, and nations. According to Timmins (2015), system leaders can operate across services and organisations, especially in complex situations. System leaders succeed by "being comfortable with chaos" (Timmins, 2015, p. 4).

System leaders consider problems without solutions and polarised situations to be opportunities for innovation (Senge et al., 2015). They are reactive problem solvers and proactive creators of value. System leaders demonstrate that individual and collective success depends on the condition of the broader systems in which everyone exists. System leaders are not unique, heroic individuals who accomplish the impossible through extraordinary abilities (Timmins, 2015). Instead, they are collaborators and alliance builders who influence others to collectively solve the unsolvable. System leaders in multiple fields have solved seemingly impossible problems, and system leadership is an effective model for achieving sustainability. System leadership for sustainability requires leaders who can overcome artificial boundaries and barriers, have a worldview based upon the natural environmental structure, see the big picture, and influence entire systems (Beehner, 2020). Although these leadership abilities are necessary to overcome the impossibilities of circularity, it may be impossible to empower enough system leaders to achieve circularity in the limited time available.

How can system leadership assist leaders in overcoming the impossibilities of circularity

Wicked problems are frequently delegated to policymakers or disregarded as too overwhelming to solve (Kolko, 2012). However, these problems impact society and every community (Kolko, 2012) and can only be overcome through collective, systemic action. History is replete with examples of humankind achieving impossible feats. While some achievements were motivated by competition or curiosity, many were motivated by crises or disasters. Humankind currently faces multiple crises requiring collective action to achieve the impossible. However, the impossibilities of circularity present a challenge of greater scale than any previous challenge and an extremely limited timeframe. Rather than consider *if* humankind can overcome these impossibilities, this chapter focuses on *how* they will be overcome.

The 9R's framework represents increasing levels of circularity, ranging from resource recovery to complete refusal of resource use. The "refusal" strategy requires complete decoupling of the economy from resource consumption, resulting in economic degrowth. Absolute resource decoupling is an impossibility that must be overcome to achieve sustainable development and the EGD; it can only be achieved by "doing without". However, the contemporary economic system resembles a development agenda of wealth extraction "with an apparatus for setting up deregulation policies and the capture of institutions to enable those who have wealth to influence political outcomes in order to give themselves more wealth" (Thurm, 2021, p. 22). Circularity requires leaders who understand complex systems, have a strategic perspective, and can influence across visible and invisible boundaries. However, system leaders may believe circularity is impossible because eight billion people will not agree on any economic model which requires sacrifice or change. Having eight individuals and families controlling half of private global wealth (Thurm, 2021) makes agreement more impossible. Even system leaders recognise limitations and impossibilities.

Achieving systemic change is difficult because few actors think systemically or grasp the interconnectedness of economic, environmental, and social systems. According to Webster (2017), "...ordered, complex, intertwined mutually interdependent systems are the new normal..." and the "circular economy is an expression of system thinking" (p. 43). Systems thinking is a management approach based on understanding organisations or industries as systems, and analysing relationships among system components (Tate, 2009). Systems thinking differs from the "silo" approach because it requires a comprehensive approach to understand how organisations function within social-ecological systems (Williams et al., 2017). The problems humankind faces result from operating on a "business-as-usual" basis, unwilling or uninterested in changing established methods and systems. A new type of leadership is required to challenge business-as-usual behaviour (Fullan, 2004). Overcoming the impossibilities of circularity requires leaders who can align people and resources across multiple systems to achieve systemic change.

The essential elements of successful system change are: equal representation of all stakeholders throughout the process; a clear outline of system components and interdependence; and, a sense of trust among all stakeholders (Confino, 2012). Achieving system-level change requires: recruiting a coalition of the willing, building an evidence base, embracing all stakeholders, combining perseverance with flexibility, and stable leadership (Timmins, 2015). The social and environmental problems identified in this chapter are a result of humankind behaving as if we exist independent of each other and nature. Therefore, overcoming the impossibilities of circularity will require systemic change and recognition of interdependence with each other and nature. Achieving circularity will require leaders who can influence diverse stakeholders to collaborate for common good in ways that may conflict with traditional roles and expectations.

How can leaders develop and apply system leadership?

In this section, we explore how leaders can develop and apply system leadership. Most system leaders have little or no awareness of the system leadership model, yet unknowingly use this model and have mastered many system leadership competencies. The competencies of systems thinking, strategic management, and interpersonal competencies are integral to system leadership and are discussed in this section. These competencies enable system leaders to overcome artificial boundaries and barriers, have a worldview based upon the natural environmental structure, see the big picture, and influence entire systems (Beehner, 2020).

The problems faced by Europe and the world do not respect boundaries. Rising sea levels, polluted air and water, and natural resource degradation do not cease at artificial or natural borders. Therefore, achieving circularity requires leaders who influence across geopolitical and socioeconomic boundaries. Becoming a boundaryless leader requires understanding every actor's interests and point of view. Boundaryless leadership requires cultural, national, religious, and political differences be acknowledged and respected. However, these leaders must engage all stakeholders based on common interests and the mutual benefits of circularity. System leadership does not easily conform to traditional, hierarchical, or bureaucratic structures.

Civilisation has removed humankind from nature, enclosing us within buildings, neighbourhoods, cities, and nations. Nature has become something that is "out there" that we occasionally visit and admire. Solving our problems requires a worldview based on recognising and respecting the natural environmental structure (Beehner, 2020).

Because circularity is a systems concept requiring comprehensive systemic change, systems thinking must be understood, developed, and applied. The development of systems thinking requires an understanding of key system characteristics: the role and purpose of inputs and outputs, creating energy requires energy, creating goods and services requires energy, sustaining life requires preserving a healthy environment, and politics matters (Siebert, 2018). However, although systems thinking is a mental model, this model is incomplete if the emotional, physical, and spiritual dimensions are excluded (Stroh, 2015). Understanding social, economic, and environmental systems requires identifying emotional attachment to beliefs and assumptions and how those attachments restrict perspectives. The coordination of emotional and mental dimensions occurs in the physical dimension. Finally, the spiritual dimension encourages recognising interconnectedness, the availability of both positive or negative choices, and developing individual character and behaviours to make appropriate choices (Stroh, 2015). "Systems thinking is a team sport" (Stroh, 2015, p. 207) because stakeholders with different perspectives can collaborate to develop a shared agenda for collective action.

Strategic management requires making decisions that consider time periods longer than one week, month, fiscal quarter, or year. Strategic thinkers consider the impacts of their actions beyond their existing and future roles, timeframes, and boundaries. Developing this ability requires seeing the broader picture, including components, organisations, and actors, which may be concealed. Strategic managers develop these abilities by asking probing questions about how and why an event occurred, or a task was performed.

Interpersonal competencies are the skills and abilities to interact with others individually and collectively. These competencies enable individuals to negotiate, communicate, develop relationships, and build and lead teams. While teaching these abilities is beyond the scope of this chapter, useful tips can be found at the European Academy for Executive Education (EURAC, n.d.). The essential leadership skills identified by EURAC are: active listening, teamwork responsibility, dependability, patience, flexibility, motivation, and empathy. In addition, they define essential interpersonal competencies of emotional intelligence, valuing people, empowering others, and teaming skills which can be developed by improving communication skills, learning to manage differences, and maintaining personal integrity.

Developing system leadership is an ongoing, dynamic process because the circumstances we find ourselves leading are constantly changing. However, developing systems thinking, strategic management, and interpersonal competencies provide the foundation for overcoming artificial boundaries and barriers, cultivating a natural environmental structure worldview, seeing the big picture, and influencing entire systems. The systemic change required to achieve circularity requires a new vision for individuals, organisations, sectors, and societies. System leaders can develop a vision through which all stakeholders can collaboratively overcome the impossibilities presented by circularity.

Discussion

No single entity can achieve the scale of environmental, social, and economic change required to overcome the challenges faced by humankind (Confino, 2012). Therefore, scalability of circularity across every organisation, industry, and sector is necessary for the impossibilities to be overcome. While the transition to a circular economy has demonstrated progress, the achievement of circularity actors can be amplified through collaboration, communication, and cooperation. System leadership is an effective method for amplifying circularity.

Overcoming the impossibilities of achieving circularity requires impossible effort by all stakeholders. Because a free, competitive market with limited regulation is the nature of capitalism, one of the challenges faced is the competitive aspect of business. Businesses operating in a competitive environment may be unwilling to collaborate or cooperate across organisations and industries. This unwillingness results from concern for the loss of market share, profit, and proprietary information, and the potential appearance of collusion or engaging in monopolistic activities. Moreover, national boundaries pose physical, cultural, and legal barriers, and have become more problematic since the nationalist and populist movements that began with the 2015 UK Brexit vote.

Overcoming the impossibilities of circularity requires a paradigm shift. Paradigm shifts in business commonly begin with expansive societal shifts (Valente, 2010), based upon frustration with the overall business behaviour (Valente, 2012). Gladwin et al. (1995) identified an emerging "sustaincentric" paradigm, integrating the existing technocentric and ecocentric paradigms (which have failed to significantly contribute to sustainable development or natural resource conservation). The fundamental elements of sustaincentrism are: recognition of the universality of life; stewardship principles common in major religions; the field of ecological economics (Costanza et al., 1991); natural resource preservation and management (Norton, 1991); and the complexity and self-organising attributes of nature (Botkin, 1990; Prigogine & Stengers, 1984; Wheatley, 1992). A paradigm shift to a sustaincentric worldview is an impossibility that must be overcome to achieve circularity.

When faced with complex, seemingly impossible problems, typical responses include: blaming other people for the lack of resources, emphasising successes while deemphasising failures, and viewing other actors as competitors (Stroh, 2015). We tend to succumb to the leadership mindtraps of being trapped by simple stories, rightness, agreement, control, and ego (Berger, 2019). However, systemic change can only be accomplished by system leaders who transcend failure, blame, or competition, and seek collective, collaborative effort (Beehner, 2020). The impossibilities of circularity require a revolutionary, boundaryless approach, perceiving failures as learning opportunities. There is no time to blame or find fault – there is only time for immediate action.

Achieving circularity requires a shift from a Newtonian, linear, mechanistic worldview to a holistic, systems perspective. Webster (2017) suggested linear thinking is a result of educating people based on the Prussian nation-building education system. When we view our world as a machine, we become alienated, finding it difficult to identify with or exist as a machine component. The Earth is not a machine – it is a living system with an abundance of life and history (Wheatley & Kellner-Rogers, 1999). Instead of trying to manage the planet and its complex, interconnected systems, humankind must adopt a more holistic and harmonious natural worldview. While the natural world seeks organisation, it does not need human assistance to achieve organisation (Wheatley & Kellner-Rogers, 1999).

Conclusion

Humankind faces wicked problems which seem unsolvable. While circularity offers an approach to solving these problems, circularity presents impossibilities that must be overcome. Achieving circularity requires entire systems to be influenced and changed. While humankind may espouse the noble belief that anything is possible, the level of systemic change required to achieve circularity may be impossible. Achieving systemic influence and change requires leaders who can think systemically. System leadership is appropriate for achieving sustainability and overcoming the impossibilities of economic circularity. While many system leaders are working to achieve circularity, countless more are needed to overcome the impossibilities and achieve significant scale and impact. However, the time for action is now, and a sufficient number of system leaders may not emerge in time to achieve circularity scale and impact.

The wicked problems faced by humankind appear unsolvable, and our destiny is uncertain. Taking the necessary steps to solve these problems requires economic circularity. Nelson Mandela was a system leader who transformed a nation of 40 million inhabitants. Transforming the economic system of a planet with nearly eight billion inhabitants might seem impossible. However, Mandela would remind us: "It always seems impossible until it's done" (n.d). Future generations will experience (and judge) the outcome of our present efforts.

References

Beehner, C. G. (2020). Systems leadership for sustainability. Routledge.

Berger, J. G. (2019). Unlocking leadership mindtraps. Stanford Briefs.

Botkin, D. B. (1990). Discordant harmonies: A new ecology for the twenty-first century. Oxford University Press.

Confino, J. (2012). The art of systems thinking in driving sustainable transformation. www.theguardian.com/sustainable-business/systems-thinking-sustainable-transformation

Costanza, R., Daly, H. E., & Bartholomew, J. A. (1991). Goals, agenda and policy recommendations for ecological economics. In R. Costanza (Ed.), Ecological economics: The science and management of sustainability (pp. 1–20). Columbia University Press.

de Man, R., & Friege, H. (2016). Circular economy: European policy on shaky ground. *Waste Management & Research: The Journal for a Sustainable Circular Economy*, 34(2), 93–95. https://doi.org/10.1177/0734242X15626015

Doppelt, B. (2017). Leading change toward sustainability: A change-management guide for business, government and civil society. Routledge.

Elkington, J., Tickell, S., & Lee, M. 2007. Sustainability. 20 Years of global leadership [online]. Sustainability. www.sustainability.com.

Ellen MacArthur Foundation. (2021). Concept. Author. www.ellenmacarthurfoundation.org/circular-economy/concept

European Academy for Executive Education (n.d.). Interpersonal competencies of global leaders and how to develop them. Global Leadership Magazine. https://eurac.com/interpersonal-competencies-of-global-leaders/#:~:text=Interpersonal%20competence%20is%20the%20ability,capacity%20for%20interdependence%20and%20collaboration.

European Commission. (n.d.). A European Green Deal: Striving to be the first climate-neutral continent. https://ec.europa.eu/info/strategy/priorities-2019-2024/european-green-deal_en

Friedman, M. (1970). The social responsibility of business is to increase its profits. *New York Times Magazine*, 32–33, 122–124.

Fullan, M. (2004). Systems thinkers in action: Moving beyond the standards plateau. DfES Innovation Unit/NCSL.

Fullan, M. (2005). Leadership and sustainability: System thinkers in action. Sage.

Ghate, D. (2015). System leadership: Expanding understanding of leadership drivers in whole systems. The Colebrooke Centre for Evidence and Implementation. www.cevi.org.uk

Gladwin, T. N., Kennelly, J. J., & Krause, T-S. (1995). Shifting paradigms for sustainable development: Implications for management theory and research. *The Academy of Management Review*, 20(4), 874–907. https://doi.org/10.5465/AMR.1995.9512280024

Jones, P., & Upward, A. (2014). Caring for the future: The systemic design of flourishing enterprises. In: Proceedings of RSD3, Third Symposium of Relating Systems Thinking to Design, 15–17 October 2014, Oslo, Norway. http://openresearch.ocadu.ca/id/eprint/2091/

Kochhar, R. (2021). The pandemic stalls growth in the global middle class, pushes poverty up sharply. Pew Research Center. www.pewresearch.org/global/2021/03/18/the-pandemic-stalls-growth-in-the-global-middle-class-pushes-poverty-up-sharply/

Kolko, J. (2012). Wicked problems: Problems worth solving. A handbook & a call to action. Austin Center for Design.

Mandela, N. (n.d.). Nelson Mandela quotes. www.quotes.net/quote/49925.

Marcus, J., Kurucz, E. C., & Colbert, B. A. (2010). Conceptions of the business–society–nature interface: Implications for management scholarship. *Business & Society*, 49(3), 402–438. https://doi.org/10.1177/0007650310368827

Moss, K. (2019). Here's what could go wrong with the circular economy – And how to keep it on track. World Resources Institute. www.wri.org/insights/heres-what-could-go-wrong-circular-economy-and-how-keep-it-track

Northouse, P. G. (2016). Leadership: Theory and practice (7th ed.). Sage.

Norton, B. G. (1991). Toward unity among environmentalists. Oxford University Press.

Population Reference Bureau. (2020). 2020 world population data sheet. https://interactives.prb.org/2020-wpds/

Potting, J., Hekkert, M. P., Worrell, E., & Hanemaaijer, A. (2017). Circular economy: Measuring innovation in the product chain (No. 2544). PBL Publishers.

Prigogine, I., & Stengers, I. (1984). Order out of chaos. Bantam Books.

Reday, G., & Stahel, W. R. (1976). Potential for substituting manpower for energy. Battelle Memorial Institute.

Senge, P., Hamilton, H., & Kania, J. (2015). The dawn of system leadership. *Stanford Social Innovation Review*, 13(1), 27–33. https://ssir.org/articles/entry/the_dawn_of_system_leadership

Starik, M., & Kanashiro, P. (2013). Toward a theory of sustainability management: Uncovering and integrating the nearly obvious. *Organization & Environment*, 26(1), 7–30. https://doi.org/10.1177/1086026612474958

Stroh, D. P. (2015). Systems thinking for social change. Chelsea Green.

Tate, W. (2009). The search for leadership: An organisational perspective. Triarchy Press.

Thurm, R. (2021). The big sustainability illusion – Finding a maturation pathway for regeneration & thriving. www.r3-0.org/wp-content/uploads/2021/04/Opinion-Paper-1-Ralph-Thurm-The-Big-Sustainability-Illusion-March-2021.pdf

Timmins, N. (2015). The practice of system leadership: Being comfortable with chaos. The King's Fund. www.kingsfund.org.uk/sites/default/files/field/field_publication_file/System-leadership-Kings-Fund-May-2015.pdf

Valente, M. (2010). Demystifying the struggles of private sector paradigmatic change: Business as an agent in a complex adaptive system. *Business & Society*, 49(3), 439–476. https://doi.org/10.1177/0007650310369376

Valente, M. (2012). Theorising firm adoption of sustaincentrism. *Organisation Studies*, 33(4), 563–591. https://doi.org/10.1177/0170840612443455

Walker, B., Barrett, S., Polasky, S., Galaz, V., Folke, C., Engstrom, G., & de Zeeuw, A. (2009). Looming global-scale failures and missing institutions. *Science*, 325(5946), 1345–1346. https://doi.org/10.1126/science.1175325

Webster, K. (2017). The circular economy: A wealth of flows (2nd ed.). Ellen MacArthur Foundation Publishing.

Wheatley, M. J. (1992). Leadership and the new science: Learning about Organization from an orderly universe. Berrett-Koehler.

Wheatley, M. J., & Kellner-Rogers, M. (1999). A simpler way. Berrett-Koehler.
Whiteman, G., Walker, B., & Perego, P. (2013). Planetary boundaries: Ecological foundations for corporate sustainability. *Journal of Management Studies*, 50(2), 307–336. https://doi.org/10.1111/j.1467-6486.
Williams, A., Kennedy, S., Philipp, F., & Whiteman, G. (2017). Systems thinking: A review of sustainability management research. *Journal of Cleaner Production*, 148, 866–881. https://doi.org/10.1016/j.jclepro.2017.02.002
World Bank. (2020). Poverty and shared prosperity 2020: Reversals of fortune. www.worldbank.org/en/publication/poverty-and-shared-prosperity

16 From closed to open systems

Applying systems thinking to reframe strategic decision-making

Sandra Hoomans and Martin Welp

Introduction

Resource depletion, excessive land use as well as air, water and soil pollution are increasingly jeopardising the Earth's life-support systems (Rockström et al., 2009; Meadows et al., 2004; WWF, 2020). Humanity however depends on high-quality and resilient ecosystems, for which the degree of biological diversity is a key indicator.

The Industrial Age meant a shift from an organic view of the human-nature relationship towards a mechanistic view. In this view, humans are not part of but rather dominate nature, resources are available without limit (Krutilla, 1967; Merchant, 1979) and the economic system functions independently of environmental constraints (Beder, 2011; Holden et al., 2017). Sustainability science is about the balance between human aspirations and nature's well-being, and the mental models and worldviews that humans have with respect to this relationship. It is a normative science with a holistic view of social-ecological complexities (Glaser et al. 2012). In practical terms, it is a contributor to complex decision-making (Jacobs et al., 2016; Van Kerkhoff, 2016). At the core of sustainability science is systems thinking, and it is providing solutions for systemic errors humans make when organised, making decisions and designing an economic system (Murray et al., 2017). At the centre of organisational behaviour (ranging from family-level to international corporations) is the process of decision-making (Simon, 1976), and especially strategic choice (Eisenhardt & Zbaracki, 1992). Strategic decision-making is aimed at the resilience of organisations and characterised by an integrative, long-term, and diverse nature; it is based on the values of individuals and groups within the organisation. Costanza et al. (2017) argue that the use and non-use values of ecosystem services should be at the centre of the fundamental change that is needed in economic theory and practice. This implies that these values should be integrated in strategic decision-making too. The industrial economy values, such as profit maximisation, maximisation of production, and rational choice, conflict with basic ecological principles. Developments with respect to the valuation of externalities (such as the concept of True Price), placing a monetary value on biodiversity, or creating new concepts for sustainability such as Circular Economy (abbrv. CE) do not result in bringing

DOI: 10.4324/9781003244196-19

about a change in the values used by people to make choices and therefore do not directly result in a change of behaviour. It is important to challenge and criticise the contribution of any newly devised concept or practice against the urgency to restore the disturbed balance between humans and nature. The question with respect to CE is therefore whether it provides a solution to the above-mentioned global change problems.

Balancing systems

Considering the fact that the current economic system is designed by humans and that humans live within the boundaries of system Earth, the starting point of any discussion or debate about changing systems goes back to the way we view and think about our relationship with the natural environment and the way we integrate these thoughts in designing the economic system. The triple bottom line – economic, social and ecological (Elkington, 1999) – is meant to focus on this connection, including not only the present state of affairs but taking future generations into account. Every concept, problem or challenge that we face can be brought back to the logical necessity between events occurring in the social and ecological system. Balancing systems is about human-nature coexistence.

Therefore we describe some basic principles of the functioning of ecosystems and social systems and concludes with key issues at the core of social-ecological complexities.

Ecological principles

Much can be learned from the functioning and "design principles" of ecosystems for our current social and economic systems. How ecosystems function can be viewed from many different perspectives (e.g., Holling, 2001). In the following, we distinguish between three kinds of attributes: (bio)mass, networks as well as information and energy flows. These key ecological attributes describe the functioning in the sphere of ecosystems. Ecosystems build up (bio)mass – a stock variable, which enables the system to be more resilient against external shocks. Let us take old-growth forests as an example; the forest accumulates biomass in the soil, roots systems, tree trunks and thus provides the basis of living for many species. Small disturbances (e.g. falling old trees, small-scale forest fire) will create a patch for new trees to grow but do not endanger the integrity of the ecosystem. Ecosystems thus create buffers and are not operating "at the edge" or "at the limit" of functioning, in contrast to our economic system, where small disturbances – to take a recent example the blocking of the Suez Canal by a freight ship – can create great disturbances in the global economy. "Disturbances" of this kind, such as droughts, do occur in natural systems. However, ecosystems as mentioned above invest in, for example, water storing soil layers, living organisms, such as grasslands in under surface biomass and root systems, in order to make them resilient to external shocks.

Networks refers to nested subsystems: ecosystems are connected to each other and build complex networks. Terrestrial ecosystems have an impact on marine ecosystems and vice versa. These complex interactions have evolved over a very long time span, adapting to changing conditions, such as non-anthropogenic climate change. In contrast to anthropogenic climate change, which is taking place extremely fast, it creates a great challenge for natural subsystems and eventually for the global ecosystem.

Information flows are the essence of social systems but are similarly important in ecosystems. To take the example of forests: trees are able to communicate with each other, and this flow is essential for the functioning of an ecosystem. Evolution has brought up more and more distinguished forms of communication, including the evolutions of human language.

Efficiency can be regarded as the main driver of system evolution. The ecological system aims at minimising energy and material throughput to other subsystems and investing in cyclic processes. Ecological systems are not closed but the material is rather kept within the (sub-)ecosystems. The basic assumptions of our current economic system causes people's desire to maximise gains from ecosystems but it is impossible to continue striving for economic growth without a stable ecological and societal base (Edwards, 2021). People are bounded by rationality (Simon, 1976); trust in rational economics, markets and institutions is misplaced (Ariely, 2009).

Social and economic system

Talking about the functioning of the social system means talking about organisational behaviour and strategic choice as its determinant. Contemporary organisations function in an economic system that is fundamentally based on scarcity, bargaining and assuming stable preferences, coordination of the market through a system of prices and allocation of resources, rational choice and economic agents driven by maximising utility (Coase, 1960; Eggertsson, 1990; March, 1997; March & Simon, 1967). The time dimension and institutions are the underlying determinants of economic performance (North, 2010).

Efficient markets are created when competition is strong enough via arbitrage and efficient information feedback. Informational and institutional requirements necessary to achieve such efficient markets are stringent. Players must not only have objectives but know the correct way to achieve them. But actors typically act on incomplete information, information feedback is not sufficient due to bounded rationality, and institutions are not necessarily or even usually created to be socially efficient; they are created to serve the interests of those with bargaining power (North, 2010).

Goals of maximising utility, or production, which means trying to obtain the highest possible yield out of ecosystems by extracting and harvesting resources against the lowest possible price (efficiency criterion) conflict with the basic structure of vital ecosystems (Odum, 1969; Gardner & Stern, 2002). Individuals do not, as suggested by the expected utility paradigm, maximise their preferences due to the framing of decision options (Tversky and Kahneman, 1992).

The time element has become a massive contributing factor to ecosystem deterioration. There is a discrepancy between the time frames used in strategic decision-making and the time frames that we need to consider in ecological development or recoveries of ecosystems. Although shifts in the collective minds can be noticed, most investors, politicians, businesses, media and even so-called green funds still focus on economic performance on a yearly or quarterly basis, emphasising growth in economic terms (Edwards, 2021) and short-term profits (Senge et al., 2008), neglecting causes of the current crises and neglecting the urgent need for taking long -term values into account in decision-making. There is a tendency to foreshorten the time horizon applied to investment decisions (Elkington, 1999; Jonker et al., 2011, Laverty, 1996; Liljeblom & Vaihekoski, 2009).

A key issue is that how resources are used is dependent on decision-making by organisations and not directly on the operation of the market (Coase, 1960). In current decision-making, the value of ecosystem services is often ignored or underestimated. Futhermore, most ecosystem services do not find their way to the marketplace, in spite of their fundamental importance to every organisation. A solution to this issue as suggested by the World Business Council for Sustainable Development (2010) is to develop valuation techniques and tools that monetise or quantify the economic value of ecosystem services (ES) (Sukhdev & Kumar, 2008). Although these tools support decision-makers in identifying values and assessing the consequences of alternative management options, in this way decisions are still based on economic values and assume stable preferences (Menzel, 2013). The incommensurability of ES and their valuation is a problem frequently pointed at by ecological economists.

Strategic choice is a transformational process through which an organisation adapts to the environment (Stacey, 1995). It is based on the values systems of decision-makers (Keeney, 1996; Marcus et al., 2015). Strategic decision-making begins with the deliberate search for or identification of an issue or decision situation (Simon, 1976; Mintzberg et al., 1976; Mintzberg, 2009). Enactment is about the action of seeing changes in the environment, then selecting possible meanings and retention of what has been learned (Weick, 1995). Seeing requires a connection between the frame of a decision-maker and the issue. Frames, defined as internalised values systems, reside in the minds of decision-makers and are used in a mostly unconscious, automatic way as filtering devices (Goffman, 1974; Keeney, 1996; Kolkman, 2005). They offer a way of simplifying unstructured, complex decision situations or problems (Mintzberg et al., 1976) and develop through interactional processes of communication (Goffman, 1974).

Internalisation of values is a response to social influence; values change only slowly, also because there is a state of tension between values associated with individuality and values associated with conformity (Aronson, 1995). Changing values requires neuroplasticity, which is defined as the ability of the human brain to change, remodel and reorganise for the purpose of enhancing the ability to adapt to new situations (Demarin et al., 2014).

Sustainability implies viewing problems in human-environment relationships from multiple perspectives and incorporating ecological, economic and social aspects and values in decisions, to reach balanced and sustainable decisions and subsequently sustainable organisational behaviour (Bonn & Fisher, 2011; Elkington, 1999; Gardner & Stern, 2002, Jacobs et al., 2016). Most decisions indeed are based on economic values and overlook social and ecological values (Bieker & Waxenberger, 2001; Elkington, 1999; Sekerka & Stimel, 2012; Senge et al. 2008).

We urgently need to accept that our morality is bounded – influenced by time, limited rational capabilities and selective attention. We have internalised frames that enable us to make decisions in a routine and fast way but the values systems that we use need reordering and become much more based on multiple values systems.

Identifying and challenging the assumptions of circular economy

As with the concept of sustainability, the CE concept is defined in many different ways. For example, Kirchkerr et al. (2017) found 114 definitions. However, there is not much argument about the assumption that the concept is grounded in industrial ecology, technology-focused and considers basically the economic functions of the environment (Andersen, 2007; Murray et al. 2017). Through promoting the use of technology and using the system of prices (micro economy), the concept is aimed at economic prosperity. So is our common future going to be circular?

When evaluating the basic principles on which circularity stands against the principles of the ecological and social system, one can detect impossibilities of the concept. These impossibilities will be described briefly.

- CE is about a new economic system aimed at reducing, reusing, recycling and recovering of materials (Barros et al., 2021; Kristensen & Mosgaard, 2020; Murray et al., 2017; Velenturf & Purnell, 2021). The basic idea of CE is to extend the lifecycle of products, materials or resources (Gregson et al., 2015).

The good element of a CE is the awareness that the current economic system needs reordering and the focal point of minimising the use of (natural) resources. This is at least a departure from the industrial economic principle of unlimited availability of resources and not taking the responsibility for waste of production and consumption.

CE provides the economic system with an alternative, cyclical material cycle model instead of the traditional linear extract-produce-use-dump model (Korhonen et al. (2018). But circularity will hardly be possible or economically viable in all spheres of production. As an example, one can mention the problems in (endless) recycling plastics or metals, which contain mixes of dozens of materials.

- CE aims at minimisation of resources based on allocative efficiency, and adopting cleaner technologies.

(Velenturf & Purnell, 2021)

In industrial societies, organisations have grown accustomed to the limitless availability of natural resources or assume that they are somehow replaceable by technological innovations (Odum & Barrett, 2005). However, technological progress only temporarily and partially compensates for the depletion of natural resources (Farla et al., 2012). Technology, together with the scale and intensity of (growing) human activity, causes environmental damage, and thus resources are no longer unlimitedly available (Gardner & Stern, 2002).

- CE considers the environment from an economic view – the economic functions of the environment being provision of amenity values, a resource base and sink for economic activities and life-support systems – and monetising externalities.

(Andersen, 2007)

By monetising externalities only a partial and incomplete picture of the environmental costs at stake (Murray et al. 2017) is given. The challenge is how to valuate the non-use values of ES, or biodiversity and integrate these values in decision-making. CE only addresses anthropogenic focused use of ES (Buchmann-Duck & Beazley, 2020), which prevents a transition towards a view in which biodiversity as a prerequisite for ecosystem functioning is central.

Even if social and environmental externalities are monetised, for example in the concept of True Price, they are not integrated with the pricing mechanism, and products with a "True Price" do not find their way to the marketplace.

- The objective of CE is the optimisation of production and consumption (Feng et al. 2007), it is however deeply embedded in the dominant growth paradigm of economic thinking.

CE as well as concepts such as Green Growth are deeply embedded in a growth paradigm with a focus on maximisation of utility (Brown and Sibley, 2015; Miles et al., 1978; Tversky and Kahneman, 1992). So far on a global scale economic growth, based on a mechanistic worldview, has gone hand in hand with the degradation of biodiversity and the quality of ecosystems (e.g., contamination of soils and seas with microplastic, decline of forested area and the decline of the quality of forests due to conversion to monocultures and secondary forests). For example, the parts of a car are produced worldwide using raw materials that are sourced globally. The transport and logistics sector cannot grow infinitely without causing serious environmental degradation and biodiversity loss (Ibisch et al. 2016).

Circularity in a globalised economy will be challenging – SDGs are also deeple embedded in the growth paradigm CE puts the traditional economic system and economic prosperity first, followed by environmental quality, neglecting social equity and future generation's concerns. It does not state that a shift in systems thinking is necessary in order for our world to become a sustainable world – rather the contrary.

For the post-industrial businesses, CE is perhaps easier to imagine, faster to realise and delivering success by means of integrated reports that show how good businesses perform in reusing and recycling materials and measuring easily identifiable key performance indicators. But foremost, it is aimed at economic prosperity, which is attractive for many people since we gained a lot from the industrial system economy. People have difficulties in sacrificing money today for more gains tomorrow. So CE appeals to behaviour and goals that gave success and welfare in the past, brought by the industrial economy.

The main arguments against the concept of CE so far focus on the undisturbed but unsustainable economic principles, the unintended consequences and over-simplified goals of cleaner technologies and neglecting the social dimension. In the next section, the systems thinking approach is used as an assessment frame to point to the impossibilities of the CE concept.

From circularity to holistic systems thinking

Is CE just a whirl in the river heading towards dangerous rapids? Thinking in cycles means perhaps a too narrow view of the transition to sustainability. Considering the global economy's rising demands on ecosystems and the decline in biodiversity, biocapacity and ecosystem quality, it is impossible to focus on economic prosperity without looking into biodiversity and the Earth's biological productivity.

The complexity of sustainability and the 17 SDGs does not mean that organisations only have to pay attention to some of them and show their best performance but to prioritise the life supporting SDG 15 (Life on Land), 14 (Life below Water), 13 (Climate Action) into their decisions and behaviour. Reframing strategic decision-making thus means that a diversity of values is included in every stage of deciding (seeing, analysis, thinking and choice). Sustainability has an integrative character. As Bateson (1972) already argues, the difficulty is not studying the components of ecosystems separately, but studying the patterns of interactions and relationships in them and the stability of our living system. How to move towards integrative, holistic thinking and reframe strategic decision-making, acknowledging that humans are part of and dependent on ecosystems. systems? This we consider an essential question to every concept, idea or method designed to move towards a sustainable society.

The ecological principle of constant evolution (and accumulation of information in more complex subsystems) implies that the collective mind needs to be a reflective and learning mind. Applying systems thinking and systems dynamics to strategic decision-making and putting values central in this process means it is important to understand strategic decision-making as an emerging pattern of interactions among informal and formal decision-makers. It also means paying attention to the emotions and cognitions of actors and integrating multiple values in decision alternatives cf. Krause & Welp (2012); Hoomans (2018). The challenge is to find balance in a diversity of values in the selection of an alternative and use both positive and negative feedback mechanisms.

The desire to conform to the group may limit the number of values systems used in decision-making. But diversity is believed to lead to more integrated decision-making. From a systems perspective, diversity determines systems change (Mowles et al., 2008). However, too much diversity results in conflicts and difficulties in pattern stability, too little diversity means minimum systems change, and continuation of the domination of economic values in strategic decision-making. CE is an example of a concept that shows too little diversity when looking at the current economic systems.

How to reframe strategic decision-making and aim for a holistic way of deciding which reorders our economic system? Or, how to balance a diversity of values in strategic decision-making? According to Weick (1995, 2011) reframing starts with the ability of actors to have an open mind. Required for strategic seeing and connecting to changes in the organisational environment is sensitivity to observe and see patterns. Humans are selective in their ability to see issues and bounded in their rationality. When confronted with disruptive events, actors firstly respond in an emotional manner, after which the event may remain ignored. Complexity, ambiguity and uncertainty cause actors to use routine ways of coping with events (Weick, 1988; Welp & Frost, 2012). Most judgments and choices are made intuitively (Kahneman, 2003). Having a reflective mind means starting with an in-depth review of our emotions, analyse the way we label events and connect and challenge our values. Emotions and feelings then become signals to start consciously making sense of events that may disrupt our system, and enact them. Repressing emotions as fear, denial of feelings result in uncontrollable and inadequate responses to changes in the environment.

Viewing strategic decision-making from a neuroscientific and sociological eye (Whittington, 2007; Jarzabkowski & Kaplan, 2015) may offer ways for reframing the collective mind. Attention to the learning processes of actors to reframe their underlying values systems collectively and use of a more balanced frame may result in sustainable organisational behaviour (Hoomans, 2018). Central to achieving a shift in routines is neuroplasticity. Neuroplasticity points to the possibility of our frames and values systems and embraces different perspectives. Learning comes from challenging the values systems used in the current economic system. Enhancing collective neuroplasticity provides an opportunity to redesign the economic system.

An economic value that urgently needs reframing is maximisation. The key to long-term growth in human and nature prosperity is adaptive rather than allocative efficiency, adaptive in a sense that economic growth is possible only within planetary boundaries. The adaptive cycle is a dynamic process of adjusting to environmental change and is key to the strategic choice approach (Miles et al., 1978). This means decision-making has to rank ecological values first.

Conclusions

The principles of CE resemble in some respects those of ecosystems. However, it is very much framed as a technical approach and limited to a too narrow view of system boundaries. The promise of CE is overestimated in a globalised economy. It is not addressing the dynamics and complexity of social-ecological systems, and our argument is that our economic systems need much more profound changes. It is an illusion to think that circularity results in solving the ecological crisis and creates a profound shift in the collective mind. CE lures us to believe that only minor transformation in production technologies enables us to continue rushing on a path of continuous economic growth. There is not much empirical evidence that on a global scale – taking into account the many facets of environmental degradation – this is possible. Aligning socio-economic systems with ecological principles asks for emphasising adaptive efficiency and recognising positive and negative feedback loops in social interactions and in human-nature interactions.

Solving the conflict between humans and their natural environment starts with seeing the larger systems of which we humans are part of. Seeing this is not just a small step, it changes mental models and the values that are determinant in decision-making. Biodiversity is ä key indicator of the functioning of the social-ecological system. But many organisations do not address biodiversity in their strategic decisions. CE as well ignores the need for integrated seeing and thinking and the required change in values systems. But without reframing our economic system and its principles, tension between nature and humans will continue to exist. The question is how to reframe decision-making in such a way that a diversity of values is integrated in choices and shifts the collective mind. The true Tragedy of the Commons is that many human communities seem unable to overcome our own unsustainable nature. Training our reflective mind and enhancing our neuroplasticity enable us to move away from short-term responses to changes in the environment and overcome our largely emotional, routine and biased way of making decisions with long-term consequences. We believe it is essential to accept that as individuals, we respond to change in an emotional way first and accept our own impossibilities to deal with a complex environment. The challenge is to design mechanisms for sustainable decision-making in an organised way that simplifies but creates a more rational and systemic way and leads to decisions based not overly on sustainable values.

References

Andersen, M.S. (2007). An introductory note on the environmental economics of the circular economy. *Sustainability Science*, *2*(1), 126–140.

Ariely, D. (2009). The end of rational economics. *Harvard Business Review*, *87*(7–8), 78–84.

Aronson, E. (1995). *The Social Animal, 7th ed*. New York: W.H. Freeman and Company.

Barros, M.V., Salvador, R., do Prado, G.F., de Francisco, A.C., Piekarski, C.M. (2021). Circular economy as a driver to sustainable business. *Cleaner Environmental Systems*, 2, 1–11.

Bateson, G. (1972). *Steps towards an Ecology of Mind*. New York: Ballatine Books.

Beder, S. (2006). *Environmental Principles and Policies: An Interdisciplinary Introduction*. London: Earthscan.

Bieker, T., & Waxenberger, B. (2001). Sustainability Balanced Scorecard and Business Ethics Developing a Balanced Scorecard for Integrity Management. *10th International Conference of the Greening of Industry Network, Sweden*, 1–25.

Bonn, I., & Fisher, J. (2011). Sustainability: the missing ingredient in strategy. *Journal of Business Strategy*, *32*(1), 5–14.

Brown, A. D., Colville, I., & Pye, A. (2015). Making sense of sensemaking in organization studies. *Organization studies*, *36* (2), 265–277.

Buchmann-Duck, J., & Beazley, K. F. (2020). An urgent call for circular economy advocates to acknowledge its limitations in conserving biodiversity. *Science of the Total Environment*, *727*, 138602.

Coase, R. H. (1960). The problem of social cost. *Journal of Law and Economics*, 3, 1–44.

Costanza, R., de Groot, R., Braat, L., Kubiszewski, I., Fioramonti, L., Sutton, P., … Grasso, M. (2017). Twenty years of ecosystem services: How far have we come and how far do we still need to go? *Ecosystem Services*, 28, 1–16. http://doi.org/10.1016/j.ecoser.2017.09.008

Demarin,V., Morivic,S., Béné,R. (2014). Neuroplasticity. *Periodicum Biologorum*, *116*(2), 209–211.

Edwards, M.G. (2021). The growth paradox, sustainable development, and business strategy. *Business Strategy and the Environment*, *30*(7), 1–16. https://doi.org/10.1002/bse.2790

Eggertsson, T. (1990). *Economic Behavior and Institutions*. Cambridge: Cambridge University Press.

Eisenhardt, K., & Zbaracki, M. (1992). Strategic decision-making. *Strategic Management Journal*, *13* (S2), 17–37.

Elkington, J. (1999). *Cannibals with Forks: The triple bottom line of 21st century business*. Oxford: Capstone.

Farla, J., Markard, J., Raven, R., & Coenen, L. (2012). Sustainability transitions in the making: A closer look at actors, strategies and resources. *Technological Forecasting and Social Change*, *79*(6), 991–998. http://doi.org/10.1016/j.techfore.2012.02.001

Feng, W., Mao, Y.R., Chen, H., & Chen, C. (2007). Study on development pattern of circular economy in chemical industry parks in China. *Xiandai Huagong/Modern Chemical Industry*, *27* (3), 7–10.

Gardner, G. T., & Stern, P. C. (2002). *Environmental Problems and Human Behavior*. Boston: Pearson Custom Publishing.

Glaser, M., Krause, G., Ratter, B., and Welp, M. (eds.) 2012: *Human-Nature Interactions in the Anthropocene: Potentials of Social-Ecological Systems Analysis*. Routledge. 232 p.

Goffman, E. (1974). *Frame analysis: An essay on the organization of experience*. Harvard University Press.

Gregson, N., Crang, M., Fuller, S., Holmes, H. (2015). Interrogating the circular economy: the moral economy of resource recovery in the EU. *Economy & Society*, 44(2), 218–243. https:// doi.org/10.1080/03085147.2015.1013353

Holden, E., Linnerud, K., & Banister, D. (2017). The Imperatives of Sustainable Development. *Sustainable Development*, *25*(3), 213–226. http://doi.org/10.1002/sd.1647

Holling, C. S. (2001). Understanding the complexity of economic, ecological, and social systems. *Ecosystems*, *4*(5), 390–405.

Homan, T. (2005). *Organisatiedynamica: Theorie en praktijk van organisatieverandering*. Den Haag: BIM Media.

Hoomans, S. (2018). *Elephants in the Boardroom? Sustainable values-based strategic decision-making in a Dutch Housing Association*. Delft: Delft University of Technology.

Ibisch, P. L., Hoffmann, M. T., Kreft, S., Pe'er, G., Kati, V., Biber-Freudenberger, L.,... & Selva, N. (2016). A global map of roadless areas and their conservation status. *Science*, *354*(6318), 1423–1427.

Jacobs, S., Dendoncker, N., Martín-López, B., Barton, D. N., Gomez-Baggethun, E., Boeraeve, F., … Washbourn, C. L. (2016). A new valuation school: Integrating diverse values of nature in resource and land use decisions. *Ecosystem Services*, 22 (December), 213–220. http://doi.org/10.1016/j.ecoser.2016.11.007

Jarzabkowski, P., & Kaplan, S. (2015). Strategy tools-in-use: A framework for understanding "technologies of rationality" in practice. *Strategic Management Journal*, *36*(4), 537–558.

Jonker, J., Diepstraten, F., & Kieboom, J. (2011). *Inleiding in Maatschappelijk Verantwoord en Duurzaam Ondernemen*. Deventer: Kluwer.

Kahneman, D. (2003). A perspective on judgment and choice: mapping bounded rationality. *American psychologist*, 58 (9), 697.

Keeney, R. L. (1996). Value-focused thinking: Identifying decision opportunities and creating alternatives. *European Journal of Operational Research*, 92(3), 537–549. http://doi.org/10.1016/0377-2217(96)00004-5

Kirchherr, J., Reike, D., Hekkert, M. (2017). Conceptualizing the circular economy: an analysis of 114 definitions. *Resources, Conservation and Recycling*, *127*, 221–232. https://doi. org/10.1016/j.resconrec.2017.09.005

Kolkman, M. J. (2005). *Controversies in Water Management; Frames and Mental Models*. Enschede: Universiteit Twente/CSTM.

Korhonen, J., Honkasalo, A., Seppsälä, J. (2018). Circular economy: The concept and its limitations. *Ecological Economics* *143*, 37–46. https://doi.org/10.1016/j.ecolecon.2017.06. 041

Krause, G. and Welp, M. (2012). Systems Thinking in Social Learning for Sustainability. In: Glaser, M., Krause, G., Ratter, B., and Welp, M. (eds.) Human-Nature Interactions in the Anthropocene: Potentials of Social-Ecological Systems Analysis. Routledge. p. 13–33.

Kristensen, H.S., Mosgaard, M.A. (2020). A review of micro level indicators for a circular economy–moving away from the three dimensions of sustainability? *Journal of Cleaner Production*, *243*, 118531. https://doi.org/10.1016/j.jclepro.2019.118531.

Krutilla, J. V. (1967). Conservation reconsidered. *The American Economic Review*, *57(4)*, 777–786.

Laverty, K. J. (1996). Economic "Short-Termism": The Debate, the Unresolved Issues, and the Implications for Management Practice and Research. *Academy of Management Review*, *21*(3), 825–860. http://doi.org/10.5465/AMR.1996.9702100316

Liljeblom, E., & Vaihekoski, M. (2009). Corporate ownership and managerial short-termism: Results from a Finnish study of management perceptions. *International Journal of Production Economics*, *117*(2), 427–438. http://doi.org/10.1016/j.ijpe.2008.12.008

March, J. G. (1997). Understanding How Decisions Happen in Organizations. In Shapira, Z. (Ed.). (2002). *Organizational Decision Making*. Cambridge: Cambridge University Press.

March, J., & Simon, H. (1967). *Organizations*. New York: John Wiley & Sons.

Marcus, J., MacDonald, H. A., & Sulsky, L. M. (2015). Do personal values influence the propensity for sustainability actions? *Journal of Business Ethics*, *127*, 459–478.

Meadows, D., Randers, J., & Meadows, D. (2004). *Limits to Growth: The 30-year update*. London: Earthscan.

Menzel, S. (2013). Are emotions to blame? – The impact of non-analytical information processing on decision-making and implications for fostering sustainability. *Ecological Economics*, 96, 71–78.

Merchant, C. (1979). *The Death of Nature: Women, Ecology and the Scientific Revolution*. San Francisco: Harper & Row Publishers.

Miles, R. E., Snow, C. C., Meyer, A.D., & Coleman Jr., H.J. (1978). Organizational Strategy Structure and Process. *The Academy of Management Review*, *3*(3), 546–562.

Millennium Ecosystem Assessment. (2005). *Ecosystems and Human Well-Being: Opportunities and Challenges for Business and Industry*. Washington, DC: World Resources Institute. Retrieved from www.unep.org/maweb

Mintzberg, H., Lampel, J., & Ahlstrand, B. (2009). *Strategie Safari, Uw complete gids door de jungle van strategisch management*. Amsterdam: Pearson Education Benelux.

Mintzberg, H., Raisinghani, D., & Théorêt, A. (1976). The Structure of "Un-structured" Decision Processes. *Administrative Science Quarterly*, *21*, 246–275.

Mowles, C., Stacey, R., & Griffin, D. (2008). What contribution can insights from the complexity sciences make to the theory and practice of development management? *Journal of International Development*, *20*, 804–820. http://doi.org/10.1002/jid

Murray, A., Skene, K., Haynes, K. (2017). The Circular Economy: An Interdisciplinary Exploration of the Concept and Application in a Global Context. *Journal of Business Ethics*, *140*, 369–380.

North, D. (2010). Economics and Cognitive Science. *Procedia Social and Behavioral Science*, 2, 7371–7376. doi:10.1016/j.sbspro.2010.05.099

Odum, E.P. (1969). The strategy of ecosystem development. *Science*, *164*(3877), 262–270.

Odum, E. P., & Barrett, G. W. (2005). *Fundamentals of Ecology, 5th ed*. Belmont: CA: Thomson, Brooks/Cole

Rockstrom, J., W. Steffen, K. Noone, A. Persson, F. S. Chapin, III, E. Lambin, T. M. Lenton, M. Scheffer, C. Folke, H. Schellnhuber, B. Nykvist, C. A. De Wit, T. Hughes, S. van der Leeuw, H. Rodhe, S. Sorlin, P. K. Snyder, R. Costanza, U. Svedin, M. Falkenmark, L. Karlberg, R. W. Corell, V. J. Fabry, J. Hansen, B. Walker, D. Liverman, K. Richardson, P. Crutzen, and J. Foley. (2009). Planetary boundaries: exploring the safe operating space for humanity. *Ecology and Society 14(2)*, 81–87. http://doi.org/10.1007/s13398-014-0173-7.2

Sekerka, L. E., & Stimel, D. (2012). Environmental sustainability decision-making: Clearing a path to change. *Journal of Public Affairs*, *12*, 195–205. http://doi.org/10.1002/pa

Senge, P., Smith, B., Kruschwitz, N., Laur, J., & Schley, S. (2008). *The Necessary Revolution; How individuals and organizations are working together to create a sustainable world*. London: Nicholas Brealey Publishing.

Simon, H.A. (1976). *Administrative Behavior: A study of decision-making processes in administrative organizations*. New York: The Free Press.

Stacey, R. D. (1995). The science of complexity: An alternative perspective for strategic change processes. *Strategic Management Journal*, *16*(6), 477–495.

Sukhdev, P., & Kumar, P. (2008). The Economics of Ecosystems and Biodiversity (TEEB). *Wesseling, Germany, European Communities*, (May). Retrieved from www.teebweb.org/

Tversky, A., & Kahneman, D. (1992). Advances in prospect theory: Cumulative representation of uncertainty. *Journal of Risk and Uncertainty*, 5(4), 297–323. http://doi.org/10.1007/BF00122574

Van Kerkhoff, L. (2016). Thaddeus Miller: Reconstructing Sustainability Science: Knowledge and Action for a Sustainable Future, (February), 51–53. https://doi.org/10.1007/s10745-015-9786-5

Velenturf, A.P.M., Purnell, P. (2021). Principles for a sustainable circular economy. *Sustainable Production and Consumption 27*, 1437–1457.

Weick, K.E. (1988). Enacted sensemaking in crisis situations. *Journal of Management Studies*, 25(4), 305–317.

Weick, K. E. (1995). *Sensemaking in Organizations*. Thousand Oaks: Sage Publications.

Welp, M. and Frost, I. 2012. Non-knowledge and organisational learning. In: Ibisch, P., Geiger, L. and Cybulla, F. (eds.) Global Change Management: Knowledge Gaps, Blindspots and Unknowables. Nomos. 250 p. 213–222.

Whittington, R. (2007). Strategy practice and strategy process: family differences and the sociological eye. *Organization Studies*, 28(10), 1575–1586.

World Business Council for Sustainable Development (2010). Energy Efficiency in Buildings. www.wbcsd.org/Projects/Energy-Efficiency-in-Buildings, date of retr. 2017/01/10

WWF (2020). *Living Planet Report 2020* – Bending the curve of biodiversity loss. Almond, R.E.A., Grooten M. and Petersen, T. (Eds). Gland, Switzerland: WWF.

17 Truly circular economies require deep collaboration

The principles underlying successful circular economies

James L. Ritchie-Dunham

A great idea

> The circular industrial economy manages stocks of manufactured assets such as infrastructure, buildings, vehicles, equipment and consumer goods; to maintain their value and utility as high as possible for as long as possible; and stocks of resources at their highest purity and value.
>
> (Stahel, 2019, p. 6)

With this statement, Stahel defines the circular economy through the concepts of value, stock management, and efficiency of using goods. Value brings in (1) different perspectives of natural resources and labour-enhanced resources (Costanza et al., 1997) and (2) the capacity to learn and adjust the quality and use of the stock of these natural and labour-enhanced resources. Stock management focuses on the net effect of the inflows and outflows of those resources (Stahel, 2016). The efficiency of using these natural and labour-enhanced resources compares the amount of natural and labour-enhanced resources for a given use of them, over time. According to Stahel, these are the required elements of a circular economy.

Today's logic cannot get you there

The current logic of a linear industrial economy cannot get you to a circular economy. While the linear logic expresses itself in forms that range from standalone, siloed companies to integrated supply chains, they focus on seeing value as extractive. One group extracts its value from another, defining efficiency as scaling the amount of resources extracted per unit of effort (Daly & Farley, 2004). Value is defined by the extractor (Hoeschele, 2010). Resources are managed by looking at the outputs, not the net effect of the inflows and outflows on the sustainable availability of the resources. While circular-logic efficiency includes the percentage of inputs utilized and how many times these inputs are utilized, linear-logic efficiency looks at the amount of output generated per unit of input. While this linear logic has proven its success in scaling value generated

DOI: 10.4324/9781003244196-20

for some, by extracting value from natural resources and from others, it cannot generate a circular economy, as defined above.

Three requirements for a circular economy

The circular economy requires three elements that are not in the current linear industrial economic logic. It requires (1) explicit feedback loops; (2) coordination across a set of feedback loops; and (3) the capacity to learn and adjust across this set over time. Linear economic logic does not include these three required elements. The circular economic logic can.

Explicit feedback loops. Explicit feedback loops describe the impact of A on B, B on C, and C on A, in the next time period (Senge et al., 2008). Said another way, the decisions of today affect your capacity to make those same decisions tomorrow. Or the way you made those decisions in the past affects your capacity to make those same decisions today. The number of people serving in the kitchen today increases the number of meals served, which reduces the number of people going hungry today. A affects B affects C. The success of feeding people might increase demand, thus an increase in the number of people serving today. C affects A. The linear logic of economic value drivers, and simple theories of change, only look at how A affects B and then B affects C, linear, by definition (McDonough & Braungart, 2002). There is no feedback. Feedback is required to be able to calibrate, to learn and adjust from what has happened in the past. Linear logic does not do this. Feedback logic does.

Coordination across a set of feedback loops. Feedback loops make explicit the dynamics of accumulation and uses of each resource. Understanding the interrelated dynamics of natural and labour-enhanced resources requires defining and coordinating across a set of feedback loops. A set that might include the interweaving dynamics around the people serving in the kitchen, the food inputs, the meals served, and the people fed. Important feedback loops for each element become more valuable as you understand the dynamics across the set of these feedback loops. Understanding dynamics across a set of feedback loops requires coordination of information from different systems and how they fit together.

Capacity to learn and adjust across this set over time. Understanding this set of dynamics over time requires the ability to work with different perspectives, as they change, over time. Maintaining the value, optimizing the net flow of the stocks, and increasing the efficiency of using resources require the capacity to coordinate a set of feedback loops over time, learning and adjusting from what was learned.

Doing these three elements of circular logic well and evolving your capacity to do these well over time, with others, require making these three elements explicit. Part of the conscious design of the system. This interweaves technical and social innovations of instruments and awareness. What do the instruments help you perceive, and how do you make sense of it? These three elements are not part of linear industrial economic thinking. Many people say that they are talking about the circular economy, but they are assuming linear economic thinking (Mayers et al., 2021). These three required elements of learning across coordinated sets of feedback loops are not allowed in linear thinking. Simply put, this means that circular logic is impossible with a linear logic. These three elements require circular thinking. What else is required in circular economic thinking?

What is required in circular economic thinking?

For the circular economy to work, you need to be able to define the ecosystem you are working with, and how you will know if it is better off (Frishammar & Parida, 2021)?

Defining your ecosystem. To know if your ecosystem is better off, you must start by defining your ecosystem. What is included and what is not included? Without explicit ecosystem boundaries, you cannot define what is included or not in your ecosystem. You cannot know whether it is representative or not, because you have not defined what it is trying to do. Three common responses in linear logic of what to include or not are: (1) to keep it simple, by including only a couple of variables, for example, in a simplified theory of change; (2) to include everything imaginable, for example, using current practices around big data; or (3) to include a very specific set of variables, for example, those described in a specific theory on the cycle of poverty. These three responses cover the continuum, from hardly any variables to an infinite number of variables. There is no guidance on how many variables to include or which ones to include. What is needed is a way to define the boundaries of the ecosystem, in a way that can be agreed upon by the involved stakeholders (Ritchie-Dunham, 2004).

Better off. To know how well an economic ecosystem is maintaining value, optimizing stock management, and increasing efficiency, you need to be able to define whether the ecosystem is better off because of those activities. This requires defining the health of the ecosystem. Multi-stakeholder approaches to defining why this ecosystem is relevant, what it produces for them, describes their deeper shared purpose (Frishammar & Parida, 2021). This might be reducing the years of life lost to chronic disease in vulnerable communities. It could be the level of self-empowerment for women receiving micro-finance. Or it could be the regenerative capacity of your farm. With this proxy for the health of your ecosystem, you can assess how well the current ecosystem has achieved that purpose over time (*Industrial Environmental Performance Metrics: Challenges and Opportunities*, 1999)—historically and today. If the ecosystem continues to operate in the same way going forward, what is the most probable outcome, using this proxy, for the health of the ecosystem? What level of outcome for the health of your ecosystem is required going forward? The gap between the most probable and desired levels provides the motivation for changing the ecosystem (Senge et al., 2008). This definition of the historical, current, and future outcomes for the health of your ecosystem gives you clues into the feedback dynamics that could generate what you have experienced, in the past, and what you need to experience going forward. Where the trend is flat, at the same level, balancing feedback loops dominate (Sterman, 2000). Where you see growth or decline, reinforcing feedback loops dominate.

One way to assess the health of your ecosystem, which works well with circular economic thinking, is the total value generated within the ecosystem. In a circular economy, all of the stakeholders are better off because of the ecosystem. In an extractive economy, some stakeholders are better off than others, because they extracted value from them (Dietz & O'Neill, 2013). The total value in the ecosystem stays the same or deteriorates. To build towards a circular economy, the total value that the ecosystem generates increases for all stakeholders. Assessment of the total value of the ecosystem is straightforward. By defining the critical stakeholders involved in generating the health of the ecosystem, as described above, you can now assess the value experienced by each stakeholder. For each stakeholder, the value they experience, now, is the direct financial value and the indirect experiential value. Characterizing these two elements of value experienced as direct and indirect is a simple, clear way to assess the baseline and current state. What do they value, and where do they stand in achieving that? This is the baseline, for each stakeholder. For a family in your ecosystem, the direct financial value might be their combined level of financial income and liquid assets, and the indirect value of their ability to grow and flourish (VanderWeele, 2017). For an employee, this might be the level and stability of their wages (direct value), and their experience of being engaged and respected at work (indirect value). For an investor, the direct value might be the return on equity of their investment and the indirect value of the impact their investments have on communities.

To bring in and make explicit the deep value available in a regenerative, circular economy, the total value generated framework makes explicit four levels of regenerative value: the noun level of outputs, the verb level of outcomes, the potential level of impacts, and the ecosystem level of total value generated (Arthur, 2021; Ritchie-Dunham, 2014).

Noun level of outputs. There is value in the things one has. The amount of a specific resource, whether of nature or labour, is enhanced. These are the nouns. Linear economic thinking focuses on this level (Arthur, 2021). It integrates the change over time to be able to ask the question of how much is there right now (Marshall, 1890). The answer to this question is the quantity available, which allows you to then ask the question of the price at which you can exchange this quantity. This is the elegant formulation that provides the intersection of supply and demand curves. Price and quantity. While this is a powerful insight, economic thinking at the level of independent accumulations of things leads to transactional, in-the-moment-only exchange. By definition, these exchanges are extractive. What is the value that I can extract from another in this moment of exchange?

Verb level of outcomes. There is also value in the inflows and outflows of the things one has and in the development of capacities and relationships over time (Arthur, 2021). This type of thinking requires putting time and space back into the equation, or never taking it out, which you must do to count the quantity of things you have right now. Connecting to others is an extension over space.

Learning is extension over time. By looking over space and time, you can begin to see the outcomes of your actions and the effects on others of what you do, in addition to your noun-level of outputs. Extending your focus, over space and time, allows for relational exchanges. These can be win-win interactions. What is the value that you and I can experience together in this series of exchanges?

Potential level of impacts. Additionally, there is value in living into one's potential, individually and as a group (Ehrenfeld & Hoffman, 2013). This is where creativity and innovation live. Seeing and manifesting something new, a new possibility. When seeing the feedback from what worked or did not work in the past, you can learn at the verb level to improve what you did before, or you can learn at the potential level and see something new. Potential-level thinking allows you to see the impacts of your outcome in distant parts of your ecosystem. This is the realm of generative, transformational exchanges. Together we co-generated a future that neither of us saw alone.

Ecosystem level of total value generated. And there is value in learning from the potential that was seen, manifested through verb into noun, providing you the feedback of what happened when you instantiated the potential you saw. You can learn and evolve, changing the potential you see, the pathways of verbs to manifest the potential, and the noun-level things those verbs generate. This is the realm of regenerative evolutionary exchanges. How can you and I continuously improve the capacity of our ecosystem to regenerate itself?

The total value generated framework (Figure 17.1) highlights three questions: How much value is generated at each of the four levels of regenerative value? How common are these four levels? What is required to engage each level? Our initial survey research from over 130,000 groups in 126 countries and field research in 49 countries shows that the value generated at each level increases 100 to 1,000-fold. For example, network logic at the verb level generates far more value than hierarchical-only logic at the noun level, thus the massive valuations of network-based enterprises (Cooper Ramo, 2016). If you go back and look at each of these four levels (noun, verb, potential, and ecosystem), you experience them all on a regular basis. Our research across the globe, over the last 20 years, shows that everybody experiences all 4 levels. The question is whether the organization is set up to support all four levels. Circular thinking requires all four levels. Linear economic thinking does not allow for the verb, potential, ecosystem levels, in its very definition—to find the quantity and price here now, you integrate out these dimensions (Arthur, 2021; Marshall, 1890). Yet, our research shows that human beings innately work in the four-level ways. The trick then to engaging all four levels is to stop disengaging them. It is natural for human beings to see possibilities that they then manifest, getting feedback and adjusting over time. This is creative work. This is the life of designers. This is imagination in movement. Shutting down this creativity is creating high entropy, taking that creativity, that creative energy, and making it useless for the purpose being served. Decreasing that entropy is increasing the engagement, transformation, and transference of that creative energy, in service to a deeper purpose (Ritchie-Dunham, forthcoming).

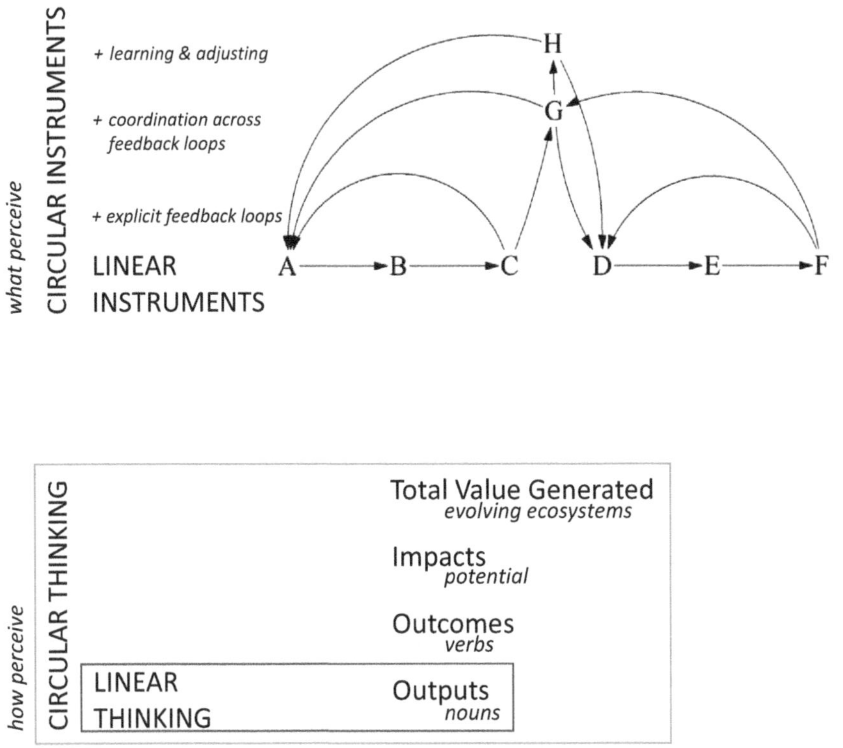

Figure 17.1 What is required and possible in linear and circular instruments and thinking?
Source: Own depiction, ISC research.

The entropy in linear and circular economies

Because human beings are innately creative, they see new potential, how to manifest it, and learn from the outcomes of that process. They evolve. You can assess the entropy, the energy lost, that results from disengaging this creative process. Two simple questions can give you an idea of the level of entropy you are experiencing. First, with the people that you paid to have in the room for a specific period of time (you might call it a meeting), how many of the creative ideas and insights that they had were shared and worked with? When I ask this question in linear thinking, noun-focused group, they typically share less than 10% of their creative ideas. When asked why, they usually say that it was because they were not asked or there was no space for sharing. You paid creative people to be in the room and to engage, which they did, but you lost most of it—high entropy. In verb-focused groups, they tend to share 50% of their creative ideas. In potential-focused groups, they share most of their creative ideas and evolve them together. In ecosystem-focused groups, they share, co-generate, and evolve their

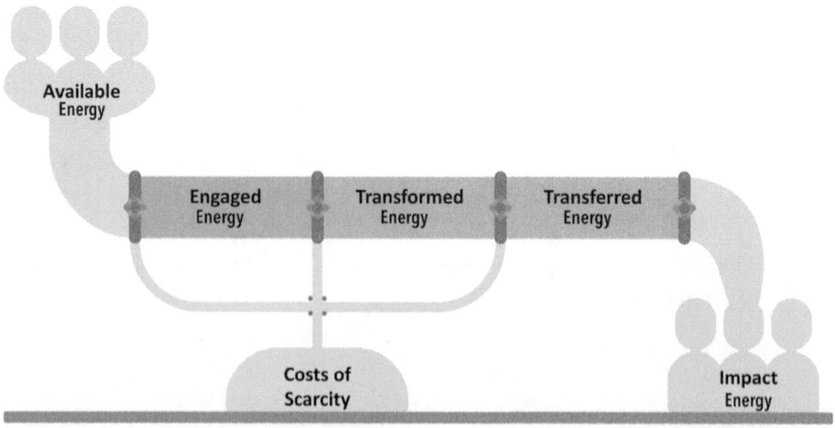

Figure 17.2 Three activities of engaging, transforming, and transferring human creative energy and natural resources.
Source: Own depiction, ISC research.

insights (Waddock, 2020). A second simple question also emerges from thinking about the energy lost in a creative process. Who are you able to bring into that room? We find that very creative, high-performing people avoid high-entropy groups that disengage the creative process.

These four levels of entropy are found in the three activities of engaging, transforming, and transferring human creative energy and natural resources into something that someone else wants (Figure 17.2). The circular economy designs in higher levels of these three activities, which are nearly impossible in linear economic thinking. Engaging human creative energy requires connecting to the deeper purpose you are serving—your source for this creative energy—bringing in the multiple perspectives required to understand the whole of the dynamics you are looking at and sharing these insights. Transforming these insights requires organizational structures that support and work ecosystemically with the noun, verb, potential, ecosystem levels of human creativity, sustainably providing the resources, and decision processes that value evolutionary learning and development of potential over time. These inputs are then transformed into services and products that others want. Transferring requires the involvement of those who are to receive these products and services, determining if they want them, and whether they are able to receive them in the form they are offered. These three activities of engaging, transforming, and transferring at these four levels of noun, verb, potential, and ecosystem are critical for the circular economy. They are impossible to achieve in a linear economy.

By dismissing change over time and space, linear economic thinking cannot include feedback. This makes explicit feedback loops impossible. Thus, one cannot coordinate across feedback loops, and one cannot learn and adjust across this set over time. That is impossible from linear logic. And it is completely doable from circular logic. By understanding these four levels (noun, verb, potential, and ecosystem) and these three activities (engaging, transforming, and transferring), you can differentiate between groups that are rooted in linear logic and circular logic. You can assess what they see, explicitly, at each of these four levels and in each of these three activities, what that indicates about what they can do, whether they are capable of linear or circular economic thinking, the amount of entropy they generate with their available human creative energy and natural resources, and thus the total value they generate, across all of their critical stakeholders. With this, you can then connect the way they think to the results they achieve, the total value generated in the ecosystem of their economy.

What this looks like

Through this framework, our global research-practitioner network has identified thousands of groups operating at a very high level of engagement and total value generated, through the regenerative practices of a circular economy. Four brief examples: In Europe, the BuildUpon initiative brings together tens of thousands of stakeholder groups across the building and energy efficiency industries to reduce dramatically the greenhouse gas emissions generated by Europe's building stock (*BUILD UPON2: A Tool to Deliver the Renovation Wave*, 2021). They started by coming together to describe the deeper shared purpose that united them. Reducing greenhouse gas emissions dramatically through building renovations and energy efficiency in ways that generated equitable economic opportunities, healthier people, greater funding, and a more engaged citizenry. In South Africa, communities are designing their own regenerative water, energy, building, and food systems, engaging youth ambassadors and complementary currencies to collaboratively build the regenerative capacity of their community (Ziervogel et al., 2016). In the USA, stakeholders across the state of Vermont come together to create an equitable structure for generating their energy needs within the state, moving from zero per cent generated within Vermont to a very high percentage within a generation (Colnes, 2013). In Costa Rica, a national initiative is demonstrating the capacity to bring together many different initiatives to demonstrate that sustainable, regenerative agriculture is possible across thousands of communities at the national level (Müller, 2018).

In these four initiatives and thousands of others we have identified, these groups are working to engage the human creativity available to them. Because they are dramatically reducing the entropy of energy lost to disengaging people, they are benefiting from high engagement and high performance. They are learning how to collaborate deeply. Three of the critical elements for this deep collaboration are the ability to make feedback loops explicit, to coordinate across a set of feedback loops, and the capacity to learn and adjust across this set. These three critical elements differentiate circular economies from linear economies. Talking about being circular without these three critical elements is linear in disguise.

Shifting to circular agreements

In describing and identifying high-performing, highly engaged groups, we have learned how to support groups in shifting to more regenerative, circular economic agreements. We call this the Agile Vibrancy Move process (Ritchie-Dunham, 2014).

In Step One, you identify your purpose, what you have achieved in accomplishing that purpose, and what you need to be able to achieve in service to the purpose. This sets up the gap between your actual and desired state.

In Step Two, you identify groups that are experiencing your desired level of outcomes. This is very different than linear economic thinking, which tries to improve on what you are already doing from your own logic (Frishammar & Parida, 2021). The kind of thinking needed to achieve your desired state is usually not available within your current thinking. That is why you have not achieved it yet. What we found from groups that successfully transitioned was that they found inspiration in groups that were already living the desired experience. Once you identify these groups, then you can see what you observe that they do differently than you do. For example, if your group currently focuses more on noun-level, output-focused thinking, you might discover this higher-performing group has agreements that support verb level, outcomes-focused thinking, such as enquiry and mentoring, allowing them to engage far more creativity and learning over space and time.

In Step Three, you look at your own agreements, structures, and processes to see how your own differ from those you saw in the other group. They are achieving something that you are not. What is it that you can see that they are doing that you are not (Cooperrider & Whitney, 2005)?

In Step Four, you begin to try some of the new practices that you observed, learning from what happens within your system. What worked? What did not work? What might you try differently next time? What might other groups within your ecosystem now try? This is the agile learning process (Jensen Clayton, 2021). Through this process, hundreds of groups have been able to shift their agreements towards circular economic agreements. They collaboratively agree on what they know they are here to do, their shared purpose, and how important it is to them to achieve it. They learn about the kinds of agreements that support the level of engagement, transform, and transference that they have not yet experienced, but must (Hinske, 2017). They then begin to experiment with those processes, building the capacity to learn and adjust over time. They begin to evolve towards regenerative, circular economies.

In the shift to circular agreements, you move from measuring inputs to outputs to outcomes to impacts to the total value generated. Is the ecosystem better off because of your circular economy? Is the value generated for each stakeholder greater than when you started, leading to the generation of a greater value for the whole ecosystem? This value is measured for each stakeholder and the whole ecosystem in direct financial terms and indirect flourishing terms—greater health and performance. Health in a sustainable ecosystem of regenerated resources is measured in how people can access them more equitably (MacArthur, 2019). Performance is measured by how those natural and human-enhanced resources generate outcomes and impacts (Keller & Schaninger, 2019).

The circular economy is a great idea that linear economic logic cannot achieve. The circular economy requires making feedback loops explicit, coordinating across a set of feedback loops in service to a deeper shared purpose, while learning and adjusting across the set over time. These three requirements are only achievable through deep collaboration (MacArthur, 2019), where human creativity is engaged, transformed, and transferred, simultaneously integrating the levels of nouns, verbs, potential, and ecosystems. This is the full human expression, in relationship with nature, that creates regenerative circular economies. Thousands, maybe millions, of groups are figuring out how. It is only impossible from the linear economic mindset. It is completely possible from the natural human understanding of collaboratively engaging the creative process. Now is the time, and here is the space for truly circular economies. We can agree to this.

References

Arthur, W. B. (2021). *Economics in Nouns and Verbs*. https://arxiv.org/abs/2104.01868

BUILD UPON2: A Tool to Deliver the Renovation Wave. (2021). www.worldgbc.org/build-upon

Colnes, A. (2013). Energy Action Network Annual Report 2013 published at www.eanvt.org.

Cooper Ramo, J. (2016). *The Seventh Sense: Power, Fortune, and Survival in the Age of Networks*. Little, Brown and Company.

Cooperrider, D. L., & Whitney, D. (2005). *Appreciative Inquiry: A Positive Revolution in Change*. Berrett-Koehler.

Costanza, R., Cumberland, J., Daly, H., Goodland, R., & Norgaard, R. (1997). *An Introduction to Ecological Economics*. St. Lucie Press.

Daly, H. E., & Farley, J. (2004). *Ecological Economics: Principles and Applications*. Island Press.

Dietz, R., & O'Neill, D. (2013). *Enough Is Enough: Building a Sustainable Economy in a World of Finite Resources*. Berret-Koehler.

Ehrenfeld, J. R., & Hoffman, A. J. (2013). *Flourishing: A Frank Conversation About Sustainability*. Stanford Business Books.

Frishammar, J., & Parida, V. (2021). The Four Fatal Mistakes Holding Back Circular Business Models. *MIT Sloan Management Review*. https://sloanreview.mit.edu/article/the-four-fatal-mistakes-holding-back-circular-business-models/

Hinske, C. (2017). *Agreements of Transformation: Experience-based Research Exploring the Patterns and Specifics of Societal-scale Transformations in Different Cultures*. U. Bundesamt.

Hoeschele, W. (2010). *The Economics of Abundance: A Political Economy of Freedom, Equity, and Sustainability*. Ashgate Publishing Company.

Industrial Environmental Performance Metrics: Challenges and Opportunities. (1999). The National Academies Press. https://doi.org/doi:10.17226/9458

Jensen Clayton, S. (2021). An Agile Approach to Change Management. *Harvard Business Review*. https://hbr.org/2021/01/an-agile-approach-to-change-management?utm_source=feedburner&utm_medium=feed&utm_campaign=Feed%3A+harvardbusiness+%28HBR.org%29

Keller, S., & Schaninger, B. (2019). *Beyond Performance 2.0: A Proven Approach to Leading Large-Scale Change*. Wiley.

MacArthur, E. (2019). *The Virtuous Circle*. European Investment Bank.

Marshall, A. (1890). *Principles of Economics*. MacMillan and Co.

Mayers, K., Davis, T., & Van Wassenhove, L. N. (2021). The Limits of the "Sustainable" Economy. *Harvard Business Review*. https://hbr.org/2021/06/the-limits-of-the-sustainable-economy

McDonough, W., & Braungart, M. (2002). *Cradle to Cradle: Remaking the Way We Make Things*. North Point Press.

Müller, E. (2018). Regenerative Development in Higher Education: Costa Rica's Perspective. In N. W. Gleason (Ed.), *Higher Education in the Era of the Fourth Industrial Revolution* (pp. 121–144). Springer Singapore. https://doi.org/10.1007/978-981-13-0194-0_6

Ritchie-Dunham, J. L. (forthcoming). Agreements_Your Choice. In I. f. S. Clarity (Ed.).

Ritchie-Dunham, J. L. (2004). A Framework for Achieving Clarity for You and Your Organization. *The Systems Thinker*, *15*(7), 7–8.

Ritchie-Dunham, J. L. (2014). *Ecosynomics: The Science of Abundance*. Vibrancy Publishing. ecosynomics.com

Senge, P., Smith, B., Kruschwitz, N., Laur, J., & Schley, S. (2008). *The Necessary Revolution: How Individuals and Organizations Are Working Together*. DoubleDay.

Stahel, W. R. (2016). The Circular Economy. *Nature*, *531*(7595), 435–438. https://doi.org/10.1038/531435a

Stahel, W. R. (2019). *The Circular Economy: A User's Guide* (T. E. M. Foundation, Ed.). Routledge.

Sterman, J. D. (2000). *Business Dynamics: Systems Thinking and Modeling for a Complex World*. Irwin McGraw-Hill.

VanderWeele, T. J. (2017). On The Promotion of Human Flourishing. *Proceedings of the National Academy of Science*, *114*(31), 8148–8156. https://doi.org/https://doi.org/10.1073/pnas.1702996114

Waddock, S. (2020). Thinking Transformational System Change. *Journal of Change Management*, 20(3), 189–201. https://doi.org/10.1080/14697017.2020.1737179

Ziervogel, G., Cowen, A., & Ziniades, J. (2016). Moving from Adaptive to Transformative Capacity: Building Foundations for Inclusive, Thriving, and Regenerative Urban Settlements. *Sustainability*, 8(9), 955. www.mdpi.com/2071-1050/8/9/955

18 Development and implementation of resource labelling

Klaus M. Dosch and Alexa K. Lutzenberger

The problem–introduction

At over 90 billion tonnes, global material use has more than tripled compared to the 1970s. According to current UN estimates, this trend will continue. Forecasts expect a doubling to 180 billion tonnes by 2050 (IRP, 2017; see also OECD Global Material Resources Outlook 2060).

Resource consumption is a direct cost factor and a key driver of major global environmental problems (IRP, 2017). Through the accompanying degradation of ecosystems and biodiversity and the acceleration of climate change, resource consumption is already having a negative impact on our livelihoods. People in unstable, conflict-ridden regions are particularly at risk from increasing distribution struggles. The link between climate change and resource consumption is becoming increasingly apparent in society, and the call for a resource transition is growing louder (Sharp 2020). Its goal is to ensure equitable resource use within the limited capacities of our planet (Steffen et al. 2015; Dittrich et al. 2019; Giljum et al. 2014; Hirschnitz et al. 2017; Klaus et al. 2019).

The global construction industry must face up to these correlations. China needed more cement between 2011 and 2013 than the USA did in the 20th century. The construction industry causes 40% of the current resource and energy consumption. By 2050, more than 75% of the population will live in megacities, and 3 billion homes will have to be built for them (Swanson 2015).

To meet this challenge, the resource consumption linked to construction must be significantly reduced. In addition to climate- and resource-friendly building materials and constructions, measurement methods for resource consumption in construction are necessary that calculate greenhouse gas emissions, primary energy and raw material consumption as realistically as possible. However, due to the long lifespan of buildings, the assessment of the circularity and the effects of a circular economy in construction reach its systemic limits.

How the problem should be solved

The systematic improvement of the environmental performance of buildings and settlements in Germany and Europe has been limited to increasing energy

DOI: 10.4324/9781003244196-21

efficiency. In Germany, this was started very successfully in the 1970s with the first Heat Insulation Ordinance (EnEG: Law for saving energy in buildings enacted in 1976 Federal Republic of Germany). Today, the specific energy consumption for heating buildings and supplying hot water has been reduced from more than 350 kWh/(m^2a) in the early 1970s to around 50 kWh/(m^2a) with the current Building Energy Act (Gebäudeenergiegesetz: Act on the Saving of Energy and the Use of Renewable Energies for Heating and Cooling in Buildings from 08.08.2020 Federal Republic of Germany). This corresponds to about 7/8 of what is theoretically possible. Further increases in energy efficiency are hardly possible since the expected marginal expenditure of further measures necessary for this often exceeds the achievable marginal benefit. Therefore, expending more material for lower energy savings only in the use phase is the wrong way to go.

Nevertheless, in Europe, the Performance of Buildings Directive and the Energy Efficiency Directive, and in Germany the current Building Energy Act, also focus exclusively on energy consumption during building use. Greenhouse gases and mass flows – and thus the recycling of raw materials – have not been considered.

There is tremendous untapped potential for reducing greenhouse gas emissions and the consumption of non-renewable primary energy and non-renewable raw materials in other phases of the life cycle.

Systems for assessing the sustainability of buildings, such as DGNB, BNB, Leed or Breeam, use a variety of criteria and indicators. Therefore they are more of a comprehensive assessment system for the quality of buildings than their environmental performance. As a result, they sometimes even create distortions in the measurement of resource use (Hirschnitz et al. 2015). Moreover, indicators on mass flows and greenhouse gases – if available at all – only account for a negligible share of the overall assessment. Furthermore, the comprehensive methods for assessing the sustainability of buildings are not suitable for a clear and easy-to-understand communication of the contribution of certified buildings to the energy and resource transition and climate neutrality.

Currently, the most urgent problem in the field of environmental sustainability is the mitigation of climate change through the drastic reduction of greenhouse gas emissions, the energy transition and the decline of the consumption of non-renewable raw materials, for example, through partial substitution with renewable or recycled raw materials.

The calculations of buildings with life cycle assessments in which deconstruction and recycling are credited are also controversial. It is completely unclear whether and when a building will be deconstructed. Moreover, it is hardly possible to seriously estimate which deconstruction or disposal technology will be available in 50, 80 or more years and what resource requirements will be associated with it. Therefore, in the case of durable goods such as buildings, it is more than questionable whether life cycle phases C (disposal and recycling) and D (credits or burdens outside the actual scope of the system boundaries) may be taken into account in their life cycle assessment, since their valuation is carried out with today's technology.

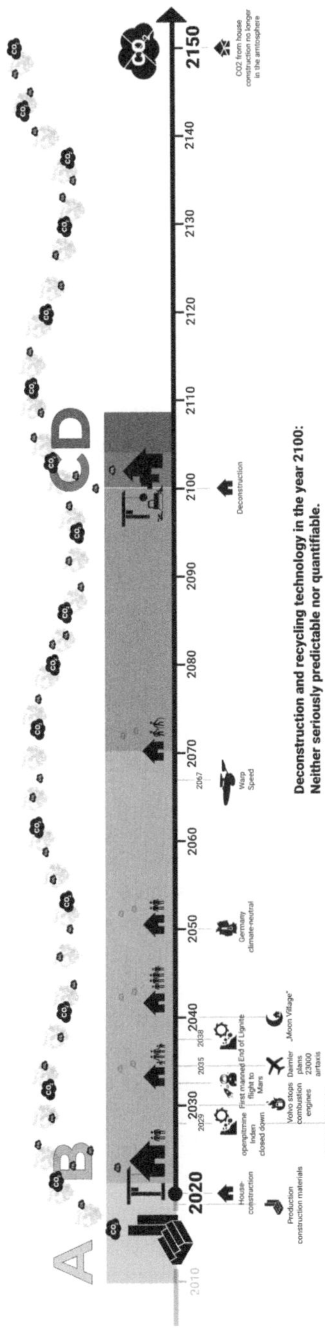

Figure 18.1 Timeline building life.

Source: Own depiction.

End-of-life or cradle-to-cradle approaches do not solve this problem. When a building is constructed, all greenhouse gases associated with the production of the building are emitted or raw materials are degraded in a close temporal connection with the construction of the building, thus causing environmental damage. Greenhouse gases are in the atmosphere for at least 150 years from this point onwards and intensify the greenhouse effect; environmental damage due to the extraction of raw materials has occurred. If CO_2, energy or raw material savings related to disposal, recovery or potential recycling after the deconstruction of the building in 50, 80 or more years are already credited in the construction phase of buildings, this leads to systematic errors. The same applies to the damage to ecosystem services caused by raw material extraction.

If LCA phases C or even D are taken into account for very durable goods such as buildings, the actual emission of greenhouse gases, primary energy consumption or consumption of non-renewable raw materials caused during the construction of the building does not match the data determined by LCA, for example, in procedures for assessing the sustainability of buildings such as the DGNB, LEED or BREEAM methods.

Besides, the technological framework conditions for deconstruction and recycling after the end of a building's useful life are completely unknown. It must be assumed that in 80 or 100 years, fundamentally different forms of energy and raw material extraction will prevail. A consideration of dismantling or credit for recycling based on today's technologies is therefore not justifiable.

What is essential for the containment of climate change and the reduction of natural resource consumption is actual material flows into the atmosphere or from and into nature and not hypothetical accounting constructs.

Considering the limits of the circular economy in buildings

This is where the present work on the Resource Score comes in, which as a label evaluates and depicts the use of natural resources. In its conception, the success criteria of proven labels were taken into account.

The Resource Score was primarily designed for buildings. It focuses on three major societal challenges: energy transition, climate neutrality and resource transition. It deliberately leaves out other quality parameters because these can just as easily be formulated in tenders, specifications and so on. It also ignores all aspects of economic sustainability, which are taken into account by investors anyway.

For classifying a building into efficiency classes from A to G in the three resource categories, a simplified life cycle assessment is required, which takes place anyway as part of the preparation of environmental product declarations. It is necessary to optimise the resource consumption of buildings in the early planning phases. Only in early planning phases decisions can be made that have a major influence on the building's resource consumption. Ideally, a sensible system should be able to handle ex-ante and ex-post consideration of buildings.

For example, a standardised procedure has been established through eco-balancing in accordance with ISO 14040/44, but strategic control is lost in the complex presentation of input-output analyses and the critical assessment of the end-of-life life cycle phases. A solid and clear information basis on resource use per building has been lacking up to now. As a result, it is currently possible neither for those involved in the value chain nor for consumers to see at-a-glance whether a building is actually resource-efficient or even resource-saving.

The introduction of the resource label Resource Score is a corresponding instrument with a far-reaching steering function.

Only three key criteria are used for the Resource Score. They reflect essential tasks of the necessary transition of industrial societies:

1. Climate score: Mitigation of climate change by reducing the release of greenhouse gases into the atmosphere.
2. Energy score: conversion of the energy system by substituting non-renewable primary energy with renewable energy.
3. Material score: Resource transition from a linear economy based on abiotic raw materials to a circular economy increasingly based on renewable raw materials.

With the classification of energy efficiency in the use of buildings, an established and generally known scheme is available.

The Resource Score takes up this basic idea of classification but modifies and expands it fundamentally to assess the contribution of buildings to the energy and resource transition and to climate neutrality.

The Resource Score thus fills a gap that is increasingly being created by the ever-improving energy efficiency during the use of products. If buildings require less and less energy during their use, which in the course of the energy transition also consists of steadily increasing shares of renewable energies, the upstream and in part also downstream value creation phases of buildings become more important. Considerable energy and raw material consumption, as well as greenhouse gases, are released in the phase of building product manufacture and the upstream stages of raw material extraction, the production of materials and auxiliary materials, the necessary transport processes and the downstream processes such as the possible recycling or disposal of the product.

Resource label based on tried and tested Factor X methodology

Factor X becomes the Resource Score. It brings the tried and tested, regionally oriented Factor X approach, which has been successfully applied in the Rhenish lignite mining district (Dosch 2018), into a form that can be applied nationwide. In addition, the Resource Score creates a recognisable and self-explanatory label for resource and climate protection in buildings.

As part of the work of the Factor X Agency of the Indeland development company, buildings in seven new construction areas in the Rhenish lignite mining region have so far been assessed with regard to the consumption of non-renewable primary energy (PENRT: primary energy non-renewable total), the consumption of non-renewable raw materials ($RI_{abiotic}$ = ∑ cumulative resources effort CRE, unused extraction NCE) and greenhouse gas emissions (GWP_{100}).

In these settlement areas, only buildings were allowed to be constructed that had a maximum of 50% of the demands of an EnEV (Energy Efficiency Regulation)-compliant comparative house built in a customary manner in all three resource categories (factor 2).

Meanwhile more than 800 buildings, single-family houses and multi-family houses with up to 100 residential units and commercial buildings were calculated.

For a nationwide application of the Factor X principle, its originally intended regionality is an obstacle. For example, a house in Bavaria must have the same improvement factor X as an identical house in North, East or West Germany. This is not the case with the current approach because regional or even local benchmarks are used. So far, this has been correct and purposeful to develop and evaluate the methodology locally and regionally and to create a robustly applicable procedure.

Resource score

The Resource Score is determined in the three subscores: non-renewable primary energy, greenhouse gases and non-renewable raw materials, as done successfully with the Factor X approach. The allocation of the class boundaries of the efficiency classes A to G is designed to be dynamic.

The best efficiency class A is defined as an efficiency not previously available on the market with regard to the resource category presented. It creates an incentive for innovation in the construction industry. Efficiency class A is coloured blue, in contrast to the common traffic light colouring of energy efficiency or the Nutri-Score (green-yellow-red), and thus stands out from efficiency class B in a recognisable way. In class B, the best buildings currently available on the market are found in relation to the respective score. The gradation up to efficiency class G, which reflects the lowest resource efficiency observable on the market, is linear. An aggregation of an overall score is not initially planned for the Resource Score.

The climate score evaluates the life-cycle-wide release of greenhouse gases in CO_2 equivalents without end-of-life assessments. Endpoint A (blue) is defined as at least CO_2 neutral. The minimum requirement for climate neutrality is that no CO_2 emissions may emanate from the building over the life cycle of 50 years. The endpoint G is defined by the worst observed value of an EnEV 2016-compliant building. As with the other scores, the time limit is 50 years without later demolition or disposal of the building materials. France is currently following a similar path. With the RE2020 Regulation, France is also the first country in the EU to limit greenhouse gas emissions associated with building construction. Until 2027, the requirements correspond to climate score D; from 2028, a limit value corresponding to climate score C will be required for new buildings in France (Ministère de la Transition écologique 2020)

The energy score creates the link to the previous energy efficiency classes of buildings. In contrast to this, however, the energy score evaluates the

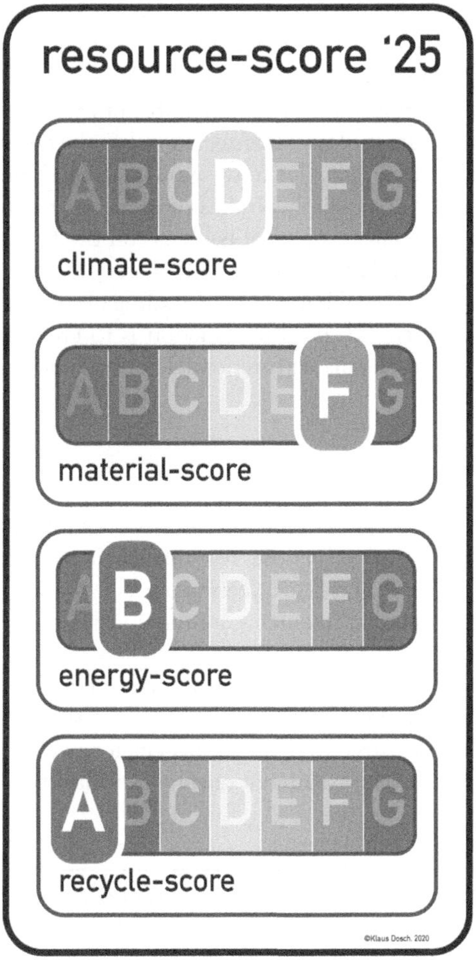

Figure 18.2 Resource score.
Source: Own depiction.

non-renewable primary energy consumption during the use phase and the "grey" non-renewable primary energy associated with the building. Analogous to the climate score, the scale ranges from A (blue) to G (red). A building with an energy score of A is an extreme low-energy building, that is, it requires less than 500 kWh/($m^2$50a) [per year: < 10 kWh/(m^2a)] of non-renewable primary energy over its life cycle of 50 years. The endpoint is defined by the worst observed value of an EnEV 2016-compliant construction. As with the other scores, the temporal balance limit is 50 years without subsequent demolition or disposal of the building materials.

The material score evaluates the life cycle consumption of non-renewable raw materials. The indicators cumulative raw material input (CRE) and unused extraction during raw material extraction (NCE of VDI 4800.1) (guideline on resource efficiency) are applied. This indicator fulfils a triple function: On the one hand, it addresses the shortage of available non-renewable raw materials. In most cases, this is not a shortage in the geological sense, but rather the decline in the availability of the raw material, especially due to the growing competition for land in heavily populated regions. Secondly, this indicator promotes the recycling of building products, as it places all "ecological burdens" on the first use of building material. In the case of secondary use or building materials made from recycled raw materials, only the "ecological burdens" of recycling or reprocessing into a new building material are incurred. Its third function is to promote the substitution of non-renewable raw materials with renewable raw materials such as wood or other natural fibres.

Efficiency classes

For the classification of the efficiency classes of the Resource Score for buildings, more than 800 buildings were evaluated, whose resource consumption was determined over the life cycle phases A and B (50 years of use).

This resulted in the following specific resource consumption related to the heated square metre:

The following limits were derived from this for the classification of the Resource Score. For efficiency class A, limits were chosen that define a "not yet available best in class" and thus create an incentive to achieve this efficiency class. The currently best-observed results justify the assignment of efficiency class B.

Table 18.1 Specific resource consumption/square metre

RI abiotic [kg/(m²50a)]	*GWP 100 [kg CO_2 eq./(m²50a)]*	*PENRT [kWh/(m²50a)]*
Min: 1.797 Max: 6.780	Min: −205 Max: 1.546	Min: 1.139 Max: 6.697

Table 18.2 Efficiency categories

Efficiency class	*RI abiotic [kg/(m²50a)]*	*GWP 100 [kg CO_2 eq/(m²50a)]*	*PENRT [kWh/(m²50a)]*
A	<1.500	< 0	< 1.000
B	1.500–2.399	0–279	1.000–1.999
C	2.400–3.299	280–559	2.000–2.999
D	3.300–4.199	560–839	3.000–3.999
E	4.200–5.099	840–1.119	4.000–4.999
F	5.100–5.999	1.200–1.399	5.000–5.999
G	≥6.000	≥1.400	≥6.000

Table 18.3 Resource score of a benchmark building in a factor 2 settlement area

RI abiotic [kg/(m²50a)]	*GWP 100 [kg CO_2 eq/(m²50a)]*	*PENRT [kWh/(m²50a)]*
5.311 Material score: F	1.534 Climate score: G	6.373 Energy score: G

Table 18.4 Resource score factor 2 building

RI abiotic [kg/(m²50a)]	*GWP 100 [kg CO_2 eq/(m²50a)]*	*PENRT [kWh/(m²50a)]*
2.800 Material score: C	750 Climate score: D	3.200 Energy score: D

Efficiency class G marks the worst observed value of the class. The classes in-between are distributed linearly.

According to this classification, a reference building – a conventionally solidly constructed single-family house according to the valid EnEV – has the following Resource Score:

The minimum target for a factor 2 single-family house must achieve the following goals:

Key findings

The Resource Score is a lean and efficient method. It is applicable in the early planning stages where there is still a considerable influence on the choice of fundamental building construction and building materials. Using the well-known traffic light scheme from energy efficiency labelling, the Resource Score can also provide planners unfamiliar with life cycle assessments with an at-a-glance view of the performance of buildings with regard to the climate, energy and raw material change in construction. The class boundaries on which the classification into A to G is based were determined on the basis of more than 800 calculated buildings. Residential buildings of all types as well as office buildings were considered. By cutting off the life cycle assessment after 50 years of use, it is ensured that a deconstruction of the building that lies far in the future and, moreover, is uncertain in its probability of occurrence and the associated disposal of building materials or their recycling is not taken into account. The consistency between actual and calculated emissions and resource consumption is thus maintained. We know from the efficiency classification of white goods, for example, that such an easily understandable label has a considerable steering effect with regard to the supply of highly efficient products. A similar effect can therefore be expected for buildings.

Further outlook

In the meantime, local authorities are beginning to set up minimum standards for the Resource Score in building tenders. For example, in Stolberg and Aachen (North-Rhine-Westfalia, Germany), tender competitions for building plots based on the Resource Score will be decided and carried out in 2022. The Resource Score will initiate innovations in climate- and resource-friendly buildings. It shows the differences between climate- and resource-efficient properties, projects and neighbourhoods compared to traditional concepts.

References

Campolmi, G. (2005) Proceedings of the 3rd World Biomass Conference – Biomass for Energy, Industry and Climate Protection, III Vol., p. 981.

Dittrich, M. et al. (2019) Monitoring internationale Ressourcenpolitik. Abschlussbericht. Hg. v. Bundesministerium für Umwelt, Naturschutz und nukleare Sicherheit (BMU). Dessau-Roßlau (TEXTE 51/2020).

Dosch, K. (2018) Resource Efficiency in the Building Sector. In: Lehmann H. (eds) Factor X. Eco-Efficiency in Industry and Science, vol 32. Cham: Springer. https://doi.org/10.1007/978-3-319-50079-9_19

EnEG: Law for saving energy in buildings enacted in 1976. Federal Republic of Germany.

Gebäudeenergiegesetz enacted 08.08.20 in BGBI I p.1728 Federal Republic of Germany.

Giljum, S.; Hinterberger, F. (2014) The Limits of Resource Use and their Economic and Policy Implications. In: Harry Lehmann, Michael Angrick and Andreas Burger (Hg.) (eds) Factor X. Policy, Strategies and Instruments for a Sustainable Resource Use, Bd. 29. Dordrecht: Springer Dordrecht (Eco-efficiency in Industry & Science, 29), S. 3–17.

Hirschnitz-Garbers, M.; and Werland, S. (2017): Ressourcenpolitik und planetare Grenzen: Analyse möglicher naturwissenschaftlicher Begründungszusammenhänge für ressourcen- politische Ziele. Vertiefungsanalyse im Projekt Ressourcenpolitik 2 (PolRess 2).

Hirschnitz-Garbers, M; Lutter, S.; Giljum, S.; Srebotnjak, T.; and Gradmann, A. (2015) Weiterentwicklung von Material- und Rohstoffinputindikatoren – Methodendiskussion und Ansätze für widerspruchsfreie Datensätze. Endbericht des UFOPLAN-Vorhabens FKZ 3713 93 150. Hg. v. Umweltbundesamt (UBA). Dessau-Roßlau. www.ecologic.eu/sites/files/publication/2015/bf_endbericht_inputindikatoren_fkz371393150_final.pdf.

IRP (2017). Assessing global resource use: A systems approach to resource efficiency and pollution reduction. Bringezu, S., Ramaswami, A., Schandl, H., O'Brien, M., Pelton, R., Acquatella, J., Ayuk, E., Chiu, A., Flanegin, R., Fry, J., Giljum, S., Hashimoto, S., Hellweg, S., Hosking, K., Hu, Y., Lenzen, M., Lieber, M., Lutter, S., Miatto, A., Singh Nagpure, A., Obersteiner, M., van Oers, L., Pfister, S., Pichler, P., Russell, A., Spini, L., Tanikawa, H., van der Voet, E., Weisz, H., West, J., Wiijkman, A., Zhu, B., Zivy, R. A Report of the International Resource Panel. United Nations Environment Programme. Nairobi, Kenya.

Klaus, J.; and Postpischil, R. (2019) Governance einer effizienten und nachhaltigen Ressourcennutzung. Abschlussbericht im Projekt Ressourcenpolitik 2 (PolRess 2). Unter Mitarbeit von Lisa Graaf und Martin Hirschnitz-Garbers Friedhelm Keimeyer.

Ministère de la Transition écologique. (2020) *Réglementation environnementale RE2020.* Ministère de la Transition écologique. Retrieved December 3, 2021, from www.ecologie.gouv.fr/reglementation-environnementale-re2020

OECD (Ed.) (2018) Global Material Resources Outlook to 2060. Economic drivers and environmental consequences, OECD Publishing, Paris. oe.cd/materials-outlook.

Sharp, H.; and Mohaupt, F. (2020) Ressourcenwende. Eckpfeiler und Rahmenbedingungen einer neuen ressourcenpolitischen Vernetzung von Zivilgesellschaft und Wissenschaft. Diskussionspapier. Ed. Bundesumweltministerium und Umweltbundesamtes, Berlin. www.ressourcenwende.net/wpcontent/uploads/2020/02/Ressourcenwende_Diskussionspapier.pdf.

Swanson, A. (2015) How China used more cement in 3 years than the US did in the entire 20th century. Published in Washington Post March 24, 2015.

19 Circularity's stumbling blocks

How stuttering implementation and socio-metabolic root causes adversely interact

Willi Haas

Introduction

Despite convincing promises, the implementation of the circular economy (CE) lacks behind expectations. The literature on implementation barriers draws a bleak picture. CE is seen as a niche discussion among experts, and implementation encounters resistance to change. Overall the literature shows that while low-hanging fruits in mainly recycling niches can be harvested, the more fundamental changes are envisaged, the more insurmountable the barriers. Against this backdrop, socio-metabolic root causes of circularity-impeding barriers are discussed: A decarbonisation that fosters stock growth with a narrow option space for circularity strategies, a stock growth dynamic inscribed in socio-metabolic systems that limits reuse and recycling and a long-standing open-loop management of biomass. The socio-metabolic analysis demands fundamental changes. Given the literature on implementation barriers, exactly these far-reaching changes seem to be out of reach. Concluding, instead of doing more of the same and tarnishing against rubber walls, it is more promising to focus on this interwoven texture of barriers and stumbling blocks to discover leverage points that might widen the circularity space in the future.

Why have we not been circular for a long time?

Over the last two decades, the concept of the circular economy has received increasing popularity in academia, business and politics (Ghisellini et al., 2016; Harris et al., 2021; Merli et al., 2018). Proponents from all sectors argue that a CE reduces environmental impacts since it opts for reducing inputs and outputs of the societal metabolism. Inputs are reduced as secondary materials replace primary materials extracted from nature, and outputs are scaled down as end-of-life waste destined for release to nature is diverted into material cycles that provide secondary materials or products for reprocessing or reuse, among other, more far-reaching CE strategies such as lifetime extension. In recent years, the CE is also promoted as a strategy to particularly combat climate change (Cantzler et al., 2020). In addition to these environmental benefits, proponents claim the

DOI: 10.4324/9781003244196-22

transition to a CE will lead to higher economic growth, improve security of supply and create more jobs (Rizos et al., 2019; Webster, 2017; Wijkman & Skanberg, 2016). Overall, the CE is sometimes described as the long-awaited silver bullet to achieve a transition to sustainability.

Given these advantages, one would expect the number of CE initiatives to rapidly increase at an accelerated pace with visible changes in the societal metabolism. However, the evidence paints a different picture. Global material extraction is increasing and CE efforts are not noticeable (Hart & Pomponi, 2021). In contrast, the global circularity has declined over the last century and has stagnated at a historic low for the last two decades (Haas et al., 2020). Some scholars and key players of the CE might point to a number of successful cases and contradict this diagnosis. While I agree that there are successful cases, my point is that closing and slowing loops are drowned in the still ongoing mainstream developments that generally foster and prefer non-circularity. Therefore, in my view, instead of doing more of the same and extending the list of potential societal benefits of a hypothetical CE, it is more rewarding and high time to think critically about the reasons for the lack of progress. What is hindering the implementation of an effective CE? Are the promises too optimistic or even not correct at all? Or are proponents overlooking serious obstacles and failing to give them the attention they deserve? Only if barriers are well understood, CE can step out of a too narrow and pure business imperative, and a targeted and evidence-based development strategy can be developed by employing a reflexive and adaptive approach to meet social and environmental goals.

In the first part, this essay summarises the findings from the literature on implementation barriers to the CE, then discusses complementary and underlying socio-metabolic stumbling blocks and finally draws conclusions on what changes are needed to make the CE work.

Different scholarly perspectives on implementation barriers

Hindrances for the EU to become circular

In a survey-based study, Kirchherr et al. (2018) explore the question of why the implementation of the CE in the European Union has made little progress so far, despite high attention. They start off that most scholarly studies point at various technological barriers. In contrast, they find cultural barriers to be the most important hindrances. In particular, the interviewed corporate and political interviewees highlight a lack of consumer interest and awareness, as well as a hesitant corporate culture, as the main barriers. In their analysis of interactions, they link the hesitant corporate culture to barriers resulting from the linear system culture they operate in and further link it with market barriers related to low virgin material prices and high upfront costs. These well-known and long-standing market barriers require synergistic governmental interventions to accelerate the transition towards a CE. However, government policies do not address these main barriers. Their research also revealed that technological barriers are not among the most pressing obstacles to the CE.

Overall, they draw a quite disillusioning conclusion. First, referring to an earlier work (Kirchherr et al., 2017, p. 228), they state "[CE is not] a 'quick win', but a major long-term undertaking". Secondly, at the present stage they classify the CE as a niche discussion among sustainable development professionals. Their work can be understood as a call for a fundamental shift in government intervention strategies from a superficial to a deep level of intervention in order for the CE to maintain its momentum.

The country case of Italy: recycling centeredness as a barrier to CE

Another study investigates the CE transition in Italy (Ghisellini & Ulgiati, 2020). They draw on a sample of 292 organisations and survey their perception of the transition to a CE at company, meso and macro levels. Among the 6R practical framework (reduction, repair, reuse, recover, remanufacturing and recycling), recycling is the most preferred strategy along the whole supply chain. Other strategies such as repair, reuse, remanufacturing are making good progress, especially in small businesses. Companies specialised in promoting the CE in its full bandwidth of strategies offer the opportunity of shifting the concept beyond the recycling bias. In their study, they identify seven main types of barriers. (1) As legislative barriers they name inadequate and incomplete legislative framework, a lack of vertical environmental policy integration and a lack of incentives for the use of recycled materials. (2) The economic barriers they detect are low investment in research and development and the Italian industrial structure which is dominated by small family businesses. (3) The market barriers are constituted by the higher prices for secondary materials compared to virgin materials. (4) In financial terms there is a lack of availability of capital risk, adequate investment tools and credit access for eco-innovation research. (5) Networking barriers exist due to a lack of platforms for brokering materials over multiple cycles and sectors. (6) Advanced technologies for reuse are assessed as a bottleneck. (7) Finally, they name the cultural barriers as a lack of attention to waste prevention strategies (design, sustainable production and consumption, industrial and urban symbiosis).

While authors note non-negligible changes in the structure, culture and practices of Italian societal (sub-)systems, they state that CE in Italy is currently only recycling-centred. Given the range of CE strategies and their hierarchy (Potting et al., 2017), this recycling focus needs to be questioned as an adequate entry point for a CE. Morseletto (2020) argues that recovery and recycling do not necessarily promote a CE because these activities destroy products' integrity. "Recycle and Recovery have limited benefits in terms of the (partial) reclamation of materials and energy recovery" (Morseletto, 2020, p. 10). Therefore, more powerful CE strategies should be favoured.

Circularity of the built environment hampered by cultural and financial issues

Since the transition to a CE is an endeavour re-constituting societies as a whole, heterogeneity needs to be considered and demands a more tailored understanding and approach. Hart et al. (2019) focus on barriers and drivers for the case of the built environment, where buildings and infrastructure feature numerous and different stakeholders with different interests and incentives in different phases of long lifespans and hundreds of components. They structure their barriers after a review process of more than 200 references to barriers and enablers in a similar way as Ghisellini and Ulgiati and Krichherr et al. into the categories cultural, regulatory, financial and sectoral. Their sectoral barriers are of special interest here. They name complexity and confused incentives (S2), long product life cycles (S3), technical challenges regarding material recovery (S4) and lacking standardisation (S5) as well as insufficient use or development of CE-focused design and collaboration tools, information and metrics (S6). In this chapter, a lack of bandwith (S1) is identified as a more fundamental barrier, which authors see as not explicitly addressed in the literature. With this they point at competing and overlapping priorities and uncertainty by stakeholders to what extent the CE framework has an overarching quality or is subdue to other frameworks, such as sustainable development. As another sector-specific cultural barrier, they discuss the sector itself (S6). They state "that the sector is its own enemy in terms of CE. By nature it is wary of innovation, and takes an adversarial, risk-averse approach to contractual terms on liability that can restrain innovation further" (Hart et al., 2019, p. 622).

In their concluding remarks, they emphasise that while many technical and regulatory challenges are still in place, the cultural and financial/market issues are the built environment's big circularity obstacles, in particular, the lacking collaboration with other actors along the supply chain and a lacking strong business case for circular models.

Supply chain circularity inhibited by lack of awareness in society and by consumers

To add another complementary perspective, a systematic review on drivers, barriers and practices regarding circularity in the supply chain is to be provided here. Govindan and Hasanagic (2018) examined 60 articles and identified 39 barriers which were categorised into eight clusters as government, economic, technological, knowledge and skills, management, CE framework, cultural and social, and market issues. The evaluation of barriers in literature shows that the most mentioned is that "consumer perception towards components that are reused is bad and therefore it is more difficult to implement CE strategies". It is followed by "technological limitations by tracking recycled materials" and "lack of public awareness and therefore it is difficult to reuse, recycle and remanufacture products". To a lesser degree but still high ranking is "a lack of enthusiasm towards CE in supply chain" (Govindan & Hasanagic, 2018, p. 300).

The study summarises as key barriers a lack of awareness of the CE in society and by consumers and asks managers and decision-makers to address these issues. This overall assessment of a systematic review is less guiding an effective process to overcome barriers than a statement that shows that underlying causes are not well understood yet.

How differing stakeholder perceptions of the CE implementation become barriers

The perception of different stakeholder groups namely researchers, economists and administrators was explored in a study by Sven Kevin van Langen et al. (2021). Researchers in this study are 80 participants of an European project studying the CE; economists comprise 114 academics in economics, management, business economics and finance of Parthenope University of Naples, Italy; and administrators are 141 public officials of the Metropolitan City of Naples, Italy. The survey shows that administrators envisage a CE predominantly as a "zero waste economy" and focused on utilising CE for economic growth and job creation. Researchers and economists perceive a CE as a far-reaching re-design of the economy and society in a more regenerative manner and mainly expect a reduction of environmental benefits from the CE transition. Interesting enough they agree in their views that a successful implementation of CE depends on the governance of the process by key actors and instruments. When it comes to the question of how governance initiative should look like, they differ again. A holistic top-down approach is favoured by researchers and a bottom-up approach guided by the civil society (companies and citizens/consumers) is rated as most promising approach by economists and administrators. It needs to be critically noted that this mismatch in perception is already an obstacle in itself: One of the groups sees the ball in the government's court, while the other two groups including administrators shift the initiative to two very distinct stakeholder groups, one of which has high economic stakes and the other is a relatively powerless group expected to champion environmental concerns.

The authors summarise their findings on the main relevant perceived barriers as "resistance to change", the "low awareness and know how", "lack of policies/ regulations" and "current linear design of products". In line with other studies, they identify the need to deepen political intervention to further accelerate the transition, citing "regulatory measures", "the provision of financial support to companies" and dedicated instruments useful to "increase the level of CE awareness on consumers" as the main avenues to pursue.

Socio-metabolic root causes as circularity-impeding stumbling blocks

Given the insights generated from the literature on CE barriers, implementation lacks far behind expectations of the CE. Reasons provided are that it is a niche discussion among sustainable development professionals and that the deeper and more far-reaching interventions are the more fundamental implementation barriers play out against a transition. In addition to implementation, there is another, often overlooked, circularity-impeding layer of socio-metabolic root causes that impede circularity.

The present dominant mode of subsistence in high-income countries can be described as an industrial regime. This is a regime that replaces the agrarian one and was made possible by fossil fuels that allowed to overcome the constraints of area-bound biomass as a primary energy source. Fossil fuels became a more and more abundant energy source which allowed for large and growing infrastructures in combination with increasing energy services with smaller and smaller devices whenever and wherever demanded by a large share of the population (Fischer-Kowalski & Haas, 2016; Haas & Andarge, 2017). This radically transformed the spatial organisation and consequently the nature of social metabolism. Quantitatively energy and material use were increased by a factor of three to five from the agrarian to the industrial regime. The share of non-energy use of materials could be increased by a factor of three to ten (Krausmann et al., 2016). The fossil fuel energy regime paved the way for a 23-fold rise in global socioeconomic material stocks over the 20th century which demanded roughly half of the annual resource use (Krausmann et al., 2017). The industrial regime is characterised by its fossil-fuelled energy base which goes hand in hand with related structural interactions between sub-systems, self-reinforcement processes and power relations that allow it to change only under specific circumstances. Against this backdrop, I want to focus on three aspects that illustrate how socio-metabolic stumbling blocks limit a transition towards material circularity.

Decarbonising economies means large-scale replacement of material-intensive stocks

An ideal net zero around 2050 results in a reduction of the extraction of fossil fuels for energy use. If we consider in a thought experiment that net zero is already achieved in 2015, this means that 13.8 Gt or 15% of non-circular fossil fuels for energy use (Haas et al., 2020) needs to be replaced by renewable energy sources. For the ease of discussion here the replacement is only considered by a shift to wind, water and solar power for electricity production which in parts can be used to produce hydrogen. This means a fundamental change in the electricity infrastructure. There are three effects to be considered: First, electricity demand will increase due to the electrification and use of hydrogen in the transport sector and decarbonisation of heating systems in countries with cold winters; second, material demand per TJ is far higher for renewable power generation in a mix of wind, water and solar power compared to fossil fuel-based electricity; and third, additional electricity storage systems are required to balance a more volatile electricity generation.

To illustrate the second aspect separately: The material intensity of electricity generation in tonnes per TJ electricity in a medium estimate for coal is 0.26, for gas is 0.09 and oil is 0.11. For wind the value is 1.72 (onshore) and 2.51

(offshore), for PV 0.26 (rooftop) and 2.5 (ground-mounted) and for water 7.8 (run-of-river) and 16.7 (storage) (Kalt et al., 2021).

Given all these developments together, the electricity sector will require a significant increase in annual material demand with regard to generation, transmission and storage towards 2050 (Deetman et al., 2021). The 2050 material inflows for a 2-degree world scenario are considered to rise from roughly 223 Mt to 327 Mt per year. Metal used for the electricity sector was about 38 Mt (0.6% of global metal use) in 2015 and would almost triple in a 2-degree world scenario in 2050 (own calculation based on Deetman et al., 2021).

Decarbonisation means as well a complete shift in the transport sector, which makes up a substantial part of today's energy regime. Individual mobility based on the automobile is a cornerstone of the global economy. In the pre-pandemic years, the global vehicles fleet counted 1.21 billion automobiles (about 5% in Germany); 8.3 million automobiles were added annually resulting in a global level of motorisation of 160 cars per 1000 people, with some countries like the US and Germany ranging at around 600-700 cars per 1000 people (Schlögl, 2017). If cars with combustion engines are just replaced by electric vehicles and 1.5 t are assumed as the average vehicle weight for both drive technologies, this means that 12.5 Gt of cars need to be replaced. While recycling is an option for some components, this is challenging to be organised and hindered by recycling losses, even with a complete collection. One of the best practiced recycling is for steel. According to Pauliuk (2018), a hypothetical closed-loop recycling system for passenger cars shows an average steel lifetime in the socioeconomic system of 110 years, about eight full 15 years of use cycles. And in reality, he resumes, secondary steel from cars is downcycled mostly into buildings. A reason for this is the relatively lower purity demands on material quality in buildings compared to high-tech applications in cars and other machinery (almost no residual alloys can be tolerated). This would suggest even for the relatively simple case of steel in automobiles that the perpetuation of recycling practices of the past requires a continued growth of building stocks to absorb the huge quantities of secondary steel. This would satisfy the call for more recycling but would contradict a transition to a sustainable CE that needs to reduce material inputs from and outputs to nature.

With regard to buildings, climate targets demand the decommissioning and refurbishing of buildings and replacing fossil-fuelled heating systems. What is needed are new and different building stocks, but existing buildings have lifespans of decades to centuries (Hertwich et al., 2019). These long lifespans have led to lock-ins of specific use patterns which no longer meet current needs or reflect the current state of energy efficiency (Reyna & Chester, 2015). When it comes to CE strategies, recycling is the only option for the old and outdated stocks. The construction and demolishing waste is a huge share of the overall solid waste of societies and constitutes for example about 50% of all solid waste in the EU28 (Mayer et al., 2019). In practice, construction minerals like concrete are most often downcycled to coarse aggregates and not all uses result in environmental benefits (Hertwich et al., 2019).

When retrofitting is the strategy, a Swiss study hints at the particularly problematic thermal insulation material. In their modelling they show that material flows will increase considerably by 2035 with insulation material becoming the fraction with highest environmental impacts. They find disposal to be problematic, as in the past it was often contaminated with flame retardants (Heeren & Hellweg, 2019).

Growing stocks limit circularity

While secondary materials show a 20-fold increase, the socioeconomic cycling rate remains modest at only 6% input cycling. This is only partly due to poor recycling performance, but growing stocks constitute a deep-rooted structural barriers in the dynamics, scale and composition of socioeconomic metabolism (Haas et al., 2020).

Closing material loops completely is not compatible with physical stock growth, since the additional material demanded for new stocks can't be satisfied from the outflow from relatively smaller stocks of previous years or decades. Even with continued efficiency gains, a doubling or even tripling of global resource use has been projected (Krausmann et al., 2018; Schandl et al., 2016). Taken together, 86% of all processed materials are currently used to manufacture or operate stocks. The limits of this stock growth to circularity might be best illustrated with metals: In 2015, 1.4 Gt of primary metals were processed while only 0.8 Gt was accrued as end-of-life waste, with 49% being recycled. This means only 22% of all metal inputs could be satisfied by secondary material; thus a thermodynamically impossible 100% could only substitute 57% of metal inputs.

In addition, we know that materials might be contaminated or might not meet the high standards for high-tech production processes. In the latter case, new products might be invented to absorb secondary materials or might lead to cheaper products that increase the overall market of products in material terms. Such phenomena are described by Zink and Geyer (2017) as CE rebounds. Further, secondary materials might occur in large quantities in world regions that have already very high per capita stocks and where extension of stocks should be halted or even reduced. In world regions where per capita stocks are low and where stock expansion from very low levels is needed to improve quality of life, there is a lack of secondary materials. Wiedenhofer et al. (2021) show large inequalities in per capita stocks from 450 t in the Industrialised "New World", 280 t in the Industrialised "Old World", 220 t in China, 40 t in India to even 20 t in Sub-Sharan Africa. Transporting bulk flow secondary materials over longer distances, leaving alone from one continent to another, entails a huge environmental burden (Butera et al., 2015).

Another stock-related limiting factor for circularity is the so-called "hibernating stocks" in sub-surface layers like foundations or sewers, as well as unused roads. Material is difficult to recover because surface soil needs to be removed or material is spread out in the landscape while it has only limited value (Hertwich et al., 2019; Lanau et al., 2019).

The open loop of a renewable source: Biomass

In a preliminary assessment ecological cycling contributes a lion's share to circularity and was around 91% in 1900 and about 76% in 2015 (Haas et al., 2020). In most CE strategies, biomass does not receive critical attention but is assumed to be renewable, circular and sustainable by its nature. This assumption needs to be scrutinised critically, since biomass production can deteriorate ecosystems, interrupt carbon, nitrogen and phosphorus cycles (Navare et al., 2021), can lead to a loss of biodiversity and even foster zoonotic diseases (Rohr et al., 2019). Bio-fuels are an example where a push towards bioeconomy can lead to increased environmental and social pressures (Gomiero, 2018; Searchinger et al., 2008). In acknowledgement of this problem, Navare et al. (2021) have developed circularity criteria for biomass. Thus the transition towards circular biological cycles needs (1) to ensure "renewability of biotic resources"; (2) to optimise the "cascading use of biotic resources'"; (3) to "close the nutrient cycle" by enhanced separability and biodegradability, reduced hazardous substances and by increased return of nutrients sustaining the regeneration of the ecosystem; (4) to minimise the "environmental impact" on ecosystem services, in particular, resulting from land-use interventions and resource depletion and to minimise the global climate impact. However, the IPCC Special Report on climate change, desertification, land degradation, sustainable land management, food security and greenhouse gas fluxes in terrestrial ecosystems (Shukla et al., 2019) critically shows that the activities in agriculture, forestry and other land use represent 23% of total net anthropogenic emissions of GHG, thus showing that biomass production is everything but sustainable.

How implementation barriers and socio-metabolic stumbling blocks interact

Summarising insights from the socio-metabolic perspective show that decarbonisation will likely lead to an enormous additional building of societal stocks, while continued rapid stock growth is already determining huge material inflows in the future (see also Reyna & Chester, 2015). And, what becomes clear is that stock growth is fundamentally undermining circularity. It limits circularity rates, but more importantly, it tightly limits the absolute reduction of non-circular inputs from and outputs to nature. Thus, the socio-metabolic post-fuel regime requires a far-reaching transition with deep interventions. To decarbonise the industrial regime without changing deeper structures hinders a transition towards a CE. This adversely interacts with insights from the literature on implementation barriers, which provides the picture that the deeper and more far-reaching circularity interventions are, the more fundamental is the resistance to change. One stumbling block may be that the required deep circularity shift needs to be implemented against existing power structures dominated big transnational and material-intensive extraction and production enterprises. Therefore, the circularity shift also requires a shift in power towards locally rooted small and medium enterprises of the service sector that design and service slim and low maintenance infrastructures and that repair and refurbish products close to consumers. A focus on this problem leads circularity professionals out of their comfort zone; however, such a focus on fundamental stumbling blocks can be instrumental to systematically generate knowledge on the most rewarding leverage points that promise exit strategies that might open new windows of opportunities in the steps to follow.

References

Butera, S., Christensen, T. H., & Astrup, T. F. (2015). Life cycle assessment of construction and demolition waste management. *Waste Management*, *44*, 196–205. https://doi.org/10.1016/j.wasman.2015.07.011

Cantzler, J., Creutzig, F., Ayargarnchanakul, E., Javaid, A., Wong, L., & Haas, W. (2020). Saving resources and the climate? A systematic review of the circular economy and its mitigation potential. *Environmental Research Letters*. https://doi.org/10.1088/1748-9326/abbeb7

Deetman, S., de Boer, H. S., Van Engelenburg, M., van der Voet, E., & van Vuuren, D. P. (2021). Projected material requirements for the global electricity infrastructure – generation, transmission and storage. *Resources, Conservation and Recycling*, *164*, 105200. https://doi.org/10.1016/j.resconrec.2020.105200

Fischer-Kowalski, M., & Haas, W. (2016). Toward a Socioecological Concept of Human Labor. In H. Haberl, M. Fischer-Kowalski, F. Krausmann, & V. Winiwarter (Eds.), *Social Ecology: Society-nature Relations across Time and Space* (pp. 259–276). Springer.

Ghisellini, P., & Ulgiati, S. (2020). Circular economy transition in Italy. Achievements, perspectives and constraints. *Journal of Cleaner Production*, *243*, 118360. https://doi.org/10.1016/j.jclepro.2019.118360

Ghisellini, P., Cialani, C., & Ulgiati, S. (2016). A review on circular economy: The expected transition to a balanced interplay of environmental and economic systems. *Journal of Cleaner Production*, *114*, 11–32. https://doi.org/10.1016/j.jclepro.2015.09.007

Gomiero, T. (2018). Large-scale biofuels production: A possible threat to soil conservation and environmental services. *Applied Soil Ecology*, *123*, 729–736. https://doi.org/10.1016/j.apsoil.2017.09.028

Govindan, K., & Hasanagic, M. (2018). A systematic review on drivers, barriers, and practices towards circular economy: A supply chain perspective. *International Journal of Production Research*, 56(1–2), 278–311. https://doi.org/10.1080/00207543.2017.1402141

Haas, W., & Andarge, H. (2017). More Energy and Less Work, but New Crises: How the Societal Metabolism-Labour Nexus Changes from Agrarian to Industrial Societies. *Sustainability*, 9(7), 1041. https://doi.org/10.3390/su9071041

Haas, W., Krausmann, F., Wiedenhofer, D., Lauk, C., & Mayer, A. (2020). Spaceship earth's odyssey to a circular economy – A century long perspective. *Resources, Conservation and Recycling*, *163*, 105076. https://doi.org/10.1016/j.resconrec.2020.105076

Harris, S., Martin, M., & Diener, D. (2021). Circularity for circularity's sake? Scoping review of assessment methods for environmental performance in the circular economy.

Sustainable Production and Consumption, *26*, 172–186. https://doi.org/10.1016/j.spc.2020.09.018

Hart, J., & Pomponi, F. (2021). A Circular Economy: Where Will It Take Us? *Circular Economy and Sustainability*. https://doi.org/10.1007/s43615-021-00013-4

Hart, J., Adams, K., Giesekam, J., Tingley, D. D., & Pomponi, F. (2019). Barriers and drivers in a circular economy: The case of the built environment. *Procedia CIRP*, *80*, 619–624. https://doi.org/10.1016/j.procir.2018.12.015

Heeren, N., & Hellweg, S. (2019). Tracking Construction Material over Space and Time: Prospective and Geo-referenced Modeling of Building Stocks and Construction Material Flows. *Journal of Industrial Ecology*, *23*(1), 253–267. https://doi.org/10.1111/jiec.12739

Hertwich, E. G., Ali, S., Ciacci, L., Fishman, T., Heeren, N., Masanet, E., Asghari, F. N., Olivetti, E., Pauliuk, S., Tu, Q., & Wolfram, P. (2019). Material efficiency strategies to reducing greenhouse gas emissions associated with buildings, vehicles, and electronics – A review. *Environmental Research Letters*, *14*(4), 043004. https://doi.org/10.1088/1748-9326/ab0fe3

Kalt, G., Thunshirn, P., Wiedenhofer, D., Krausmann, F., Haas, W., & Haberl, H. (2021). Material stocks in global electricity infrastructures – An empirical analysis of the power sector's stock-flow-service nexus. *Resources, Conservation and Recycling*, *173*, 105723. https://doi.org/10.1016/j.resconrec.2021.105723

Kevin van Langen, S., Vassillo, C., Ghisellini, P., Restaino, D., Passaro, R., & Ulgiati, S. (2021). Promoting circular economy transition: A study about perceptions and awareness by different stakeholders groups. *Journal of Cleaner Production*, *316*, 128166. https://doi.org/10.1016/j.jclepro.2021.128166

Kirchherr, J., Reike, D., & Hekkert, M. (2017). Conceptualizing the circular economy: An analysis of 114 definitions. *Resources, Conservation and Recycling*, *127*, 221–232. https://doi.org/10.1016/j.resconrec.2017.09.005

Kirchherr, J., Piscicelli, L., Bour, R., Kostense-Smit, E., Muller, J., Huibrechtse-Truijens, A., & Hekkert, M. (2018). Barriers to the Circular Economy: Evidence From the European Union (EU). *Ecological Economics*, *150*, 264–272. https://doi.org/10.1016/j.ecolecon.2018.04.028

Krausmann, F., Weisz, H., & Eisenmenger, N. (2016). Transitions in sociometabolic regimes throughout human history. In *Social Ecology* (pp. 63–92). Springer.

Krausmann, F., Lauk, C., Haas, W., & Wiedenhofer, D. (2018). From resource extraction to outflows of wastes and emissions: The socioeconomic metabolism of the global economy, 1900–2015. *Global Environmental Change*, *52*, 131–140. https://doi.org/10.1016/j.gloenvcha.2018.07.003

Krausmann, F., Wiedenhofer, D., Lauk, C., Haas, W., Tanikawa, H., Fishman, T., Miatto, A., Schandl, H., & Haberl, H. (2017). Global socioeconomic material stocks rise 23-fold over the 20th century and require half of annual resource use. *Proceedings of the National Academy of Sciences*, *114*(8), 1880–1885. https://doi.org/10.1073/pnas.1613773114

Lanau, M., Liu, G., Kral, U., Wiedenhofer, D., Keijzer, E., Yu, C., & Ehlert, C. (2019). Taking Stock of Built Environment Stock Studies: Progress and Prospects. *Environmental Science & Technology*, *53*(15), 8499–8515. https://doi.org/10.1021/acs.est.8b06652

Mayer, A., Haas, W., Wiedenhofer, D., Krausmann, F., Nuss, P., & Blengini, G. A. (2019). Measuring Progress towards a Circular Economy: A Monitoring Framework for Economy-wide Material Loop Closing in the EU28: Progress towards a Circular

Economy in the EU28. *Journal of Industrial Ecology*, *23*(1), 62–76. https://doi.org/10.1111/jiec.12809

Merli, R., Preziosi, M., & Acampora, A. (2018). How do scholars approach the circular economy? A systematic literature review. *Journal of Cleaner Production*, *178*, 703–722. https://doi.org/10.1016/j.jclepro.2017.12.112

Morseletto, P. (2020). Targets for a circular economy. *Resources, Conservation and Recycling*, *153*, 104553. https://doi.org/10.1016/j.resconrec.2019.104553

Navare, K., Muys, B., Vrancken, K. C., & Van Acker, K. (2021). Circular economy monitoring – How to make it apt for biological cycles? *Resources, Conservation and Recycling*, *170*, 105563. https://doi.org/10.1016/j.resconrec.2021.105563

Pauliuk, S. (2018). Critical appraisal of the circular economy standard BS 8001:2017 and a dashboard of quantitative system indicators for its implementation in organizations. *Resources, Conservation and Recycling*, *129*, 81–92. https://doi.org/10.1016/j.resconrec.2017.10.019

Potting, J., Hekkert, M., Worrell, E., & Hanemaaijer, A. (2017). *Circular Economy: Measuring innovation in the product chain*. 46. https://dspace.library.uu.nl/handle/1874/358310

Reyna, J. L., & Chester, M. V. (2015). The Growth of Urban Building Stock: Unintended Lock-in and Embedded Environmental Effects: Urban Buildings, Lock-in, and Environmental Effects. *Journal of Industrial Ecology*, *19*(4), 524–537. https://doi.org/10.1111/jiec.12211

Rizos, V., Elkerbout, M., & Egenhofer, C. (2019). *Circular economy for climate neutrality:* (p. 11). Centre for European Policy Studies (CEPS).

Rohr, J. R., Barrett, C. B., Civitello, D. J., Craft, M. E., Delius, B., DeLeo, G. A., Hudson, P. J., Jouanard, N., Nguyen, K. H., Ostfeld, R. S., Remais, J. V., Riveau, G., Sokolow, S. H., & Tilman, D. (2019). Emerging human infectious diseases and the links to global food production. *Nature Sustainability*, *2*(6), 445–456. https://doi.org/10.1038/s41893-019-0293-3

Schandl, H., Hatfield-Dodds, S., Wiedmann, T., Geschke, A., Cai, Y., West, J., Newth, D., Baynes, T., Lenzen, M., & Owen, A. (2016). Decoupling global environmental pressure and economic growth: Scenarios for energy use, materials use and carbon emissions. *Journal of Cleaner Production*, *132*, 45–56. https://doi.org/10.1016/j.jclepro.2015.06.100

Schlögl, R. (2017). E-Mobility and the Energy Transition. *Angewandte Chemie International Edition*, *56*(37), 11019–11022. https://doi.org/10.1002/anie.201701633

Searchinger, T., Heimlich, R., Houghton, R. A., Dong, F., Elobeid, A., Fabiosa, J., Tokgoz, S., Hayes, D., & Yu, T.-H. (2008). Use of U.S. Croplands for Biofuels Increases Greenhouse Gases Through Emissions from Land-Use Change. *Science*, *319*(5867), 1238–1240. https://doi.org/10.1126/science.1151861

Shukla, P., Skea, J., Calvo Buendia, E., Masson-Delmotte, V., Pörtner, H., Roberts, D., Zhai, P., Slade, R., Connors, S., Van Diemen, R., & others. (2019). *IPCC, 2019: Climate Change and Land: An IPCC special report on climate change, desertification, land degradation, sustainable land management, food security, and greenhouse gas fluxes in terrestrial ecosystems.*

Webster, K. (2017). *The circular economy: A wealth of flows* (Second edition). Ellen MacArthur Foundation Publishing.

Wiedenhofer, D., Fishman, T., Plank, B., Miatto, A., Lauk, C., Haas, W., Haberl, H., & Krausmann, F. (2021). Prospects for a saturation of humanity's resource use? An analysis of material stocks and flows in nine world regions from 1900 to 2035. *Global Environmental Change*, *71*, 102410. https://doi.org/10.1016/j.gloenvcha.2021.102410

Wijkman, A., & Skanberg, K. (2016). The Circular Economy and Benefits for Society Jobs and Climate Clear Winners in an Economy Based on Renewable Energy and Resource Efficiency. https://circulareconomy.europa.eu/platform/sites/default/files/the-circular-economy-czech-republic-and-poland.pdf

Zink, T., & Geyer, R. (2017). Circular Economy Rebound: Circular Economy Rebound. *Journal of Industrial Ecology*, *20*(4), 719–729. https://doi.org/10.1111/jiec.12545

Part IV

What opportunities do we see?

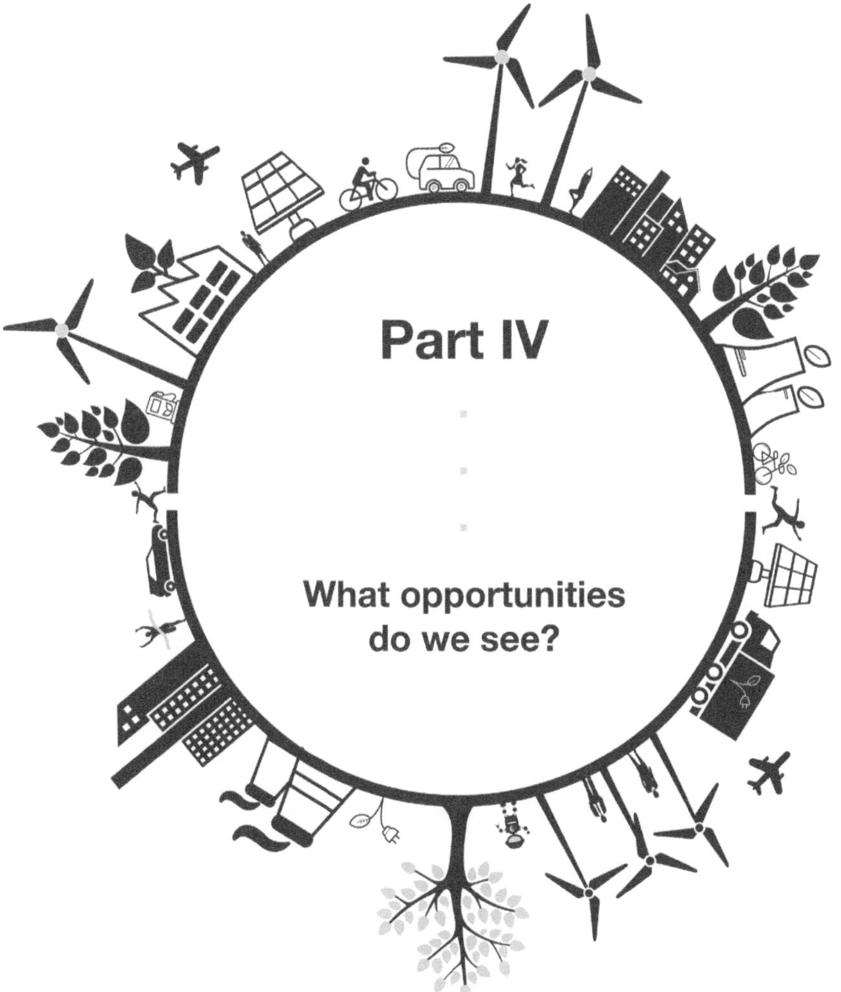

20 Global resource use and the future

Any room for the circular economy?

Ole van Allen, Harald U. Sverdrup, and Anna Hulda Olafsdottir

Introduction

The demand for raw materials is increasing due to a growing world population. Per capita consumptions of materials increased additionally, because of the positive economic development of many developing and threshold countries. Global material consumption had increased from 43 billion tonnes in 1990 to 92 billion tonnes in 2017, an increase of 113 per cent. That is an increase of 113 per cent. The depletion of natural resources and its negative impacts have accelerated rapidly since the beginning of the 2000s. Without developing globally effective policies, the material consumption will increase to 190 billion tonnes by 2060 (UNEP SDG's Report 2019, Sverdrup and Ragnarsdottir 2014). The debate about the increasing consumption of resources and the associated consequences has shifted from the scientific community into the public and political debate in the last 30 years. With the rising awareness of the problem, several solutions and ideas for change have emerged in the discussion. We briefly present the most common approaches.

1. UN Sustainable Development Goals are 17 interlinked global goals intended to serve as a "blueprint for a more sustainable global future for all". In 2015, the goals were established by the United Nations General Assembly with the intent to achieve them by 2030 (SDG's Report 2016). They are not independent, and no proper linking of them using causal loop diagrams has been done. The goals do not have operational definitions yet but do make good declarations of intent.
2. Circular economy is an alternative to the traditional linear production and consumption model (take-produce-use-dispose). The circular economy aims to preserve existing materials and products as long as possible. The life cycle of materials and products should be extended to reduce the necessary resource input and, at the same time, reduce waste to a minimum. The materials contained in products should be retained in the system as long as possible.
3. Decoupling is broadly understood as the goal of breaking the link between economic growth and environmental degradation, as well as resource use. In the current global economy, the growth of GDP increases environmental degradation and intensifies resource use. Environmental degradation or

DOI: 10.4324/9781003244196-24

environmental impacts involve large-scale global chemical pollution, physical disturbances, climate change and ecosystem destruction. The decoupling strategy was first adopted as a goal by the OECD in 2001. Since then, decoupling has been included in several policy action plans. Increasing GDP with lower resource requirements is referred to as relative decoupling or efficiency increase. Absolute decoupling is when the GDP rises while material and energy use stagnates or declines.

4. 4 R's strategy includes the goals Reduce, Reuse, Recycle and Recover. The application area of this strategy can be applied to many areas of our economy. These principles are also found in previously mentioned approaches such as the circular economy.
5. Technical efficiency where the primary approach is increased production efficiency and reduction of transaction losses. All "energy and materials 'savings'" were no savings as they were all used to expand other activities, and thus accelerating consumption and impacts.

In the context of the sustainability discussion, the need to change consumption patterns is often mentioned, but in the same breath, more efficient production and economic growth are also mentioned. According to SDG's Report (2016 and 2019), the consumption of materials and products increases each year, despite the reduction in resource and energy intensity during the extraction and production of these materials and products. The increase in efficiency cannot keep up with the increased consumption of multiple products. Additionally, the ongoing economic growth fosters further increased consumption rates of products, which is reinforced by planned obsolescence and short product lifetime to scale up consumption even faster. In the field of consumption reduction, no serious attempts have been made to date to reduce consumption. Consumption reduction would require a mental shift from a capitalistic growth-focused society with a strong desire for new and luxury products to a non-consumption and no growth-oriented societal approach (Costanza et al. 2014). Consumption reduction is not compatible with the political goal of sustained economic growth. If sustainability is the primary goal, seriously questioning and changing our consumption patterns is a need (Beddoe et al. 2009; Wiedmann et al. 2020). Concepts and approaches that are not discussed outside of the scientific arena should also enter the discussion. There's a variety of items that are not much discussed on a political and public level, of which some have the potential to affect sustainable resource use, each with their caveats and requirements:

1. Global average life satisfaction has not significantly improved since 1975 (Costanza et al.,2009, 2014, Kubiszewski et al. 2013). If wealth were distributed more equally on a global scale, it would appear to be economically possible to support a population of 9 billion people at about 7,000 $ per capita with the current world GDP, but this is assuming the natural resources for this to be available (Bardi 2013, Bardi et al. 2019, Kubiszewski et al. 2013, Sverdrup and Ragnarsdottir 2014).

2. Natural resource ownership, responsible use, and the delineation between individual ownership and the ownership of the global commons is a necessary topic for discussion. Systemic change of the economic, social and financial system instead of putting faith in technology to increase the efficiency to the needed extent (Jackson 2009).
3. Discussion about the population size and what that means for the living standard to be sustainable. Additionally, the economic contraction approach is necessary to delegate resource consumption and emissions towards the planetary boundaries. From a materials mass balance perspective, there does not appear to be any sustainable population size above 3 billion people in the long run (Ehrlich et al. 1992, Sverdrup and Ragnarsdottir 2011, 2014, Sverdrup et al., 2014, 2020a).
4. Redistribution of opportunities for income, with it the linked resource use as an opposing strategy of constant growth to lift the living standards in the poorest countries, has been suggested. However, this requires good governance, democracy, limiting corruption and closing of tax havens to be a valid strategy, which is an enormous challenge in many countries (Rothstein 2011, Acemoglu and Robinson 2013).

Integrated assessment models are currently the best way to evaluate policies to tackle this problem. This chapter presents outputs from a systems analysis and the WORLD7 and WORLD0 models, specially designed for such a purpose. Based on the system analysis of the problem, no "one-trick pony" will suffice to resolve the global natural resource sustainability issues, a systemic approach is required and necessary. A systemic approach is required and necessary. For this purpose, we tested several combinations of concepts against a Business-as-Usual (BAU) case to identify various ideas that might help to reach sustainable resource use.

Scope and objectives

The scope of this study is to assess and pedagogically present how BAU is grossly unsustainable and leads to typical exponential growth and subsequent decline and subsequent decline, the task is to evaluate to what degree. The task is to evaluate to what degree. We will explore different strategies using both WORLD7 and the simplified WORLD0, to be implemented from 2030 and forward in time to 2500 AD. Four different policy scenarios have been examined:

1 Keep Business-as-usual but improve by adjusting some parameters

1.1 Business-as-usual (BAU), talk, but do nothing

1.2 BAU and enhanced resource recycling (adjusting parameters for recycling and renewables)

1.3 BAU enhanced recycling, increased renewable resources input and improved natural resource use technical efficiency (adjusting parameters)

1.4 Introduce a systemic change strategy, systemic changes in structure, social system, power system and economic paradigms. External finite natural resource system input reduction to below sustainability limit, enhanced recycling and increase renewable natural resources, switch ecosystem exploitation to sustainable for agriculture, forests and oceans, change consumption pattern by increased consumption resource use efficiency and lifestyle changes

For the analysis, we will use our earlier experience and findings from running a complex integrated assessment model WORLD7 (Lorenz et al. 2017, Olafsdottir and Sverdrup 2020, Sverdrup and Olafsdottir 2019, Sverdrup et al. 2020a,b, 2017a,b, 2021) as well as exploratory studies based on the simplified version named WORLD0.

Theory

Theoretical foundation

From a systems perspective, global resource use is different from resource use in a circular context inside the system. It is technically possible to have a system net resources impact contraction, simultaneous with an expanding internal resource use within the circularity loop, with transaction losses, assuming that the population and the consumption per capita do not increase. This is, however, not the case at present. Beyond the bending point, GDP and the associated resource's use are no longer the most significant contributors to life quality. This has been illustrated in Figures 20.1 and 20.2 and explained below (Hotelling 1931, Diamond 1997, Heinberg 2011, Fraumeni 2021). In the different versions of economic policies that use GDP as an indicator, it is assumed that GDP correlates with available purchasing power. It is to a certain degree, but with some imperfections (Fioramonti 2013).

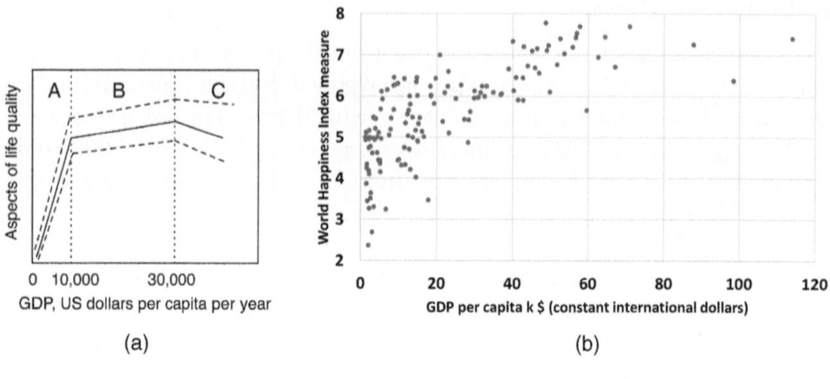

Figure 20.1 (a and b) An example of the relationship between GDP and aspect of life quality.

GDP is an indicator of economic activity and annual turnover, without considering what that activity consists of. Thus, the cost of construction and destruction is deemed equal and added up. War and peace, achievements, and disaster, all add up. GDP was used actively to promote the industrial economy and was very successful during major wars. In some way, both construction and destruction were a part of the overall goal. However, after WWII, that assumption was no longer valid. Building up industries counts as positive, but also cleaning up pollution or treating people who get ill from the pollution (Fioramonti 2013, Heinberg 2011, Kubizsewky et al. 2013). When plotting GDP/per capita against the material footprint/per capita (tonnes), we do get a linear correlation, suggesting strongly that decoupling does not really occur. Thus, promoting GDP growth has so far been equivalent to promoting more physical resource use (Bringezu et al. 2004, Burton 2016, Fletcher 2014, Fletcher and Rammelt 2017).

Figures 20.1 and 20.2 say that life quality is a function of disposable purchasing power up to a certain limit when all the essentials for sustaining life have been provided. Beyond a certain limit of GDP, there is a break in the curve somewhere in the range of 7,000–10,000 US dollars per capita, per year, depending on the data source. This is when we shift from zone A to zone B in Figure 20.1. In zone A in Figure 20.1a, every increase in purchasing power can be used to ease the burden of life and make life easier. For this reason, GDP is an important indicator for developing nations that start from a low level. In zone B in Figure 20.1a, a relatively large increase in disposable purchasing power, measured as the proxy variable GDP, will give a relatively modest increase in quality of life, if any. In zone B in Figure 20.1a, the actual increase in life quality comes from the benefit of social processes minus the cost of human vices in society. In zone C in Figure 20.1a, the economic activity is so intense that the potential for making substantial physical or social damage is significant.

The diagram shows how the countries with high GDP can contract their GDP with little or no impact on life quality. The increase in life quality at GDP above 10,000 $/capita depends more on social factors than money. (b) An example of data supporting the illustration 20.1a in Figure 20.1b was taken from Fraumeni (2021).

We can detect a strong correlation between GDP and resource consumption. The coefficient of determination $r^2=0.72$. Number of countries is 168. [GDP data from the World Bank (March 2021, World Development Indicators). Material footprint data: http://gapm.io/dmfootp]

For quality of life (as attempted to be captured by indicators like GPI), we may propose the following equation (20.1), based on diagrams like Figures 20.1 or 20.2 (Anielski and Soskolne 2001, Kubizsewky et al. 2013, Fraumeni 2021, Schutz 1994):

$$\text{Quality of life} = f(\text{disposable purchasing power}) + g(\text{social factors}) - j(\text{disaster}) \quad (20.1)$$

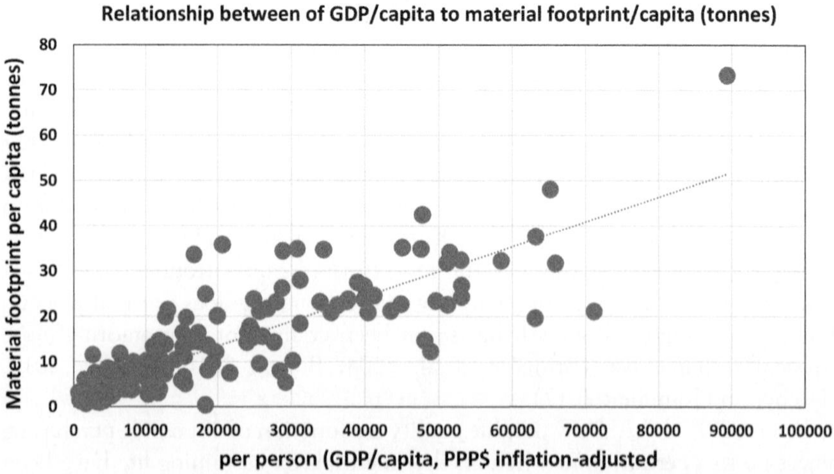

Figure 20.2 The relationship between GDP per capita in (PPP$ inflation-adjusted) and material footprint per capita in tonnes.

Disposable purchasing power is different between countries, as it is a function of disposable income and the price of the commodities essential for quality of life. g (social factors) is a term containing the effects of social factors on the personal level (subsistence safety, physical safety, personal comfort), interpersonal level (social trust, perceived social differences, social tolerance) and of society. This implies such things as public social trust, the efficiency of the institutions in society (justice system, health care system, education system, general governance), the absence of corruption and abuse of power and limitation of crime. j (disasters) are the costs of the adverse effects of activities in society, physical, environmental and social GDP adjusted like this is sometimes called the GPI (Kubizsewki et al. 2013).

As a causal loop diagram, we have drawn up the relationship between population size, affluence, GDP and economic activity, shown in Figure 20.3 GPI (Anielski and Soskolne 2001) or the Gross National Happiness, as launched by the Kingdom of Bhutan, are alternative measures.

One major confounding issue in the transition to sustainable energy and resource use is the delays caused by stocks-in-use. This is because the flow from use does not automatically match the flow into use. It has been argued that much of the treatment of scarcity can be relieved by substitution and decoupling. When studying decoupling and substitution closer, it appears that this may not be correct. On the global scale, decoupling and substitution are not tools that can be worked with, as they generally do not occur or have a negligible effect in the big picture (Bringezu et al. 2004, Burton 2016, Fletcher and Rammelt 2017, Fletcher 2014). Much because the decoupling effect is not there, partly that what has been posted as decoupling turned out to be production moved to another

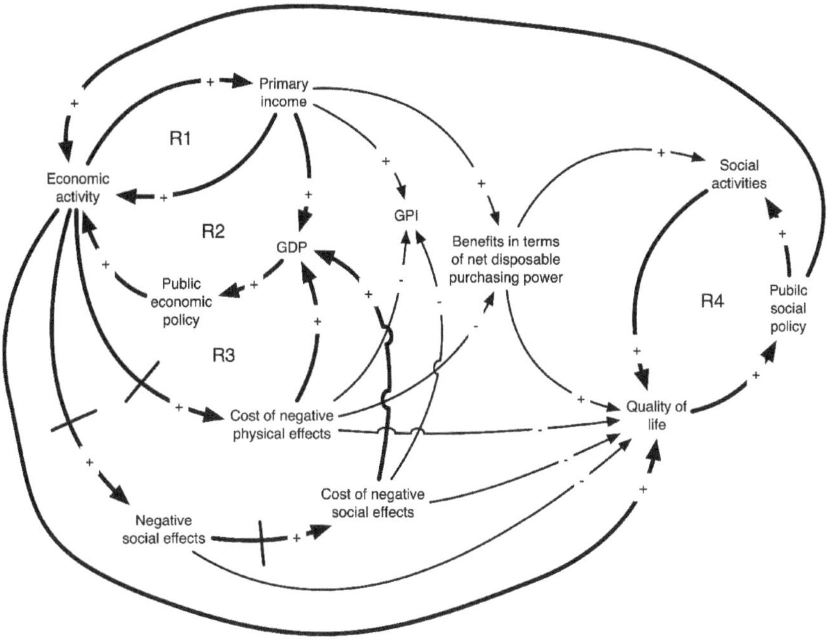

Figure 20.3 Creating a causal loop linking GDP, GPI, social- and environmental effects as well as the quality of life.

country, often having larger impact there. Substitution does not work for two reasons, one that it is only possible to substitute with a more plentiful resource, and secondly, because most resources are already booked for a certain use and are not freely available. Increased natural resource efficiencies and increased production efficiency have caused price decreases, which have been returned as higher consumption by other activities. The final effect is increased resource depletion.

Note how policies based on GDP give policy promotion from both positive and negative effects. The negative effects are normally delayed in the system, thus the positive effect on the quality of life initially appears as larger but later declines when the feedbacks kick in. The social effects have longer delays and thus a longer time will pass until the social and environmental effects become fully manifested and will have feedbacks on the economic and political systems.

Model tools used: WORLD7 to WORLDO simulations

An assessment using the WORLD7 model for fossil energy supplied and metals and materials have shown that a combination of measures is required: increased recycling in the broadest context, reduction of the net input of finite resources into the system, improved resource use efficiency, better circularity, contraction of the resource use of the developed part of the world and growth for the under-developed part of the world (Sverdrup 2019, 2020, Sverdrup et al. 2018, 2020). Figure 20.4 shows the WORLD7 model. Figures 20.5 and 20.6 show the flow chart for resources and the associated causal loop diagram for WORLD0. The simple model is used because it is straightforward and has fewer outputs that are easier to understand and communicate. The basic response pattern of WORLD7 and WORLD0 are similar. The credibility is secured through the comparison with the complex model, which in turn has been verified on real-life data (Sverdrup et al. 2017, 2018, 2019, 2021, Sverdrup and Olafsdottir 2018, 2019, 2020, Olafsdottir and Sverdrup 2020). Figure 20.7 (a–d) shows selected examples of some of the WORLD0 runs made.

Every transaction has a transaction loss term, and thus when circularity is cascaded, the overall efficiency may be mediocre even if the efficiency of individual steps is very good.

Figure 20.7 (a–d) provides the overview of the outputs from the WORLD0 model for the different scenarios listed in the text. All scenarios lead to long-term finite resources depletion (grey line) and thus only push the limit issue forward in time. The conclusion is that it does not solve the problem.

Discussion

The results of simulations with WORLD0 and WORLD7 indicate that we are depleting our resources in an unsustainable way. Soon we will face challenges regarding resource scarcity. Population size combined with the desired consumption level is a significant variable, and with population degrowth, the challenges would be easier to overcome. Several proposed solutions are available, but the social challenges associated with behavioural change and personal patterns, preferences and norms appear the most difficult challenge. The shift from the BAU case to systemic change will require carefully chosen and thoroughly tested policy measures that can influence the intervention points. The study indicates that it is impossible to rely on a circular economy concept alone to solve the main challenges. Six problems regarding the circular economy approach got already identified by earlier research from Korhonen et al. (2018). According to the model result, there are four additional problems that further highlight the difficulties of the CE to tackle the resource sustainability issues. These are:

1. Ongoing population growth with a growing economic power, leads to an adaptation of industrial nations' consumption patterns, and an increase in resource consumption. The efficiencies gain of circular economy are not able to reduce the overall all consumption efficiently because of system delays and lack of adaption of the concept in a wide range of our society.
2. The desire for perpetual economic growth as a global political goal as well as on the personal level even in a world that is already in resource overshoot. Constant growth will outgrow a circular economy because renewable

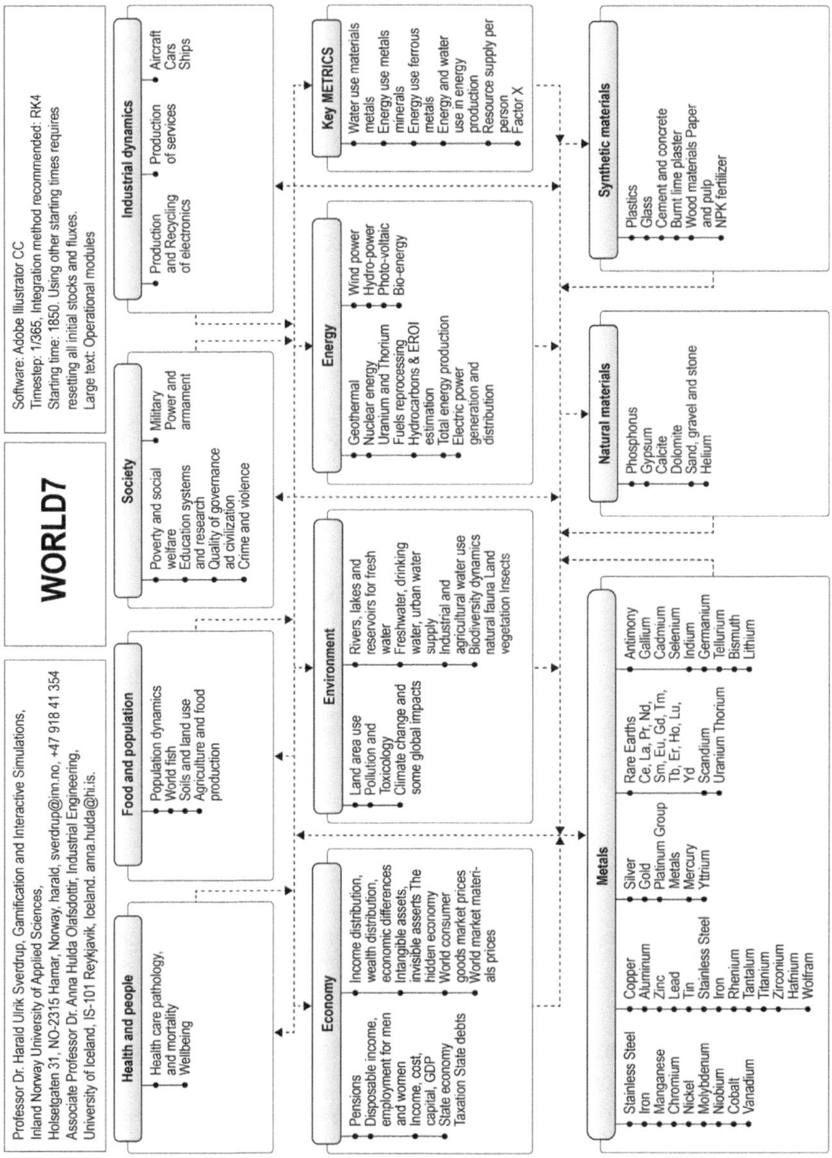

Figure 20.4 The WORLD7 model overview, connecting economy, natural resources energy, social aspects and ecology.

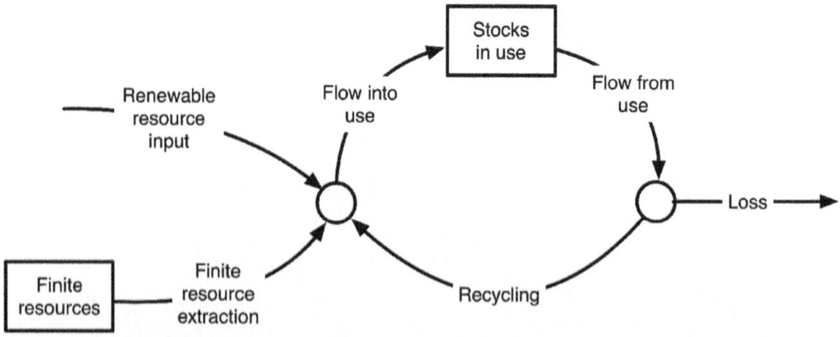

Figure 20.5 Simple flow chart for resources in WORLDO.

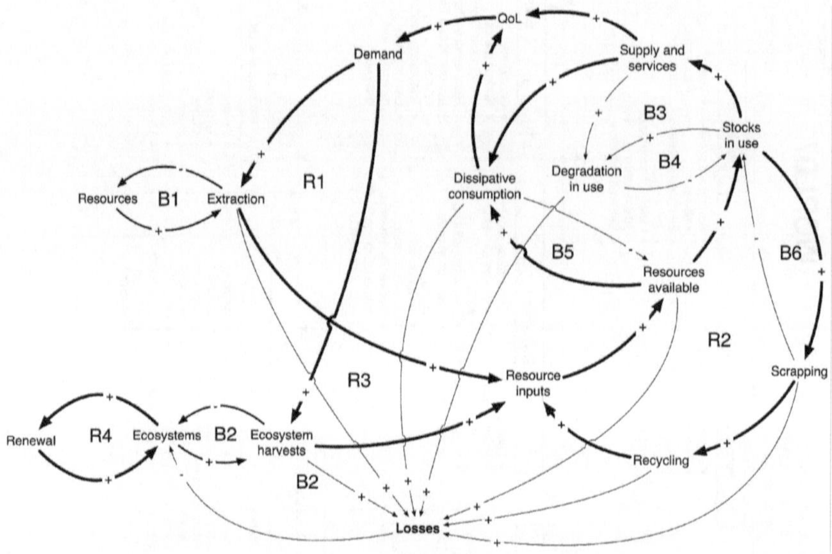

Figure 20.6 A simple causal loop diagram representing the mechanisms involved in WORLDO.

resources have regeneration time, setting limits to the rate at which resources can be extracted from the ecosystem.

3. The impossibility to substitute most finite physical resources with renewable ones is a problem of order of magnitude. The dependence on finite resources for the products that make up our modern society (computer, machinery, etc.) and the limitations to the extent to which these resources can be recycled and remain in the product cycle, because several steps of transition losses leading added up to major losses of resources, during the recovery.

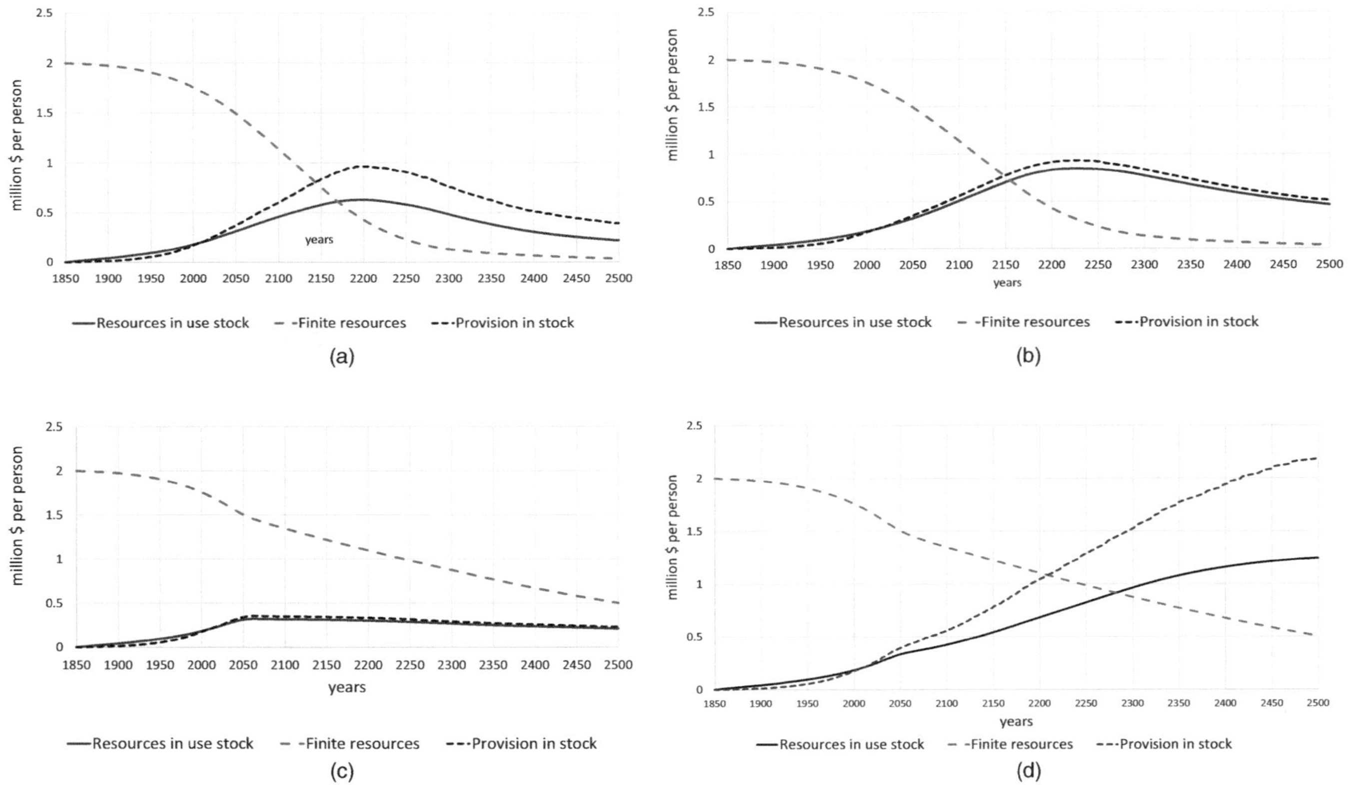

Figure 20.7a Scenario Business-as-usual; Talk about sustainability, but no real action.
Figure 20.7b Scenario Business-as-usual and enhanced recycling.
Figure 20.7c Scenario Resource use reduction, all else business-as-usual.
Figure 20.7d Scenario Resource use reduction, enhanced recycling, more renewables, better resource use efficiency and circular economy.

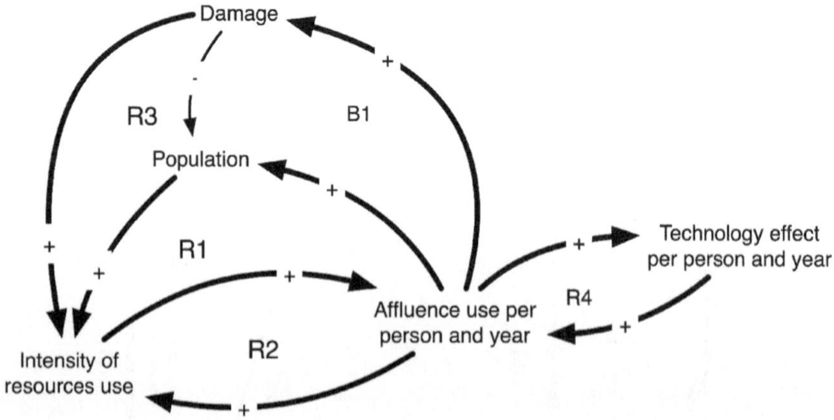

(a)

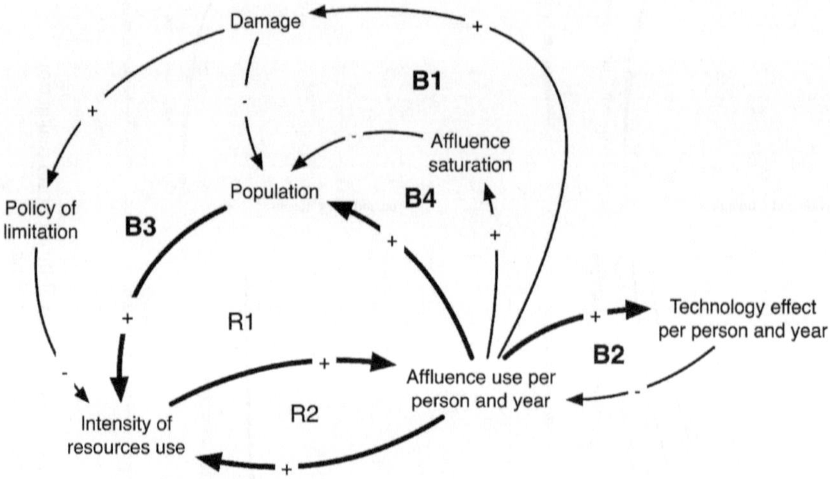

(b)

Figure 20.8a (CLD1) shows the setup in our society at the moment. Several factors drive the system, increasing resource consumption, with very few limitations in the system. Since every efficiency gain is used to increase consumption, then increased resource use is actually damaging. Applying circular economy to system CLD1 (Figure 20.8a) will make things worse, not better.

Figure 20.8b (CLD2) shows that circular economy still has a meaning when the savings are actually saved, leading to less resource use and when affluence increases, leading to populations going down. Circular economy alone does not save the day but may contribute to it. A systemic change dealing with population overshoot and affluence use beyond the breaking point between A and B in Figure 20.1a would be needed.

4. System delays must be considered in the circular economy, as resources are locked up in use for a substantial amount of time. Recycling may take as long as the delay time to bring material back is long, sometimes up towards 100 years. Thus, it may take a very long time to reach circularity, and certainly more time than we have available to resolve the first stages of energy-, resources-, and climate crisis. This emphasises the need and requirement for integrated assessment modelling in policy development.

Different strategies involving system change are needed to prevent a resource crisis and achieve an internally stable economic situation (Acemoglu and Robinson 2013). However, there is a great resistance to discussing real actions on systems change particularly with respect to population, corruption and lifestyle (Kotter 2014, Schutz 1994, Sverdrup and Ragnasdottir 2014, Costanza et al. 2014).

It does not appear that BAU can be sustainable in the long run, without contraction of finite resources use. Any solution must include a significant reduction of the use of finite resources to below the global sustainability level. At the same time the internal cycling of resources can be amplified through recycling, reuse, improved efficiency, improved consumption efficiency, improved lifetime of goods and improved lifestyles. The intervention points require further research to form policy measures that will lead to more sustainable resource use and internal sustainable growth. Decoupling capacities of GDP and resource use are currently not occurring. Any solution must be socially sustainable to be a valid proposal, and the sole reliance on technology alone is neither sufficient nor sustainable (Schutz 1994, Rothstein 2011, Sverdrup and Ragnarsdottir 2014). Our current population size, combined with the demand for materials and desire to continuously foster economic growth, exceeds most planetary boundaries. Lower population numbers will ease the pressure on the global resource demand and contribute to long-term sustainability.

Conclusions

For all policy development, frequent use of Integrated Assessment Models is a necessity and a requirement before any policy is implemented. Policies cannot be left to be based on political opinion alone; it is a requirement that Integrated Assessment Models are used to check that proposed policies really will achieve the goals envisioned. Failing to do so is taking unchartered risks and potentially may lead to damaging policies.

All BAU scenarios with improvements used in the simulations show peak behaviour, end up with resource exhaustion and failure to achieve sustainability. Transaction losses, delays and the lack of available renewable substitutes for finite resources lead to resource and energy losses. The approach of circular economy alone cannot resolve all these issues. Efficiency improvements in an economic system that requires growth will at best only delay the risk of system malfunction unless the resource savings really become real physical savings and that the saved resources are not rolled forward into increased consumption. The models show that a system based on constant growth outgrows any finite physical resource supply capacity, no matter how efficient the system is. This is regardless of using renewables or finite resources.

References

Acemoglu, D. and Robinson, J.A., 2013. Why nations fail. The origins of power, prosperity and poverty. Profile Books Ltd, London. 529 pp. ISBN 978-1-84668-430-2

Anielski, M. and C. Soskolne. C., 2001. Genuine Progress Indicator (GPI) Accounting: Relating Ecological Integrity to Human Health and Well-Being. Just Ecological Integrity: The Ethics of Maintaining Planetary Life, eds. P., Miller and L., Westra. Lanham, Maryland: Rowman and Littlefield: pp. 83–97.

Bardi, U. 2013 Extracted. How the quest for mineral wealth is plundering the planet. The past, present and future of global mineral depletion. A report to the Club of Rome. Chelsa Green Publishing, Vermont. 299pp. ISBN 978-1-60358-541-5

Bardi, U., Falsini, S., Perissi, I., 2019. Toward a General Theory of Societal Collapse. A Biophysical Examination of Tainter's Model of the Diminishing Returns of Complexity. Biophysical Economy and Resource Quality. 4: 1–9.

Beddoe, R., Costanza, R., Farley, J., Garza, E., Kent, J., Kubiszewski, I., Martinez, L., McCowen, T., Murphy, K., Myers, N., Ogden, Z., Stapleton, K., Woodward, J. 2009. Overcoming systemic roadblocks to sustainability: The evolutionary redesign of worldviews, institutions, and technologies. Proceedings of the National Academy of Sciences 106, 2483–2489.

Bringezu, S., Schütz, H., Steger, S., Baudisch, J. 2004. International comparison of resource use and its relation to economic growth. Ecological Economics, 51, 97–124.

Burton, M. 2016. A gain and again: Supposed evidence for decoupling emissions from growth is not what it seems. Degrowth blog. March 28. Retrieved from www.degrowth.de/en/2016/03/once-again-supposed-evidence-for-decoupling-emissions-from-growth-is-not-what-it-seems/

Costanza, R., Hart, M., Posner, S., Talberth, J., 2009. Beyond GDP: The Need for New Measures of Progress. The Pardee paper, No. 4, 46pp. Frederick S. Pardee Center for the Study of the Longer-Range Future. Boston University. Boston, Massachusetts

Costanza, R., Kubiszewski, I., Giovannini, E., Lovins, H., McGlade, J., Pickett, K.W., Ragnarsdottir, K.V., Roberts, D., de Vogli, R., Wilkinson, R., 2014. Development: Time to leave GPD behind. Nature, 505, 282–285.

Ehrlich, P., Daily G., Goulder L., 1992. Population growth, economic growth and market economics. Contention 2, 17–35.

Fioramonti, L. 2013 Gross Domestic Problem: The Politics Behind the World's Most Powerful Number. ZED Books.

Fletcher, R. 2014. Taking the chocolate laxative: Why neoliberal conservation fails forward. In B. Büscher, W. Dressler, R. Fletcher (Eds.), Nature Inc.: Environmental conservation in the neoliberal age (pp. 247–258). Tucson: University of Arizona Press.

Fletcher, R. and Rammelt, C., 2017 Decoupling: A Key Fantasy of the Post-2015 Sustainable Development Agenda, Globalizations, 14, 450–467.

Fraumeni, B. M. (n.d.). *Gross domestic product: Are other measures needed?* https://doi.org/10.15185/izawol.368

Heinberg, R. 2011, The end of growth. Adapting to our new economic reality. New Society Publishers, Gabriola Island, Canada.

Hotelling, H. 1931. The economics of exhaustible resources. Journal of Political Economy 39, 137–175.

Jackson, T., 2009. Prosperity Without Growth. Economics for a Finite Planet. Earthscan, London.

Korhonen, J., Honkasalo, A., Seppälä, J. 2018 Circular Economy: The concept and its limitations, Ecological Economics, 143, 37–46.

Kotter, J.P. 2014. Leading change; Why transformations efforts fail. Harvard Business Review – OPoint 30-37. Originally published in Harvard Business Review April 1995.

Lorenz, U., Sverdrup, H.U., Ragnarsdottir, K.V., 2017. Global megatrends and resource use – A systemic reflection. Chapter 3. In: The Factor X book. Lehman, H. (Ed). 67–77. Springer Verlag, Frankfurt.

Meadows, D.H, Meadows, D.L, Randers, J, Behrens, W. 1972. Limits to growth. Universe Books, New York

Meadows, D.H, Meadows, D.L, Randers, J. 1992. *Beyond the limits: confronting global collapse, envisioning a sustainable future*. Chelsea Green Publishing Company.

Meadows, D.H, Randers, J., Meadows, D.L 2005 *Limits to Growth, the 30-year Update*. Earthscan, Sterling Virginia.

Olafsdottir, A.H., and Sverdrup, H., 2020, System dynamics modelling of mining, supply, recycling, stocks-in-use and market price for nickel. Mining, Metallurgy & Exploration. 1–22. 10.1007/s42461-020-00370-

Rothstein, B., 2011. The quality of government. Corruption, social trust, and inequality in international perspective. University of Chicago Press, Chicago 286pp. ISBN-13: 978-0-226-72957-2

Schutz, W. 1994 The Human Element: Productivity, Self-Esteem and the Bottom Line. San Francisco, CA: Jossey-Bass.

Sverdrup, H.U., 2019. The global sustainability challenges in the future: the energy and materials supply, pollution, climate change and inequality nexus. In: J. Meadowcroft, D. Banister, E. Holden, O. Langhelle, K. Linnerud, G. Gilpin. (Eds), Our Common Future, What Next for Sustainable Development? Our Common Future at Thirty. Monograph Chapter. Chapter 4: 49–75, Edward Elgar Publishing.

Sverdrup, H., 2020. What remains, Our natural resources, The World's bookkeeper. Cover story on the P+ Magazine, 18: 1–6. www.p-plus.nl/nl/nieuws/The-Worlds-Bookkeeper-AVANS

Sverdrup, H.U., and Ragnarsdottir, K.V., 2014. Natural Resources in a planetary perspective. Geochemical Perspectives, 2(2, October issue): 1–156. European Geochemical Society.

Sverdrup, H.U., Olafsdottir, A.H., Koca, D., 2020a. How large is the global population when limited by long term sustainable global metals-, energy- and phosphate supply? Presented at the International System Dynamics Conference, 21–24 July 2020, Bergen University, Norway. Peer-reviewed abstract in International System Dynamics Conference Proceedings. 18 pages. https://proceedings.systemdynamics.org/2020/papers/P1345.pdf

Sverdrup, H., Lorenz, U., Olafsdottir, A.H., 2020b. The world at the ultimate crossroads: natural resources, energy transitions, climate change, environmental impacts, social challenges and quality of governance. In: Lehmann, H (Ed)., Sustainable Development and Resource Productivity The Nexus Approaches. Routledge, Berlin, 120–140 ISBN 9780367429546

Sverdrup, HU., Ragnarsdottir, K.V., Koca, D. 2017. An assessment of global metal supply sustainability: Global recoverable reserves, mining rates, stocks-in-use, recycling rates, reserve sizes and time to production peak leading to subsequent metal scarcity. Journal of Cleaner Production, 140: 359–372.

Sverdrup, H, Olafsdottir, A.H., Ragnarsdottir, K.V., 2021. Development of a biophysical economics module for the global integrated assessment WORLD7 model. In: Cavana, R., Pavlov, O., Dangerfield, B., Wheat, D. (Eds) *Modelling Feedback Economics*. Chapter 10, 41 pages. Springer Verlag, Frankfurt. ISBN 978-3-030-67189-1.

Tainter, J.A. 1988. The Collapse of Complex Societies. Cambridge: Cambridge University Press. 177pp.

Tainter, J.A. 1995. Sustainability of complex societies. Futures 27: 397–407.

UN 2016. The Sustainable Development Goals Report 2016. doi: 10.18356/3405d09f-en

United Nations Department of Economic and Social Affairs. 2016. *The Sustainable Development Goals Report 2016*. UN. https://doi.org/10.18356/3405d09f-en

Wiedmann, T., Lenzen, M., Keyßer, L.T., Steinberger, J.K. 2020. Scientists' warning on affluence. Nature Communications 11: article 3107.https://doi.org/10.1038/s41467-020-16941-y

21 Regenerative economy

The embedding of circularity

Daniel Dahm

Nearly 30 years ago, in 1992, the Earth Summit took place in Rio de Janeiro. Since then, people's view of their planet has changed fundamentally. The fact that sustainable development is needed for a future worth living has settled in most people's minds.

Humans and the planet have moved closer together, almost intimately, since the global limits and the resulting ecological (and thus also economical) limitations have become an integral part of our world experience: the planet Earth is more or less spherical and bounded. Homo sapiens are living beings in planetary interconnectedness, embedded in the diversity of the Earth's habitats and united in their variety of cultures and ways of thinking from about 1.4 million years of human (co-)evolution.

Life between syntropy and entropy

Around 3.8 billion years of biological evolution fundamentally have shaped the interplay of material and energetic flows on our planet, transforming the geosphere over hundreds of millions of years into a biogeosphere with all its ecological interconnections.

Everything that is moves towards the greatest possible entropy. Living things are constantly engaged in counteracting this move towards disorder with the most stable states of order possible. As selectively open (Schroedinger, 1951), living systems and living beings are constantly striving to optimize their own order and that of their habitat. They form cell membranes and skins to protect themselves from the outside; they stabilize themselves with lignifications, cornifications, calcifications, with fibres, tissues, and inner and outer skeletons; they create structures, burrows, and nests, form families, herds, and swarms and incorporate themselves into entire communities in soils, forests, and reefs (Gell-Man, 1995). They can only maintain their high degree of order as organisms if they supply themselves with the necessary energy in their life process, which enables them to continue to survive away from thermodynamic equilibrium, that is, to resist the entropic gradient. The energy of order necessary for this is also called negative entropy or syntropy (Duerr, 2011a). The living creates syntropy and uses free energy (e.g., light and heat), transforms other states of order (e.g., inorganic

DOI: 10.4324/9781003244196-25

matter into organic matter), and binds it (e.g., in biomass). Energetically, this is fed endogenously (= coming from inside) by the material and thermal turnover along the material flows and food chains of the Earth system, as well as exogenously (= coming from outside) primarily by solar radiation, which is the energetic source for photosynthesis. Our planetary system needs the input of free energy and its biological binding that enables the living evolution. It must constantly "pump" itself energetically. Pure circulation does not exist here. The idea that we can survive without the steady rebuilding of ecological order is esoteric.

This energetic buildup of syntropy is predominantly carried out by plants. Plants are capable of building up the inorganic matter of high entropy into more complex organic matter of low entropy, thus making it available as a primary source for the global food chains. With the help of mainly photosynthesis, negative entropy is "imported" by using sunlight to build up inorganic substances into energetically higher-value organic matter such as glucose, ATP, or DNA. This is then cascaded through the complex food chains of all living organisms and metabolized as a source of energy and carbon. Simplified, eating a fruit serves a living being to maintain its physical integrity or physical order dynamically, that is, to be alive. For this purpose, the organic-material order energy of the fruit is physically and chemically liberated and imported and further used to maintain its own state of order.

The construction and reconstruction of biological life systems are constantly pumped by solar energy and maintain their states of order through continuous energetic turnover. If the process of dynamic stabilization can no longer be maintained, entropy increases again, and "death" occurs. The remaining order energy bound in organic matter is then absorbed by other living organisms and recycled, or deposited in sediments and soils, in water and in fossil deposits (e.g., peat, coal, and oils). In this way, it becomes energetically available to all again via the cooperative linking of utilization stages.

Nature never produces garbage. Aliveness is always the (thermo)dynamic play between (systemically open) living beings in and with their environment (Heisenberg, 1969). To maintain or increase the order of a subsystem, the disorder of the surrounding total system increases at least to the same extent (compare the First and Second Law of Thermodynamics) (Planck, 1897). The order of an individual living being always increases the disorder of its environment at the same time, from which the energy of order is taken; unless the available energy of order of the direct environment or of the total system is increased at the same time through energetic binding (e.g., biochemically in organisms). In this way, the basis of all life and all ecosystems on Earth is created from inorganic and organic matter, together with the exogenous energy input through solar radiation.

> Every process, every event, every happening [...], in short, everything that happens in nature, means an increase in the entropy of that part of the world in which it happens. Thus a living organism continuously increases its entropy – or, as one could also say, it produces a positive entropy – and thus

strives towards the dangerous state of maximum entropy, which means death. It can only keep away from it, i.e. live, by continually withdrawing negative entropy from its.

(Schroedinger, 1951)

Again and again, the living must resist an entropic gradient, which it cannot achieve through circularity by itself. For this, it needs a continuous inflow from outside.

In evolutionary terms, the interaction of living beings within a common habitat always serves to mutually optimize their living development and to increase the possibilities of their individual and common life. Ecosystems with the diversity of biological life forms, communities, and habitats are the manifestations of their ordering processes. Since the capacity for dynamic stabilization is a fundamental property of living things, the development and maximization of adaptability to a dynamically changing living environment are vital consequences. For this, diversity, difference, as well as constant transformation are necessary, optimizing properties that can develop in the best possible way in the interaction of species and within ecosystems as well as between them.

The climate-ecological crisis –decline of planetary resilience

Between human imagination and planetary limitation, there has been the rise of a glaring mismatch in the interplay between the anthroposphere and the biogeosphere, especially in the 20th century. As a result, all areas and spaces of life have been transformed. Biogeoecological resources have been increasingly consumed and depleted, and their regenerative capacity has been exceeded, sometimes irreversibly. Together with excessive emissions of toxins, waste, and gases into landscapes, waters, and the atmosphere, this led to the climatic, bioecological, and humanitarian crises we are facing today. Humanity's mental and cultural space is destructively colliding with the Earth's natural planetary ecosystem.

The concept of Global Overshoot (Global Footprint Network, 2010) offers a plausible representation of the consumption of basic livelihoods, which "*depicts the consumption of global common goods in annual cycles on a global level, and [...] also represents this for the respective geo-economic reference areas*" (Dahm, 2012). The biocapacity symbolizes the ability and capacity of the Earth's ecosystem to bind solar radiation into biomass via biological activity, thus building up syntropy – negentropy or energy of order – and making it available to the living. The ecological footprint, on the other hand, describes the degradation of syntropy and the damage to ecosystems in their ability to rebuild this order energy.

Any value creation process [is] necessarily linked to a value destruction process [...] that overcompensates it. This physical regularity also dominates our technical production, which, however, is not always understandable for us, since we usually do not perceive the value destruction process running parallel to the value creation

> *or consider it insignificant. For this value destruction process, this consumption of syntropy, happens, as it were, in secret.*
>
> (Duerr, 2011a)

The extent of the consumption of syntropy becomes visible through the illustration of the overshoot of the biocapacity, which, by means of the overshoot, illustrates the damage to the natural boundaries by mankind. It cumulates in the *Earth Overshoot Day*, the date on which the full global biocapacity of planet Earth is consumed for the entire year by humanity's ecological footprint. From that day on, humanity lives off the ecological substance of the Earth. In 1970, *Earth Overshoot Day* can be calculated as December 29, in 2000 it was already on September 23, and since then it has moved forward year by year, falling on July 29 in 2021 (Global Footprint Network, 2021). The possibility of building up syntropy is being steadily reduced by the gradual depletion of biocapacity, thus depriving planetary life of the available bases of life. Circulation is not an adequate solution in view of these losses, it is rather cynical. It shows more how out of touch with life the sustainability scene also argues and thinks. The complex ecological-energetic-material interrelationships of the planetary living context are largely not understood.

The comprehensive reduction in the productivity of global ecosystems is complemented by the peak of everything (Heinberg, 2010, Dahm, 2015). Since the beginning of industrialization, economic development and the paradigm of unlimited economic growth have been based on the unlimited availability of raw materials, biological reserves, and the productive power of humans. It was not until the middle of the 20th century that these basic assumptions were increasingly called into question. The awareness of the vulnerability of the biogeosphere was now joined by the experience of the exhaustibility of natural resources (fossil and nuclear energy sources, rare earths, metals, etc.) (Bardi, 2014). The scarcity of finite raw material reserves is forcing more costly raw material extraction and recycling, and this is causing a creeping increase in production costs, initially in small steps.

Geographically, the overshoot of the ecological footprint beyond the capacity of the biosphere can be viewed as a virtualization of economic growth space. However, this can only be sustained over a limited period of time. The consideration of regeneration processes and limits of use, however, is the prerequisites for long-term conservation of use. In a limited space, however, continuous growth is not possible without externalization, that is, the outsourcing or passing on of growth costs. The abstraction "externalization" must not be misunderstood and obscure the fact that externally within a planetary limited ecosystem is only relative to the originally considered subsystem. The "outside" of a subsystem is not separated in an integrated overall view but embedded in the whole of the planet, there it is "inside"; all externalizations are always ecologically internalized (= counter-process to externalization), with all their consequential effects. In the economic production process of previous capitalist practice, externalizations usually gradually transfer the values and benefits of the commons into private, mostly commodity-like goods. Due to the excessive consumption of energy, resources, and land, high increases in productivity and at the same time reductions in production costs have been achieved, especially in the last 150 years. However, this economic growth development of the past continues to be extrapolated into the biogeoecological space and ignores the inherent material and energetic limitations of the global living system. This is ecologically destructive and dangerous, and the social, market, and political consequences are humanitarian catastrophic.

The economist Herman Daly describes the underlying erroneous thinking very catchily in his Full World Economics (Daly, 2015). Daly's basic intellectual figure is based on the finding that the economic strategy and practice of the present are oriented to an experience of a world that is empty for humans, which enabled an economic mode of unlimited expansion over many generations, traditionalized it, and thus culturally legitimized it. If trees grow faster than they can be chopped down, then there is no need to pursue sustainable management. Only in a full world do we experience the planetary limitation of nature, which casts doubt on the economic paradigm of a world with inexhaustible resources, and thus it becomes the occasion for new strategies of economic cultivation. A full world economy follows a necessity for the reproduction and regeneration of natural resources and livelihoods, to avoid the consequences severely affecting all life on our planet including humankind.

Nevertheless, the old orientations and wrong strategies are continued until today and spread globally.

With old thinking into the final century

Thereby, the institutional, technical, and socio-economic infrastructures follow the outdated old thinking and continue to optimize the process of overexploitation of the fundamentals of life by communicative, technological, and political-regulatory means with all its devastating effects on our future. The rush of mass consumption and easily generated wealth legitimize the crimes against the future. Nevertheless, the irreversible consumption of the foundations of life in favour of short-term production successes and financial advantages are communicated as "economic achievements" in the media.

The energetic turbocharging (IPCC, 2021) and the tilting of the climate system with spatial and seasonal shifts of climate zones and precipitations, a rapid dynamization of weather patterns with extreme events like droughts, storms, heavy rains, and floods, are negative externalities of this (IPCC, 2021). Other dimensions of this ecological crisis include rising sea levels, the collapse of marine circulation systems and ocean food chains, losses of freshwater, dwindling fertile soils, large-scale erosion and landscape degradation, and irreversible losses of biodiversity (IPBES, 2019, IPCC, 2021). The planetary boundaries (Rockstroem, 2009) clearly show where the major challenges lie. The functional diversity of all ecosystems is threatened, as landscapes, forests, steppes, and peatlands, also the oceans are pushed out of their natural equilibrium and destroyed by overuse – deforestation, industrial agriculture, overgrazing, overfishing, and littering. And with them, the biogeochemical cycles of substances such as nitrate and phosphorus, which affect soils, waters, and all life processes, weakening ecosystems and food chains. Climate change is only one prominent symptom of this life-threatening planetary transformation. Our obsession with CO_2 is becoming increasingly fatal, because here even the idea of closed circles appears to be coherent – if humans and ecosystems would not constantly need nourishment.

The entropy of the climate-ecological system is increasing, and the capacity to build up negentropy – order energy – continues to crumble. The degradation of bioecological difference, biological productivity, and the disruption of material cycles and climatic stability correlate negatively, amplify each other, and accelerate the process exponentially.

The ongoing destruction of ecological and socio-economic livelihoods worldwide, and especially in the regions and countries of origin of refugee migrations, results primarily from the politically and economically dominant interests of the old industrial societies of Western-European character. For generations, we kept other countries and regions weak to realize our energetic, material, and geopolitical interests. Political power dominance, an insane materially and energetically intensive consumerism, and centuries of overexploitation and economic-political polarization destabilized entire regions of the world. Greed destroys, fear prevents. All, that gives us the courage to be alive, falls by the wayside. "*No future is now*". The development path followed by the last generations cannot be continued. The economic practice of the last decades perverted the Enlightenment idea of a just and liberal economy with fair markets and turned it upside down. Led by industrial and mass consumer societies, humanity has maneuvered itself into an end-of-pipe scenario. What was supposed to create prosperity, freedom, justice, and peace resulted in an all-out attack on all of life. Today, many people have solely fled as a perspective for the future – or a life of poverty and deprivation.

We may have entered the last century of humanity – the "final century" (Rees, 2003) – as Lord Martin Rees puts it – and he is not just anyone, but Royal Astronomer of England, professor for astrophysics at Cambridge and the 20th president of the Royal Society of Science.

A peaceful, just, and liveable future is possible. But today, in the 2020s, appellative calls for an end to overexploitation, an exit from the fossil growth mindset, and pleas for renunciation, retrenchment, and frugality are by no means enough. It requires a clear departure from the economic-political ideologies and feasibility fantasies of the old 20th century. A reorientation of economic action towards ecological principles such as diversity and difference, and freedom and connectedness are the necessary answer to the climate-ecological and cultural-humanitarian situation of mankind.

Energetic and material circulation as an element of future-oriented economies

But instead of jointly competing for future-oriented and life-serving alternatives to previous path dependencies, the vacuum of vision and ethics becomes the reactionary legitimation of the self-optimization of an outdated system. And so, the old fossil thinking, which founded a linear robber economy in which matter and energy were simply degraded, consumed, and turned into wastes (not existing at all in the bioecological evolution before humans), is wrapped in a new garment.

The naïve narrative fanatics are celebrating frenetically "green" technologies and are cheering when a line is bent to a circle. Nevertheless, to direct stupidity in circles makes no sense within an energetically and materially open system. Trash remains trash. Strictly speaking, the one-dimensional focus on increasing efficiency through circular management hinders the necessary innovation breakthroughs towards true ecological effectivity.

We do ourselves no favour to optimize the same old wrong in such a way that some of its negative symptoms do not manifest themselves so vehemently. What now appears as innovation is only the highly optimized peaking of the old linear logic of utilization. In this manner, we are again creating infrastructures that will take a lifetime to get rid of, resulting in renewed path dependencies on old, rutted routes. In their inelasticity, they will once again hinder the much more important, life-serving, and regeneration-oriented systemic innovations that will be needed for our future. In this way, profound innovation is prevented and, what needs fundamental change, a systematic transformation towards an ecological buildup becomes infrastructurally perpetuated.

Here, the call for a future-rescuing circular economy is simply naïve. Moreover, it ignores the urgent need to rebuild global biocapacity, which is constantly dependent on the input of syntropy through the capture of exogenous energy. Only this can ensure that the demands of all life forms, including humans, can be sustained.

Instead, circular economy is still often understood (and abused) as a legitimation figure for the proceeding of the old fossil development path. Or, as Michael Braungart told me in a phone call on the 1st of December 2021: "*Making the wrong perfect only makes it perfectly wrong. This is what efficiency means. In contrast, being effective means doing things right*". To achieve, what is urgently needed, the permanent spin-off of bioecological beneficial effects, and a restoration of our degraded ecosystems within a truly regeneration-oriented economy, we need more than primitive efficiency. We need ecological effectivity, a life-serving economy within regenerative cultures.

Capitalistic economy precludes sustainability and destructs market economy

Only when the sources of value creation are understood in their ecological interconnectedness and dependence and are strategically included, a strong and pluralistic economy can emerge in which the diversity of capitals, instead of counteracting each other, can mutually grow and dynamically stabilize themselves.

The previous (numerical-quantitative) yardsticks for economic development (e.g., GDP/year) are inadequate; they only represent the numerical-monetary measurable value-added and exclude expenditures of economic activities and for their results that cannot be calculated in monetary equivalents.

The "growth economy" of the last decades was a consumption economy, fossil and nuclear-powered wasting of resources. It destroyed the functionality of markets and their preconditions. Financial capitalism burnt the bases of production and pushed the plurality of economic actors out of the market. The practical and publicly circulated equation of market economy and (financial) capitalism is certainly one of the great faults of the recent past.

1. If we diagnose the externalization of burdens as a counter-process to sustainability in that it damages the foundations of life (which are also the foundations of production); and
2. if we recognize that financial productivity has so far been based on the externalization of costs into nature and society, then
3. financial capitalism is correctly identified as the externalization engine. It must therefore
4. be understood as a counterstrategy to sustainable development.
5. Through the private accumulation of financial capital and economic goods among fewer and fewer people,
6. the majority of the many other people are pushed out of the market; they can no longer participate in market events as independent actors.

Conclusion: Financial capitalism – "capitalism" – destroys the production bases of the market economy and deprives the markets of market participants. This makes dynamic and innovative market activity completely dysfunctional or impossible. Capitalism must be seen as a counter-process to the market economy.

The exploitation of the global division of labour and supply chains turns predation into a competitive advantage and the accumulation of financial profits among the few becomes the driver of investment. In this way, higher financial profits can be generated, and sustainability-oriented companies and value chains are outcompeted. Monetary profitability and short-term profit optimization in competition against all are still considered indispensable. Financial capitalism is enforced by the state in terms of regulatory policy by not adequately protecting the common natural resources against private profit interests. The natural commons are being consumed and destroyed, the diversity of market participants is being suppressed and innovation is being prevented. The misunderstood growth mindset, which with a look in the rear-view mirror of the 20th century is to be assessed primarily as a steady increase in the consumption of nature, raw materials, and ecological carrying capacity, was based on this misunderstanding. (Financial) capitalist competition makes sustainable development impossible on the one hand and a functioning (social and ecological) market economy on the other. This contradicts all ecological reasons.

However, if sustainability were to become a qualitative condition and a defined goal of anthropogenic action, then the analysis and evaluation of economic activities and their results could not be limited to financial capital and economic capital alone. Nature offers the bioecological basis of all economic activity as well as the anthropogenic basis of all economic processes, the community of people, and their institutions. Planet Earth, in all its material and immaterial interactions and transformations, forms the common ground that also supports our human life.

As a consequence of an assessment of successful economic practice along its positive effects on the biogeosphere and anthroposphere, the externalization of beneficial effects on the planetary life system, including humans, has to be a transformative driving force for economic action. This aims at the realization of the (re)generation of the weakened and partly destroyed foundations of human life, the regenerating of its material and immaterial qualities within their dynamic balance. The resilience and sustainability of the planetary habitats and relationships require the restoration and strengthening of the biological diversity, fertility, and potentiality of our world, the only living space that Homo sapiens has.

Sustainability Zeroline – benchmarking a sustainable economy

As a starting point and orientation basis for a regenerative economy, which must be measured against the living potential of the Earth and its biocapacity, the Sustainability Zeroline (Dahm, 2019) defines the fictitious state of a total balance between the global biocapacity and the global ecological footprint as a Zeroline-yardstick – as a minimum requirement for sustainability – which, however, is obviously not fulfilled so far.

> Sustainability begins at a zero line along which the full integrity of the biogeosphere, including humans, is maintained. If the sum of (1) externalization of negative effects, (2) internalization, (3) compensation/compensation measures and (4) positive effects is less than or equal to zero, then this is not a sustainable economic activity; it produces more harm than good and would be better left out. As a formula, the Sustainability Zeroline is defined as follows: (internalisation + compensation + good impact) – (externalisation of negative effects) ≤ 0. Sustainability is not, if negative effects on biogeosphere and anthroposphere common goods arise and remain. From the Sustainability Zeroline onwards, the preservation of the natural and cultural basis of life is guaranteed. Only here sustainability begins.
>
> (Dahm, 2021)

Accordingly, sustainability presupposes much more than avoidance and mitigation, namely that economic activities and fixed capital bring about the strengthening of the common goods of the biogeosphere and the anthroposphere.

> Sustainability, in addition to preserving and protecting the commons of the biogeosphere and anthroposphere, accomplishes their enrichment, strengthening, and vitalization. Future viability performs beyond avoidance, internalization, and compensation the building up and promotion of the

> planetary life potential. "Life-serving" (= good impact) becomes the key here.
>
> (Dahm, 2021)

So, if sustainability is to be life-serving, this requires more than substance preservation. Only the (re)construction of the degraded life systems and the renaturation and recultivation of the damaged biocapacity of the planet create real sustainability. The most important achievement that humanity must accomplish is to balance the debt to the planetary commons so that we can write an ecological "black zero" – a sustainability zero. Where we need to act is easy to see; after all, the causes of the planetary ecological crisis and the necessary areas for action are right at our feet.

Regenerative economy – rise of a paradigm of abundance

A new paradigm is emerging in which circularity is an element, but not the driving force. This is the regeneration and restoration of the bioecological substance of our habitats, their interconnections, and interactions.

At the core of a regenerative economy are its livelihood-related economic goals to secure everyday needs, good living conditions, and peaceful and sustainable development – the stabilization of food chains and biogeochemical fluxes, the strengthening of biological and functional diversity of ecosystems, the fertility of soils, landscapes, and waters, and the storage of CO_2 in biomass. In addition, there is the development of infrastructural livelihoods to secure social coexistence and everyday supply in the areas of energy and water, health and education, transport, and traffic, in agriculture, and in entrepreneurial value and logistics chains.

For decades, natural capital was converted into financial capital on a grand scale; now it is time to invest financial capital in natural capital and systematically rebuild it on a broad scale, a generational project. It will be our task to re-create nature reserves and protected zones, to recultivate floodplain landscapes, to reforest, to revitalize peatlands and wetlands, to sequester carbon and nitrogen, to cleanse and strengthen oceans and food chains, to support and vitalize natural landscapes and seas. If this succeeds, then sustainability becomes possible for all of us.

To initiate the necessary transformation process for the economy and its institutions, all economic effects, negative as well as positive, on natural livelihoods must be included in corporate balance sheets – along the zeroline of sustainability. This requires a ("true cost") integration of all natural impacts into accounting standards (commercial and tax balance sheets): an integrated sustainability accounting. This is because all burdens on the ecological basis of life must not only be fully compensated for by reinvestment but must be overcompensated and transformed into life-sustaining in their effectiveness.

> In practice, future-oriented economic restructuring of companies will require the comprehensive technological conversion, rehabilitation and renewal

> of the infrastructures for production, logistics and distribution. Particular emphasis is placed on maximising operational energy and material efficiency and resource and energy productivity. This includes closing the value-added cycles with recycling stages with as little loss as possible and, ideally, real eco-efficiency (Braungart & McDonough, 2002), in which the waste from the first recycling stage becomes food for the next.
>
> (Dahm, 2021b)

For this, a systematic expansion of entrepreneurial methods and economic practices will be necessary, ranging from sustainability assessment, financial analysis, risk management, and business valuation to new investment instruments and logics.

All of this requires inspired, bold, and strong governance to create and enforce the legal and regulatory, as well as the institutional and international frameworks that will make a life-serving future possible. Never before has the need for pioneering policy decisions and courageous positioning been greater than today.

Our culturally and ecologically vibrant world is the result of a 3.8-billion-year-old evolution of bioecological diversity and differences in constant dynamic balance. Now it is time to embrace transformative ideas for the future and to open new paths of development, instead of trying to preserve the rigid, centralized, and mechanistic models of the order of the past.

Bibliography

Bardi, U. (2014). Extracted: How the Quest for Mineral Wealth Is Plundering the Planet. Chelsea Green Publishing.

Dahm, D. (2012). Preventing Day after Tomorrow. A level playing field for sustainability. Lecture, Conference "Sicherung der Welternährung und Armutsbekämpfung als Herausforderung für Frieden und Nachhaltigkeit". Georg-August-Universität Göttingen, Vereinigung Deutscher Wissenschaftler.

Dahm, D. (2015). Corporate Sustainable Restructuring (CSR). In. Depping, A., Walden, D. [Ed.]. CSR und Recht. Juristische Aspekte nachhaltiger Unternehmensführung erkennen und verstehen. Springer.

Dahm, D. (2019). Benchmark Sustainability: Sustainability Zeroline. Das Maß für eine zukunftsfähige Ökonomie. Transcript.

Dahm, D. (2021). The Sustainability Zeroline – a severe standard for a truly sustainable, a regenerative economy. In: Goydke, T., Koch, G. (Eds). Economy for the Common Good. A Common Standard for a Pluralistic World? Studies in International Management, Politics and Economies No. 1. Tredition.

Dahm, D., Koch, G. (2021b). The Sustainability Zeroline serving as an initial concept for an Economy of the Anthropocene. Knowledge for the Anthropocene. Elgar.

Daly, H. (2015). Economics for a Full World. Great Transition Initiative. https://greattransition.org/publication/economics-for-a-full-world

Duerr, H.-P. (2011): Das Lebende lebendiger werden lassen. Oekom.

Gell-Man, M. (1995). The Quark and the Jaguar: Adventures in the Simple and the Complex. Henryholt.

Global Footprint Network (2010). Ecological Footprint Atlas. www.foot-printnetwork.org.
Global Footprint Network (2021). Earth Overshoot Day. www.footprintnetwork.org/earth-overshoot-day.
Heinberg, R. (2010). Peak Everything: Waking Up to the Century of Declines. New Society Publishers.
Heisenberg, W. (1969). Das Teil und das Ganze. Gespräche im Umkreis der Atomphysik. Piper.
IPBES Intergovernmental Science-Policy Platform on Biodiversity and Ecosystem Services (2019). Global assessment report of the Intergovernmental Science-Policy Platform on Biodiversity and Ecosystem Services. IPBES secretariat.
IPCC Intergovernmental Panel on Climate Change (2021). Climate Change 2021. The Physical Science Basis. Contribution of Working Group I to the Sixth Assessment Report of the Intergovernmental Panel on Climate Change. Cambridge University Press.
Planck, M. (1897). Vorlesungen über Thermodynamik. Veit & Comp.
Rees, M. (2003). Our Final Century? Will the Human Race Survive the Twenty-first Century? William Heinemann.
Rockstroem, J., Steffen, W., Noone, K., Persson, A., Chapin, F. S., Lenton, T. M., Scheffer, M., Folke, C., Schellnhuber, H. J., Nykvist, B., de Wit, C. A., Hughes, T., Rodhe, H., Soerlin, S., Snyder, P. K., Costanza, R., Svedin, U., Falkenmark, M., Karlberg, L., Corel, R.W., Crutzen, P., Foley, J. A., et al. (2009). Planetary boundaries. Exploring the safe operating space for humanity. In: Nature, Vol 461. Macmillan Publishers Limited.
Schroedinger, E. (1967). What is life? Mind and Matter. Cambridge University Press.

22 Circular Economy through a system change lens

Tilmann Vahle, Janez Potočnik, and Martin Stuchtey

Introduction

For the first time in human history, we are surpassing or risking to surpass several of the critical planetary boundaries that support human life on Earth (Stockholm Resilience Centre, 2015). Unfortunately, our economic model is poorly adapted to limit our growth: Since the Enlightenment, it has been designed to maximize throughput as proxy for development. It under-values and under-rewards human capital and does not value most natural capital (such as clean water, air, and soil) at all. Market forces thus tend to over-exploit natural and human resources and thereby threaten to exceed planetary boundaries. Large-scale system change is urgently needed (Waddell et al., 2015). While some argue that we have started to create "more from less" (McAfee, 2020), data shows that global total resource consumption is still rising, and resource productivity has been stagnant for the last 20 years (Oberle et al., 2019). Today, according to the UN International Resource Panel (UN IRP), resource extraction accounts for 50% of anthropogenic carbon emissions and 90% of biodiversity impacts and is expected to double by 2060 (Oberle et al., 2019). It is therefore vital that humanity decouples resource consumption from economic development and human well-being to ensure the long-term existence of our civilization (Oberle et al., 2019).

Circular Economy (CE) measures, corresponding to "Resource Efficiency Strategies" as proposed by the UN IRP, have significant potential to lower our environmental footprints and thereby decouple human well-being from material consumption (Hertwich et al., 2020). Therefore, they are considered effective levers to protect a human-friendly ecosphere alongside decarbonization strategies. As described by the UN IRP and the EU (COM, 2020), the CE encompasses a range of strategies to extend product life, raise productivity, slow material throughputs through the economy, and ultimately recirculate them.

Notwithstanding theoretical potential, CE measures have not yet led to resource decoupling. Based on their experience in academia as well as political and economic decision-making processes, the authors outline five key

DOI: 10.4324/9781003244196-26

socio-economic mechanisms that they have found to be underlying the slow pace of change towards a sustainable and CE. The authors then discuss nine fundamental limits to the CE from physics, the economy, and human nature. They close by proposing definitions of systemic solutions, recommending principles to put them into action, to push those limits and to create an economic model that is fit to support humanity in the future.

Five socio-economic mechanisms that inhibit systems change

The authors suggest that based on their experience, the following five mechanisms in particular keep us locked in our current unsustainable system:

> **First**, addressing challenges like climate change or biodiversity loss requires sustained, system-wide and coordinated action long before their impacts are visible, since the most severe impacts happen after tipping points are passed and damages accelerate irreversibly (Fiona Harvey, 2021). However, our institutional governance structures (both in politics and in economic organisations) largely follow much shorter-term, non-complex rhythms along electoral cycles or short-term economic success – which penalises long-term action. **Second**, our production and consumption systems are optimised for consumerism, meaning the Key Performance Indicators are focused on maximising turnover, output, and Gross Domestic Product. None of these represent the actual utility of our economic activities well, meaning human needs and natural ecosystem effects are only captured coincidentally, if at all (UNDP, n.d.) (infamously, an increase in prison inmates has a positive GDP effect, with arguably few benefits for society). **Third**, inversely, negative externalities are under-priced (Barrett, 1990). Applying pricing and valuation mechanisms like carbon certificates to other key functions of society, like wellbeing, mobility, or biodiversity, could effectively decrease such externalities on those utilities by giving them value, but establishing such mechanisms has proven prohibitively complex so far. **Fourth**, existing lock-ins and vested interests in the status quo create enormous interests in maintaining our current systems, to the extent that even pioneers who want to drive change face high risks as their existing investments risk being stranded (Bos & Gupta, 2019). **Fifth** and last, environmental and social agendas are still typically discussed as distinct, although the opposite is true. Most measures that protect the environment have significant social benefits (MacArthur, E. et al., 2015) – after all, population groups of lower socio-economic echelons are particularly affected by environmental degradation. Nevertheless, these societal benefits of environmental action are often not communicated effectively enough, which lowers their likeliness of success (Meadows & Wright, 2008; RNE, 2021).

Nine impossibilities of Circular Economy

Keeping in mind the above socio-political hurdles and learnings, the authors propose the following **nine impossibilities of the CE** to be central to describing limits to the concept.

Physics, #1: Thermodynamics

Every human activity has a physical footprint on our natural environment, and every material transformation requires energy. The more refined and complex a product, the higher the physical work and energy embedded in it.

Therefore, higher-value "R-strategies" – as defined by the Recycling Hierarchy (European Commission, 2021) – should be the focus of Resource Efficiency Strategies (Allwood, 2014). By sheer physical necessity, deeper levels of material deconstruction (aka, recycling) create higher thermodynamic losses than more direct reuse. Avoidance of material consumption avoids cascades of waste and losses along the value chain that cannot be recovered through end-of-life recycling. Not least, the dissipation of materials in material composites and products across the economy leads to ever-increasing extraction- and search "costs" both in terms of economic value and energy (Reuter et al., 2019). Therefore a 100% perfectly closed loop system is thermodynamically impossible. Due to these fundamental necessities, focusing CE on recycling limits it to a fraction of the full potential of CE; other circularity strategies should be prioritized (acatech/CEID/SYSTEMIQ (Eds.), 2021a). These facts may be clear to circularity practitioners and academics, but they are often unclear to decision-makers in policy and business as well as the general public, who often confuse CE with circular waste management (SRU, 2020).

Moreover, increasing the share of renewable energies across all of the economy is critical for CE: since material dissipation and entropy are bound to increase as products are distributed across the economy and materials are blended, even in a more efficient CE the remaining energy needs must be decarbonized in order to become compatible with climate targets (Reuter et al., 2019). While discourse is ongoing on whether a 100% renewable energy system is possible (Roberts, 2018), it has been proposed as possible for Germany (Klaus et al., 2010) and more recently the USA (Jacobson, 2021) based on founded analyses.

Even at lower rates of renewable energies, CE measures decrease environmental footprints as they reduce the energy consumption of the system and can provide lower-impact alternatives to products and materials. Some lower-echelon R-strategies that are particularly energy-intensive may be exceptions to the rule – think of chemical recycling of plastics that sometimes have larger carbon footprints than comparable virgin feedstocks (acatech/CEID/SYSTEMIQ (Eds.), 2021b).

Physics, #2: Time

As time passes, most materials suffer certain ageing that reduces performance. In the case of biological materials, this ageing is most clearly seen in the form of decomposition. While we can use this process (e.g., composting for soils or biodigestion for energy), the original material utility is invariably lost. Plastics, being composed of organic chemistry, lose material performance as time passes and external stresses on the material cumulate, and can therefore not be reused or recycled indefinitely (acatech/CEID/SYSTEMIQ (Eds.), 2021b). To increase the remaining value of materials, technical analysis can help to determine the state of materials/products for their optimal use at the end-of-life (keeping in mind the fundamental limit outlined in point 1), but it would be impossible to avoid the general mechanism altogether.

At the business model level, planning for the future needs to take into account compounding risks and uncertainties. Especially for long-lived products and in markets with high innovation speed, this makes business planning for business models that apply to product end-of-life (e.g., refurbishment or recycling) sensitive to uncertainties that increase capital costs and business risks. Consequently, these business models suffer from lower risk-adjusted returns than shorter-term business models. As a result, circular business models such as X-as-a-Service models based on long-lived products are complex to develop, capital intensive, and typically only work in economic conditions that are comparatively stable – a condition that is true for ever fewer markets (Butler, 2016). More complex financial modelling, agile business models and scale (which result in lower capital costs) can balance these risks, but the mathematics remains relentless.

Lastly, as time passes, innovation causes improvements to technology and markets. A successful innovative technology or business model devalues existing products and business models (Schumpeterian Disruption) (Spencer & Kirchhoff, 2006). As innovation speed has been increasing across all economic sectors (Butler, 2016), previous product generations are devalued at increasing speed. This is not good news for business models that bank on the longevity of products.

One way of counteracting this relentless force is to raise the utilization intensity of products to extract their utility (useful service to its user) in a shorter amount of time. This way, each product reaches end-of-life faster, so that business models that depend on end-of-life products can take place sooner.

Physics, #3: Nature

The biosphere is characterized by natural cycles, which highly depend on local conditions and cannot be changed indefinitely (e.g., local solar irradiation and climate are largely set by geography) and creates hyper-locally specific needs (e.g., dependent on soil, micro-organisms, and hydrological conditions) (EMF, 2019). Therefore, circularity action in the biosphere such as nature-positive or regenerative agriculture (one that maximizes the value of natural resources, minimizes ecotoxic inputs, and regenerates biological capital) must be tailored to local conditions (FOLU, 2021).

To learn to manage these local particularities better, expanding knowledge of the locally specific requirements is key; technology is a boon for this, as more affordable sensory (remote and micro) technology and analytical tools can process far greater numbers of variables than traditional farming could. Combining these with traditional farming approaches with higher socio-ecological integration (FSNE, n.d.) could create more circular, resilient agricultural systems (FOLU, 2019).

Of course, natural conditions can be controlled in certain circumstances, the greenhouse being one prime example. Controlled environment farming and molecular agriculture (e.g., lab-grown meat and dairy) are recent developments that promise a step-change in how resource-efficient food can be produced irrespective of external natural conditions. The higher energy needs through artificial lighting and ventilation should be covered through renewable energy sources (Vahle & Stuchtey, 2019).

Economics, #1: Dissipating data and transaction costs

"Waste is matter without information" (Rau & Oberhuber, 2019): between the production and end-of-life of most products, most of the information about the product is never transmitted across value chain steps or is lost. This is particularly true for fast-moving consumer products (Götz et al., 2021). This lack of information inhibits higher value R-strategies, as transaction costs – such as locating a product, identifying appropriate actions to take, locating spare parts, and safely transporting it – increase (Götz et al., 2021).

Not least, citizens and consumers need the information to make rational decisions, including those for circularity. Also, if systemic impacts and rebound effects are not considered in policy making and business decisions (e.g., transaction costs for shared services; decreasing costs from efficiency leads to more consumption), outcomes are bound to be sub-optimal at system level.

Recent technologies create hope that we may address such information shortcomings much better than in the past: various actors including the European Commission propose digital product passports to support sustainability and circularity across a product's lifetime (VDMA, 2021). Policy makers have an important role in mandating more extensive and harmonized disclosure of information, including via such digital product passports. Moreover, education – about the scientific principle, systemic thinking, and environmental education – needs to consider these issues to help people make better decisions (acatech/CEID/SYSTEMIQ (Eds.), 2021a).

Irrespective of information, every action involves transaction costs. Automation can help lower these, for example, in the case of algorithm-based digital service models. They can also be reduced by prioritizing products with high-value retention potential (like buildings instead of consumer packaging) and markets with high scale and high density (e.g., in car sharing, looking at larger cities). Nonetheless, transaction costs mean that higher-value circularity action can never be suitable for 100% of products – which substantially limits their total system-wide impact potential.

Economics, #2: Value add and value loss

Products increase in value with every manufacturing step. As humans derive utility from products and services beyond their mere objective function, including social status, pleasure, or other emotional effects, this process includes non-physical process steps like design and marketing, whereby intangible values are imbued into a product or service (Patrick Ward, 2021).

Consequently, materials are bound to represent only a share of a product's economic value. With the increasing wealth of consumers and increasing complexity of products, this share of value decreases. These intangible, seemingly non-rational values overlay basic human needs. For CE, this means: Firstly, materials comprise only a small share of product value that decreases with further economic development and complexity of products. Secondly, products lose value as they age compared to innovation in the market, irrespective of their physical condition. Thirdly, when trying to raise the productivity of assets by creating a "utility economy", that is, a sharing economy based on providing for human needs such as mobility, decision-makers need to consider consumers' non-material needs and want to design effective interventions.

Therefore, the image of a CE that is narrowly focused on providing basic human needs is impossible in reality. Also, it is impossible that those CE strategies that focus merely on "end-of-life material value" are valuable compared to the overall economy. They decrease in value potential the further down the life cycle and the more directly to the products' mere materials they apply (Point 1).

Thus, a systemic perspective focuses first on how to satisfy a human need and what products are needed to satisfy it (SYSTEMIQ & Club of Rome, 2020) and focuses on further upstream CE strategies.

Economics, #3: Demand focus

Local demand for CE business models, especially sharing offers, needs to be sufficiently high so that unit transaction costs remain low, economies of scale are sufficient, and utilization justifies the cost of capital (Araghi et al., 2010). Therefore, when introducing sharing economy concepts, operators will focus on high-density markets first. It is impossible that lower-density markets are as attractive to economic operators as high-density ones. Policy makers should ensure service to less attractive markets through regulation or subsidies.

Temporal demand: while cars famously stand idle >90% of the time (MacArthur, E. et al., 2015), not all of that can be avoided – at night, most people sleep, and they require transportation, especially during rush hours. During the days, offices are occupied, while at night they are generally not. Something well known to utility providers, from public transport to energy: a system must be designed for peak demand (Jara-Díaz et al., 2020). This could be amended by smoothing out demand peaks through more home-office and workspace flexibility. This way, infrastructure might be used more productively.

Dynamic demand – Rebound effects: As utilization and longevity improvements lower the monetary cost and increase the convenience of services, usage tends to increase – a rebound effect (SYSTEMIQ, 2021). This principle is so enduring in the mobility sector that it has been coined the "fundamental law of congestion": building more roads to reduce congestion leads to more cars on the road, until congestion returns to previous levels (Duranton & Turner, 2011). It is therefore impossible that all savings from CE measures lead to reduced environmental impacts without rebound. However, rebounds can be minimized through smart and systemic public action. For example, instituting dynamic mobility infrastructure and fuel pricing or pricing externalities can shift people's behaviour at large. However, this only works if lower-footprint alternatives are available and attractive.

Economics, #4: Incentives

It is hypothesized that by shifting from selling products to "X-as-a-Service" (XaaS) or "product-service-systems" business models, businesses are incentivized to use products more efficiently to provide their services, rather than aiming to 'sell more stuff'. This should incentivize decoupling prosperity from material consumption (Görög, 2018; SYSTEMIQ, 2021).

While XaaS is a promising concept, there are various challenges associated with this (Beuren et al., 2013). These include: Firstly, product-as-a-service users may not be incentivized to use those products carefully, leading to higher depreciation or fuel consumption (as the ironic saying "do not be gentle, it is a rental" captures well). Secondly, companies may optimize for other values than cost, such as convenience, brand value, or other emotional factors. In that case, servicization of products might even lead to higher resource consumption. Thirdly, transaction costs for such business models add further cost and environmental burden (Point 4) like in ride-hailing services, where passenger pick-up journeys may double the total distance driven (OECD/ITF, 2021). Fourth, materials and fuel rarely constitute a substantial share of business costs and thus may not be worth optimizing.

In short, X-as-a-Service business models have not consistently been shown in practice to create the environmental benefits that proponents often claim; for this to work, they need to be designed and operated with that in mind. It may be impossible to overcome these business incentives for non-circular cost- and non-cost optimizations. Still, policy makers can support such models, for example, through regulatory requirements and changing economic conditions via taxation, levies, or subsidies, by shifting from labour taxes to resource taxes (Ex'tax, n.d.), instituting carbon prices (European Commission, n.d.-b), or instating road pricing schemes (Ubbels & de Jong, 2009).

People, #1: Understanding impact

The range of CE solutions is large across product and service lifecycles but differs in impact potential. To prioritize the most effective actions, understand their impacts on human needs and ecosystems across their lifecycles (SYSTEMIQ & Club of Rome, 2020). Appropriate metrics and impact assessment tools are needed.

However, many policies lack consideration of lifecycle effects (e.g., EU vehicle emission performance standards only consider end-of-pipe carbon effects and disregard emissions at other parts of the value chain) (European Parliament and European Council, 2019). Also, the very tools needed to make such regulation possible in the first place still require further development (European Commission, n.d.-a; Mugnier et al., 2010). Of course, lifecycle assessment (LCA) methodologies have been applied widely and routinely for decades. However, their application rests on data and assumptions that are often spurious, limited by confidentiality requirements, or hard to generate (Ballweg et al., 2021). Given the near-unlimited variations of product designs and business model combinations, it may be a true impossibility for CE to make LCA fully comparable.

Nonetheless, more comprehensive assessments of the effects of CE measures on the economy, the environment, and labour markets are possible. Measurement tools, metrics, and lifecycle assessment methodologies need to be evolved and harmonized to assess impacts consistently. Recent technological developments like remote sensing, machine learning, and digital product passports raise hopes that impact assessments' quality, comparability, and timeliness may dramatically improve in the coming years. For example, it is now possible to assess power plants' carbon emissions from space in real-time (Jupiter Intelligence, n.d.).

Building on such improved impact assessment, a comprehensive taxonomy of CE should be developed (as initiated by the European Institutions (European Commission, n.d.-c)) to support capital to flow at scale into the most impactful solutions and to create the scale of solutions needed.

People, #2: Institutional capacity and mental models

A lack of understanding or prioritization of scientific principles among decision-makers limits how decision-makers consider systems and scientific issues. Chiefly, those include planetary boundaries and the likely consequences of overstepping them (Stockholm Resilience Centre, 2015), entropy and electrochemical fundamentals and their relentless effects on comparative efficiencies of different R-strategies (Reuter et al., 2019), or exponential effects and tipping points. In any organization, there is a strong natural selection for those factors that primarily drive that organization's benefit, irrespective of societal impacts. In practice, this is leading to structurally sub-optimal long-term outcomes for society, especially regarding complex issues such as ecosystem health, climate change, or social cohesion. While this may appear like an issue that may be addressed simply through better education or training, it appears that due to deeply rooted institutional and organizational dynamics, such capacity constraints are hard to address. While scientifically founded information and better systems understanding can be taught and provided to an extent – and increasing funding is key to achieving this – (acatech/CEID/SYSTEMIQ (Eds.), 2021a), the dynamics that underpin the self-selection described are impossible to overcome without more fundamental changes in how performance is rewarded in organizations and the economy at large.

Conclusion: Stretching the limits of the Circular Economy through systemic thinking

Circular Economy or Resource Efficiency Strategies may help decouple human well-being from environmental impacts, alongside decisive decarbonization and energy efficiency strategies (Hertwich et al., 2020). They reflect a change of perspective from economic growth to a focus on improving human well-being and ecosystem health by making more from less.

In this chapter, the authors have reflected on five mechanisms that inhibit systems change and outlined nine impossibilities of the CE that decision-makers should consider designing effective interventions. The authors have argued that systemic thinking and solutions that are mindful of the impossibilities and limits of CE help create effective system change interventions.

Building on the Circular Economy Initiative Deutschland CE Roadmap for Germany (2021a) and the System Change Compass developed by SYSTEMIQ and the Club of Rome (2020), endorsed by EU Commission President Ursula von der Leyen, the authors propose four criteria to describe systemic solutions and make recommendations for systemic action to maximize the potential of CE. These are broadly compatible with other change theory frameworks (Waddell et al., 2015).

Describing systemic solutions:

1. They **focus on outcomes** – they seek to achieve certain objectives such as societal needs and environmental outcomes such as planetary boundaries, and optimize across value chains and sectors towards that outcome, instead of optimizing production within sectors.
2. They **complement supply-side measures with demand reduction** – as (downstream) demand creates upstream footprints, modulating demand has outsized leverage for impact (as stipulated, for example, by the term "Negawatts").
3. They **consider feedback loops**, especially in the form of **rebound effects and non-linear cause–effect relationships.** They do not focus on demanding individual action but on modulating the behaviour of entire systems, and take care to use efficiency gains for further acceleration of impact, rather than allowing rebound effects to lead to more consumption.
4. They consider **action from all stakeholders relevant to the cross-value chain optimization**, across ministries, across sectors.

To put systemic solutions into practice, the authors suggest the following:

1. **Be science-based and realistic:** acknowledge limits to circularity. Consider thermodynamic and physical conditions including climate science. Acknowledge impossibilities.
2. **Clarify discourse:** identify suitable metrics; separate outcome metrics from impact metrics to be able to track both progress in measures and their intended effects (Kick et al., 2021). Dedicate effort early to creating common understandings to avoid misunderstandings down the road.
3. **Focus:** do not get sidetracked by measures with likely minor effects, even though they may be popular. Given the little time we have left to avoid a catastrophic climate crisis and ecosystem collapse, incremental action does not help – it delays. We need to prioritize those issues and measures that have the potential to make substantial differences. Systems approaches such as the DPSIR framework (Ness et al., 2010) can help.
4. **Embrace complexity, put action first:** hypothesize what needs to be done and consider non-linear and chaotic effects. Then act fast: in complex challenges, there is never one optimal answer, and the solution space constantly changes. Attempting to pinpoint it leads to analysis paralysis. Visioning methods like the Three Horizons Framework (International Futures Forum, n.d.; Sharpe, 2020) (acatech/CEID/SYSTEMIQ (Eds.), 2021a) can be useful tools to support charting the way. The best way to predict the future is to create it.
5. **Work with the market:** companies produce what we consume. They need to be allies in transforming the system, as they will ultimately put changes into action. Therefore, work with businesses that build the future. Punish those that do not. Set firm boundaries and drive incentives through prices. Support innovation for alternatives to allow behavioural change to happen.
6. **Be mindful of social impacts:** as with every change, there will be losers when societies transform to be more circular and sustainable. Their fears and pains are legitimate. They must be anticipated and addressed, both in communication and action, otherwise they could block the change.
7. **Keep at it:** organize structures that can sustain change processes – across time, political divides, and electoral cycles – can coordinate the process and have the mandate and resources to take effective action (RNE, 2021).

By following these principles and recommendations, the authors argue that systemic solutions can push the limits of a CE up to its true impossibilities and thus become a springboard for innovation, fulfilment of societal needs, and a rich field of entrepreneurial activity. They challenge us to leave behind incremental solutions, set new 'north stars' for outcome-oriented action, and enter a new field of societal discussion and industrial revolution that are compatible with planetary boundaries. Nonetheless, practitioners need to humbly accept the limits and impossibilities of the CE.

References

acatech/CEID/SYSTEMIQ (Eds.). (2021a). *Circular Economy Roadmap for Germany*. Circular Economy Initiative Deutschland. https://static1.squarespace.com/static/5b52037e4611a0606973bc79/t/61482d35b9cffc5bb5816d1e/1632120122091/Circular+Economy+Roadmap+for+Germany_EN.pdf

acatech/CEID/SYSTEMIQ (Eds.). (2021b). *Plastics packaging in a closed loop – Potentials, conditions, challenges*. Circular Economy Initiative Deutschland. www.circular-economy-initiative.de/s/VP_Gesamtbericht_EN

Allwood, J. M. (2014). Squaring the Circular Economy. In *Handbook of Recycling* (pp. 445–477). Elsevier. https://doi.org/10.1016/B978-0-12-396459-5.00030-1

Araghi, Y., Larco, N., Bouma, G., Doll, C., Vonk Noordegraaf, D., & Krauß, K. (2010). Drivers and barriers of mobility-as-a-service in urban areas. *8th Transport Research Arena*. Transport Research Arena Conference (TRA), Helsinki, Finland. http://publica.fraunhofer.de/dokumente/N-633316.html

Ballweg, M., Potocnik, J., Stuchtey, M., Vahle, T., & Marie, W. (2021). *Paving the Way: EU Policy Action for Automotive Circularity*. World Economic Forum. www3.weforum.org/docs/WEF_Circular_Cars_Initiative_Paving_the_Way_2021.pdf

Barrett, S. (1990). The problem of global environmental protection. *Oxford Review of Economic Policy*, 6(1), 68–79. https://doi.org/10.1093/oxrep/6.1.68

Beuren, F. H., Gomes Ferreira, M. G., & Cauchick Miguel, P. A. (2013). Product-service systems: A literature review on integrated products and services. *Journal of Cleaner Production*, 47, 222–231. https://doi.org/10.1016/j.jclepro.2012.12.028

Bos, K., & Gupta, J. (2019). Stranded assets and stranded resources: Implications for climate change mitigation and global sustainable development. *Energy Research & Social Science*, 56, 101215. https://doi.org/10.1016/j.erss.2019.05.025

Butler, D. (2016). Tomorrow's world: Technological change is accelerating today at an unprecedented speed and could create a world we can barely begin to imagine. *Nature*, 530(7591), 398+. Gale Academic OneFile.

COM. (2020). *A new Circular Economy Action Plan For a cleaner and more competitive Europe* (COMMUNICATION FROM THE COMMISSION TO THE EUROPEAN PARLIAMENT, THE COUNCIL, THE EUROPEAN ECONOMIC AND SOCIAL COMMITTEE AND THE COMMITTEE OF THE REGIONS COM/2020/98 final). European Commission. https://eur-lex.europa.eu/legal-content/EN/TXT/?qid=1583933814386&uri=COM:2020:98:FIN

Duranton, G., & Turner, M. A. (2011). The Fundamental Law of Road Congestion: Evidence from US Cities. *American Economic Review*, *101*(6), 2616–2652. https://doi.org/10.1257/aer.101.6.2616

EMF. (2019). *Cities and circular economy for food*. Ellen MacArthur Foundation. https://emf.thirdlight.com/link/7ztxaa89xl5c-d30so/@/preview/1?o

European Commission. (n.d.-a). *Environmental Footprint Pilot Phase: Policy Background*. Retrieved 4 November 2021, from https://ec.europa.eu/environment/eussd/smgp/policy_footprint.htm

European Commission. (n.d.-b). *EU Emissions Trading System (EU ETS)*. Retrieved 4 November 2021, from https://ec.europa.eu/clima/eu-action/eu-emissions-trading-system-eu-ets_en

European Commission. (n.d.-c). EU taxonomy for sustainable activities. What the EU is doing to create an EU-wide classification system for sustainable activities. Retrieved 4

November 2021, from https://ec.europa.eu/info/business-economy-euro/banking-and-finance/sustainable-finance/eu-taxonomy-sustainable-activities_en

European Commission. (2021). *Waste prevention and management*. https://ec.europa.eu/environment/green-growth/waste-prevention-and-management/index_en.htm

European Parliament and European Council. (2019). REGULATION (EU) 2019/631 OF THE EUROPEAN PARLIAMENT AND OF THE COUNCIL of 17 April 2019 setting CO2 emission performance standards for new passenger cars and for new light commercial vehicles, and repealing Regulations (EC) No 443/2009 and (EU) No 510/2011 (recast). European Parliament and European Council. https://eur-lex.europa.eu/eli/reg/2019/631/2021-03-01

Ex'tax. (n.d.). *The Ex'tax Project*. Retrieved 4 November 2021, from https://ex-tax.com/

Fiona Harvey. (2021, June 23). IPCC steps up warning on climate tipping points in leaked draft report. *The Guardian*. www.theguardian.com/environment/2021/jun/23/climate-change-dangerous-thresholds-un-report

FOLU. (2019). *Growing Better: Ten Critical Transitions to Transform Food and Land Use*. Food and Land Use Coalition. www.foodandlandusecoalition.org/wp-content/uploads/2019/09/FOLU-GrowingBetter-GlobalReport.pdf

FOLU. (2021). *Accelerating the 10 Critical Transitions: Positive Tipping Points for Food and Land Use Systems Transformation*. Food and Land Use Coalition. www.foodandlandusecoalition.org/wp-content/uploads/2021/07/Positive-Tipping-Points-for-Food-and-Land-Use-Systems-Transformation.pdf

FSNE. (n.d.). *The Sood Solutions New England Pledge*. Retrieved 4 November 2021, from https://foodsolutionsne.org/the-food-solutions-new-england-pledge/

Görög, G. (2018). The Definitions of Sharing Economy: A Systematic Literature Review. *Management*, 175–189. https://doi.org/10.26493/1854-4231.13.175-189

Götz, T., Adisorn, T., & Tholen, L. (2021). *Der digitale Produktpass als Politik-Konzept*. Wuppertal Institut. https://epub.wupperinst.org/frontdoor/deliver/index/docId/7694/file/WR20.pdf

Hertwich, E., Lifset, R., Pauliuk, S., & Heeren, N. (2020). *Resource Efficiency and Climate Change: Material Efficiency Strategies for a Low-Carbon Future*. International Resource Panel. United Nations Environment Programme. www.resourcepanel.org/reports/resource-efficiency-and-climate-change

International Futures Forum. (n.d.). *Three Horizons*. Retrieved 4 November 2021, from www.iffpraxis.com/three-horizons

Jacobson, M. Z. (2021). 100% clean, renewable energy and storage for everything. Cambridge University Press.

Jara-Díaz, S., Fielbaum, A., & Gschwender, A. (2020). Strategies for transit fleet design considering peak and off-peak periods using the single-line model. *Transportation Research Part B: Methodological*, *142*, 1–18. https://doi.org/10.1016/j.trb.2020.09.012

Jupiter Intelligence. (n.d.). *Jupiter Intelligence*. Retrieved 4 November 2021, from https://jupiterintel.com

Kick, M., Kadner, S., Greiff, K., Jarchow, S., Stuchtey, M. R., Weber, T., & Kobus, J. (2021). Making the Circular Economy Count. An analysis of available circular economy metrics to develop a practical, implementable set for national progress monitoring. SYSTEMIQ, SUN Institute Environment & Sustainability, acatech. www.systemiq.earth/wp-content/uploads/2021/08/CE-Metrics-Report_Final.pdf

Klaus, T., Vollmer, C., Werner, K., Lehmann, H., & Müschen, K. (2010). *Energieziel 2050. 100% Strom aus erneuerbaren Quellen* (Broschüren). Umweltbundesamt. www.umweltbundesamt.de/publikationen/energieziel-2050

MacArthur, E., Stuchtey, M. R., & Zumwinkel, K. (2015). *Growth Within: A circular economy vision for a competitive Europe*. Ellen MacArthur Foundation. https://emf.thirdlight.com/link/8izw1qhml4ga-404tsz/@/preview/1?o

McAfee, A. (2020). More from less: The surprising story of how we learned to prosper using fewer resources – and what happens next. Simon & Schuster.

Meadows, D. H., & Wright, D. (2008). *Thinking in systems: A primer*. Chelsea Green Pub.

Mugnier, E., Mairet, A., & Boucher, J. (2010). *Product Carbon Footprinting – a study on methodologies and initiatives*. European Commission DG Environment. https://ec.europa.eu/environment/eussd/smgp/pdf/Product_Carbon_Footprint_study.pdf

Ness, B., Anderberg, S., & Olsson, L. (2010). Structuring problems in sustainability science: The multi-level DPSIR framework. *Geoforum*, *41*(3), 479–488. https://doi.org/10.1016/j.geoforum.2009.12.005

Oberle, B., Bringezu, S., Hatfeld-Dodds, S., Hellweg, S., Schandl, H., Clement, J., Cabernard, L., Chen, D., Droz-Georget, H., Ekins, P., Fischer-Kowalski, M., Flörke, M., Frank, S., Froemelt, A., Geschke, A., Haupt, M., Havlik, P., Hüfner, R., Lenzen, M., … Zhu, B. (2019). *Global Resources Outlook 2019: Natural Resources for the Future We Want*. International Resource Panel. United Nations Environment Programme. www.resourcepanel.org/reports/global-resources-outlook

OECD/ITF. (2021). *The Innovative Mobility Landscape: The Case of Mobility as a Service* (p. 126) [Research Report]. Organization for Economic Cooperation and Development/International Transport Forum. www.itf-oecd.org/innovative-mobility-landscape-maas

Patrick Ward. (2021, October 24). *Value-Add: Term Meaning and Usage in Business*. https://nanoglobals.com/glossary/value-add/

Rau, T., & Oberhuber, S. (2019). Material matters: Wie wir es schaffen, die Ressourcenverschwendung zu beenden, die Wirtschaft zu motivieren, bessere Produkte zu erzeugen und wie Unternehmen, Verbraucher und die Umwelt davon profitieren (I. Wilhelm, Trans.; 2. Auflage). Econ.

Reuter, M. A., van Schaik, A., Gutzmer, J., Bartie, N., & Abadías-Llamas, A. (2019). Challenges of the Circular Economy: A Material, Metallurgical, and Product Design Perspective. *Annual Review of Materials Research*, 49(1), 253–274. https://doi.org/10.1146/annurev-matsci-070218-010057

RNE. (2021, October 5). Zirkuläres Wirtschaften: Hebelwirkung für eine nachhaltige Transformation. *Stellungnahme*. www.nachhaltigkeitsrat.de/wp-content/uploads/2021/10/20211005_RNE_Stellungnahme_zirkulaeres_Wirtschaften.pdf

Roberts, D. (2018, February 7). Is 100% renewable energy realistic? Here's what we know. Reasons for skepticism, reasons for optimism, and some tentative conclusions. [News website]. *Vox.Com Energy and Environment*. www.vox.com/energy-and-environment/2017/4/7/15159034/100-renewable-energy-studies

Sharpe, B. (2020). *Three horizons: The patterning of hope* (Second edition). Triarchy Press.

Spencer, A. S., & Kirchhoff, B. A. (2006). Schumpeter and new technology based firms: Towards a framework for how NTBFs cause creative destruction. *International Entrepreneurship and Management Journal*, 2(2), 145–156. https://doi.org/10.1007/s11365-006-8681-3

SRU. (2020). *Kreislaufwirtschaft: Von der Rhetorik zur Praxis* (p. 86) [Umweltgutachten]. Sachverständigenrat für Umweltrat. www.umweltrat.de/SharedDocs/Downloads/DE/01_Umweltgutachten/2016_2020/2020_Umweltgutachten_Kap_03_Kreislaufwirtschaft.html

Stockholm Resilience Centre. (2015). *Planetary boundaries*. www.stockholmresilience.org/research/planetary-boundaries.html

SYSTEMIQ. (2021). Everything- as-a-Service XaaS. How businesses can thrive in the age of climate change and digitalization. SYSTEMIQ. www.systemiq.earth/wp-content/uploads/2021/09/XaaS-report_ES.pdf

SYSTEMIQ, & Club of Rome. (2020). *A System Change Compass. Implementing the European Green Deal in a time of recovery*. www.systemiq.earth/wp-content/uploads/2020/11/System-Change-Compass-full-report_final.pdf

Ubbels, B., & de Jong, G. (2009). *Review of Evidence on the Effects of Road Pricing*. European Transport Conference 2009. http://citeseerx.ist.psu.edu/viewdoc/download?doi=10.1.1.678.4872&rep=rep1&type=pdf

UNDP. (n.d.). *Human Development Index (HDI)*. Retrieved 4 November 2021, from http://hdr.undp.org/en/content/human-development-index-hdi

Vahle, T., & Stuchtey, M. (2019). Urban agriculture: Boon or bust? In *Urban agriculture, another way to feed cities*. Veolia Institute. www.institut.veolia.org/en/urban-agriculture-boon-or-bust

VDMA. (2021, August 16). *Digital Product Passport. Protect essential knowledge and know-how*. https://pr.euractiv.com/pr/digital-product-passport-protect-essential-knowledge-and-know-how-220951

Waddell, S., Waddock, S., Cornell, S., Dentoni, D., McLachlan, M., & Meszoely, G. (2015). Large Systems Change: An Emerging Field of Transformation and Transitions. *Journal of Corporate Citizenship*, 58, 5–30. https://doi.org/10.9774/GLEAF.4700.2015.ju.00003

23 Practising circular economy

Stumbling blocks for circulation and recycling

Henning Friege and Klaus Kümmerer

Stumbling blocks – a short introduction

The "stumbling blocks" were derived empirically from studies and research in waste and resource management (Friege 2012, 2018). In the following, each of the stumbling blocks is briefly explained.

Entropy (ΔS): Management of matter is confronted with the increase of entropy. Dissipative loss of energy and materials happens all along the life cycle including circulation and recycling of products and handling of waste. An important entropy-increasing step is the mixing of different constituents. This happens at all levels from atomic to product, for example, when alloys are produced or additives are added to basic polymers. Following thermodynamics, entropy may be used as a yardstick for the disorder of a closed system. Waste management means to upgrade highly entropic wastes to low entropy raw – or "recovered" – materials (Rechberger/Graedel 2002). To achieve this higher material order in a system, external energy has to be fed to the system, and some of it will end up as entropy again accompanied by material waste. It is therefore impossible to close technical loops completely (Stumm/Davis 1974). The planet can at least get rid of the dissipative heat in principle. But it cannot get rid of the materials' dissipation which is reflected in the law of material conservation on the one hand and levelling off concentrations in the long run.

Dissipative use (D!): This stumbling block refers to the loss of products and their constituents as a consequence of their use. The dissipation rate depends among others on the number of users, for example, it is far higher for consumer goods as compared to equipment for industry. The owner of the product decides if and when the item in question is handed over to the trash collector (see also ΔS and Δt). If the consumer does not hand it over, the product and its constituents may be lost along the further life cycle (see ΔS).

Hazardous compounds vs. resources (H↔R): Products may contain harmful substances that are necessary for the intended function or application. In the case of recycling, hazardous components must be extracted and separated to obtain secondary raw materials of sufficient quality. Efforts for the segregation of contaminants depend on the type of bonding between the contaminant and the basic material (i.e., chemically bonded, adsorbed, loose material mix, see also ΔS).

DOI: 10.4324/9781003244196-27

Missing information (I?): If used products shall be re-used, information is required about their previous service life and functionality. In the case of recycling, information on the chemical composition and, if applicable, on suitable dismantling processes is needed. Unwanted degradation or loss of components can change composition over lifetime (see Δt). The quality and extent of information that is available for a waste fraction are often linked to the degree of mixing of different products and materials (see also ΔS, D!) and often lost over time.

Time (Δt): Time is a crucial challenge for two reasons: (1) Mass flows of materials in waste and the ones of waste itself change over time at various rates of change for size, place, and composition. The opportunity for recycling of used products depends on their availability, which is determined by their service life, distribution, and location (see also D!, I?). This is a dynamic process that is difficult to track and even more difficult to control. (2) Scientific knowledge about the properties of substances grows over time and can lead to new, often negative assessments of substances (see also H↔R).

Economy (EcY!): Materials and products are placed on the market by economic drivers, that is, supply and demand. This holds also for products that shall be remanufactured or re-used and for materials that shall be recovered from waste. Re-use of products depends on the decision of individual consumers who compare the quality and functionality of used products with new items. Secondary raw materials must compete with primary materials on the market, that is, quality and price. High costs for recycling are among the most important economic obstacles for secondary raw materials.

Differences in income and wealth (ΔEcY): For most waste fractions disposal and treatment are linked to costs (negative price). If the waste contains valuable constituents, owners can decide whether they segregate and sell the valuables. Such a decision is linked to opportunity costs that are a function of the given economic situation. Therefore, high-income disparities in society cause informal sector activities related to waste (Cavé 2014).

The stumbling blocks do not cover cultural or regulatory barriers, though these may be very important for overcoming problems in the circular economy but can also create new challenges.

In the following we will elaborate on the stumbling blocks using examples (see Table 23.1) that are important for a circular economy focusing on recycling, remanufacturing, and re-use.

Boundaries caused by entropy and dissipation

Collection, sorting, and recovery of materials from used electric appliances (WEEE)

Modern electronic devices include a broad spectrum of complex materials including constituents in low concentrations, for example, indium for LCD screens, cadmium telluride for PV cells, but also gold, silver, copper, rare earth metals, and so on, as well as different polymers including additives. Metals have

Table 23.1 Examples used in the text

Recycling (1), remanufacturing (2), re-use (3) of used products	*Entropy* (ΔS)	*Dissipative use (D!)*	*Hazardous compounds vs. resources (H↔R)*	*Missing information (I?)*	*Time* (Δt)	*Economy* (EcY!)	*Differences in income and wealth* (ΔEcY)
Plastic package for meat (1)	XX	XXX		X		XX	
Electric and electronic devices (1,2,3)	XXX	XXX	(X)	X	XX	XX	XX
Used textiles (1,3)	XX	XXX		X	XX	X	
Automotive batteries (1,2)	XX	XX	XX	X	XXX	X	X
PVC floor tiles (1)	XX	XX	XXX	XXX	XXX	X	
FeNdB magnets for wind turbines (1)	XXX	X		X	XX	XX	
LCD TV screen (1)	XX	XXX	XX	X	XX	X	X
CdTe PV modules (1,3)	XX	XX	XXX	X	XXX	X	
High-grade steel (1)	XXX	X	X	X	X		
PVC cable sheaths (1)	XX	XX	XXX	X			

Note: Stumbling block must be considered (X), is important (XX), is fundamental (XXX).

an enormous ecological footprint that is due – inter alia – to the cumulated energy demand, for example, 194 MJ/kg for primary aluminium and 23.8 Mg/kg for aluminium from scrap (Graedel et al. 2019). These come along with dissipative losses of material too. All these materials exhibit specific functions, for example, Neodymium (NdFeB alloy) in strong magnets in gearless windmills or cobalt and lithium in high-performance accumulators. The demand for these metals is sharply increasing and leads to extremely volatile prices. Moreover, the supply is critical (European list of "strategic minerals" (EU COM 2020)). Recovery of these resources will thus

- substitute primary metals and lower dependency from primary sources,
- decrease the amount of energy needed for the production of metals,
- ensure further substitution of fossil energy by renewable one.

The recovery of the metals for example is hampered by many stumbling blocks. Functional materials in electronic appliances or cars, construction, or machinery are often based on special grades of alloys, for example, high-performance steel grades or non-ferrous base metals doped with other metals as well as metalloids. These alloys often cannot be fragmented into its basic elements (see below). High dissipation on one hand and very low concentrations of the desired metals in the product challenge resource recovery. Recovery of all these materials will work without any subsidies only when the price for primary materials is higher than the costs associated with the recycling process (EcY!).

Furthermore, consumer products must be separately collected from millions of users and all devices must be identified to ensure correct recovery operations to avoid the inevitable loss of constituents. We are faced with the dissipation problem (D!) here again and an enormous information gap (I?). According to the European WEEE directive, the producers and importers of electric and electronic appliances are held responsible for their products after use, that is, in the waste phase. Collection of WEEE is mostly performed by municipal authorities and retailers, but costs must be borne by the producers or importers. The collection of consumer products after their useful life close to 100% is per se impossible, specific reasons are behaviour of consumers, knowledge and temporal gaps, missing or improper legislation, and infrastructure. Most EU Member States even do not reach the actual collection target of 65% but less than 50% on average. There are numerous recipes aiming at higher collection rates (Tesfaye et al. 2017) for example, more information, higher density of collection points (WEEE Forum 2021, Friege et al. 2015), introduction of economic incentives (Shevchenko et al. 2019), but there will remain large gaps caused by dissipation.

For the targeted, effective, and efficacious mining of resources from waste, information about composition, concentration, and location is needed. The improvement of the recycling efficiency of valuable and/or scarce elements depends to a large extent on a priori knowledge of materials and material distribution (Ueberschaer et al. 2017), which is normally not available in detail. For this reason, only particularly hazardous constituents are usually removed during initial dismantling, for example, flammable batteries or climate-damaging refrigerants. Afterwards, the appliances are shredded or otherwise destructed aiming at disaggregation (singularization) of often still heterogenic composed particles to be sorted on a conveyor belt. Thus, discrete valuable materials can be picked out of the mass flow if appropriate sorting technologies are available. Magnetic and eddy current separation are used for the recovery of iron, steel, chromium, copper, aluminium, and some other frequently used metals. Rare metals are often lost, because they can be adsorbed on plastic particles or on grains based on iron or aluminium (Wäger et al. 2014). Shredding results in mixing and increases the material entropy leading to higher demand for energy and costly separation techniques.

Further problems come up with different service lifetimes and storage times of appliances (Thiébaud et al. 2017), that is, the temporal dynamics of mass flows (Δt): 15% of all private laptops are used for a maximum of three years, but more than 15% are used for eight years or longer. The composition of electronic devices changes considerably over time. This makes it difficult to refurbish or dismantle used equipment, especially since information on the content of certain materials can only be made available if the equipment in question is precisely identified (I?).

Dissipation and loss of metals

Statements like "Steel loses no quality during recycling and can be recycled endlessly" can be found in popular news. Unfortunately, this is not correct. The main route of metal recycling covers scrap collection, sorting, and input to foundries, steelworks, or non-ferrous metal smelters. High-quality (cold-rolled) steel is applied in the automotive and machinery industry. If a scrap of high-quality steel is not recycled directly to the same product line and same quality level, down-cycling of steel into hot-rolled construction steel, for example, for concrete reinforcement, is unavoidable. Moreover, some material is lost during the recovery and re-melting stages. According to model calculations, losses of steel may be up to 50% within this century (Pauliuk et al. 2017) caused by material entropy (ΔS) and dissipation (D!).

The recovery of metals is increasingly hampered by the growing diversity of alloys. In the case of steel, the chase for lightweight car bodies is an important driver for the development of high-performance alloys with complex compositions. On the basis of thermodynamic distribution tendencies, most alloying elements cannot be separated from steel scrap. Typical steel alloying elements, such as manganese, chromium, and vanadium, tend to migrate into the slag which is often used in roadbeds. Metals buried in the slag are often not accessible for further use anymore; some metals, however, can leach over a long time and pollute the environment. Copper, nickel, molybdenum, cobalt, and so on remain in the metal phase (Ohno et al. 2014) but only if the process is done right from the very beginning. Some other elements, mainly zinc, can be recovered from the dust in a rotary kiln under reducing conditions. Rare earth metals that are present in low concentrations are thus lost (Andersson et al. 2017). "Tramp metals" are also traces in important carrier non-ferrous metals. The "Metal Wheel" (Reuter et al. 2018) visualizes the circular economy's carrier metals processing infrastructure.

However, on top of these unintended losses, there are also cases where the dissipative loss of materials is a consequence of its function like zinc in sacrificial anodes to protect submerged metal structures from corrosion, plating with chromium as a corrosion inhibitor for numerous products, pigments based on metals oxides, and so on. These inevitable losses are partially due to technical desires that support the longevity of applications; they may be summed up by the term "lost by design" (Ciacci et al. 2015).

Recycling of plastic products

Plastic materials are tailored for their intended use, for example, for food packaging (polyethylene, polypropylene, polystyrene, etc.), water and lemonade bottles (polyethylene terephthalate), insulation material (polystyrene, polyurethane), and so on. Desired functions of plastic products can be achieved by additives. Typical additives are:

- stabilizers against heat and sunlight,
- plasticizers to make plastics malleable and flexible,
- flame retardants,
- oxygen barriers to avoid the spoilage of packaged goods, mostly food,
- fillers.

In total, more than 10,000 additives are in use (Wiesinger et al 2021). They add to the chemical diversity of the polymers themselves, in some cases up to 50% by weight. PVC floorings for example contain about 50% additives (stabilizers, plasticizers, fillers) (ECHA 2017). Special functions of plastic products are achieved by the combination of several layers, for example, plastic films laminated with aluminium, adhesives, and so on. Additives and polymer combinations lead to high material diversity and entropy (ΔS) that can be reversed only in special cases by a combination of targeted collection, separation, and cleaning processes with an appropriate input of energy.

For the recycling of plastic products, some different levels can be defined: mechanical reprocessing into a material with equivalent properties, mechanical reprocessing into materials of inferior quality ("down-cycling"), and recovery of chemical constituents (i.e., monomers by depolymerization) which needs more resources. The higher the necessary energy and material input, the less useful and economically viable is the recycling process. Assessments based on statistical entropy as well as chemical exergy associated with the chemical potential and differences in chemical compositions can be used as a benchmark (Ignatenko et al. 2007). If the energy used for a recycling process falls below the chemical exergy of the products obtained, the process is not reasonable. Additives that cannot be separated hamper the recovery of high-quality polymers resulting in down-cycling applications, for example, use of low-quality plastics as replacement for bituminous binder in asphalt (White 2020). It is clear that this type of product cannot be recycled again into “plastics”. As the number of such applications is limited, incineration with partial energy recovery (Andreasi Bassi et al. 2017) is the only left rational. This example demonstrates that so-called recycling is often a down-cycling by adding just one circle before the final loss of materials.

Boundaries caused by contamination

While the doping of pure, high-quality material by additives is an intended contamination, many used products and residues of materials contain critical substances that are carried unintentionally over into the secondary material during recycling processes (H↔R). Hazardous substances

- are or have been added to achieve certain properties, for example, brominated flame retardants in different polymers,
- can be regularly present also in primary material, for example, cadmium in products made from zinc,
- can also originate from the use phase (cross-contamination, chemical aging).

From a profound investigation of plastic waste from households using a wide range of sorting and material recovery configurations, it was concluded that at best 55% of the collected plastic waste was suitable for recycling due to contamination (Eriksen et al. 2018).

European bodies aim at “non-toxic material cycles, so that recycled waste can be used as a major, reliable source of raw material” (EP 2018). The term “non-toxic material cycles” should not be taken literally, because the entropy dilemma (ΔS) impedes complete material recovery and completely pollutant or additive-free material from waste. Moreover, both goals conflict with each other depending on the case in question (Friege et al. 2019). Balancing the opportunities for resource efficiency against the risk of contamination is difficult. An interesting example is PVC cable sheaths containing Diethylhexyl phthalate (DEHP). Since 2015, DEHP may no longer be placed on the European market. The Commission granted an exemption with a limit of 20% DEHP in recyclates. Due to the high concentration of phthalates in soft PVC compounds, it was not possible to produce a material that met this threshold value (VINYLOOP 2019).

Boundaries caused by time

As demonstrated by the DEHP example, our increasing knowledge over time (Δt) can lead to a much more critical classification of previously used chemicals turning them into “legacy chemicals”. However, previous decisions on product composition cannot be reversed as the products are already on the market.

On the other hand, our technical skills improve over time, making it possible to recover valuable materials which have not been accessible before. Suitable technology must be available and affordable at the moment of recycling. Materials from cars have a time gap of up to 20 years or more, from buildings at least decades and electronic appliances only a few years. In all these cases the "fading" of their use and trailing are often much longer than these time scales which are crucial for understanding systems (Kümmerer 1996). The current discussion about lithium and cobalt for the construction of rechargeable batteries shows the importance of dynamic considerations about the mass flows (Müller et al. 2014, Fellner et al. 2017, Kümmerer et al. 2020). As a large share of these metals is still used and thus accumulates in the material stock of the technosphere, the potential for substitution of primary metals by recycled material is extremely low. Due to the unsecured availability of primary lithium and cobalt, a rapid switch to e-mobility is at risk.

Boundaries caused by economic problems

Many processes in the circular economy

- require information (I?) that is costly to obtain, if possible at all
- and/or considerable amounts of energy to reduce dissipative processes (D!, ΔS) and are therefore expensive (EcY!).

They often do not take place under market conditions. Therefore, the implementation of goals like recycling rates and the creation of appropriate economic incentives are challenging allocation processes (see Wiesmeth (2021), chapters 7, 9, and 18).

Economic imbalances within a society or between different societies (wages, service costs, etc.) are important drivers for informal sector activities (ΔEcY). As long as no public waste management is established, the informal sector can take the first steps towards recycling. However, the strictly economic motivation (EcY!) results in a focus on the most rewarding products and/or constituents and can lead to serious environmental damage as well as loss of other constituents. An example is the informal reclamation of electronic waste for the extraction of metals such as gold or copper in some developing countries.

Extending the boundaries

Thinking in systems (Matlin et al. 2016) is a crucial prerequisite for extending resource management barriers and not ending up very early in physical, chemical, material, energetic, and economic blind lanes. "Circular economy" is a highly complex system consisting of diverse building blocks at all levels from atomic and molecular to materials in products and products themselves. Normally, plans for material recovery start in the waste phase. There are increasingly precise sorting techniques based on different spectroscopic methods that support material separation (Gaustad et al. 2012, Pauliuk et al. 2017). But products to be recycled must often be grinded or shredded, both energy-intensive processes. Generally, a shift from a material-centric approach to a product-centric approach is necessary, that is, bringing both together from the very beginning (Kümmerer 2017, Kümmerer et al. 2020), because considering only one material means neglecting the effect of all other materials in the product not only in relation to performance and function but also for lifetime circulation and recycling. Through a product-centric approach, "a fully fundamental basis is established to estimate resource efficiency in the circular economy ...This inclusion of liberation and particulate quality as a function of design and comminution, and hence recyclate quality, into the description of a recycling system is crucial for understanding and optimizing recycling" (Reuter & van Schaik 2015). A design for disassembly (Ferrão & Amaral 2006) is necessary, which includes planning of repair and recycling according to available technology in the phase of manufacturing. This is even more important for complex products, which preferably should have a modular structure (Reuter et al. 2018). It is clear that progress of this type affords adequate education and information (I?) that is accessible even after the useful life of a product. In future, digitalization will support information transfer along the value chain.

Information is also necessary to avoid or at least recognize the carry-over of contaminants from used materials (H↔R) into recycled resources. The recently introduced database ("SCIP") covering substances of very high concern in products is complex and not useful for recycling companies (Friege et al. 2021).

There are opportunities to achieve less hazardous and even "benign by design" chemicals (Kümmerer 2007, Leder et al. 2015, Suk et al. 2020, Leder et al. 2021) based on the Concept of Sustainable Chemistry (Kümmerer 2017). But it should be clear that hazardous substances will still be needed sometimes to deliver the functionalities needed for certain applications (H↔R). Systemic thinking (Matlin et al. 2016) within this concept also means taking the entropy dilemma seriously by "reducing total substance flows, material flows, product flows, and connected energy flows at all spatial and temporal scales and dimensions especially with respect to volume and complexity" (Kümmerer et al. 2020).

The distribution of products in billions of households is an inevitable process in present societies (D!, Δt). The consequences of dissipation can be reduced by information transfer (I?) along the value chain (see above) and by demand-oriented business models, where the product is taken back by the producer after use or service is paid for instead of owning a product. The leasing of vehicles, solvents, and the rental of professional clothing are examples of well-known business models widely limited to B2B but increasingly reaching out to consumers. Business models will only succeed if all parties involved can happily answer the question "what is in it for me?" (EcY!).

Recommendations

The basic laws of nature tell us there will be neither a zero-waste society nor a 100% circular economy. Approaches to circular economy should be assessed according to their contribution to resource conservation, the energy required, waste generated in present and future, and their social and economic impacts. Legal definitions of "circular economy" need to be framed accordingly.

Recycling is not a goal in itself but a tool of resource management (Velis & Brunner 2013). The quality of secondary materials is key. Therefore, a shift from quantity-based recycling policy (the higher the recycling target, the better) towards life cycle metrics as governing policy principle is necessary (Anshassi et al. 2018).

Material-oriented waste management is good, product-oriented resource management is better! Reducing the complexity of materials and combinations of materials in a product with regard to its disassembly after use must be a priority target in the design phase. Sustainable chemistry principles (Kümmerer et al. 2017, Halpaap 2021) should be integrated in resource policy as an enabler for environmentally sound materials and products.

The recovery of products and materials with high quality after use affords smart management of the value chain including the consumer. Regulations based on extended producer responsibility must take into account the relationships of all actors along the value chain and align their (economic) interests (Friege 2018) to avoid losses due to lack of information and indifference.

References

Andersson M, Söderman M L, Sandén BA (2017): Are scarce metals in cars functionally recycled? Waste Management 60: 407–416.

Andreasi Bassi S, Christensen TH, Damgaard, A (2017): Environmental performance of household waste management in Europe – An example of 7 countries, Waste Management 69: 545–557.

Anshassi M, Laux S, Townsend TG (2018): Replacing Recycling Rates with Life-Cycle Metrics as Government Materials Management Targets, Environ. Sci. Technol. 52: 6544–6554.

Cavé J (2014): Who owns urban waste? Appropriation conflicts in emerging countries, Waste Management & Research 32(9): 813–821, DOI: 10.1177/0734242X14540978.

Ciacci L, Reck BK, Nassar NT, Graedel TE (2015): Lost by Design, Environ. Sci. Technol. 49, 9443–9451.

ECHA (2017): Committee for Risk Assessment (RAC) and Committee for Socio-economic Analysis (SEAC): Annex to the Background Document to the Opinion on the Annex XV dossier proposing restrictions on Lead compounds-PVC. 5 December 2017. https://echa.europa.eu/documents/10162/1b0e3c59-16a3-6221-6237-2f3d34820d68, accessed 28-10-2020.

Eriksen M.K., Damgaard A., Boldrin A., Astrup T.F. (2018): Quality Assessment and Circularity Potential of Recovery Systems for Household Plastic Waste, J. Ind. Ecol. 23 (1):156–168.

European Commission – EU COM (2020): Critical Raw Materials Resilience: Charting a Path towards greater Security and Sustainability, COM(2020) 474 final; https://ec.europa.eu/docsroom/documents/42849

European Parliament – EP (2018): Resolution of 13 September 2018 on implementation of the circular economy package: options to address the interface between chemical, product and waste legislation (2018/2589(RSP)).

Fellner J, Lederer J, Scharff C, Laner D (2017): Present Potentials and Limitations of a Circular Economy with Respect to Primary Raw Material Demand, J. Ind. Ecol. 21 (3): 494–496.

Ferrao P, Amaral J (2006): Design for recycling in the automobile industry: New approaches and new tools, Journal of Engineering Design 17(5):447–462; doi:10.1080/09544820600648039

Friege H (2012): Resource recovery from used electric and electronic equipment: Alternative options for resource conservation, Waste Management & Research 30 (9), S3–S16.

Friege H (2018): Separate Collection of Waste Fractions – Economic Opportunities and Problems, In Dornack C, Maletz R, Ziyang L (Eds.): Source Separation and Recycling – Implementation and Benefits for a Circular Economy, 11–30 (2018), ISBN 978-3-319-69071-1, Springer International Publishing, https://link.springer.com/chapter/10.1007/698_2017_24

Friege H., Kummer B., Steinhäuser K. G., Wuttke J., Zeschmar-Lahl B. (2019): How should we deal with the interfaces between chemicals, product and waste legislation? Environ Sci Eur 2019 31:51. https://doi.org/10.1186/s12302-019-0236-7

Friege H, Zeschmar-Lahl B, Kummer B, Wagner J (2021): The new European data base for chemicals of concern: How useful is SCIP for waste management? Sustainable Chemistry and Pharmacy 21: 100430; https://doi.org/10.1016/j.scp.2021.100430

Graedel TE, Reck BK, Ciacci L, Passarini F (2019): On the Spatial Dimension of the Circular Economy, Resources 8, 32; doi:10.3390/resources8010032

Halpaap A (2021): Green and Sustainable Chemistry: Framework Manual; https://wedocs.unep.org/handle/20.500.11822/35312?show=full, accessed 12-10-2021.

Ignatenko O, van Schaik A, Reuter MA (2007): Exergy as a tool for evaluation of the resource efficiency of recycling systems, Minerals Engineering 20: 862–874.

Kümmerer K (1996): The ecological impact of time. Time Soc 5: 219–235.

Kümmerer K (2007): Sustainable from the very beginning: rational design of molecules by life cycle engineering as an important approach for green pharmacy and green chemistry. Green Chem. 9: 899–907.

Kümmerer K (2017): Sustainable Chemistry: A Future Guiding Principle. Angew. Chem. Intern. Ed. 56, 16420–16421, doi: 10.1002/anie.201709949

Kümmerer K, Clark, JH, Zuin, VG (2020): Rethinking chemistry for a circular economy. Science, 367 (6476), 369–370, 10.1126/science.aba. 4979.

Kümmerer K, Amsel AK, Bartkowiak D, Bazzanella A, Blum C, Cinquemani C (2021): Key Characteristics of Sustainable Chemistry, ISC_3 Dialogue Paper, www.isc3.org/en/service/policy-papers.html, accessed 3-10-2021

Leder C, Rastogi T. Kümmerer, K (2015): Putting benign by design into practice-novel concepts for green and sustainable pharmacy: Designing green drug derivatives by non-targeted synthesis and screening for biodegradability. Sust. Chem. Pharm. 2: 31–36, doi: 10.1016/j.scp.2015.07.001

Leder C, Suk M, Lorenz L, Rastogi T, Peifer C, Kietzmann M, Jonas D, Buck M, Pahl A, Kümmerer K (2021): Reducing Environmental Pollution by Antibiotics through Design for Environmental Degradation. Sus. Chem. Eng. https://doi.org/10.1021/acssuschemeng.1c02243

Matlin, S.A., Mehta, G., Hopf, H., Krief, A. (2016): One-world chemistry and systems thinking. Nat. Chem. 8, 393–396. https://doi.org/10.1038/nchem.2498

Matlin SA, Mehta G, Hopf H, Krief A, Keßler L, Kümmerer K (2020): Material circularity and the role of the chemical sciences as a key enabler of a sustainable post-trash age. Sust. Chem. Pharm. 17: 100312; https://doi.org/10.1016/j.scp.2020.100312

Müller E, Hilty LM, Widmer R, Schluep M, Faulstich M (2014): Modelling Metal Stocks and Flows: A Review of Dynamic Material Flow Analysis Methods, Environ. Sci. Technol. 48: 2102−2113; dx.doi.org/10.1021/es403506a

Ohno H, Matsubae H, Nakajima K, Nakamura S, Nagasaka T (2014): Unintentional Flow of Alloying Elements in Steel during Recycling of End-of-Life Vehicles, J. Ind. Ecology 18 (2): 242–253; doi: 10.1111/jiec.12095

Pauliuk S, Kondo Y, Nakamura S, Nakajima K (2017): Regional distribution and losses of end-of-life steel throughout multiple product life cycles – Insights from the global multiregional MaTrace model, Resources, Conservation and Recycling 116: 84–93.

Rasmussen KD, Wenzel H, Bangs C, Petavratzi E, Liu G (2019): Platinum Demand and Potential Bottlenecks in the Global Green Transition: A Dynamic Material Flow Analysis, Environ. Sci. Technol. 53 (19): 11541–11551; doi: 10.1021/acs.est.9b01912

Rechberger H, Graedel TE (2002): The contemporary European copper cycle: statistical entropy analysis, Ecological Economics 42: 59–72.

Reuter MA, van Schaik A (2015): Product-Centric Simulation-Based Design for Recycling: Case of LED Lamp Recycling, J. Sustainable Metallurgy 1:4–28; doi: 10.1007/s40831-014-0006-0

Reuter MA, van Schaik A, Ballester M (2018): Limits of the Circular Economy: Fairphone Modular Design Pushing the Limits, World of Metallurgy – ERZMETALL 71 (2): 68–79.

Rojas A, Yabar H, Mizunoya T, Higano Y (2018): The Potential Benefits of Introducing Informal Recyclers and OrganicWaste Recovery to a Current Waste Management System: The Case Study of Santiago de Chile, Resources 2018, 7, 18; doi:10.3390/resources7010018

Shevchenko T, Laitala K, Danko Y (2019): Understanding Consumer E-Waste Recycling Behaviour: Introducing a New Economic Incentive to Increase the Collection Rates, Sustainability 2019, 11, 2656; doi:10.3390/su11092656

Stumm W, Davis J (1974): Kann Recycling die Umweltsbeeinträchtigung vermindern? In: Recycling – Lösung der Umweltkrise, Ed.: Gottlieb Duttweiler-Institut Rüschlikon, Verlag Ex Libris, Zürich, Deutsche Verlags-Anstalt GmbH, Stuttgart, 29–41.

Suk M, Haiß A, Westphal J, Jordan A, Kellett A, Kapitanov IV, Karpichev Y, Gathergood N, Kümmerer K (2020): Design rules for environmental biodegradability of phenylalanine alkyl ester linked ionic liquids. Green Chem. 22, 4498–4508.

Tesfayea F, Lindberg D, Hamuyuni J, Taskinen P, Hupa L (2017): Improving urban mining practices for optimal recovery of resources from e-waste. Minerals Engineering 111: 209–221

Thiébaud E, Hilty LM, Schluep M, Böni HW, Faulstich M (2018): Where Do Our Resources Go? Indium, Neodymium, and Gold Flows Connected to the Use of Electronic Equipment in Switzerland, Sustainability 2018, 10, 2658; doi:10.3390/su10082658

Ueberschaer M, Geiping J, Zamzow M, Flamme S, Rotter VS (2017): Assessment of element-specific recycling efficiency in WEEE pre-processing. Resources, Conservation & Recycling 124, 25–41

Velis C, Brunner PH (2013): Recycling and resource efficiency: it is time for a change from quantity to quality, Waste Management & Research 31: 539–540

VINYLOOP: Closure of operation in Italy / Phthalates issue under REACH brings down European PVC recycling project. www.plasteurope.com/news/VINYLOOP_t240095/. Accessed 25 April 2019.

Wäger P, Widmer R, Restrepo E, Fernandes M (2014): Seltene technische Metalle in Fraktionen aus der maschinellen Aufbereitung von WEEE. (Ed.: Bundesamt für Umwelt), Bern.

White G (2020): A Synthesis on the Effects of Two Commercial Recycled Plastics on the Properties of Bitumen and Asphalt, Sustainability 2020, 12, 8594; doi:10.3390/su12208594

Wiesmeth H (2021): Implementing the Circular Economy for Sustainable Development, Amsterdam; ISBN 978-0-12-821798-6.

Wiesinger H, Wang Z, Hellweg S (2021): Deep Dive into Plastic Monomers, Additives and Processing Aids, Environ. Sci. Technol. 55, 13, 9339–9351; doi:10.1021/acs.est.1c00976

Zhang L, Xu Z (2016): A review of current progress of recycling technologies for metals from waste electrical and electronic equipment, Journal of Cleaner Production 127: 19–36.

24 Implementation of refuse derived fuel technology towards achieving a sustainable circular economy

Potentials and compatibility in Bangladesh

ANM Safiqul Alam

Introduction

Solid waste management (SWM) in developing countries is a real environmental and social concern because the most applicable treatment option is final disposal in open landfills or in unsuitable sanitary landfills (Al-Khatib et al., 2010; Ravindra et al., 2015; Maheshi, 2015; Ferronato et al., 2017). Sustainable measures must be introduced, incorporating low-carbon solutions and appropriate technologies (Papargyropoulou et al., 2015). For this purpose, the shift from a linear economy to a circular economy (CE) that will preserve the environment, generate new economic growth and spread environmental awareness of the population, can be considered the most adaptive way to improve the current SWM worldwide (Diaz and Otoma, 2013). As stated by Stahel (2016), "The CE system would convert out-of-service goods into resources for others." However, each waste source and each physical part can be included in an independent scheme CE, while collection and treatment systems must be evaluated differently in cities, towns or small communities, as well as in regions with geographic frameworks and special tourist areas (Ciudin et al., 2014). For this purpose, municipal and "private" waste must be assessed in an integrated manner although in low-middle income countries no distinction is made between these streams and the environmental impacts of solid waste influx to final disposal sites of concern, where materials are mixed with hazardous fractions (such as hospital waste, oils, slaughterhouses) and all waste sources deliver materials in the same collection system.

The initial challenge is introducing the concept of refuse derived fuel (RDF) which is an efficient technique to turn 100% of the generated waste into usable product and fuel. If that can be implemented, it will boost up the economy by converting the garbage into asset. By reconsidering the entire waste management cycle, it is possible to resolve not only the challenge of inadequate waste management but also create employment, promote economic growth, improve public health and ecosystems and mitigating climate change. It is possible to reduce the quantity of waste, reuse the existing resources and recycle what is really not

DOI: 10.4324/9781003244196-28

needed. Advanced technologies such as RDF by MTB technique can be a great help for this sector.

This study aims to address the problem of circular economy through SWM as well as the promotion of sustainable practices and appropriate technologies for the reduction of environmental impacts and for the recovery of resources in Bangladesh.

Formal circular economy

The circular economy is an economic system of closed cycles in which raw materials, components and products lose their value as little as possible, renewable energy sources are used and systems thinking is essential. In this chapter, we will explain this definition in more detail.

Informal circular economy

Usually, in both rural and urban areas street hawkers collect refuse materials in form of broken tools and parts in exchange for other low-priced products, or in some cases small amounts of money. Then the hawkers resell those to secondary collector enterprises who usually do a basic screening, categorize the items and sell them to small recycling companies. Those companies manufacture consumer products from recycled materials and ship them to the market for the consumers. In these ways, informal circular economy preexists in Bangladesh.

Elements of the circular economy

According to Korhonen, Nuur, Feldmann and Birkie (2018), definitions that focus on system change often emphasize three elements, which are explained in more detail below:

(1) Closed cycles
(2) Renewable energy
(3) Systems thinking

Some researchers argue that social inclusiveness is also a necessary part of the circular economy (Korhonen, Honkasalo and Seppälä, 2018).

Waste-to-energy approach

Municipal governments across the world are facing choices about how to manage the unending blast of waste generated by their residents and businesses. In certain places, landfills and dumpsites are filling up and leak into environmental surroundings. As populations continue to grow, the problem of waste gets to be more urgent and more difficult. Although enhancing recycling technologies reduces a substantial fraction of waste, still a sizable percentage of municipal solid waste results in landfills. Landfilling waste means losing resources and landfill sites. Also, risk toxins leach into soil and water and produce emissions of methane (CH_4) and carbon dioxide (CO_2) that subscribe to climate change (USEPA, 2019).

Using a combustible fraction of solid wastes that cannot be recycled as an energy source is just one efficient solution to decrease the quantity of landfilled waste (Habib et al. 2021). The combustible fraction of waste is called "Refuse Derived Fuel (RDF)". RDF covers an array of waste products that have been processed to fulfil guidelines and regulatory or industry specifications mainly to reach a higher calorific value (Ragazzi et al., 2007). RDF production technology plays a part in the "waste-to-energy" approach, reduces the carbon footprint and is essential for diverting waste from landfills (Mostakim et al., 2021). RDF captures the energy in non-recyclable and combustible waste and turns it into an alternative for fossil fuels like coal or oil. RDF is a renewable solid fuel that is used to build energy. The RDF may be utilized in the cement industry; steel furnaces; power stations, substituting coal and oil; or perhaps incinerated in energy-from-waste plants (Grillo, 2013).

The benefits of harnessing this otherwise wasted energy are obvious. Energy harvesting from RDF eliminates a huge quantity of carbon dioxide equivalent gases (mostly CO_2 gas and methane) from being emitted each year through the burning of fossil fuels. Not just that but also every ton of waste that is diverted from landfills eliminates 0.54 tons of carbon dioxide equivalent from being emitted in landfill gas. This can be an important saving in greenhouse gas emissions (Rezaei, 2020).

The further processing of RDF to improve its physical and chemical properties strongly depends upon the following application. Even taking into consideration transport costs, this often offers a cheaper replacement for landfills (Abdel-Shafy & Mansour, 2018). It also reduces emissions associated with air pollutants that donate to climate change, while the waste is burnt cleanly and efficiently to extract the maximum quantity of energy as you can.

Strategic and legal aspects of solid waste management in Bangladesh

There is no existing separate legal institutional framework or holistic sustainable approach for SWM in Bangladesh. Some government agencies like city corporations, municipal authorities, local government, Department of Environment, in cooperation with NGOs and donor organizations, are taking some initiatives to manage the waste in a sustainable manner, but it's not enough. Bangladesh is a juvenile nation that is still struggling with their basic needs such as food, shelter, medication, education and so on since the day of independence in 1971. So, it is hard to allocate massive funds to waste management sectors and policies. But circular economy might help the situation as income generation is involved in the process rather than just spending.

Potentials and compatibility in Bangladesh

Existing practice of circular economy in Bangladesh

The circular economy is not a new concept in Bangladesh. People have been doing this for a long time with their indigenous knowledge and technique, particularly, in the informal sector. However, circularity has been ignored by the policymakers because it is practiced informally. Usually, in both rural and urban areas street hawkers collect refuse materials in form of broken tools and parts in exchange for other low-priced products, or in some cases, small amounts of money. For example, hawkers collect damaged electronics, broken furniture, cooking pots, and all sorts of household garbage that is recyclable and has an existing market value. In exchange, they offer a variety of alternative products like a new cooking pot in exchange for several broken cooking pots. Mainly women are the main customers for those hawkers. Sometimes, to attract their attention, hawkers prefer cosmetics, beauty products or other female staff in exchange for the garbage. In some rural areas, like villages of Barisal division, farmers separate their paddy into three segments with their indigenous technique which involves blowing the paddy by the wind and the wind separates the heavier well-grown paddy in the first segment, then lightweight premature paddy into the second segment then the paddy with no rice in it at the last segment. After this primary separation, farmers keep the first segment to harvest rice for their family and sell a portion to the market and the last segment which contains no rice is used as cattle food or fuel. However, the second segment is exchanged for products like mud pots and other household staff from hawkers. These light paddies then find their way to Dhaka and are processed for broken rice (popularly known as Khud rice in Dhaka). Then the hawkers resell those to secondary collector enterprises who usually do a basic screening, categorize the items and sell them to small recycling companies. Those companies manufacture consumer products from recycled materials and ship them to the market for the consumers.

Existing practice of circular economy and waste generation and management scenario has been illustrated from Bangladeshi perspective.

Waste generation and management scenario in Bangladesh

In Bangladesh, there are more than 522 towns and cities, which are hubs of rapid economic development and population growth, and generate thousands of tons of waste from domestic, industrial, commercial, health care facilities and agricultural sources that must be managed daily. Low collection coverage, unavailable transport services and lack of suitable treatment, recycling and disposal facilities are responsible for unsatisfactory waste management, leading to water, land and air pollution, and for putting people and the environment at risk.

Table 24.1 Relationship of GDP and population with waste generation

Year	*Urban population*	*Total urban waste generation (on/day)*	*Per capita waste generation rate in urban areas (kg/cap/day)*	*Per capita GDP*
1991	20.8 million	6493	0.31	US$ 220
2005	32.76 million	13,332	0.41	US$ 482
2025	78.44 million	47,000	0.60	-

Source: Amin (2007).

The situation of waste generation in Bangladesh

Total volume of municipal solid wastes in urban areas 4,866,505 (2005) = 13,332.89 tons/day × 365 = 3,000 tons/day in Dhaka (2005) as stated by Waste Concern (2005) and JICA (2005). According to Waste Concern and Swiss Contact 2007, the amount of agricultural waste was estimated as 65 million metric tons per year. Hazardous industrial waste such as waste from textile, hospital clinics, tannery, pesticides, fertilizer, oil refinery and paper and pulp were estimated as 109.47 million/cubic metre/year (wastewater), 0.113 million ton/year (sludge) and 26,884 tons/year (solid waste) as per Waste Concern and ADB (2008). In the case of per capita waste generation, the figures were urban: 0.41 (2005), Dhaka City: 0.56 (2005) and agricultural: 1.68 (based on 2008 rural population) in Kg/day as stated by Waste Concern (2008) and JICA (2005). There are also some projections about future waste generation scenarios, for example, according to the projection made by UMP (1999), as cited by Waste Concern (2008), Waste Concern and ADB (2008), by 2025 hazardous waste will be generated as follows: 17,155,000 tons/year = 47,000 tons/day × 365 = 0.60 kg/day per capita in urban areas, 2472.07 million/cubic metre/year (wastewater), 2.81 million metric ton/year (sludge) and 53,874 metric ton/year (solid waste).

According to a study by Waste Concern (2005), the collection of waste (% of waste generated) was 44.30–76.47% in major urban cities. Primarily, solid waste disposal facilities were mainly uncontrolled landfilling (except for the sanitary landfill at Matuail site in Dhaka, supported by JICA). No site or facility for treatment, recycling and disposal of hazardous waste as stated by Dhaka City Corporation and JICA (2007). A significant quantity of electrical and electronic waste is being generated each day in a major urban area of Bangladesh, especially in Dhaka. Use of electronic goods in year 2006: mobile phones: 22,000,000 units, personal computers: 600,000 units and televisions: 1,252,000 units as per Waste Concern (2008). Waste recycling in Bangladesh is mainly dependent on the informal sector as the formal sector can hardly be seen. According to Waste Concern (2005), 120,000 urban poor from the informal sector were involved in the recycling trade chain of Dhaka City: 15% of the total generated waste in Dhaka (mainly inorganic) amounting to 475 tons/day were being recycled daily. Savings through recycling in Urban Areas of Bangladesh is almost US$ 15.29 million/year (in 2005).

Division-wise waste generation and potential CO_2 emission scenario

A report presented in 2nd Meeting of the Regional 3R Forum in Asia, Kuala Lumpur, Malaysia, 2010, stated that in Dhaka total annual waste generation was 4,634.52 tons and potential CO_2 emission was 760,000 tons, in Chittagong total annual waste generation was 1,548.09 and potential CO_2 emission was 250,000, in Rajshahi total annual waste generation was 172.83 and potential CO_2 emission was 30,000, in Khulna total annual waste generation was 321.26 and potential CO_2 emission was 50,000, in Barisal total annual waste generation was 134.38 and potential CO_2 emission was 20,000, in Sylhet total annual waste generation was 142.76 and potential CO_2 emission was 20,000, in all Paurashava total annual waste generation was 4,678.40 and potential CO_2 emission was 770,000, in other urban centres total annual waste generation was 1,700.65 and potential CO_2 emission was 280,000 (GoB, 2010). See Figure 24.1 for infographics.

Introduction of refuse derived fuel in Bangladesh

The concept of circular economy preexists in Bangladesh. As it is not an entirely new concept, it is easy to adopt in Bangladesh. But initial challenge is introducing the concept of RDF which is an efficient technique to turn 100% of the generated waste into usable product and fuel. If that can be implemented, it will boost up the economy by converting the garbage into an asset.

Bangladesh is a lower-middle-income country with a struggling economy. The garment sector is the most contributing sector in the country's economy but most of the raw materials are coming from abroad which has a tremendous effect on our foreign reserve. Some other important sectors are significantly contributing to the GDP like metal industry, household amenities, electrical and electronics products, plastic products and other manufacturing industries. All of them are dependent on imports for their raw material supply. As being a linear economy-based country, Bangladesh basically imports all of its raw material needs. If a recycling-based circular economy can be formed as a formal sector, it might reduce the burden on foreign imports.

Another important sector that is crucial for industrial production is energy. The majority of the power plants are coal fuel-based and the proven reserve of coal in Bangladesh is almost close to nothing. Bangladesh is dependent on India and other foreign nations for coal import. And it costs a lot which is negatively impacting the economy. Here is a window where RDF can come into play. RDF is an extremely combustible material and significantly less expensive but can perform as good as costly fuel-like coal can do.

So, using RDF instead of diesel fuel has been proved to be more efficient and economically sustainable. Same can be applied for producing electricity power instead of coal fuel. Some industries brick factories use wooden logs and coal to

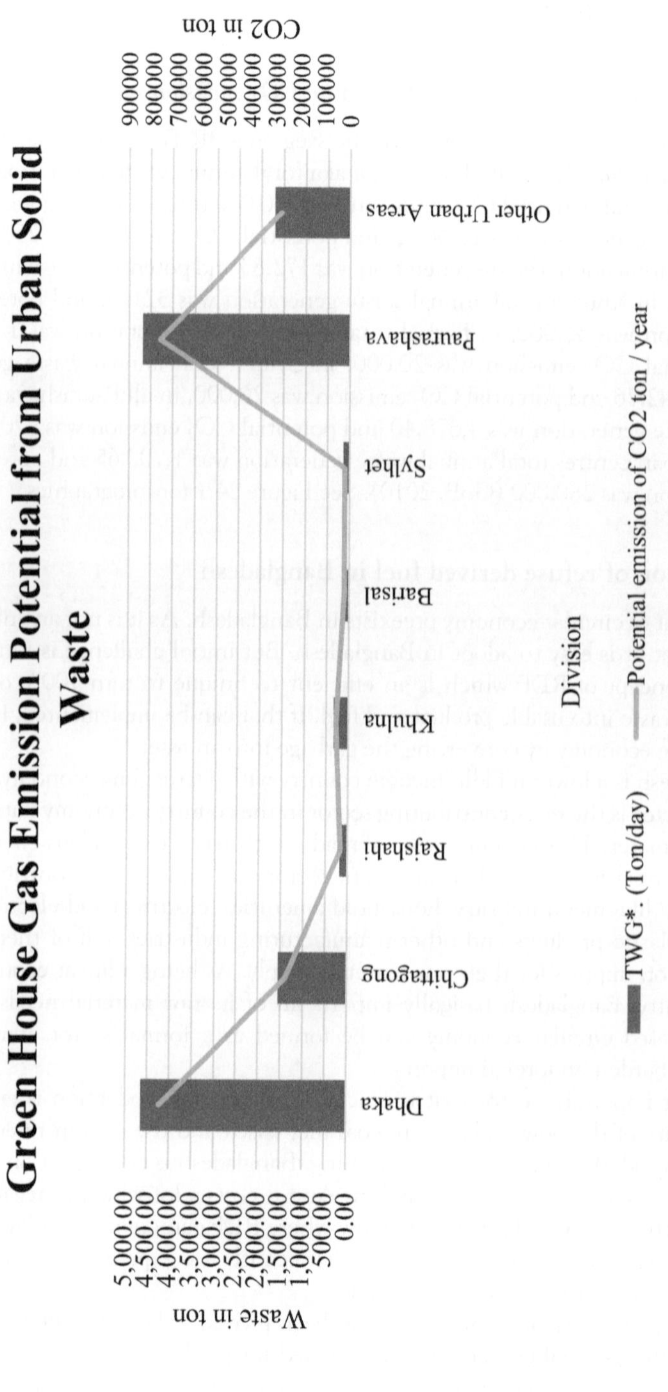

Figure 24.1 Green house gas emission potential from urban solid waste.
Source: Own depiction, data Source: GoB (2010).

produce heat. RDF can be an ideal fuel source for them as well. In this process, we can not only save money but also can save the environment by saving trees. Additionally, wasting land for dumping waste is also being controlled in this process because there will be nothing to dump.

Every year the government of the people republic of Bangladesh has to compensate a lot to provide fertilizer to the farmers (GoB, 1999) while there is a cheaper alternative. A portion of the biodegradable waste can be processed to make compost fertilizer with minimal cost.

So, there are limitless benefits of RDF-based circular economy if can be implemented in Bangladesh. At the first stage of RDF, it separates the metallic components so that they can be recycled for reuse in manufacturing industries. Then the flammable portion of the waste is cut into small peaches and dried to become extremely combustible dry fuel (Breeze, 2018). A portion of the biodegradable waste is separated for making compost and biogas. In short, the total amount of the waste will be reused for different purposes and no waste will be wasted anymore. If this sector can be introduced as a formal economic sector, a lot of job opportunities will also be created. Solid waste which was once considered as a burden would become an asset and might contribute to country's formal economy and the GDP as well as reducing the burden of foreign imports making the country self-sufficient. Transforming from linear to circular economy is the key to achieve economic solvency as well as international recognition as being a totally green economy.

Impossibilities to implement circular economy in Bangladesh

It's not so easy to meet the requirements of the true circular economy, even the best companies run into obstacles when attempting to meet them. It is practically impossible to transform 100% of materials from the old used product into reusable new products without external energy inputs, for example, materials like glass, iron, aluminium, plastic, gold, copper and so on need to be melted down to reshape which requires heat, and to generate heat energy input such as electricity or burning of fossil fuel is required. No matter can be transformed by itself without external influence and that denies the core principle of circular economy to be closed in a circle. Completing a circle requires to be confined in a circle, in this case, the same materials are supposed to be reused entirely over and over again without depleting external resources, otherwise, it is a cost-effective alternative of the traditional linear economy, not an entirely closed circled circular economy. For the very basic concept of circular economy, it is the biggest impossibility.

The essence of circulation is the gradual elimination of waste. Waste is usually found at the end of the value chain, so cooperation between all parties involved is essential. Furthermore, products and services must be developed in such a way that the materials can be reused, preferably multiple times. For this reason, it is extremely important to share knowledge among potential customers, product developers, recyclers, and other potential stakeholders who can reuse the product. At the moment, cooperation across the ends of the supply chain is still very limited. In the future, everyone should participate, share the same perception of the importance of the circular economy and trust each other's approaches.

The majority of supply chain companies lose control of products and raw materials at their individual point of sale. This means that they must regain consumer access at the end of a product's life. High-tech organizations favour rental and subscription models because the product will come back to them automatically.

One of the key challenges is to collect and centralize end-of-life products to process them economically. The majority of supply chain organizations work with waste suppliers, raw material suppliers, and reverse logistics providers to perform their operations.

The circular economy has yet to operate within economic limits. Goods with a cheap residual value are less likely to be recycled. Although there may be differences in the environmental impacts between materials, most of the organization's decisions are based on economy and risk.

There are several reasons why it may be attractive to salvage end-of-life materials with a low residual value, as salvaging these assets can serve as a hedge against price volatility and increase the safety of a commodity. Scaling up circular techniques is often a big challenge because circular products require a different mentality from customers. Not all consumers appreciate the prospect of sharing instead of owning, for example. In addition, most substantial-level circularity strategies require some influence on the part of consumers, such as repairing a product, bringing it back to the rental facility and so on. Unfortunately, for circularity to become important, consumers must derive value from it beyond mere sustainability. Circular products also need to be less expensive, more reliable or more useful and be the right product at the right time. Customer sentiment towards certain forms of materials such as single-use plastics has also changed, posing a reputational risk, which has been a catalyst for action.

Product complexity is always an annoying problem for electronics buyers. The less complex the product, the easier and cheaper it is to reprocess. One of the easiest ways to get around the complexity is through recycling to recover the raw materials, but recycling leads to a loss of value, as the manufactured product is put down in the process.

The circular economy is a great philosophy for integrating business value and sustainability. It offers many options to close loops and optimize resource use, from designing for recycling to using recycled materials to entirely new business models. However, we still have a long way to go before rethinking, redesigning, opening up channels of collaboration, and really thinking outside the box can really help us embrace the circular economy.

Developing countries like Bangladesh has the best potential to explore the potential of the circular economy. With limited resources, the Bangladeshi industrial sector is mainly dependent on foreign sources which is very costly and hard to get. Countries like Bangladesh are dependent on exports but they can rely on recycling instead. The main problem in Bangladesh is that there are not many formal sectors working on it. The circular economy exists here but it is informal. Investment is also very less in this field, skilled manpower is not available yet, there is also a lack of formal technical education in this field, people are not aware of the potential of circular economy and its advantages on the environment. Another regrating fact is that circular economy is not formally introduced or integrated in nation level planning and policy making here in Bangladesh. The lack of government support and encouragement through the provision of funding opportunities, training, effective taxation policy, import duty and so on is widely recognized as a significant barrier in the uptake of circular economy in Bangladesh. These are the major impossibilities for circular economy to be implemented in Bangladesh.

Similar good practices of circular economy

Seven-hundred-tons per day capacity composting project for Dhaka City Corporation area. This project is expected to produce compost of 50,000 tons every year, creating job for 800 urban poor, saving municipal waste management costs, improving the environment and reducing 89,259 tons of CO_2 e/year. This Certified Emission Reduction from composting organic waste has created a new source of revenue for a composting initiative (GoB, 2010).

Biogas technology provides an alternative source of energy mainly from organic wastes and livestock waste. It is obtained in the process of biodegradation of organic materials under anaerobic conditions, which allows the extraction of energy from organic matter without destroying nutrients contained in it. In Bangladesh so far 60,000 Biogas Plants have been established with funding from IDCOL (GoB, 2010). The target is 200,000 rural biogas plants. Domestic biogas installations can reduce greenhouse gas (GHG) emission in two different ways:

(1) Substituting fossil fuels and non-renewable biomass for cooking (smaller extent for lighting) with biogas
(2) Replacement of chemical fertilizer with the organic fertilizer

Conclusion

In developing countries with limited natural resources like Bangladesh, RDF-based circular economy can be a game changer. With the help of RDF-based technology, it is not only possible to reduce the number of imports by turning into a circular-based economy from linear economy but also a big opportunity to job creation and formation of large industry and business opportunity and saving the environment at the same time. So, it is high time to realize the fact and work accordingly. Government agencies must formulate policies and strategies as well as provide a budget for supporting this initiative.

References

Abdel-Shafy, H. I., & Mansour, M. S. (2018). Solid waste issue: Sources, composition, disposal, recycling, and valorization. *Egyptian journal of petroleum*, *27*(4), 1275–1290.

Al-Khatib, I. A., Monou, M., Zahra, A. S. F. A., Shaheen, H. Q., & Kassinos, D. (2010). Solid waste characterization, quantification, and management practices in developing countries. A case study: Nablus district–Palestine. *Journal of environmental management*, *91*(5), 1131–1138.

Amin, A. N. (2007). Country chapter. State of 3Rs in Asia and Pacific: The People'sRepublic of Bangaldesh. Accessed from www.researhgate.net/publication/322332160_Bangladesh_Country_Chapter_State_of_the_3Rs_in_Asia_and_the_Pacific.

Andritz. (2021). Refuse Derived Fuels. Accessed from www.andritz.com/products-en/recycling/recycling/rdf-production-plants.

BEZA (2021). Bangabandhu Sheikh Mujib Shilpa Nagar Master Plan. Accessed from www.beza.gov.bd/economic-zones-site/government-owned-sites/mirsorai-chittagong/

Breeze, P. (2018). Chapter 4 – Waste to Energy Technologies. Energy from Waste. Pages 29–37.

Ciudin, R., Isarie, C., Cioca, L., Petrescu, V., Nederita, V., & Ranieri, E. (2014). Vacuum waste collection system for an historical city centre. *UPB Scientific Bulletin, Series D*, *76*(3), 215–222.

Diaz, R., & Otoma, S. (2013). Constrained recycling: a framework to reduce landfilling in developing countries. *Waste management & research*, *31*(1), 23–29.

Ellen MacArthur Foundation. (2015). Towards a circular economy: Business rationale for an accelerated transition.

Ferronato, N., Rada, E. C., Portillo, M. A. G., Cioca, L. I., Ragazzi, M., & Torretta, V. (2019). Introduction of the circular economy within developing regions: A comparative analysis of advantages and opportunities for waste valorization. *Journal of environmental management*, *230*, 366–378.

Ferronato, N., Torretta, V., Ragazzi, M., & Rada, E. C. (2017). Waste mismanagement in developing countries: A case study of environmental contamination. *UPB Sci. Bull*, *79*(2), 185–196.

Geissdoerfer, M., Savaget, P., Bocken, N. M., & Hultink, E. J. (2017). The Circular Economy–A new sustainability paradigm. *Journal of cleaner production*, *143*, 757–768.

GoB (1999), National Agriculture Policy. Ministry of Agriculture, Government of the People's Republic of Bangladesh. Accessed from http://dae.portal.gov.bd/sites/default/files/files/dae.portal.gov.bd/page/dd7d2be1_aeef_452f_9774_8c23462ab73a/NAP.pdf

GoB (2010). Country Presentation Bangladesh. 2nd Meeting of the Regional 3R Forum in Asia. 4-6 October 2010, Kuala Lumpur, Malaysia. Retrieved from www.uncrd.or.jp/content/documents/RT2_01_Bangladesh.pdf

Grillo, L. M. (2013). Municipal solid waste (MSW) combustion plants. In Waste to Energy Conversion Technology (pp. 72–97). Woodhead Publishing.

Habib, M., Ahmed, M. M., Aziz, M., Beg, M., Alam, R., & Hoque, M. (2021). Municipal Solid Waste Management and Waste-to-Energy Potential from Rajshahi City Corporation in Bangladesh. *Applied Sciences*, *11*(9), 3744.

Kirchherr, J. W., Hekkert, M. P., Bour, R., Huijbrechtse-Truijens, A., Kostense-Smit, E., & Muller, J. (2017). Breaking the barriers to the circular economy. Deloitte. https://circulareconomy.europa.eu/platform/sites/default/files/171106_white_paper_breaking_the_barriers_to_the_circular_economy_white_paper_vweb-14021.pdf

Kirkman, R., & Voulvoulis, N. (2017). The role of public communication in decision making for waste management infrastructure. *Journal of environmental management*, *203*, 640–647.

Korhonen, J., Honkasalo, A., & Seppälä, J. (2018). Circular economy: the concept and its limitations. *Ecological economics*, *143*, 37–46.

Korhonen, J., Nuur, C., Feldmann, A., & Birkie, S. E. (2018). Circular economy as an essentially contested concept. *Journal of cleaner production*, *175*, 544–552.

Lewandowski, M. (2016). Designing the business models for circular economy – Towards the conceptual framework. *Sustainability*, 8(1), 43.

Maheshi, D. (2015). Environmental and economic assessment of 'open waste dump' mining in Sri Lanka. *Resources, Conservation and Recycling*, *102*, 67–79.

Mostakim, K., Arefin, M. A., Islam, M. T., Shifullah, K. M., & Islam, M. A. (2021). Harnessing energy from the waste produced in Bangladesh: evaluating potential technologies. Heliyon, e08221.

Münnich, K., Mahler, C. F., & Fricke, K. (2006). Pilot project of mechanical-biological treatment of waste in Brazil. *Waste management*, 26(2), 150–157.

PBL (2019). What is a circular economy? Retrieved from https://themasites.pbl.nl/o/circular-economy/

Ragazzi, M., Rada, E. C., Panaitescu, V., & Apostol, T. (2007). Municipal solid waste pretreatment: A comparison between two dewatering options. *WIT Transactions on ecology and the environment*, *102*.

Rahman, M. M., Ghosh, T., Salehin, M., Ghosh, A., Haque, A., Hossain, M. A.,... & Hutton, C. W. (2020). Ganges-Brahmaputra-Meghna delta, Bangladesh and India: a transnational mega-delta. In Deltas in the Anthropocene (pp. 23–51). Palgrave Macmillan, Cham.

Ravindra, K., Kaur, K., & Mor, S. (2015). System analysis of municipal solid waste management in Chandigarh and minimization practices for cleaner emissions. *Journal of cleaner production*, 89, 251–256.

Rezaei, H. (2020). Special Issue "Agricultural Crop Residue and Municipal Solid Waste to Refuse-Derived Fuel (RDF)". Sustainability.

Singh, J., & Ordoñez, I. (2016). Resource recovery from post-consumer waste: important lessons for the upcoming circular economy. *Journal of cleaner production*, *134*, 342–353.

Su, B., Heshmati, A., Geng, Y., & Yu, X. (2013). A review of the circular economy in China: moving from rhetoric to implementation. *Journal of cleaner production*, *42*, 215–227.

Thedailystar (2021). Big push for mega projects. Accessed from www.thedailystar.net/backpage/news/big-push-mega-projects-2104501

USEPA (2019). Overview of Greenhouse Gases. United States Environmental Protection Agency. Accessed from www.epa.gov/ghgemissions/overview-greenhouse-gases.

Wikipedia (2013). Trommel screen. Retrieved from https://en.wikipedia.org/wiki/Trommel_screen#/media/File:Trommel_Screen.png

Zurbrügg, C., Caniato, M., & Vaccari, M. (2014). How assessment methods can support solid waste management in developing countries – a critical review. *Sustainability*, 6(2), 545–570.

25 From profit to prosperity

Making the impossible possible through integral investing

Mariana Bozesan

Introduction

In *The Collapse of Complex Societies* (1988), anthropologist Joseph Tainter argued that evolved societies, such as the Mayan and the Roman Empire, ultimately collapsed due to the "Law of Accelerated Returns" (p. 93), which makes it eventually impossible for the society to pay for the increasing cost per person required to maintain the growing complexity. Since the fall of the Roman Empire, we can witness many more complex societies that have developed around the world and whose economies now operate not only in local but global economies—more later. As a result, we face grand global challenges of unprecedented scale (von Weitzsaecker & Wijkman (Eds.), 2018) that only exacerbate the load shown by the law of diminishing returns.

As opposed to the Law of Diminishing Results, we witness for the first time in human history what Ray Kurzweil (2005) calls the "Law of Accelerating Returns" (p. 35), which refers to the speed and power of the evolutionary process that increases exponentially over time and that leads to massive cost reduction and demonetization. As we will see later, the process of the consciousness evolution explodes exponentially so that *the rate of exponential growth itself grows exponentially* creating an abundance that could provide humanity with a window of opportunity to build more resilient and sustainable societies and avoid the impending collapse.

Otto Scharmer of MIT argues that "intellectual bankruptcy [...] underlies the financial and economic bankruptcy of many established organizations and institutions" causing the current grand global challenges (Scharmer, 2010, p.17). He suggests that the transition towards a regenerative, ecosystem-centered economy, must first address "the blind spot of economics and economic theory [which] is our own *consciousness*—our structure of attention and state of awareness and how it affects our individual and collective behavior" (p.17). Unfortunately, such blind spots can arguably be found also in solutions recommended by progressive thinkers including the proponents of circular economy. A series of examples for such reductionistic thinking has been delivered by researcher Barrett C. Brown (2007, 20 February, pp. 19–28). Brown performed an in-depth analysis of eight bestselling books on sustainability, circular economy, and ecological business development by renowned researchers including Brown (2006), Hawken

DOI: 10.4324/9781003244196-29

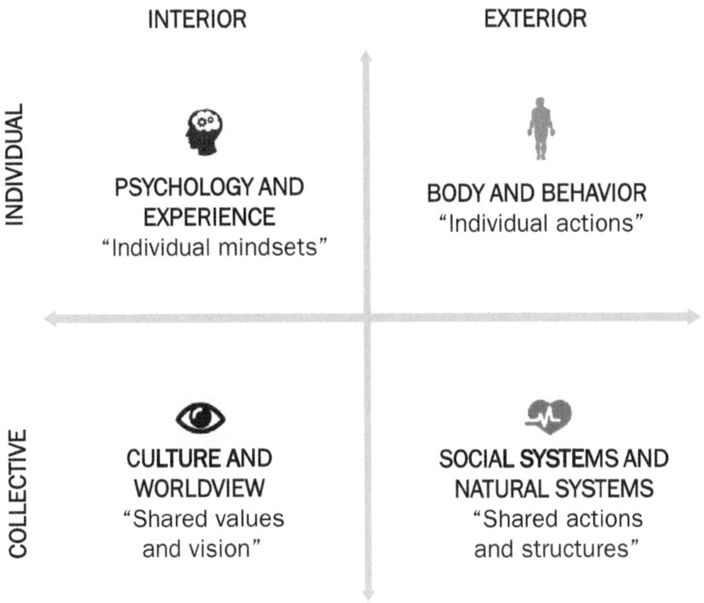

Figure 25.1 Quadrant view of the Ken Wilber's integral framework.
Source: Own picture after Wilber (2000).

(1993), Hawken, Lovins & Lovins (1999), Holliday, Jackson & Svensson (2002), McDonough & Braungart (2002), Nattrass & Altomare (1999), Holliday, Schmideiny & Watts (2002), and the World Commission on Environment and Development (2009/1987). Barrett C. Brown, whose report is titled *Four Worlds of Sustainability: Drawing upon Four Universal Perspectives to Support Sustainability Initiatives*, took an ontological approach to perform his investigation with the intention to find out how many different perspectives these progressive authors took in their effort to address humanity's crises. Under the assumption that current catastrophic risks such as climate change can only be addressed from a holistic perspective and later stages of consciousness, Barrett C. Brown used the lens of consciousness by Ken Wilber's (2000) integral theory depicted in a simplified form in Figure 25.1.

Integral theory: integrating the concealed dimensions of reality

At the foundation of Wilber's integral theory (2000) is the understanding that the perceived reality is most comprehensively represented through Plato's (1961/1938) *value spheres of humanity* exemplified as four quadrants in Figure 25.1. These value spheres are the *Beautiful* (interior-individual subjective mindset), the *Good* (interior-collective, inter-subjective/culture/worldviews/morals and ethics), and the *True* (exterior, objective individual aspects, and exterior collective/science/nature/social systems) represented through the two right-hand quadrants in Figure 25.1. These value spheres are always present, are constantly co-arising, and cannot be separated from each other whether we are consciously aware of them or not. Everything that occurs has these dimensions, perspectives, or points of view: an individual-subjective view; a collective-subjective/cultural view; an objective, provable-facts view, exterior individual; and a collective, exterior view that refers to the social structures and the ecology realms (Wilber, 2000).

In his investigation, Barrett C. Brown did not intend to provide an epistemological interpretation of the texts; instead, he analyzed every sentence in each of the eight books, classifying the sentences according to the view of the world (quadrant) on which they focused. He examined each sentence to evaluate whether it represented (1) an interior or exterior view and/or (2) an individual or collective perspective of reality. Barrett C. Brown determined that the exterior, lower-right quadrant perspective (Figure 25.1), the social systems, and the environment views dominated. The interior, subjective aspects such as the collective intersubjective, the cultural aspects, shared values, and vision, as well as the individual interior perspective, individual mindsets, or individual external behaviors and actions were significantly under-represented. Brown concludes that the lower-right quadrant is obviously the strongest and most powerful influencer for change in society. However, he also shows why there is little chance of future success if we do not take an integral sustainability approach, one that uses the entire integral framework of consciousness (Wilber, 2000) instead of just one quadrant. In the final analysis, Brown argues that the one-sided, mostly external (social and environmental) view of the world taken by all authors missed being informed by the interior dimensions of reality such as the shared vision, the collective cultural mindsets, but also emotional intelligence, the psycho-spiritual intelligence, and other dimensions of life. He concludes that this approach limited the authors' perspective of the world, biased their analyses, and unavoidably lead to the impossibility of delivering comprehensive solutions to current global grand challenges. Which additional perspectives are potentially also missing?

The exponential global

Throughout evolution, humans have been conditioned to think *linearly* and *locally* because for eons we inhabited mostly a limited geographic area, lived on average a relatively short time, and performed mostly the same occupations as our ancestors did. For generations, our lives were predetermined and *complicated* at best. But the accelerated technological growth, most visibly felt since the first industrial revolution, starting at the end of the 18th century, challenged us in unprecedented ways. Technology is the pinnacle of the human capacity to impact the world through intelligence. Why? Because, from the creation of the first life form to the creation of cells, it took biological evolution 2 billion years (Kurzweil, 2005). The technological evolution, however, needed only 14 years to move from the invention of the first personal computer in 1975 to the World Wide Web (Bozesan,

2020). In other words, biological evolution eventually led to technological evolution placing humanity at the beginning of its exponential acceleration (Tegmark, 2017) including all its ups and downfalls. Entrepreneur Elon Musk even views humanity as a "biological bootloader for digital superintelligence" in that our biology provided the small but crucial piece of code required to jump-start the AI revolution and warns of its unmitigated dangers if we want to save consciousness (Bozesan, 2020, p. 243)—more later.

Today, we live in a *global* world that is massively ruled by the *exponentially* growing complexity of technology. Life is not just complicated but has become a function of the *exponentially increasing complexity*, of which humanity can hardly make any sense, as the COVID-19 crisis demonstrates. In trying to respond to such big challenges, human ingenuity produces a myriad of theories, models, solutions, and alternatives that can increase sensemaking but how can we decide which ones to pursue and which ones to abandon? What informs our decision making?

On clarity and chaos

The innovative knowledge thinker and former IBM management consultant, Dave Snowden, used complexity science to develop the decision support framework known as Cynefin (a Welsh word pronounced kə'nɛvɪn/kuh-NEV-in) (Snowden & Friends, 2021). Cynefin enables emergent action by "looking at the dynamic interplay between deductive, inductive and abductive sense making" (p. 58). At the heart of the Cynefin framework are four natural patterns that logically and intuitively move between *Complex*, *Complicated*, *Clear*, and *Chaos* whereby each pattern is governed by varying constraints. A *complicated* domain is a domain where the governing constraints are ruled by causal relationships that can eventually be comprehended and acted upon. For example, we can develop, build, maintain, and repair a space shuttle; we can perform surgeries, and we can build smart computers and complicated algorithms. With appropriate training, best practices and expertise, the *complicated* things can be analyzed, addressed, and a wide range of answers can materialize—e.g., engineering, medicine, law, and algorithms.

The *complex* domain, on the other hand, can only be understood in retrospect because it is evolutionarily emerging and there are no right or wrong answers—e.g., markets, ecosystems, cultures, or personal growth (Hendricks & Ludeman (1996)). Human civilizations have moved well beyond the *complicated* that governed our lives in the past mostly at the *local* levels and are currently facing several global, *complex*, and *exponentially growing* domains, which are exacerbating each other—catastrophic risks threatening planetary boundaries, unsafe AI, nanotech, biotech, to name a few. For example, John von Neumann, designer of the von Neumann computer architecture, predicted already in the 1950s the impact of exponential growth within the realm of the technology acceleration (Oxtoby et al., May 1958). We are now at the pivotal point of technological evolution where its exponential growth is becoming explosive and massively *disruptive*. Thus, if we want not only to survive but also to thrive in the 21st century, we must learn to think, and most important to *act*, *exponentially* and *globally*. For example, it should worry us that the sensemaking of the billions of people on social media is increasingly governed not by high ethics and morals of democratic legislation but by AI programmers and their supervisors (at Google, Facebook, or TikTok, to name a few) who are driven by profit maximization—as demonstrated in the insightful Netflix movie *The Social Dilemma*. Within this context, Daniel Schmachtenberger (June 25, 2021, min 1:16:44) argues that we will not be able to address current issues, unless we understand the attractors determining the current "oligarchic tech feudalism" which operates outside public accountability or democratic jurisprudence. Therefore, it did not come as a surprise when concerned scientists comprising of the late Stephen Hawking, MIT professor Max Tegmark, as well as renowned entrepreneurs Elon Musk, Ray Kurzweil, and Dennis Hassabis, devised the Asilomar AI Principles to ensure the ethical application of AI (2017), accelerate AI-safety research, and prevent autonomous, super-intelligent AI (Bozesan, 2020, pp. 71–88).

Thus far, Barrett C. Brown argues that the integral theory by Ken Wilber is prone to deliver multi-perspectival solutions in a global world ruled by highly intricate economic, social, and environmental interdependencies. And Dave Snowden's Cynefin model shows how to use natural science to make better sense of the world with the intention to enable emergent action within the exponentially growing complexity at global levels. Next, we will use the lens of transdisciplinarity to deepen our analysis of additional impossibilities of circular economic models.

Transdisciplinarity and the new mindset

Transdisciplinarity is a research method that spans the boundaries of many disciplines to enable the design of new and holistic approaches to the ever-growing complexity of evolution. It transcends and includes theories and/or techniques that were originally developed by one single discipline to advance new, evolutionary ones. The term transdisciplinarity was originally introduced in 1970 by child psychologist Jean Piaget (Nicolescu, 2005) and further developed by Robert Kegan (1982) with the intention to distinguish it from interdisciplinarity, which transfers methods from one discipline to another while remaining within the framework of each individual discipline. Theoretical physicist and transdisciplinary scientist, Basarab Nicolescu (2005), postulates that (1) *Reality has several levels* of existence (2) there is an *included middle* whose logic describes the coherence of various levels of reality, and (3) there is an *ever-growing complexity*. While observing reality, we become aware that it has several levels and see that both the space between disciplines and beyond them is also filled with information. Thus, Nicolescu insists that the action logic of the *included middle* of reality has significant consequences for the theory of knowledge because it implies that knowledge remains always open and cannot be confined to a complete theory. This ties in with Barrett C. Brown's analysis of the progressive economic models discussed earlier that challenges the current mindset and understanding of consciousness that no longer serves us.

It appears that a new mindset is needed, one based on later stages of consciousness evolution; a mindset that provides answers to new questions, including: Why do we keep defining the problems too narrowly despite living in an interconnected, global world? Is human evolution self-terminating? Is human civilization self-terminating? Why have civilizations tethered between chaos and order, leading to today's tragedy of the commons? What prevents us from becoming better stewards of power? Why do civilizations fail? How can human civilization become antifragile in the presence of existential risks? Are we currently fighting a non-kinetic World War III through AI-driven tech? Is democracy itself at risk? Is democracy currently evolving or regressing? How can the tension between authoritarian nation states and the greed of capitalism (lead by exponential tech companies) be solved? Can holistic, superordinate, transdisciplinary solutions emerge within planetary boundaries? Who is asking? Who are we? What is the purpose of life? What is consciousness?

Consciousness and the case against reality

The astrobiologists Russell and Kanik (2010) maintain that the purpose of life is "the hydrogenation of carbon dioxide" (p. 1012) because from a thermodynamic point of view, life "evolves to maximize entropy and attempts to reach this state as rapidly as possible" (p. 1015). We could adopt this theory and accept that consciousness arises out of unconscious matter, a theory known as the "*hard problem of consciousness*" (Bozesan, 2020, p. 82), which assumes that space and time are foundational. We could. We could also accept Richard Dawkins' assertion that we are nothing more than the sum of our genes, "a set of instructions for how to make a body" (1976, p. 23), as described by our DNA and which could be downloaded into a robot (and live forever) as soon as technology makes it possible. Or could we? Can life—*can sentient beings*—really be reduced to a genetic code that could be entirely replicated and eventually downloaded into AIs to solve current challenges (including the impossibilities of circular economy), perpetuate, broaden, enhance, and expand life beyond Earth as the transhumanists (Bostrom, 2005) envision?

Unfortunately, the scope of this paper does not permit digging deeper into the centuries-old, ongoing dispute between mechanistic dualists, scientific materialists, cognitive psychologists, and panpsychist philosophers, to name only a few factions of consciousness theorists (Bozesan, 2020). What should be mentioned here is the (not so recent) work of cognitive scientist Donald Hoffman (2019), who is arguing that we miss important aspects of reality if we continue to assume that consciousness arises from unconscious matter. In his book, *The Case Against Reality* (2019), Donald Hoffman shows his alignment with the latest discoveries in physics such as theoretical physicist and Princeton Professor Nima Arkani-Hamed, who argues that "space-time is doomed" (2018, June 20, min. 8:35) because the current theories (e.g., quantum mechanics and gravity) do not answer several important structural questions including the very essential ones such as *Why is the universe the way it is?* In observing the new theories in physics but also Kurt Gödel's (1931) incompleteness theorems, Hoffman suggests that consciousness must be more essential and elemental than space-time. Based on his research in visual and computational psychology at MIT, Hoffman concedes that "evolution hid the truth from our eyes [to help us evolve]" and defines consciousness anew using the mathematical model of a conscious agent (Hoffman, 2019, pp. 203–205). He challenges leading scientific theories of consciousness, which assume that our senses register objective reality, and maintains that we should instead take what we see, hear, and feel, seriously but not literally. Our impression of objective reality, for example, a "tree" or a "car," Hoffman insists, is only "eye candy" that helps us navigate the world safely and with ease. The "tree" or the "car" is to be interpreted as literal as the icons on our computer screen. The icons are hiding the fact that they are, at the computer hardware level, a collection of "0" and "1," or electric impulses, if we want to go deeper. According to Donald Hoffman, space-time is "your virtual reality, a headset of your own making. The objects you see are your invention. You create them with a glance and destroy them with a blink" (2019, p. 202). He ends his book with the open question: "What happens if you take it [the headset] off?"

It could be argued that if we want to address the impossibilities of circular economy, we ought to consider exactly that: Questioning the very definition of consciousness that (potentially) created the current reality and assessing what new mindset (or level of consciousness) would help to create the reality that would not terminate human civilization. Trying to answer such questions is likely to preoccupy humanity for the duration of its existence.

Equipped with an expanded understanding of consciousness, an updated decision support system, a renewed appreciation of complexity and a multi-perspectival view of knowledge, and transdisciplinarity as a post-post-modern research method, we will focus next on the application of later stages of consciousness within the exemplification of early-stage investing and entrepreneurship.

From profit to prosperity through integral investing: a case study

It is widely accepted that humanity is currently not well prepared to address global grand challenges, particularly existential threats (Bostrom & Circovic (Eds.), 2008; Randers, 2012), but there is also hope (Bozesan, 2020; Hawken (Ed.), 2017; Pinker, 2011; Randers et al., 2018). This paper makes the case for the need for a major shift in consciousness (a mind shift) to address the impossibilities of current circular economic models. The necessary mind shift appears to be occurring as can be witnessed, for example, at the level of the European Commission that launched the European Green Deal (2019). Its action plan aims to implement a sustainable finance model that should be prepared to meet both the goals of the Paris Accord, through carbon neutrality by 2050, and the Agenda 2030 of the United Nations (with its 17 Sustainable Development Goals). Since we can only achieve what we measure, the European Green Deal is accompanied by the Financing Sustainable Growth set of documents (2019, June) that includes a *Taxonomy*, sustainability-related *Disclosures* (such as Environmental Social and Governance—ESG—criteria), as well as *Benchmarks* for climate and others. The effort of the European Commission has been joined by US President Joe Biden's *Executive Order on Tackling the Climate Crisis at Home and Abroad* (White House, 2021, January 27) and by the Chinese government whose five-year plan includes the divestment of investments from fossil fuels to green technology (UNDP, 2021 July). These efforts are providing the first regulatory and legislative steps for the greater mind shift necessary for societal, environmental, and cultural transformations including the transition to sustainable economics, finance, business, and education, to name a few.

This mind shift appears to be leading to a dramatic paradigm shift and to a major acceleration in creativity and radical product innovation in leading-edge, exponential technology start-ups as well (e.g., Bozesan, 2020; Diamandis & Kotler, 2012 & 2015 & 2020). For example, German environmentalist, high-tech entrepreneur, and founder of Hyperganic (2021), Lin Kyser shows how to use exponentially growing technologies to implement circular economic models within the context of a single start-up. He demonstrates how traditional computer-aided design can be replaced by computer-generated design; a new paradigm based on principles of highly complex, AI-based, generatively designed products that can be 3D printed. These massively customized products—e.g., airplane or satellite turbines, rocket combustion chambers, or customized bike helmets—can only be manufactured (3D printed) after being designed by highly complex algorithms that define their geometry (to be 3D printed) and whose AI (neural nets) can be transferred between products.

As more governments are providing capital and other stimulus packages, the need for accelerated digitalization and scalable investment decisions for implementing the UN SDGs within planetary boundaries by 2050 becomes our duty, particularly since start-ups like Hyperganic are desperately in need of funding that has been traditionally scarce. Small to medium enterprises (SMEs) are a substantial economic force worldwide—with a contribution of "about 90% of businesses and more than 50% of employment worldwide. Formal SMEs contribute up to 40% of national income (GDP) in emerging economies" (The World Bank, 2020); developed countries are no exception. The German Federal Ministry of Economic Affairs and Energy (2017), for example, attests that SMEs' "contribution towards Germany's economic strength, [represents] approx. 35% of total corporate turnover ... In terms of their contribution to GDP, these companies even account for close to 55%." Yet, despite the massive amount of capital available in the market and the low-interest policies of central banks since the financial crisis of 2008, SMEs are the last to partake in it due to the high risk associated with the particular asset class they represent. Better due-diligence processes are needed to solve the problem and the new green deals are coming to the rescue. The strategic direction of the various governmental new green deals represents an important guiding post for all players including investors, entrepreneurs, and businesspeople alike because it entices smart action and supports the efforts of already environmentally and socially active market leaders. From an early-stage investing perspective, we will look at *Integral Investing* (Bozesan, 2020) and its de-risking model, the Theta Model, as an integrative framework for sustainable investing based on integral theory by Ken Wilber (2000) (Figure 25.1).

De-Risking with the Theta Model

The *Integral Investing* framework pre-supposes a later-stage consciousness and mindset that integrates, transcends, and includes both traditional investing and impact investing practice and metrics with the intention to build integrally sustainable companies from the very beginning. It argues that all investment activity must be rooted in the essence of *all* existence, the later-stage levels of consciousness including culture, values, ethics, and morals as well as exterior reality, the material world, such as the social and the environment. As a result, Integral Investing shows that financial sustainability cannot be separated from the environmental, social, cultural, and an ethical impact, as well as individual self-actualization, joy, and personal happiness (in short, the *6Ps: Parity of People Planet and Profit with Passion and Purpose*); and provides an integration framework. The increased complexity of the investment process also begs the question how the entire value chain creation from the original start-up screening to the actual exit can be implemented within the context of the de-risking process. The answer can be found in the Theta Model (Figure 25.2), which makes Wilber's (2000) integral theory, at later stages of development, applicable within early-stage investing.

The five steps of the Theta Model integrate (a) traditional investing due-diligence criteria (*Step 1*: financial, legal, sales due-diligence) with (b) sustainability criteria and impact investing metrics (*Step 2*: UN SDGs within planetary boundaries, as well as Social, Environmental, and Governance (ESG) of the UN PRI) with (c) *Steps 4 and 5*: collective cultural, behavioral, and individual and collective mindset criteria, before it leads to the decision to invest or not (*Step 5*). Through its due-diligence, the Theta Model navigates the entire integral framework (Figure 25.1) as defined by Ken Wilber (2000) and has shown to be a powerful de-risking tool that enables a differentiated view not only of investees as individuals and in terms of company culture, but also of the context of investing, the exterior reality. This reality is made of a complex mesh of interdependent and intra- and interconnected *ecological* organizations, *social* and *cultural* structures, and *behavioral* factors, all of which are subject to *consciousness evolution*. The Theta Model has been successfully applied in early-stage investing since 1994 and could, of course, be used to de-risk investments in larger companies, albeit more complex than within the start-up context. The large-scale application of such a model would presuppose a world-centric level of consciousness, one that has outgrown both the egocentric (me and mine) and the ethno-centric/tribal ("make America great again" kind of thinking) mindset. The world-centric mindset focuses on the healthy development of *all humans* (everybody wins) and the flourishing of *all* life, everywhere. In 1985,

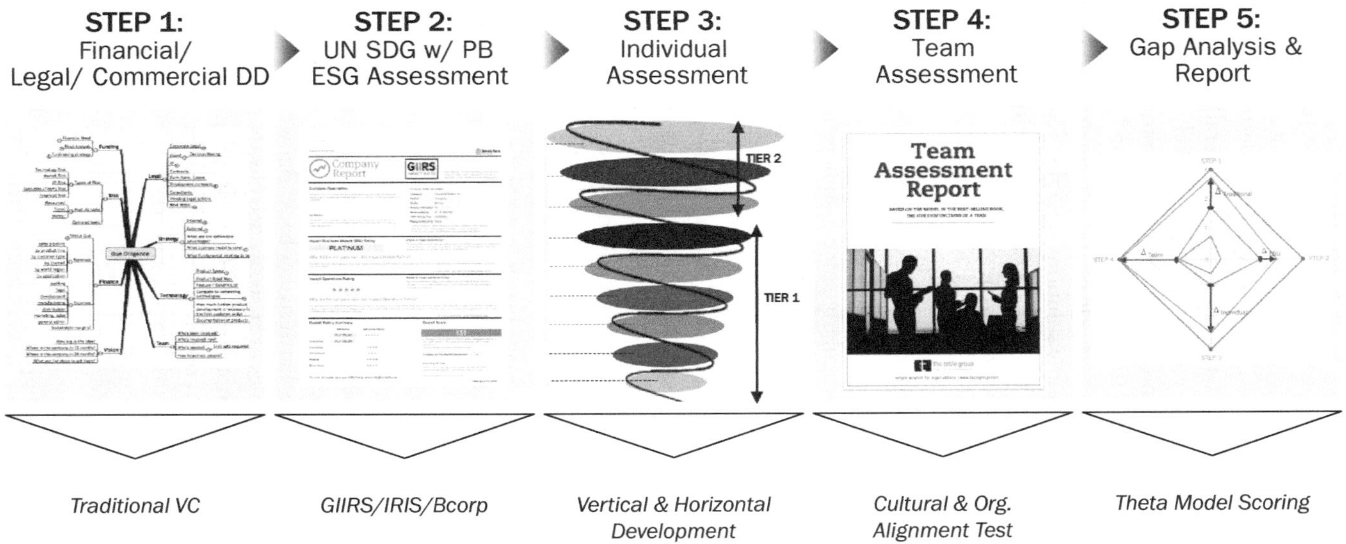

Figure 25.2 De-risking with the Theta Model.
Source: Own depiction.

Herman Daly called for "an engineering student to explain how a car can run on its own exhaust" (Daly, 1991, p. 197), which was impossible back then. Technologically, this is no longer the case due to advanced photo bioreactors, which use a wide range of micro-organisms to produce biofuels directly from CO_2 emissions using sunlight. I have personally invested in a US-based biofuel company, called BioCEE, a world-centric, integrally acting start-up that produced biofuels from CO_2 emissions. Unfortunately, the US government decided to promote fracking and fossil fuels subsidies rendering progressive biofuel companies financially unsustainable. What we can learn from this example is that the best intentions, the best ideas, and the smartest technology are not enough to make circular economy solutions feasible. The political will is more important and will win every time—as long as it remains rooted in an ethnocentric mindset instead of a world-centric one.

Summary

Only the future will show if humanity makes the transformation to a sustainable global civilization possible, particularly since a shift in mindset and the graduation to later stages of consciousness are the premise for said transformation. In this chapter, I argue that we need a new, transdisciplinary, understanding, and appreciation for multi-perspectival solutions in a global world ruled by highly intricate economic, social, and environmental interdependencies; a world in which we can deepen our understanding associated with the impossibilities of circular economic models. It is true that we cannot go beyond the first principles of science such as the law of thermodynamics. However, consciousness evolution and theoretical models such as Ken Wilber's integral theory, Dave Snowden's Cynefin model, and Donald Hoffman's new definition of consciousness could provide deeper guidance on how to make better sense of the world with the intention to enable emergent action within the exponentially growing complexity at global levels. As we have seen, we do not have to succumb to the Law of Diminishing Results and let human civilization collapse, as in previous cultures. Now, for the first time in the history of human civilization, we witness the Law of Accelerated Returns that can create an abundance that has the potential to help eradicate global poverty, address climate change, and implement the UN SDGs within planetary boundaries before the Earth strikes back. But we must do the work, and it is not going to be easy. In times of crisis, we see clearly that we cannot control what other people do, we cannot control the weather, and we certainly cannot control a pandemic. What is in our own reach, however, are our own thoughts, our emotional and psycho-spiritual states, and our behavior. We can despair, we can panic and become a burden, or we can grow emotionally and spiritually and become an inspiration and a force for good. We are the only person thinking in our heads, but we must protect the entrance to it. Consciousness evolves through us and can make the impossible possible within the laws of physics. But we do have choices. We can decide what kind of person we want to be, and we must grow if we do not want to regress as previous societies have done. Our own level of consciousness, our mindset, will determine whether we choose misery or happiness. What will you choose? Others will follow.

References

Arkani-Hamed, N. (2018, June 20). The end of spacetime. Public lecture at SLAC (Stanford Linear Accelerator Center). Retrieved September 25, 2021, from YouTube www.youtube.com/watch?v=t-C5RubqtRA

Asilomar AI Principles (2017). Retrieved September 20, 2021, from https://futureoflife.org/ai-principles/

Bostrom, N. (2005). A history of transhumanist thought. Journal of Evolution and Technology 14 (1), April 2005. Reprinted (in its present slightly edited form) in Rectenwald M, Carl L (Eds.) Academic Writing Across the Disciplines. New York: Pearson Longman, 2011. Retrieved September 20, 2021, from https://nickbostrom.com/papers/history.pdf

Bostrom, N., & Cirkovic, M.M. (Eds.) (2008). Global Catastrophic Risks. Oxford: Oxford University Press.

Bozesan, M. (2020). Integral Investing: From Profit to Prosperity. Cham, Switzerland: Springer Nature.

Brown, B.C. (2007, 20 February). Four worlds of sustainability: Drawing upon four universal perspectives to support sustainability initiatives. Integral Sustainability Center. Retrieved September 12, 2021, from https://tinyurl.com/5cf55fr2.

Brown, L.B. (2006). Plan B 2.0: Rescuing a Planet under Stress and a Civilization in Trouble. New York: W.W. Norton & Company.

Daly, H. (1991/1985). Steady-state Economics. Washington, D.C.: Island Press.

Dawkins, R. (1976). The selfish gene. Oxford: Oxford University Press.

Diamandis, P.H., & Kotler, S. (2012) Abundance: The Future Is Better than You Think. New York: Free Press.

Diamandis, P.H., & Kotler, S. (2015) Bold: How to Go Big, Create Wealth, and Impact the World. New York: Simon & Schuster.

Diamandis, P.H., & Kotler, S. (2020). The Future is Faster than you Think. New York: Simon & Schuster.

European Commission (2019, June). Financing a Sustainable European Economy. See also following documents retrieved September 28, 2021, from https://tinyurl.com/y2qq6syw, https://tinyurl.com/rkz92zx, and https://tinyurl.com/tfkv6cd

European Commission (2019, December 11). The European Green Deal. Retrieved September 28, 2021, from https://tinyurl.com/vlplq5l

German Federal Ministry of Economic Affairs and Energy (2017). SMEs are driving economic success; Facts and Figures about German SMEs: 2017-A successful year for German SMEs. https://tinyurl.com/y3cytbzf

Gödel, K. (1931). Über formal unentscheidbare Sätze der Principia Mathematica und verwandter Systeme I. Monatsh. f. Mathematik und Physik 38, 173–198. https://doi.org/10.1007/BF01700692

Hawken, P. (1993). The Ecology of Commerce: A Declaration of Sustainability. New York: HarperBusiness.

Hawken, P. (Ed.) (2017). Drawdown, the Most Comprehensive Plan Ever Proposed to Reverse Global Warming. New York: Penguin Books.

Hawken, P., Lovins, A., Lovins, L. H. (1999). Natural Capitalism: Creating the Next Industrial Revolution. New York: Little Brown & Company.

Hendricks, G., Ludeman K (1996) The Corporate Mystic: A Guidebook For Visionaries With Their Feet On The Ground. New York: Bantam Books.

Hoffman, D. (2019). *The Case Against Reality: Why Evolution Hid the Truth from Our Eyes.* New York: W.W. Norton & Company.

Holliday, Ch. Jr, Schmidheiny, S., Watts, P. (2002). Walking the Talk: The Business Case For Sustainable Development. Sheffield, United Kingdom: Greenleaf Publishing.

Hyperganic (2021). Company website viewed on September 28, 2021, at www.hyperganic.com/

Jackson, H., Svensson, K. (2002). Ecovillage Living: Restoring the Earth and Her People. Devon, UK: Green Books.

Kegan, R. (1982). The Evolving Self: Problem And Process In Human Development. Cambridge, MA: Harvard University Press.

Kurzweil, R. (2005) The Singularity Is Near: When Humans Transcend Biology. New York: Viking Penguin.

McDonough, W., & Braungart, M. (2002) Cradle to Cradle: Remaking the Way We Make Things. New York: North Point Press.

Nattrass, B., & Altomare M (1999). The Natural Step For Business: Wealth, Ecology and the Evolutionary Corporation. Gabriola Island, British Columbia, Canada: New Society Publishers.

Nicolescu, B. (2005). Transdisciplinarity: Past, Present and Future. Retrieved September 14, 2021, from https://tinyurl.com/f8y2ssn4

Oxtoby, J.C., & Pettis, B.J., & Price, G. B., von Neumann, J. (1958, May). Bulletin of the American Mathematical Society, 64(3), Part 2 (Whole No. 654). Retrieved September 14, 2021, from https://tinyurl.com/wcn7elh

Pinker, S. (2011). The Better Angels of Our Nature: The Decline of Violence in History and its Causes. London, UK: Allen Lane.

Plato (1961). The Collected Dialogues of Plato: Including the Letters. Princeton, NJ: Princeton University Press. (Original work published 1938).

Randers, J. (2012) 2052: A Global Forecast for the Next Forty Years. White River Junction, Vermont: Chelsea Green.

Randers, J., & Rockström, J., & Stoknes, P.E., & Golücke, U., & Collste, D., Cornell, S. (2018) Transformation is feasible. How to achieve Sustainable Development Goals within Planetary Boundaries. A report to the Club of Rome, for its 50th anniversary, 17 October 2018. Stockholm Resilience Center. Retrieved September 28, 2021, from https://tinyurl.com/y9epzlmk

Russel, M. J., & Kanik, I. (2010). Why does life start, what does it do, where will it be, and how might we find it? Journal of Cosmology, 5, 1008–1039. Retrieved September 20, 2021, from https://tinyurl.com/5bajas5a

Scharmer, O. (2010). Seven acupuncture points for shifting capitalism to create a regenerative ecosystem economy. Oxford Leadership Journal, 1(3), June 2010. Retrieved September 12, 2021, from https://tinyurl.com/y32cospb.

Schmachtenberger, D. (2021). [unedited] A Problem Well-stated is half-solved. Your Undivided Attention Podcast, June 25, 2021. Retrieved September 20, 2021, from https://tinyurl.com/2drxcxtd

Snowden, D., & Friends. (2021). Cynefin: Weaving Sense-making into the Fabric of Our World. Singapore: Cognitive Edge.

Tainter, J. A. (1988). The Collapse of Complex Societies. Cambridge, UK: Cambridge University Press.

Tegmark, M. (2017). Life 3.0: Being Human in the Age of Artificial Intelligence. London, UK: Allan Lane.

UNDP (2021, July). China's 14th five-year plan. Spotlighting climate and environment. Retrieved September 28, 2021, from https://tinyurl.com/4pyzjbva.

Von Weizsäcker, E. U., Wijkman, A. (2018) Come on! Capitalism, Short-Termism, Population and the Destruction of the Planet—A Report to the Club of Rome. New York: Springer Nature.

White House. (2021, January 27). Executive Order on Tackling the Climate Crisis at Home and Abroad. Retrieved September 28, 2021, from https://tinyurl.com/44k2ru3z

Wilber, K. (2000). A Theory of Everything: An Integral Vision for Business, Politics, Science, and Spirituality. Boston: Shambhala.

The World Bank SMES Finance (2020). Retrieved on September 28, 2021, from www.worldbank.org/en/topic/smefinance

World Commission on Environment and Development (2009/1987) Our Common Future. Oxford: Oxford University Press.

26 Coming full circle

Putting the social into circular economy

Corinna Vosse

Introduction

Hegemonial economic organization is damaging the planet's biospheres and by now even threatening the ecological foundation of our existence. A transformation of the economic system is urgently needed. To conceive economy, understood as the provisioning of humans for a good life, in alignment with the biospheres and therefore circular lies at the base of this transformation. The chapter looks at the representation of and the relation between the technical and the social in the idea of a circular economy (CE). The first chapter describes attributions to the circle both in technical and social contexts. It discusses definitions of circularity and requirements deduced from there and suggests two impossibilities of the mainstream concept of the circular economy. Chapter 2 further analyzes the programmatic content of the circular economy concept and substantiates the impossibilities identified. It describes assumptions of the social made in such concepts, drawing on studies in a business context, in a policy context, and in empirical research. The third chapter discusses conceptual implications and introduces a practical approach for raising the potential of the social for a circular economy.

Promises of the circle in a linear society

The circle is a positive image. It associates harmony with nature and connection to what is happening over the course of the year, in recurring seasonal cycles. More fundamentally, it evokes the cycle of life, which can best be observed in the fauna, where dying plants literally provide the base for growing plants, with a bit of time and biochemical processes involved of course—and the sun as the source of energy needed.

The technical circle takes positive connotations of the natural cycle to conjure a world of everlasting, maintenance-free products. Or it promises products that are entirely being recycled. In close association with natural cycles, product parts are supposed to become "food" for new products (Braungart/McDonough 2002). This concept evokes a strong picture, eliminating both problems of scarcity and waste. In a critical review of "imagined futures" envisioned along with the framing of a circular economy, Welch et al. describe the assumptions as

DOI: 10.4324/9781003244196-30

follows: "Resources and materials would circle through the economy based on the model of a nutrient cycle in natural ecosystems—so-called industrial symbiosis" (Welch et al. 2017, 48).

Though the nutrient cycle is a central point of reference in the circular economy discourse, the concept remains a technical one. It strongly builds on assumptions and models from industrial ecology, biomimicry, and the cradle-to-cradle concept. None of these fields much consider social actors and their interactions, values, or interests. Instead, the promise of the circular economy discourse lies in remodeling the functional principles of industrial production in order to align it with the planet's natural environments: "Idealized visions of the circular economy are of a new industrial revolution, with product designed for extended lifetimes and with near-infinitely recyclable materials and components forming a zero-waste 'closed loop'" (Welch et al. 2017, 48).

Of course, products cannot be everlasting because they are being used which causes wear (Friege et al. 2022). Even if they were not used, which matter of fact in our affluent society is a prospect to quite a few possessions; they would expire and lose functionality as they are subject to the effects of entropy. Therefore, they in any case need to be maintained and refurbished, a process requiring energy. The same is true for the recycling of products. As perfectly recyclable as a product or material may be, this process always requires energy, often even "large amounts of energy" (Potting et al. 2017, 4).

From a systemic perspective, it probably does not even make sense to differentiate between refurbishing and recycling. Recycling in the context of technical circles consequently is nothing but the refurbishing of material, since its output is the same material, in a condition that allows to re-utilize it. In some of the scholarly discourse on circular economy, much attention is put on the differentiation of R-frameworks. More and more steps are thought up and seemingly offer additional strategies in the creation of circular flows. As of now, this development culminated in the definition of a 9R framework. Meanwhile, Kirchherr et al. in their analysis of CE definitions find out that almost every fourth definition does not even include reduction—or even refusing and rethinking—as the first and probably most important step toward true circularity, given the fact that any R-strategy further down the line does require, to whatever extent, the input of material and energy. From this point of view, the differentiation from three to nine Rs seems to be part of the "circular economy babble" Kirchherr et al. speak of, referring to the lack of coherent conceptualization of CE (2017, 228).

So far, and contrary to the idea of circularity, actual recycling—or material refurbishing—often rather brings out material of lower quality, as with plastic or paper recycling, "the popularly conceived repeating circular motion of reuse and recycling is in fact a downward spiral" (Mayers et al. 2021, 1). With each turn the use quality is lowered, the potential to replace primary resources further limited, or with the words of Braungart/McDonough: "most recycling is actually downcycling; it reduces the quality of a material over time" (2002, 56). Mayers et al. describe further limitations of recycling; all things considered, it functions according to their argumentation at the most as an element in a weak sustainability strategy (2021, 3f). Potting et al. point out that "pollution and mixing of materials reduces their quality which means that very often recycled (secondary) materials cannot be applied again for the same type of product" (2017, 4). In other words, primary resources are technically still being needed in what is considered a circle in CE concepts.

The energy needed to recycle material, or to refurbish products or parts and material they are made of, is the other loose end in the story of the technical circle. It is not addressed much or simplified by referring to renewable energies, leaving out of consideration the material infrastructure needed for its provisioning—as well as rivalry with the energy demand in other sectors. When leaving the limitations in replacing primary resources and the need for energy out of the picture, there is a popular message to the story of the technical circle: We don't have to change much. Technology will once again do the job for us and get rid of all the unwanted and harmful side effects of industrial production, such as resource depletion, destruction of biospheres, and emittance of waste, including the release of carbon dioxide into the atmosphere. Accordingly, CE promises to keep current standards of material provisioning. That seems the main reason for the popularity of CE as a concept for production or, generally, as a paradigm for economic organization. It justifies the standard of living that is part of the problem.

What became apparent is that the concept of a circular economy is based on an inherent overestimation of technical solutions combined with an underestimation of limiting physical factors. This technical bias meets with ignorance toward the relevance of social determinants in bringing forward a paradigmatic shift in economic organization. This is what I consider the first impossibility of circular economy: The impossibility to leave out the social economy.

The circle is a positive social symbol as well, a symbol of cooperation and solidarity. Several people arranged in a circle becomes a group. The circle provides a supportive atmosphere to foster communication and meaningful exchange of thoughts and feelings. It supports focus and determination in a group situation as long as a certain size is not exceeded. One may say that the circle represents the community. Where people live together in large numbers, their way of organization needs to be able to manage social density. Industrialization, among other things, has led to rapid growth of the world population, and along with that, to increasing proximity in human living conditions, furthering the organization in societies. According to Tönnies, an early sociological thinker, there are some structural differences between communities and societies; they each follow an inherently different logic and bring out different institutions. When reduced to some basic thoughts, the two types can be characterized as follows: Community as a model is based on immediate, personal exchange and is supported by mutual trust. Society is based on contracts and enhanced by law and regulations (Tönnies 2019).

Nowadays, most of our social exchange is based on highly formalized principles of society, even when living in the countryside, beyond any social concentration. Just about anything we need for provisioning, for achieving the desired standard of living, like housing, food, transportation, and education, we acquire via anonymous markets, or we are offered by state-controlled systems. This is not to say that there are no meaningful social relations. But what it does imply is a significant reduction of social dependency. In society, and even more so in industrialized economies, there is little *need* for exchange and interaction even among people living in proximity or being related in some way, be it friendship or kinship (Polanyi 2001).

Positively speaking, our socio-economic organization in the society model allows for social exchange but reduces the need for it. Under those circumstances, the community seems a bit of a romantic projection to deal with feelings of social disconnectedness; the circle as an image for social relations is a misguided image for today's social reality. Meanwhile, society has become an overarching structure and an inhabited reality in industrialized countries. With most provisioning happening in industrial structures, there is little opportunity or need to organize communally, for example, to exchange surplus, to share means of production, and to manage commons. In other words, there is little practice and experience to take part in organizing and maintaining cycles of goods. Our current socio-economic organization does not require or prepare us to deal with goods in any thoughtful way beyond possessing them. This perspective suggests another kind of impossibility: A mismatch of the social challenges a truly circular system of provisioning would present on one side, and the gestalt of the social tissue on the other.

Social practice and (circular) economy

There is no doubt that humanity, in particular industrialized nations, has caused severe damage to the ecological system by extracting resources, processing them, and depositing waste material at a growing rate. Our economic system, and therefore large segments of our social organization, functions on the base of a linear mechanism of take–make–waste. The consequence of holding on to this system is by now strikingly threatening the foundation of our existence. In this situation, redesigning our economic system to be less resource demanding and wasteful is an urgent necessity. The idea of a circular economy seems intuitively a good measure, since it holds the promise to align our economy with our natural surroundings, as discussed in the previous chapter. To better understand how organizing and maintaining a circular economy is intertwined with our social tissue, the following section explores assumptions and expectations connected to the concept of CE and social implications arising from that.

With CE being a young field of research and even more, a trending topic, there is no one coherent, widely used definition. Some authors stress on what a circular economy should evoke while others define the concept from a policy perspective and include different stakeholder groups and instruments in their description. Some definitions focus on the supply side and consider a sustainable product policy framework a necessary element (EU 2020, 6) to bring out material-efficient products. Other authors stress the need for creating material recirculation opportunities and new circular business models (Material Economics, 24).

For their analysis of 114 CE definitions, Kirchherr et al. developed a coding framework consisting of 17 coding dimensions and also used this to generate a CE definition:

> A circular economy describes an economic system that is based on business models which replace the "end-of-life" concept with reducing, alternatively reusing, recycling and recovering materials in production/distribution and consumption processes, thus operating at the micro level (products, companies, consumers), meso level (eco-industrial parks) and macro level (city, region, nation and beyond), with the aim to accomplish sustainable development, which implies creating environmental quality, economic prosperity and social equity, to the benefit of current and future generations.
>
> (Kirchherr et al 2017, 224f)

This highly complex definition includes perspectives from the 114 definitions analyzed and therefore can be considered quite representative. At the same time, Kirchherr's paper provides ample proof of many definitions out there presenting strongly simplified concepts of CE.

These simplifications particularly show how social implications of a circular economy are thought about. Kirchherr's definition is proof of that itself, as it conjures business models as the foundation for a circular economy. Basically, social conditions are neither conceptualized much as a driving force to establish circular systems of provisioning nor are they analyzed as a hindering factor. Programmatically, reduction appears as a sort of precondition of CE, as the various R-frameworks show, because it is seen to "decrease the consumption of natural resources and materials applied in a product chain by less product being needed for delivering a same function" (Potting et al. 2017, 15). Yet, to reduce is not conceptualized as an activity or a decision on the side of the user/consumer. Instead, it is framed as part of the business modeling; reduction appears in terms of greater efficiency, as a strategy to reduce resource demand in production. Accordingly, there is no thought about *who* may need less and *why*. In other words, the potential of sufficiency is not explored. Humans and their wants and needs are not considered an active force in reducing the usage of resources and energy.

At the same time, the demand and use side programmatically are seen to be important for creating a circular economy. In a CE, we are all asked to take part in "making more of the materials we have already produced" (Material Economics, 10). This programmatic focus on the demand side can be explained by the structural character of the two sides. From a policy perspective, it is easier to influence the use side, since the interests of consumers are less organized and more easily compromised than the interests of producing businesses that have strong lobby groups promoting their interest, which from a systemic perspective is rather monocausal: to maintain the existence of the business. And in this, social actors can only be seen as consumers/users, not as proponents of reduction. So far, their role in a circular economy is conceptualized only for the phase when whatever good is in use already. This conceptual approach is rather negligent of rebound effects.

While allotting a role as an individual user/consumer, CE concepts show little awareness of the role of the social tissue in determining both demand and use. Often, users are more or less regarded as extensions of the production, in charge of collecting and returning used parts and products for refurbishment (Hobson 2021, 69f). Such a perspective strongly underestimates the inertia of social practice, which cannot be changed by implementing a new business model. Fortunately, implications of the social seem to slowly infiltrate the discourse. When evaluating a large number of cases in which CE transitions in product chains are central, Potting et al. were looking at what kind of innovation brings forward CE and find that "*socio-institutional change* is needed throughout the product chain when aiming at strategies for higher levels of circularity" (Potting et al. 2017, 7; italics CV). Looking at those "strategies for higher levels of circularity", as they are more or less detailed and defined in the various R-frameworks, it becomes apparent that they lie beyond what can be controlled in production or managed with technology. Those strategies are seen in the lower R numbers, namely refusing, rethinking, and reducing (Potting et al. 2017, 5). To be effective, they strongly depend on the change in social practice, in how users/consumers enliven provisioning, and how they relate to the material world.

With the social tissue at large not being considered much in CE analysis and strategy design, it remains underrated to what extent incentives, norms, and values supporting industrial production are still effective and how this interferes with establishing circularity in our economy. Looking at the individual level only, users are invited to reuse, share, maintain, and fix goods, while there is little attention to the question: what socio-institutional change is needed for that to become normality? CE strategies for business partly even depend on activities on the side of users. To have large-scale repair, refurbishment, remanufacturing, and recycling, the products at the end of a use cycle need to be available for this. Since they physically are dispersed in private households, it once more needs different routines on the side of the users. A strategic reaction to this in CE concepts is service models, where goods are not owned by the users, and return is institutionalized. Again, what remains underrated is how users are willing and able to change routines around need satisfaction—and how goods fulfill additional functions beyond provisioning, especially for social distinction, as described earlier by Veblen and coined with the term conspicuous consumption (Veblen 2009).

When looking at this mismatch between the programmatic ambitions of a circular economy and the hegemonial norms and values, practices, and rules, it becomes apparent that to bring circularity into the economy requires anticipating the social. Unfortunately, social factors not only are more important to reach higher levels of circularity, but the authors analyzing cases of CE transitions also conclude: "The results show that achieving socio-institutional change is a bigger challenge than spurring technological innovation. Radical technological innovation is even found to play a minor role only" (Potting et al. 2017, 37).

Social innovation for an economic transformation

The analysis in the previous chapters made apparent that the technical bias in CE discourse comes with negligence of the social in CE concepts and strategies, which I call the first impossibility of circular economy. The second main point was to highlight discrepancies between the social, being shaped by decades of industrialized production and ambitions of CE. This discrepancy raises fundamental questions about the feasibility of current CE concepts and presents the second impossibility. Drawing on this analysis, the final chapter discusses implications and explores possibilities to raise the potential of the social for a circular economy.

The main programmatic ambition of CE concepts lies in reducing resource consumption and waste emission in order to achieve environmental quality, economic prosperity, and social equity (Kirchherr et al 2017, 224f). Those basic targets immediately relate to a scientifically and socially widely agreed-upon problem analysis and are shared by many in various scientific fields, as well as in political and social movements. Question is not the target, but the means of reaching it—and along with that the causal model that remains implicit and is therefore difficult to assess.

Looking at definitions and strategic elements in CE discourse, they reflect an understanding of economy that is strongly related to mainstream economic theory. In the hegemonial concept of economy, it is goods and money that form a cycle, consisting of two interlinked semicircles. That is an entirely different kind of circle than the consistent regeneration of resources, as nature creates. Such economic organization, where the exchange of goods and money forms the circle, has led to an acceleration in processing resources and severe damage to ecosystems (Brand/Wissen 2017). The participants in this system learn a lot about how to exchange money for goods and vice versa. What is not required though is knowledge about managing and processing resources for provisioning.

Money, it seems, can be a strong force in the unlearning of managing limited resources. It teaches us that value does not perish and that the law of entropy has been overcome. It suggests that provisioning functions independently from natural cycles, it feeds into expectations of having anything available at all times (Blühdorn 2020b). Money influences social relations as well, which are a prerequisite for managing especially natural resources, as with commons. In neoclassic economic theory, money is seen to "act as a substitute for trust" (Gale 1982, 239). Without trust, it is more difficult to facilitate local exchange, to share goods, and to base provisioning on commons—all "strategies for higher levels of circularity" (Potting et al. 2017, 7). Further, the dominant function of money as a medium of exchange induces a preference for exchange value rather than use value, which lies in opposition to circularity. Even more, money contributes to overproduction, because at any time it represents potential demand, structurally detached of needs producers may supply goods for (Spahn 2002, 63).

An institutional setting where we basically unlearn to take responsibility for goods and to manage resources does not seem a good starting point for establishing a circular economy. An alignment of the institutional setting is one challenge that needs to be dealt with. Institutional change is known to be a key factor in any societal transformation (Sommer/Welzer 2014). Meanwhile, change in a democratic society depends on social acceptance. To raise this general acceptance, in this case transforming the system of provision toward circularity, it may be helpful to have real-world laboratories where change can be experienced, where we can become part of making the change (Vosse/Haselbach 2017, 134f).

The House of Materialization (HdM) in Berlin/Germany wants to be such a laboratory, offering fully equipped common workshops, room for sharing and swapping, repair cafes, inspiration for reuse and reappropriation, and a large inventory of goods and materials rescued from waste. With its portfolio, it aims to invite visitors to explore what it feels like to take responsibility for goods and resources, while in use or at their end of life—technically or due to abundance. In courses, it is possible to experiment with material to put it to new uses or to repair consumer goods to prolong their life span. Applied research and sustainable design generate new perspectives on the existing ones. Secondhand goods are presented in an artsy ambiance and upgraded with applied art. The HdM can be considered an urban resource center, which is "local approaches to waste prevention, re-use, repair, and recycling" (Urban Agenda for the EU 2019, 3). It aims to bring together different sectors and fields of expertise to question not only the physical dimension of our economic organization but the social dimension as well.

To repair and refurbish goods is necessary. To bring fewer goods into circulation is even more important. Circularity is not an alternative to sufficiency, as Moreau et al. point out when writing that "the magnitude of the material throughput of the economy needs to be lowered before considering the opportunities of closed material cycles" (2021, 5). Under the name of circularity, current concept look to create material cycles by solely employing technical means. Instead, we need to frame CE as one element in the necessary transformation to a resilient economy, drawing on technical solutions and social innovation. In this context, social innovations are intentional reconfigurations of our practice of provisioning, which can include a recourse to past modes of operation (Kahlenborn et al. 2019, 257). Places like HdM that go beyond commodification, that make provisioning an issue of personal involvement, provide an arena for social innovation to unfold. Such places anticipate that for the needed change we have to go further into questioning our economic institutions. CE concepts that only interfere with the cycle of goods cannot go far enough in bringing down the impact of our economy to meet the planetary boundaries, or in reference to the known proverb of Einstein: Systems built on commodification can only fail to address the problems they were part of causing.

References

Blühdorn, I. (2020a). Kein gutes Leben für Alle! Annäherung an einen Paradigmenwechsel. Blühdorn, I. Nachhaltige Nicht-Nachhaltigkeit. transcript, 47–82.

Blühdorn, I. (2020b). Die Gesellschaft der Nicht-Nachhaltigkeit. Blühdorn, I. Nachhaltige Nicht-Nachhaltigkeit. transcript, 83–160.

Brand, U., Wissen, M. (2017). Imperiale Lebensweise, Zur Ausbeutung von Natur und Mensch in Zeiten des globalen Kapitalismus. oekom.

Braungart, M., McDonough, W. (2002). Cradle to Cradle: Remaking the Way We Make Things. North Point Press.

Ellen MacArthur Foundation (2013). Towards the Circular Economy: Opportunities for the Consumer Goods Sector Report

European Commission (2020). Circular Economy Action Plan. For a cleaner and more competitive Europe.

European Commission (2015). Closing the Loop—An EU Action Plan for the Circular Economy.

Friege, H., Kuemmerer, K. (2022). Practising Circular Economy: Stumbling Blocks for Circulation and Recycling. In H. Lehmann (Ed.), The Impossibilities of the Circular Economy (Vol. 5). Routledge.

Gale, D. (1982). Money—In Equilibrium. Cambridge University Press.

Hobson, K. (2021). The limits of the loops: critical environmental politics and the Circular Economy, Environmental Politics, 30(1–2), 161–179.

Jonker, J., Navarro, N. (2018). Circular City Governance. An explorative research study into current barriers and governance practices in circular city transitions across Europe.

Kahlenborn, W., Clausen, J., Behrendt, S., Göll, E. (2019). Auf dem Weg zu einer Green Economy: Wie die sozialökologische Transformation gelingen kann. transcript.

Kirchherr, J., Reike, D., Hekkert, M. (2017). Conceptualizing the circular economy: An analysis of 114 definitions. Resources, Conservation and Recycling, 127, 221–232.

Material Economics (n.d.): The Circular Economy. A Powerful Force for Climate Mitigation.

Mayers, K., Davis, T., Van Wassenhove, L. (2021). The Limits of the "Sustainable" Economy. Harvard Business Review, 1–9. https://hbr.org/2021/06/the-limits-of-the-sustainable-economy

Moreau, V., Sahakian, M., van Griethuysen, P., Vuille, F. (2017). Coming full circle: why social and institutional dimensions matter for the circular economy. Journal of Industrial Ecology, 21(3), 497–506.

Polanyi, K. (2001). The Great Transformation: The Political and Economic Origins of Our Time. Beacon Press.

Potting, J., Hekkert, M., Worrell, E., Hanemaaijer, A. (2017). Circular economy: Measuring innovation in the product chain. PBL Netherlands Environmental Assessment Agency The Hague.

Sommer, B., Welzer, H. (2014). Transformationsdesign—Wege in eine zukunftsfähige Moderne. Oekom.

Spahn, H. (2002). Die Ordnung der Gesellschaft als Zahlungswirtschaft. Deutschmann, C. (Ed.). Die gesellschaftliche Macht des Geldes. Westdeutscher Verlag, 47–72.

Tönnies, F. (2019). Gemeinschaft und Gesellschaft. 1880–1935. Clausen, B., Haselbach, D. (Ed), De Gruyter.

Urban Agenda for the EU. (2019). Urban Resource Centres. A classification of local approaches to waste prevention, reuse, repair and recycling in a circular economy.

Veblen, T. (2009) The Theory of the Leisure Class. Oxford University Press.

Vosse, C., Haselbach, D. (2017). Kommen Sie näher, machen Sie mit! politische ökologie 35(149), 134–137.

Welch, D., Keller, M., Mandich, G. (2017). Imagined futures of everyday life in the circular economy. Interactions, 24(2), 46–51.

Zink, T. and Geyer, R. (2017). Circular economy rebound. Journal of Industrial Ecology, 21(3), 593–602.

Index

Note: Page locators in **bold** and *italics* represents tables and figures, respectively.